Consumption Studies and the History of the Ottoman Empire, 1550–1922

SUNY series in the Social and Economic History of the Middle East

Donald Quataert, editor

Consumption Studies and the History of the Ottoman Empire, 1550–1922

An Introduction

EDITED BY

Donald Quataert

State University of New York Press

Published by
State University of New York Press

Printed in the United States of America

For information, address State University of New York Press,
State University Plaza, Albany, N.Y., 12246

Production by Diane Ganeles
Marketing by Nancy Farrell

Library of Congress Cataloging-in-Publication Data

Consumption studies and the history of the Ottoman Empire, 1550–1922 : an introduction / edited by Donald Quataert.
p. cm. — (SUNY series in the social and economic history of the middle East)
Includes bibliographical references and index.
ISBN 0-7914-4431-7 (acid free paper). — ISBN 0-7914-4432-5 (pbk. : acid free paper)
1. Consumption (Economics)—Turkey—History. I. Quataert, Donald, 1941– . II. Series.
HC495.C6C66 2000
339.4'7'09561—dc21 99-24669
CIP

10 9 8 7 6 5 4 3 2 1

For Bethany

—DQ

Guide to Pronounciation of Turkish Words

C, c = "j" as in juice

Ç, ç = "ch" as in cheek

Ğ, ğ = soft "g," hardly pronounced

I, ı = without a dot, pronounced like the first syllable of "earnest"

I, i = with a dot, between "in" and "eel"

Ö, ö = as in the umlaut ö in German

Ş, ş = as in "sheet"

Ü, ü = as in the umlat ü in German

ˆ = used to denote a lenghtened vowel (a, i, and u) or to palatize a preceding g, k, or l

After Cornell H. Fleischer, *Bureaucrat and Intellectual in the Ottoman Empire: The Historian Mustafa Âli (1541–1600).* Princeton, 1986, xvi.

Contents

1

Introduction[1]

Donald Quataert

For more than a decade, scholars in European, North American, and East Asian history have been pursuing consumption studies as an important new key to unlocking the past. Materialists to the core, they argue that the consumption of goods, not their production, drives history. The comestibles, clothes, furniture, and household goods that nourish and adorn our bodies and homes, they say, define our social identities and ranks. Some, especially those in United States and European studies, go further and argue that modernity itself occurs at the moment when consumption becomes a widely dispersed, socially-accepted, and morally-proper form of economic behavior and characteristic of social differentiation. Modernity is also marked by the rise of mass consumerism, and by its ascendancy of the consumer over the producer. In sum, in their view, we are not what we make but what we eat, wear, and use.

Convinced of the centrality of consumption to the making of the modern world and of its essentiality to modern identity, consumptionists have expended enormous energies uncovering patterns of consumption in the past. For example, they have combed probate inventories, holding that the nature and the quantity of the goods possessed capture the structure, hierarchy, and mobility of a society. Hence, in one study, a scholar examined three thousand probate inventories in England, 1660–1760, to determine the kinds of goods being purchased and the changing pattern of their usage over time. At this early date, she concluded, people possessed ever-greater quantities and varieties of goods, in order to mark themselves apart—that is, for purposes of social differentiation. Thus, a consumer revolution and the modern era already had begun by ca. 1700.[2]

Some consumption studies seek to prop up the notion of United States "exceptionalism"—the American historical experience seen as fully idiosyncratic—by linking shifting consumption patterns in colonial America to subsequent democratic political developments. As the proliferation of material goods jeopardized their ability to differentiate through lavish display, American colonial elites instead began to employ refinement of taste as a social maker. That is, early eighteenth-century elites shifted over to strategies of discretion and understatement, seeking to undo middle-class efforts to rise socially via the accumulation of goods. They changed the playing field of social status and sought to replace mere wealth with refinement of taste as the hallmark of one's place in society. In the process, some historians argue, this "refinement of America" created the blurred and fluid social boundaries that thereafter have distinguished American society and political culture.[3]

Also, many histories of consumption have concluded that the emerging importance of consumer goods occurred independently of wealth. The mounting emphasis on the acquisition of goods became "oddly disconnected"[4] from economic well-being and sometimes occurred in times of general depression and decline or failing family fortunes. Thus, there are two distinctly different pictures of the seventeenth–eighteenth century past. The production image is one of real wage decline while consumption historians see a rising abundance of consumer goods. In an influential set of articles, the historian Jan deVries posited that shifts in consumption, in fashion, prompted a profound alteration in production. DeVries argued that already in the early seventeenth century there were "reallocations of the productive resources of households."[5] Experiencing a greater desire to consume, households began working harder in order to commercially produce more wares so that they could afford to buy additional consumer goods. This "industrious revolution" caused households to devote more time to producing goods for sale and in fact triggered the "Industrial Revolution."[6] Thus, DeVries believes, demand changes precede and cause production shifts in the world of consumption.[7] Hence, a society experiencing rising consumption might well be undergoing a fundamental shift in its attitude toward time, work, and money.

Embedded in these studies is the effort to explore the complex meanings that owners attached to their goods. Possession of a certain textile could mean middle-class status in one home, while in another time and place ownership of handmade "oriental rugs" provided escape from the tedium of a mechanizing, standardizing world. Our grandmothers proudly displayed rotund "happy buddhas" in their parlors surely not to denote their sinicization but for other reasons, such as to display their new prosperity.

At least one consumptionist, however, believes that material goods define values only in the West. Only there, Chandra Mukerji argues, are material interests not made subject to other social goals.[8] In my view, however, holding to such beliefs resembles the earlier, now-abandoned, insistence among modernizationists that economies must pass through particular stages of growth before they achieve economic maturity, inevitably understood as a big-factory economy with an industrial proletariat. In any event, studies of southeast Asia during the period 1450–1680 seem to contradict Mukerji's assertions about the uniquely-Western nature of the values placed on material goods.[9]

This Southeast Asian research reveals fashion cycles and consumption patterns suggestive of those in Europe and America indicating the possibility of a worldwide pattern of increasing consumption during the seventeenth century. These findings fit well into the growing consensus that capitalism was not a uniquely European phenomenon, and thus cannot be used to explain Western domination of the modern period. If the consumer revolution (and capitalism) and thus modernity were evolving autonomously in several areas of the early modern world, then subsequent European ascendancy must be reinvestigated and explained in terms other than Western particularism. Thus, Ottomanists and other Middle East specialists have much to consider when approaching consumptionist studies.

The present volume is an initial Ottomanist foray into this world of consumption. Most of the contributions herein discuss the Ottoman capital city of Istanbul and stress the eighteenth and nineteenth centuries. While it can be argued that Istanbul was the consumer leader for most of the Ottoman era, this assumption needs to be tested by additional empirical studies that focus on other regions. The emergence of port cities such as Salonica, Izmir, and Beirut offered alternative consumption models, the significance of which needs to be determined. This volume intends to provoke further studies into Ottoman consumption history and the present editor is well aware of the many questions and regions that remain unexplored.

Several of the contributions below are methodological in scope. In her wide-ranging essay, Faroqhi, for example, provides a general historiographical context and insights into the utility of a consumptionist approach for Ottomanists. She raises important issues such as that of leisure and the apparent paradox between falling incomes and rising consumption, as well as the central problem of the morality of consumption. This morality issue is, I believe, an effective prism through which much of Ottoman history can be reunderstood. Matthews, as I indicate below, enters the world of the court judge *(kadı)* in an effort to understand the utility of probate inventories for consumption history. Salzmann, in her contribution, concretely demonstrates that consumption studies can offer new interpretations of a well-known event, in this case a 1730 revolution, the so-called Patrona Halil revolt. Furthermore, she comparatively analyzes the tulip in its Asian, Ottoman, and West European settings as a means of examining the issue of changing cultural meaning on a global scale. Some of the contributors focus on the consumption of other goods—Zilfi, for her part, discusses both slaves and clothing in the context of eighteenth-century Istanbul. Jirousek, in a provocative piece, traces the changing patterns of fashion in the direction of "mass fashion dress," that, she says, is emblematic of modernity. Frierson essays the world of nineteenth-century newspaper advertising in an effort to find the modern and non-Western aspects of late-Ottoman consumer markets. In an encyclopedic manner, Artan explores the use of food. Micklewright introduces us to photography and photographs as items of consumption and insists that we treat these as texts worthy of careful analysis.

The notion of a consumer revolution clearly holds promise for its different perspectives and provocative approaches. There certainly was a sea change in Ottoman consumption habits taking place in the seventeenth century, as the spread of coffee and tobacco makes abundantly clear. Further, the widespread adoption of tobacco and coffee was occurring simultaneously across vast regions of the globe. If Ottoman, west European, southeast and east Asian consumers were behaving in a similar manner, then a shared consumer revolution was taking place. In Europe, the desire for consumer goods (according to some consumptionists), triggered technological change. In the Ottoman world, the proliferating consumption of coffee and tobacco might well explain the splendors of the Ottomans' Tulip Period (1718–1730) and its booming consumerism, discussed in Salzmann's contribution. The Ottoman industrial upswing that we now know occurred in the 1700–1760 era may have been born in the emergence of tobacco and coffee as mass consumption items.

The meanings that the various cultures attributed to these new drugs requires comparison, a simultaneity of new use that compels reconsideration of capitalism as a particularly European invention. On the Ottoman scene, historians long have noted the wrath of Sultan Murad IV and the more tempered responses of his successors to these innovations, but have remained largely uninterested in the economic, social, and cultural meanings of the new goods. Sociable activities such as drinking coffee and smoking tobacco generated an identifiable material culture that needs to be explored, as do the new public spaces of the coffeehouse. More generally, the task remains to understand and then link this transformation to other changes in Ottoman society and its polity during the seventeenth century.

We need to consider the manner in which consumption maintained or altered social boundaries. For example, as the Artan article demonstrates, the sultans distributed food to certain households physically outside the palace and thus demarcated them as belonging to Ottoman elite circles. Similarly, as Zilfi demonstrates, they distributed robes as badges of honor and esteem, elevating the recipients to a special place in the Ottoman social heirarchy. Tobacco and coffee, for their part, may well have served as instruments in the creation of a common Ottoman cultural system, as well as markers of social differentiation, as various social groups purchased different grades of the drugs.

The basic suppositions of most consumptionists regarding the significance that persons attached to material goods, as well as Mukerji's interpretation, can offer helpful guidance to Middle East historians seeking to understand the spread of consumer goods and the larger question of modernization. Middle East specialists in the past had assumed that the adoption of Western forms (of government, education, the military) indicated the westernization of the borrowers. And yet, consumption studies make clear that the ownership of Western goods—whether guns or clocks or cloth—does not mean the westernization of their users. The significance that Ottomans attached to their possession does not flow inherently from the nature of the good or its place of origin. For example, the Ottomans' acceptance of clocks does not necessarily imply their greater interest in concepts of time, although it might. Nor, more generally, does the appearance of European goods imply the increased Western-ness of their owners, although it can. After all, no one posits that, when Ottoman peasants vastly increased their consumption of India-made goods during the eighteenth century, they were being Indianized! So too, nineteenth-century Ottoman peasants did not buy cheap English cloth because they wanted to be English. Nor, when Jirousek and Zilfi suggest that Europeans were borrowing from Ottoman fashions, are they implying their Ottomanization. Similarly, Artan holds for internal, domestic explanations for changing consumption patterns, in this case, in food. We learn from our Europeanist/Asianist/Americanist predecessors in the history of consumption that the meanings of such goods must be explored, for example, through the use of literary sources.

The increased use of calicoes and Manchester cloths among peasants in part surely derives from their low cost and perhaps also from a sense of escape from the usual. Among upper levels of the social hierarchy, however, totally different meanings may have prevailed. Indian or English textiles initially may have imparted great social prestige and differentiation, at least in the early phases of their importation. During the nineteenth century, each social class smoked a particular kind of tobacco, marking their respective social boundaries. Western clocks, mirrors, weapons, and other luxury items similarly distinguished their owners from socially superior or inferior competitors. Ottoman customers obtained [foreign] goods not always for economist reasons—because they worked better or were cheaper—but sometimes for their social value. Here then are factors based on domestic Ottoman dynamics and not only externalist ones stressing imitation of foreigners as the explanation for Ottoman historical evolution.

The clothing laws promulgated by the Ottoman state offer another proof that consumption issues often are not about consumption at all.[10] These laws avowedly sought to curb excessive or extravagant consumption or mark Muslim superiority. It is true that (1) wasteful expenditures were siphoning monies out of the empire; and, (2) some non-Muslims were infringing on Muslim privileges. But these laws are important for additional reasons. *First* of all, in promulgating laws, the state was asserting its authority, reiterating its self-proclaimed monopoly on the use of force, and demonstrating a willingness to maintain control, social order, and discipline. The state also used laws to build alliances with various constituencies from whom it was seeking support. Hence, on various occasions, it took the side of those advocating probity and modesty, Muslim superiority or its opposite, the equality of non-Muslims and Muslims.

The enactment or reiteration of laws did not always reflect actual violations or changing fashions but the demands of some subjects that the state take a position on such matters. Threatened by events including foreign wars and economic precariousness, they demanded stability via reiteration of their social place, as defined by apparel. Therefore, consumptionists show us, clothing laws are about state formation as well as intrasocietal dynamics.

Second, the laws also reflect on issues relating to social differentiation. Consumption habits did not merely concern the treasury or Muslim privilege. They also distinguished among lower, middle, and upper ranks and changes in fashion imperiled those distinctions.[11] Thus, clothing laws can be about individuals and groups of one rank seeking to alter their social status by adopting the clothing or headgear of others. And, sometimes, the state permitted social blurring; for example, in one region of the empire, Tokat in northern Anatolia, it released non-Muslims who performed valuable services from the clothing restrictions particular to their group.[12]

Consumptionists once argued exclusively in favor of emulation, the percolation of tastes and fashions from the top layers of society downward as the lower elements imitated the consumption patterns of their social betters. Indeed, there are many examples of emulation both in Europe and the Ottoman Empire. Josiah Wedgewood made his pottery fortune by spectacularly manipulating emulative impulses among all classes of English buyers. In addition, Wedgewood sent goods to English ambassadors who presented them to the Ottoman court as a means of promoting sales among broader segments of the nonroyal elite Ottomans.[13] But another study shows that taste changes could travel up the social ladder: in late seventeenth-century England, socially subordinate merchants were atop the consumption hierarchy, ahead of the gentry, followed by artisans, yeomen, and then husbandmen.[14] This example suggests that emulation—from the top down—should not be assumed. Rather, we need to hold for the possibility that subordinate groups sometimes could be fashion leaders. And, if the English example has any utility, trend-setting in the fashion world by the lower ranks anticipated their move into elite political and economic status. Hence, tracing the adoption of goods outside the military-administrative *(askeri)* class will shed light on the transformation of the Ottoman polity. And, as a somewhat later corollary, the fashion leadership of Ottoman non-Muslims in the nineteenth century reflected their changing place in the political hierarchy as well.

Important vehicles for consumption research are the probate inventories *(tereke defterleri)*, for some, an "archival abyss,"[15] the use of which is hotly debated. In her contribution, Faroqhi is optimistic and offers sound advice on their use. Probate inventories may be an important key to unlocking the Ottoman consumptionist past, for they record at least some of the material possessions of recently deceased Ottomans. In an ideal world, reliably and consistently listed goods that are representative of other goods or of people's domestic behavior should reveal what other records cannot.[16] They can demonstrate which goods have become normal in everyday life—for example, establishing the consumption of coffee or tobacco through the presence of coffee cups and pipes in the inventories. Before probate inventories are used more extensively, however, Ottomanists need to better understand their nature and shortcomings.[17]

Matthews' article is a strong cautionary statement about the deeply problematic nature of these inventories and their possible misuse. She sees the probate inventories in part as a social construction, not merely a listing of goods. Hers is marvelous dissection of the probate inventory, taking it apart piece by piece in order to understand its structure and therefore its uses and shortcomings. She also offers an exceptional analysis of the Islamic courts that administered the inventories and their place in the local society. Her work is an indispensable tool for understanding how the courts really worked. Her comments suggest that the inventories must be used in a highly self-aware fashion if they are to have any utility at all.

Consumption history can further illuminate the course that Ottoman manufacturing followed during the era of European industrial hegemony. While supplyside factors affecting the trajectory of indigenous manufacturing have been presented by Ottomanists,[18] the demand side of the equation remains unclear. Local consumers' taste preferences played a crucial role in maintaining or undermining local producers. In France, for example, the bourgeoisie favored styles that emphasized comfort and careful craftsmanship rather than ostentatious display. They thus created and maintained a market for goods that were not mass produced and could only be made laboriously, in small workshops. In this manner, they dictated the overall shape of French industry as a handicraft sector that evolved quite differently from the large factory, machine, mass-produced character of English manufacturing.[19] The tastes of Ottoman consumers, I insist, shaped local manufacturing in a manner analogous to that of French industry. Their preferences for locally made goods in some cases were consciously political choices, made in the knowledge that to purchase foreign manufactures would doom Ottoman producers and thus eat away at the very fabric of Ottoman social and political life.

While the early twentieth-century boycotts against Austro-Hungarian and Greek goods are famed, such concerns are manifest in the eighteenth and early nineteenth centuries as well, as Jirousek's article demonstrates. On other occasions, consumers' selections were connected to their desire for attributes such as softness or color, qualities that mass manufactured goods lacked. When, on the other hand, they did purchase foreign-made goods, they helped to ruin indigenous manufacturers. Altogether, a consumption perspective makes it apparent that the profile of Ottoman manufacturing derives from Ottoman internal dynamics and not only foreign influences. The consumption model, in sum, enhances the sense of Middle Eastern agency.

Frierson's article demonstrates the crucial role of advertising. Advertising embraces not only sellers' presentations of goods in the newspapers and shop windows of later nineteenth-century Ottoman life. It also includes the ambassadors' presentation of Wedgewood products at the imperial court. Similarly, the promotional activities of itinerant pedlars and merchants at periodic markets and fairs were important, but remain difficult to detect. Newspapers and show-window displays reveal how the *sellers,* at least, wished their goods to be apprehended. We cannot be certain that buyers attached the same meanings to their newly acquired goods.[20] At first glance, most of the newspaper advertisements noted in Frierson appear to have publicized European made goods, hardly surprising given the venue in which they appeared. Since the purchase of foreign goods in some sense was an action against the whole Ottoman economic structure, their promotion and purchase clearly need to be better understood. This topic richly deserves further analysis.

The Ottoman world, both the state and its subjects, always consumed a mixture of foreign and domestically made goods. Whether or not there always was a distinction made between "foreign-made" or "Ottoman-made," however, is not certain. Nor is the meaning of such terms and changes in the significance attached to "foreign" and "Ottoman" as designators. Such a task seems essential to an understanding of Ottoman self-definition, not to mention cultural values, social change, and state economic policies.

Fashions and changing consumption patterns need to be related or, in the words used a few pages earlier, "oddly disconnected," from production patterns of decline or growth both at the imperial and the regional level. Similarly, comparisons of consumption patterns in the capital city of Istanbul with other administrative centers such as Belgrade or Sofia, or with centers of domestic or international trade (Izmir, Beirut), of manufacturing (Buldan, Salonica), or of mining (Zonguldak/Ereğli) will reveal much about the relationships between production and consumption, wealth and poverty. In this volume, there is a powerful emphasis, likely too much, on the imperial capital. Nonetheless, this is not entirely unwarranted. Holding three percent of the entire population of the empire, Istanbul for a long time was its major consumption center and, quite probably set consumption trends during most of Ottoman history. On the other hand, the role of the city's non-Muslims as fashion trend-setters in the nineteenth century should encourage studies comparing the consumption patterns of Istanbul with Beirut, Alexandria, and Izmir, which housed important concentrations of Ottoman non-Muslims. These port cities surely contested the capital's primacy in the consumption of goods, with implications that warrant further attention. And finally, regional variations in consumption can say a great deal about the variety or homogeneity of Ottoman culture as well as its diffusion.[21]

A focus on consumption also challenges assumptions that the state was the primary agent for change in the Ottoman world. For example, in economic history, most historians explain Ottoman agricultural commercialization as a function of state actions, governmental decisions that imposed taxes in cash and forced subjects to become involved in market economies. In this view, governmental policies—cash taxes—are seen as the crucial determinant in the shift of Ottoman producers to a market economy. A focus on consumption choices and household allocation of resources helps to redirect emphasis away from such state idolatry and back to Ottoman society as the agent of change. That is, families' own growing desire for goods explains their increasing commitment to market production. Also consider, similarly, that the Ottoman state objected strenuously to coffee as well as tobacco consumption and yet both were adopted widely. We need to reinterpret these state prohibitions in a less literal way as we already have done for the clothing laws, as negotiations and not mere prohibitions. In this case, the coffee and tobacco laws represented negotiations among the state, elements of the *ulema* opposed to the innovations and others who favored the new drugs (merchants and consumers). These debates, as both Jirousek and Faroqhi indicate, were concerned with the morality of consumption and were won by the advocates of consumption.[22] What does this tell us about state-subject relations and the control that the Ottoman state (incorrectly) is said to have maintained over society?

While there can be little doubt about Ottoman households' shift in favor of greater consumption, considerable uncertainty about the timing remains. The articles by Zilfi, Jirousek, and Frierson, for example, respectively argue for the eighteenth and nineteenth centuries as turning points. The Tulip Period (1718–1730) reveals an important increase and change in Ottoman consumption patterns, at least among certain Istanbul groups and some provincial elites. Some of the evidence presented by Salzmann argues for an earlier shift, back in the seventeenth century, at least for Istanbul, while Jirousek and Frierson both stress the later nineteenth century as the crucial turning point.

It might be useful to view the overall pattern of Ottoman consumption as one that: (1) began building in the seventeenth century with mounting coffee and tobacco consumption; (2) continued to broaden and deepen in the eighteenth century, as seen in the vast increases in the import of Indian textiles and the increasingly vital Ottoman manufacturing activities; and (3) developed still further in the nineteenth century, with the explosive rise in European imports and the continuation of local industrial production.

An "industrious revolution"[23] in my own view already was well underway in the Ottoman nineteenth century, marked by a vast increase in the number of women employed in manufacturing. Consumption historians see such a trend as part of a set of decisions within the household designed to increase its flow of money, facilitating greater demand for goods both Ottoman and domestic. We need to determine if the shift to increased use of waged female labor in fact had occurred earlier and if the Ottoman "industrious revolution" had other distinctive features.

A decrease in the number of festivals (regionally or at the imperial level) would indicate a growing emphasis on longer and harder work at the expense of leisure time as a means of obtaining the desired goods. After all, in the seventeenth and eighteenth centuries, the vast increase in the number of goods—tulips at the elite level, and of coffee and tobacco among broader elements of the populace—required cash. The elites might have gouged the taxpayers to pay for the tulips but the monies for much of the coffee, tobacco, and Indian cloth must have come from increased amounts of waged labor or commercial agriculture or savings. All this speaks to a seventeenth- and eighteenth-century propensity toward consumption and emphasis upon the production of goods rather than leisure.[24] Jirousek nonetheless argues against this chronology, maintaining that the evolution of mass fashion dress marks the later nineteenth century as radically different from preceding eras.

To sum up: consumption studies can help to disentangle modernization from Westernization, and place the internal dynamics of Middle East society closer to the center of attention. Of equal significance, a consumption focus deemphasizes the Ottoman state, which for too long has dominated our study of Ottoman history. Quite by contrast, consumption history focuses on the countless individual decisions concerning the amount of time to spend in leisure and in production. It thus places agency in the hands of households and their members.

And yet, while consumption has much to offer Ottoman and Middle Eastern studies, it is not an unproblematic concept and indeed can be a perilous business. After all, this approach removes the emphasis from work or politics and gives primacy to cultural issues over political ideology. Situating the culture of consumption as the central concern negates or might detract from efforts to build alternatives to capitalism.

Further, care must be taken to not overstate the consumption case. Societies have constructed social values around goods for centuries and not only in Europe. Also, we must not merely substitute one totem of modernity—the appearance of the industrial revolution—with that of another—the consumer revolution. Nor was there a necessary link between the two: a consumer revolution need not be a precondition for mechanical industrialization although this was the course followed in some west European countries. In the Ottoman Empire and perhaps elsewhere, consumerism's main impact on the productive sphere may have been the increased use of female labor rather than mechanization. Comparative studies is a vitally important tool and yet we cannot always be looking for replications of patterns found by the careful research of vast numbers of European and American historians.

In the end, consumption studies may be most important for the fundamental question that it poses about the role of goods in shaping and reflecting political, economic, social, and cultural behavior.

Notes

1. The present volume emerges from the Seventh Biennial Conference on the Ottoman Empire and the World Economy, held at Binghamton University, October 11–12, 1996. All of the present contributors, except Matthews and Zilfi, offered earlier versions of their papers to this conference, "Consumption in the Ottoman Empire, 1500–1923." Beshara Doumani and Sherry Vatter also contributed valuable papers; for several reasons, they are not included here.

2. Weatherill (1988); Neil McKendrick, "Commercialization and the Economy," in McKendrick, Brewer, and Plumb (1982) 9–194.

3. Compare Karin Calvert, "The Future of Fashion in Eighteenth Century America," in Carson, Hoffman, and Albert, eds. (1994), 252–83, and Bushman (1992).

4. deVries in Brewer, and Porter, eds. (1993), 101.

5. Ibid., 107.

6. de Vries, (1994), 249–70.

7. Take the example of England during the seventeenth and eighteenth centuries. In England, consumer tastes had preferred the silks and satins of France; in 1678, they were cut off by English restrictive tariff policies. Consumer demand for such unobtainable goods led to the rise of the consumption of calicoes from India. Calico appealed to the middle classes because of its silklike quality and because it was easy to clean. But laws then barred the imports of calicoes. To meet this frustrated demand for the Indian textiles, English industrialists began tinkering with machinery to make them—techno-

logical changes that led to the Industrial Revolution. Thus, the invention of capital goods proceeds from desires for material goods, an exclusive feature of Western culture. See Mukerji, (1983), esp. 186ff.

8. Mukerji (1983).

9. Reid (1988).

10. See Quataert (1997), 403–25.

11. Weatherill (1988).

12. See Tokat Şeriye Sicilleri, 1224AH, cited in Duman (1998).

13. McKendrick, Brewer, and Plumb (1982), 101–40.

14. Weatherill (1988), 195–96.

15. deVries (1993), 98–106.

16. Weatherill (1988) is an excellent model for the exhaustive and sensitive use of these inventories.

17. Also, in his remarks to the 1996 conference, Beshara Doumani strongly warned about the pitfalls of the probate inventories and was not at all encouraging about their utility.

18. See, for example, Quataert (1993), and the sources therein.

19. Walton (1992).

20. Here, I think, consumption studies can be useful, for they urge us to be careful about assuming the meaning of goods. Take, for example, Heath Lowry's personal communication about the provincial land surveys, *tahrir defterleri,* those meticulous enumerations of property and land use. In none of these surveys, he says, are we to find maps. Consumption studies here are helpful for they urge us not to deplore this absence of a good commonly found in the West (maps), as some Ottoman shortcoming or failure, but rather to try to understand its significance. For example, might the absence of maps indicate the state's effort to hoard information?

21. See Weatherill (1988) for intercity comparisons in England.

22. For models, see McKendrick, Brewer, and Plumb (1982) as well as Brewer and Porter, eds. (1993).

23. deVries (1994).

24. Cross (1993).

2

Research on the History of Ottoman Consumption: A Preliminary Exploration of Sources and Models

Suraiya Faroqhi

European Antecedents

By discussing consumption, Ottoman social and economic historians, rather belatedly, follow the lead which for the last twenty years or so has been given by Europeanists dealing with the early modern period. From about 1980 onwards, the latter have increasingly turned away from quantitatively oriented research into economic and social structures to cultural studies, with a strong emphasis on the role of small groups. On the other hand, many historians of France, England, or Italy have been unwilling to abandon a field in which they have excelled, and which moreover has helped history enhance its status as a discipline. Due to the emphasis that social and economic historians continue to place on models and quantitative analysis, ever since the 1930s this particular subdiscipline has appeared as the principal means by which history might establish itself as a social science.

Under these circumstances, the study of consumption presents particular advantages. On the one hand, it is an authentically economic phenomenon. Even if one assumes that production determines consumption and not the other way around, goods that are produced but not consumed, at least in the capitalistic context, form the reason for serious economic crisis. On the other hand by consuming—or in some instances, by declining to consume—people express cultural preferences, project self-images, and compete for status. Consumption thus impinges on both the social and cultural realms. At least where European early modern history is concerned, it enables the historian to have the best of both worlds.

At the same time, present-day emphasis on consumption certainly should be regarded as an acknowledgment of the fact that more or less "affluent societies" have existed in western Europe from the 1950s or thereabouts, and are even older in the United States of America or Canada.[1] After all it often happens that historians, when dealing with their special area, seek for the antecedents of phenomena that characterize their own world. The long period of post-World War II economic expansion, which the French have graphically named the *trente glorieuse*, did not immediately impress medievalists and early modernists. But somewhat late in the day—namely, after the period of phenomenal economic expansion and full-employment had come to an end in the early 1970s—the long-term consequences of increased popular consumption began to engage the interest of Europeanist historians. Possibly it was not merely the emergence of the "consumer society" that has stimulated historians' interest in consumption, but also the fact that the earning power and propensity of the poor to consume in industrial societies have recently come under massive attack.

Research undertaken by Europeanist historians and historical anthropologists has shown a significant misconception in the older historical literature. In the past, it had been assumed that all increases in popular consumption must have been due to some precursor or manifestation of the "industrial revolution." But now it has been discovered that at least in some parts of early modern Europe, broadly based demand for consumer goods was more than merely a nineteenth-century novelty, even though shopping trips probably first became a mass amusement during the late Victorian period. In fifteenth-century England, well to do peasants invested in farmhouses for their own use, some of them so solidly built that they are still inhabited to the present day. Where England and Holland are concerned, the period beginning with the late seventeenth century is now regarded as a time of massively expanding consumption.[2] By the late seventeenth century, as Margaret Spufford has shown us, the "great reclothing of rural England" was well underway. Pedlars made available cheap fabrics in such large quantities that even farm servants could permit themselves a change of clothing.[3] In the eighteenth century, the introduction of tea, and concomitantly of sugar, as an item of English mass consumption has attracted some scholarly attention.[4] Massive currents of both legal trade and smuggling owed their existence to the emerging sociability of the tea table, which was supplied also by "mass-produced" Staffordshire pottery and, in the wealthier homes, by Chinese porcelain.

On the continent, broadly-based consumption was all but unknown before the eighteenth century. But Daniel Roche has pointed to the large-scale use of Indian (and Syrian) cottons in eighteenth-century France.[5] This long-lasting vogue of printed cottons is interesting in a variety of ways. Cottons, due to their cheap price and the ease with which they could be washed, allowed a larger number of people to live a life of increased comfort and cleanliness, and this explains why demand was consistently high. But in addition, the stubborn presence of *indiennes* in France demonstrates that even in the homeland of royal absolutism, the prohibition to import them could not be enforced in the face of widespread consumer opposition. Probate inventories show that women's clothes, curtains, or bedcovers were frequently made out of the "forbidden" fabrics. Apparently it was almost as difficult to eradicate Protestantism as the wearing of imported cotton cloth.

Daniel Roche has also pointed out that the increasing number of prosecutions for theft in the second half of the eighteenth century may indicate an increase in cloth consumption. To be sure, such prosecutions are the result of widespread poverty and the weakening of community ties, which should have removed socio-psychological barriers against taking one's neighbors to court.[6] But at the same time there also was more to steal, particularly the sheets, shirts, and pillowcases that more people now hung out on clotheslines to dry. Extensive research into seventeenth- and eighteenth-century Parisian probate inventories has shown that in the second half of the eighteenth century many newly built houses were more comfortable than their predecessors had been.[7] More fireplaces were built, stoves made a timid appearance, and even cheap decorative objects could be found in the cramped quarters of many artisans and dependent workmen.

At the same time, there exists a countervailing tendency in historical research concerning pre-1860s Europe. This goes back to the "standard of living controversy," which raged among British economic historians of the 1960s and 1970s.[8] Scholars involved in the debate had attempted to establish whether early industrial factory workers were better or worse off than their villager ancestors had been. Researchers dealing with the history of industrialization have come to the conclusion that popular food consumption did not improve before the 1860s or even 1870s, and may even have declined in the early nineteenth century.

To the extent that demand-led growth existed, the demand must have come from the upper and middle levels of the society under discussion, which increased in numbers, and maybe in their share of total population as well. Among the poor, earnings were held down by steady population growth, which had been eroding living standards ever since the beginning of the sixteenth century, but also by the prevailing power structure. Frequently kings, noblemen, and the emerging group of bourgeois landlords in town and countryside repressed, in a most aggressive and bloody fashion, the attempts of small artisans and other members of the popular classes to counteract secular wage decline.[9] Improved distribution systems from the eighteenth century onwards were able to limit and later eliminate famines due to harvest crises, which had been so typical of medieval and early modern settings (at least as long as these crises did not take place in Ireland). But malnutrition continued to be a major problem into the last quarter of the nineteenth century, and in many places far beyond.[10]

It is difficult if not impossible to reconcile these two research tendencies and groups of findings. Both lines of argument seem to be based on solid empirical evidence. Given the priority of food needs, it is impossible to argue that undernourished people spent more on clothes, housing, or education. One might only claim that the consumption of nonfood items expanded among people who lived in privileged locations such as eighteenth-century Paris, where an enormous share of French provincial purchasing power, skimmed off in the shape of royal taxes and feudal dues, was ultimately concentrated. The Netherlands constituted another such privileged location. An abundance of capital seeking outlets for investment allowed the early modernization of both agriculture and transportation, and thus grain shortages were no longer a concern. Dutch genre painting of the seventeenth century shows that modest comforts, such as meat, "decent" clothes, bed linen and stoves, even in this early period had percolated down far into the popular classes.[11]

Another possible explanation of the contradiction between declining real wages and increasing consumption may lie in the fact that those people whose consumption is known belonged to the "better-off" strata of the population under study. This possibility seems worth investigating, particularly when we are dealing with early modern consumption in localities that did not belong to privileged regions such as the Netherlands, southern England, or Paris. It is possible that we are confronted with a growing dichotomy: an increasing group of wealthy and even modestly comfortable people and a mass of the very poor. It appears that the Paris or Toulouse artisans who joined the popular societies during the French Revolution were worried about their positions as modest earners, and well aware of the dangers of downward mobility.[12] This fact, rather than class divisions in the nineteenth-century sense of the word, is now accepted by many historians as the driving force behind the revolutionary events of 1792–95. The sources that historians of consumption have to use, such as probate inventories, may in fact be misleading, as the large number of "down-and-out"ers is underrepresented in most kinds of documentation.

Some historians have attempted to explain the dilemma by pointing out a deficiency in our concept of popular consumption. In the view of these scholars, the relationship of the traditional grains such as wheat, barley, or rye to wages may be misleading as an indicator of popular well-being. Poor people substituted cheaper alternatives for wheat more often than has been supposed.[13] In southwestern France, but also in the Balkans during the eighteenth century, maize was cultivated for local consumption, while wheat was sold. From the same time onward, potatoes became a major food crop in many parts of Europe, particularly in Ireland and the great plain that stretches from the Netherlands to Poland. During the shortages which accompanied the revolutionary wars, the population of southern France learned to live on imported rice, which had not been very highly esteemed before that time. Thus important, although not always quantifiable savings, were achieved, which, at least in peacetime, could be spent on manufactured goods.

Can This Be Relevant to the Ottomanist?

Things are, however, somewhat different when Ottoman history is at issue; to discuss consumption in the Ottoman realm is an extremely difficult and complicated undertaking. Studies dealing specifically with this issue are almost nonexistent, and to glean incidental information about consumption from work concerned basically with other issues often is not very rewarding either. Whatever merits the argument that the poor switched to cheaper foods and thus secured more disposable income may possess in the European context, the Ottoman historian will have a great many reservations about the applicability of this idea to the eastern Mediterranean. Potatoes in this region were adopted as a vegetable and not as a substitute for bread or bulgur. Rice was a modest luxury and not a popular, everyday food, and only maize in certain locations may have played the role Europeanist historians have ascribed to it.[14] The Anatolian famine of 1873–74 shows that the affected population possessed no alternative to the traditional bread grains.[15] In all likelihood, popular ability to substitute cheaper foods for older types of nourishment that had become unaffordable was linked to the position of the relevant country in world trade. If the purchasing power of incomes contracted, poorer Ottomans possessed fewer options than their French or English counterparts.

A different explanation for the contradiction between a downward trend in popular earnings and an increased consumption of nonfood goods has been proposed by Jan de Vries, who has baptized the development he postulates the "industrious revolution."[16] In the view of de Vries, populations in many areas attempted to make up for declining real wages by working longer and harder. Women and children were put to work for minimal wages in cottage industries, long before this phenomenon attracted official attention in the early nineteenth century. As a result, many goods that previously had been produced for household consumption were now made available in the market, and they were often of higher quality than could be achieved by nonspecialists. As the prices of these goods were not high, they could be purchased even by people with modest incomes. Thus we are confronted with the somewhat paradoxical situation that even though real wages stagnated or declined, more people bought small semiluxuries such as tea or a print of the Virgin Mary to hang on the wall.

This dynamic would explain how declining real wages and an increasing consumption of goods among a widening group of people could coexist. However it is difficult to imagine this development if the economic system as a whole had not achieved a relatively high degree of capitalization. For the increased numbers of poor people working for merchants, who exploited their labor in order to bring cheap goods to the market, could only be paid their wages if there was enough money around to do so. Moreover the merchants also needed to make modest outlays of capital before they could organize a cottage industry. Thus de Vries' model seems appropriate mainly to the more prosperous regions of early modern Europe, and less to the Ottoman lands.

But maybe this pessimism is not quite justified. Research into Ottoman consumption is not at present far enough advanced for us to know whether a similar contradiction between a growing abundance of goods and declining real wages did not exist in the Ottoman lands, at least in some sectors and time periods. At present "our" wage data are so fragmentary that we cannot tell what happened to wages in the long run, even in a relatively well documented sector such as the building industry. However a casual reading of inheritance inventories in the Bursa *kadı* court registers, which have been preserved from the late fifteenth century onward, does seem to indicate that the early eighteenth-century inhabitants of that particularly active center of trade and craft industries had more textiles available than their remote ancestors of the fifteenth century. At present, this is only a hypothesis, but the mere possibility of formulating it makes the work of Jan de Vries interesting for our purposes.

Moreover for the nineteenth century, Donald Quataert has pointed out that certain Ottoman crafts, particularly in the textile sector, were able to survive the competition of imported European goods, but at the price of greatly lowered real wages.[17] If we assume that some of these producers also tried to make ends meet by working longer and harder, the model developed by De Vries may be relevant at least to Ottoman historians of the nineteenth century.

Detractors of Consumption in the Ottoman Context

Given the fact that the successor states of the Ottoman Empire, including modern Turkey, have had only a very modest share of the twentieth-century abundance of goods, most Ottomanist historians have considered it unnecessary to pay any special attention to consumption. In addition the old assumption that production is somehow "moral" and consumption "immoral," which occurs in many contexts both industrial and preindustrial, has had vigorous defenders in the late Ottoman Empire and republican Turkey as well.

In late nineteenth-century novels, one of the favorite figures was the young spendthrift. This youth who became the principal tragicomical antihero was attributed *alafranga* tastes in consumption, but possessed no notion of the more serious aspects of European culture.[18] This figure incarnated the ambivalence of late Ottoman intellectuals not only toward the cultural impact of Europe in general, but more specifically toward the "consumerism" that European culture in its late-nineteenth century version had come to imply. Moreover, the popular wisdom of Anatolian peasants *işten artmaz, dıştan artar* (money is made not by increasing earnings, but by limiting the consumption of food) has probably reinforced hostility toward everything that smacks of the enjoyment of goods.

Defining the Notion of "Consumption"

Consumption as used in this paper includes not only the purchase of goods not intended for resale, but the things people do with goods once they have acquired them. This means that the goods consumed can be acquired not only through purchase but also through gift (after all, the consumption by children not yet able to contribute to the family income is made possible exclusively by gifts). Among the goods acquired by an individual, there will thus be a greater or lesser percentage passed on to other people as presents. Gift-giving is thus a significant aspect of consumption as defined here, but there are others: fabrics are made up into clothes for adult men and women, these clothes are washed and repaired, recycled as clothes for children and later as cleaning rags, and ultimately thrown away. Building materials are purchased, workers hired, and a house is built, maybe in part with family labor. Children scribble on the walls until a new coat of paint is needed. Rooms are added or changed in shape according to the growth or contraction of a family; decorations are changed in accordance with current taste. And finally the whole building is torn down in order to make way for a new one. All these different activities form part of the notion of consumption. While they have been largely neglected by historians, we can learn a great deal by studying them.

From this simple enumeration, it is obvious that consumption has at least three aspects to it. First of all, it can be studied as an economic matter—that is, we can look at the goods produced on Ottoman territory that were not exported. Marketing networks serving the distribution of such goods within the empire, while important in their own right, are regarded as the preliminary to consumption, but not as consumption itself.

Secondly, consumption can be studied as a socially embedded activity. Anthropologists have long since made us aware that in precapitalist societies, both production and consumption cannot be abstracted from their social and political contexts. Albeit to lesser degree, this is also true of capitalist settings.[19] Thus a study of Ottoman consumption must take into account the occasions at which certain goods are consumed, and the meanings attached to them. Obligations of gift-giving, whether reciprocal or not, will interest us in this context. However given the near absence of relevant studies, this remains a rather platonic interest. But we can at least approach the context of gift-giving by looking at the occasions for which certain goods, such as sweets or textiles, were produced.

Thirdly consumption in preindustrial settings is strongly linked to the demonstration of political power, with certain valuable goods restricted to rulers or courtiers. But even at lower levels of society, the right to consume certain coveted goods is used as a means of differentiating higher from lower status groups. These concerns account for the sumptuary laws so often enacted in the Ottoman Empire, and by the way, in early modern European societies as well.[20] In the present paper, I will deemphasize the economic aspect of consumption in favor of its social and cultural sides.

Possibilities and Limitations

So much for the rough overview over the research on consumption recently undertaken with respect to medieval and early modern Europe. The conclusions of these studies provide Ottoman historians with starting points for their own research. There are however some difficulties involved in this approach. One might object that transferring the results gained by Europeanists into a non-European setting smacks of eurocentrism. I do not agree with that objection. Quite to the contrary, to dwell on the "uniqueness of the East" may imply, to express it in the language of Edward Said, positing Ottoman state and society as the eternal and incommensurable "other."[21] Moreover Ottoman Rumelia and western Anatolia, in contradistinction to for instance the Arab provinces, in many fields really did exhibit features characteristic of a "borderland culture."[22] Therefore it is not illegitimate to regard the economic history of the Ottoman Empire as, among may other things, a set of developments closely connected with European history. However we must never forget that this linkage was but one, and by no means the most important, aspect of a multifaceted reality.

In addition we can increasingly "import" models and conclusions from Indian economic history, and thereby to some extent "balance" our conceptual importations from Europe.[23] Particularly promising is the notion, often used among researchers studying the Indian eighteenth century, that market-oriented production in the provinces expanded due to the state's demand for taxes paid in current coin. For in the absence of gold and silver mines on the Indian subcontinent, demands for money renewed every year should soon have led to the exhaustion of bullion reserves in the provinces, and the demise of the whole system. However by supplying goods to the capital cities of Delhi and Agra, where the money paid over as taxes accumulated, provincial Indian producers were able to "buy back" their money.[24] Thus apart from the stream of tax moneys, there was a flow of goods from the provinces to the capital. Speciality foods, fabrics of different varieties, and personal ornaments all came together in the capital cities as a result of this dynamic.

This model is especially relevant for the history of consumption, as it helps us to explain the relative abundance of material goods available in, for instance, seventeenth-century Istanbul. Not only the members of the Ottoman administration, but even the "ordinary" inhabitants of the capital city, benefited from a kind of "trickle down" effect, as goods produced in the provinces came to Istanbul in such large quantities that they became accessible even to people of small means. Price lists enumerating goods that could be purchased in seventeenth-century Istanbul shops do in fact list a great many goods of provincial origin.[25] If this model is at all appropriate to reality, the level of consumption in Istanbul should have been much higher than that prevailing in provincial towns. To a lesser degree, the same also should have been true of provincial centers, such as Cairo or Tunis. For these places were inhabited by elites who did not pass on to Istanbul all the taxes collected in the relevant province, but themselves consumed an appreciable share of local tax revenues. Thus a certain amount of bullion could be "brought back" from provincial elites as well. Istanbul was not quite the only beneficiary of the Ottoman taxation mechanism.

Indianist models have proven helpful in yet another consumption-related sector of Ottoman history. Recent students of the eighteenth century have come to the conclusion that the decline of the Mughal Empire did not lead to a collapse of market-oriented production, as had earlier been assumed by those scholars who regarded a strongly centralized tax system as the only stimulus to market production in the Indian countryside. "Revisionists" such as C. A. Bayly have pointed out that regional principalities also encouraged the manufacture of arms and luxuries as well as the cultivation of speciality crops. Of course the "buying back" model continued to be effective in the new setting as well, albeit on a smaller scale.[26] Ottomanists dealing with the eighteenth century have come to a similar conclusion. It is now assumed that the numerous notables and magnates *(ayan)* of the time, by their luxury consumption, created a local demand for artisans to build and decorate mosques, fountains, and fortified residences. At least on the demand level, the relative decline of the central power today is no longer seen as quite the catastrophe it was regarded as twenty or thirty years ago.[27]

A "rehabilitation" of the eighteenth century thus seems to be underway, and the rehabilitation of consumption is apparently connected with it. We should explore the notion that in the period before 1760, at least the inhabitants of the larger Ottoman towns experienced a greater abundance of goods. Textile manufacture revived in many places, but as the exportation of readymade textiles (as opposed to raw cotton, cotton thread, and thrown silk) was not a major feature of the eighteenth-century Ottoman economy, there must have been subjects of the sultan willing and able to buy these fabrics. Inventories of Bursa townsmen and townswomen deceased in the 1730s show a relatively large quantity of silk textiles, in the shape of clothing and as home furnishings. It thus seems worthwhile to explore the possibility that at least between 1720 and 1760, there was a certain expansion of consumption among the wealthier urban dwellers. If this hypothesis could be confirmed, our view of Ottoman economic history will be transformed.

A difficult problem confronting the historian of consumption results from the fact that Ottoman society, similar to other noncapitalist societies, used money only in certain circumscribed sectors of life. Peasant autoconsumption must have accounted for the vast majority of all goods and services produced in the Ottoman Empire, as was also true of continental European societies before the nineteenth century. And what peasants did not manufacture at home, they might have been able to obtain from neighbors or from seminomads passing through their villages. These exchanges took place by barter or in the course of fulfilling mutual social obligations, of the kind that even today are not unknown in Anatolian villages.[28] Auto-consumption has left few written records, and as long as there is almost no archeological study of Ottoman rural sites, what must have been the bulk of Ottoman consumption remains a *terra incognita.*

The Sources: Estate Inventories and their Uses

Our most useful source for Ottoman consumption are the estate inventories. Where Bursa is concerned, these lists of movable properties, houses, and gardens put together before dividing the estate of a deceased person among heirs survive from the late fifteenth century onward. In this city they were numerous enough to warrant the compilation of separate registers.[29] In other towns of sixteenth-century Anatolia, estate inventories were much rarer, and interspersed with other documents in the relevant *kadı* court registers. For Edirne, there survive sixteenth- and seventeenth-century inventories relating to servitors of the Ottoman administration, whose estates, contrary to those of "ordinary" subjects, were liable to confiscation. But for the eighteenth century, these inventories are available in much greater numbers than ever before. This was partly due to the fact that in those years the confiscation of estates had turned into a significant source of state revenue and was used as a means of asserting the central government's power over the larger and smaller notables of the empire.[30]

In addition, the Ottoman bureaucracy had expanded, so that larger numbers of records were kept even in the provinces. Both Cairo and Damascus preserve sizeable accumulations of estate inventories, and the same applies to Crete.

On the Bursa inventories, the pioneering study is that of Halil Inalcık, who used this material to show the existence of large Muslim merchants with connections to Egypt, Syria, Italy, and the lands to the north of the Black Sea.[31] Possibly the most important result of this work was the understanding that the "division of labor by religious denomination," so characteristic of Ottoman society in the nineteenth century, was by no means a permanent feature, but a historical phenomenon whose genesis needed to be investigated. Inalcık was also able to show the enormous disparity of fortune between the well to do merchants he studied and medium to upper level functionaries of the Ottoman state. Active though these merchants may have been in their own realm, they clearly were in no position to compete with men whose yearly revenue could easily surpass the wealth a successful trader might amass over a whole lifetime.

As Inalcık's research was concerned with economic activity, the consumption patterns of merchants did not interest him. The same thing applies to most other researchers who have concerned themselves with estate inventories, particularly Ömer Lütfi Barkan. Barkan's study of the central government's servitors whose estates were recorded in the Edirne registers concentrated upon the landholdings of these personages and their money-lending activities.[32] The only area where Barkan dealt with something that we would classify as an aspect of consumption was a brief analysis of the ownership of slaves. But even this is only partially true, as quite a few of the male slaves recorded in the Edirne estate registers apparently were occupied on the landholdings possessed by Ottoman officeholders, and therefore must be regarded as a productive investment of sorts.

As to the eighteenth century, Cezar's pioneering work on a small *ayan*'s holding in the region of Amasya also concentrates on the manner in which this man made a living, and not on his consumption patterns.[33] The same thing applies to my own study of an early nineteenth-century *voyvoda* of the Edremit district, who was an avid collector of olive trees and lent out money.[34]

André Raymond's analysis of eighteenth-century Cairo estate inventories, one of the most fascinating and comprehensive undertaken so far, equally neglects the consumption sector.[35] Raymond's concern is with the ups and downs of the city's economic life, and estates, when analyzed in quantity, provide some indication of the growth or decline of commerce and crafts. In addition, he has concerned himself with the "protection racket" run by janissaries, gunners, and others, which caused Muslim artisans to join the city's paramilitary corps in order to protect themselves against taxation. Thus the author has produced a graphic account of the conditions limiting consumption, not of consumption itself. The only exception to this rule is his concern with building, which includes rental housing and public baths. But even here, urbanistic concerns far outweigh the interest in consumption properly speaking.

A more recent study of eighteenth-century Damascus estate inventories, by Colette Establet and Jean-Paul Pascual, focuses on social stratification.[36] At first glance, this concern should be more germane to consumption than the economic and political concerns that play such a major role in Raymond's work. But the authors have not tried to establish consumption patterns typical for different social groups. Ways of making a living, the presence or absence of debts, and inequalities of wealth constitute the major criteria according to which social groups are distinguished from one another. Only after the book had appeared has Colette Establet, in papers that as yet remain unpublished, begun to interest herself in consumption properly speaking.[37]

One of the few aspects of "consumption" that has attracted the attention of historians dealing with Ottoman estate inventories is slavery. Barkan's study apart, there is Halil Sahillioğlu's work, which extends beyond the estate inventories to other documents from the *kadı* court registers concerning slavery. Sahillioğlu has shown how slaves both male and female were employed in weaving, while male slaves worked in the service of merchants, and at times accompanied their owners on travels.[38] But the use of slave labor in urban production was limited to the fifteenth and sixteenth centuries. Slave weavers or shop assistants were distinctly a minority phenomenon. Most Ottoman slaves and particularly slave women served as cooks, cleaners, singers, and guards, and thus provided the services permitting their owners' consumption.

Occasionally the inheritance inventories also provide information on the consumption of former slaves. Well to do townsmen and townswomen, often manumitted slaves by testament and, by establishing foundations to benefit their freed men, underwrote the latter's consumption. Young freed women had to be married off, and upon that occasion were sometimes given clothes, house furnishings, and even some modest jewelry. These donations allow us to guess what a bride of limited means normally brought with her when she entered her husband's home. In wealthy households of fifteenth-century Bursa, a manumitted slave woman sometimes (but by no means always) received as a gift the sumptuous clothes she had worn while in the household of her former owner.[39] We are free to imagine that most freed women sold these items in order to finance their trousseaus.

Evliya Çelebi's Travelogue as a Source on Consumption

Evliya's ten-volume account can be read as a loosely linked sequence of town and city descriptions.[40] In an all but invariable order, the author discusses the local citadel, mosques, theological schools, baths, dervish convents, and, outside the town's perimeter, the picnicking areas where Ottoman urbanites enjoyed their spare time. But his descriptions also included at least a few words on famous local foods, particularly fruit. Occasionally he mentioned the fabrics of which the outer wear of the inhabitants of a given town was manufactured.

Apart from these relatively standard data, Evliya recorded information about consumer goods whenever the local shops and markets were especially well stocked. For in spite of his piety and respect for dervishes, Evliya's inclinations were by no means otherworldly. Quite to the contrary, an abundance of consumable goods for him constituted a reason to praise the locality in which they were found. Evliya was fascinated by the pilgrimage fairs of Mina (Hidjaz) or Tanta (Egypt), but also by the streets of Mecca during the hajj season, when every entrance to a house offering a bit of shade was provisionally turned into a shop. In a different vein, the multiple uses the inhabitants of Trabzon made of the abundance of anchovies *(hamsi)* available in the Black Sea inspired Evliya to a page or two about the local folklore connected with this comestible.

However, courtly consumption equally incited the traveler's interest.[41] When Evliya was taken hostage by the Khan of Bitlis and obliged to spend some time in the latter's palace, he noted the entertainments in which the courtiers participated. The varied foods and beverages served at such occasions included Iranian specialities such as confiture of wild carrots. More importantly, here we also find one of the earliest references to the consumption of the tea in Anatolia. Apart from palaces (and incidentally, dervish convents) an institution whose culture and consumption greatly interested Evliya was the coffeehouse. Particularly in the case of Bursa, there is ample information on the storytellers and other entertainers who practiced their art in certain coffeehouses, making these otherwise rather plebeian locales suitable for the patronage of distinguished gentlemen.

Archival Sources on Food Consumption

Few historians have interested themselves in locating sources that may be relevant to consumption apart from the estate inventories. As a result the listing of sources given here is by no means final. New studies appear every year, and quite a few of the primary sources analyzed in them furnish information on consumption. However extricating this information is by no means a simple task, as providing information on consumption was not the principal aim, either of the original authors or of the twentieth-century historians who have studied their work. Thus the diary of a dervish by the name of Seyyid Ahmed, analyzed by Cemal Kafadar, contains information on foods served to guests, but also on Seyyid Ahmed's attitudes toward particular foods, fruit, and cheese in particular.[42] In the same diary we also find information on the use of books, which were lent out, returned, or discussed. The newly awakening interest in Ottoman everyday life is bound to enrich our information in the near future.

But as things stand today, even the accounts of pious foundations in Istanbul and Anatolia, extensively studied as sources for price history and regional economies, have scarcely been drawn upon by consumption historians. This is all the more astonishing as Ömer Barkan, in one of the earliest studies on this type of source, has pointed out that the kitchens of the major Istanbul *imaret*s served relatively high-quality food, not merely bread and charity soups. Such kitchens not only catered to *medrese* students and the poor, but to an important extent, to officeholders on brief visits to the capital, and to widows to a certain standing.[43] The foods served in the *imaret*s of provincial towns obviously were intended for a more modest clientele. But we find the *imaret* of Sultan Selim II in Konya serving the adjacent convent of the Mevlevis, well known for its close links to Ottoman officialdom.[44] Recent research moreover has shown that the accounts of foundation storehouses, which in the larger *imaret*s were kept separately from the money accounts, sometimes permit us to reconstruct the composition of dishes served. Here historians of food consumption have at their disposal a rich and still largely unexploited primary source.

During recent years, the educated reading public's interest in food and nutrition has induced a few Ottomanist historians to study this most basic sector of human consumption. Primary sources apart from foundation accounts, mostly concern the kitchen of the sultan's palace. The Topkapı Sarayı and its nineteenth-century successors Dolmabahçe and Yıldız were gigantic undertakings, where food was prepared on an everyday basis for the sultan, resident princes, pages, women of the harem, and menial service personnel. At frequently recurring special occasions, foreign ambassadors along with their often numerous retinues in addition to large numbers of janissaries were served foods of varying degrees of refinement, carefully graded according to rank.

At major festivals, the number of guests often was so large that the containers available in the palace kitchen did not suffice, and pots, pans, and dishes were borrowed from pious foundations. Careful records were kept of these proceedings, which permit us to provide a context for the meals properly speaking. But in other respects as well, officials in the service of the sultan's kitchen carefully recorded both incoming and outgoing items. The institution received certain taxes and dues without passing through the treasury. The sultan's kitchen therefore needed to account for direct money payments from taxpayers, but also for chickens or fruit acquired without recourse to the market. In addition there were purchases; from the sixteenth century onward, numerous sultanic commands survive which order this or that item for the palace kitchen, often at prices considerably below those which the ordinary consumer was expected to pay.

On the expenditure side, there survive registers that document everyday output, but also the food served to ambassadors—in certain instances, members of the latters' entourage have provided evidence that supplements the registers of the palace kitchen.[45] Palaces of princes and princesses also have produced records. Thus Feridun Emecen has discovered a kitchen register from the prince's palace in Manisa, hitherto the only representative of its kind. But in all likelihood it is simply the sole survivor of a long series.[46] Tülay Artan has studied kitchen registers documenting the lives of eighteenth-century Ottoman princesses; the latter received rations from the central palace kitchen, which were recorded in detail.[47] Moreover great festivities such as the circumcisions of 1582 or 1720 generated extensive accounts, unfortunately not always easy to decipher.

Obviously it would be a grave mistake to base our notions of Ottoman consumption on the evidence of the palace registers alone; as always, the powerful ate better than their subjects. But at least the sultan's kitchens supplied so many people that the relevant registers must have reflected the festive food consumption of well to do town dwellers, rather than merely what was consumed by the ruler and his entourage.

Sources on Women, Sources on Consumption

Ottoman nonpeasant women, that is both members of the elite and ordinary towns women, were active not so much in production as in reproduction, an activity that included consumption. As a result, the sources that historians studying Ottoman women have unearthed are often relevant for our purposes as well. In addition to the inheritance inventories already discussed, the few surviving literary texts that mention Ottoman women can be read as a record of their material culture. Particularly promising in this respect is the diary of the late seventeenth-century dervish studied by Cemal Kafadar, which we have already encountered in the section on food consumption. This educated but not exactly scholarly Istanbul gentleman must have written very much *pro domo*, as the female members of his family are given relatively great prominence. His account can probably be used in order to generate information concerning the consumption a well to do householder considered appropriate for female relatives.

Not surprisingly, however, the most informative sources concern the consumption of elite women, particularly the princesses who in the eighteenth century increased both in political importance and in (documented) consumption. Thus the growing scholarly interest both in upper-class women and in the eighteenth century has had positive repercussions on the study of consumption. Lists of clothes, jewelry, and household furnishings allotted to princesses survive. These include some lists specifying the *ceyiz*—that is, the goods a bride belonging to the sultan's family contributed to her husband's household.[48] There also exist lists of foodstuffs the central palace kitchen turned over to the kitchens of princesses' palaces. Hatice Sultan, sister of Selim III, at the end of the eighteenth century patronized the architect, decorator, and draughtsman Antoine-Ignace Melling, and some of her letters to him survive. Those that have been published deal mainly with the design of clothes and jewelry.[49]

Last but not least, there exist the memoirs of a woman who in the mid nineteenth century, was admitted to the sultan's harem as companion to a princess: Leyla (Saz)'s memoirs contain a great deal of information on the decoration of the harem sections of palaces that have since disappeared, and thus are of unique interest.[50] However often it is impossible to verify the source and therefore the reliability of her information. For though Leyla Saz saw these places with her own eyes, she was a child at the time, and before writing her memoirs at an advanced age, must have incorporated much information supplied by other people. If the "memoirs" of Melek Hanım, at one time the wife of Vizier Kıbrıslı Mehmed Paşa, should turn out to be something more than second-rate historical fiction, they will also provide information on the material culture of the Ottoman upper class.[51]

The Contributions of Archeology and Art History

In addition to written sources, art history and archaeology are also beginning to enrich our knowledge of Ottoman consumption. Archaeological data have been unearthed in Hungary, where the Ottoman elements of the castle of Buda as well as rural fortresses (*palankas*) have been examined.[52] Movable items such as potsherds or arms, and fixed installations such as water conduits, are of significance in this context. In Turkey, the pioneering works of Kâzım Çeçen on the water conduits of Istanbul can teach us a great deal about the water consumption of the capital's inhabitants, even though historians have been rather slow in making use of his contributions.[53] Museum specialists have studied one very specific branch of consumption—namely, the collection of artifacts by wealthy men and women. Unfortunately, only one major collection put together by prenineteenth-century Ottoman collectors survives—namely, that of the Topkapı Palace. Thus the study of collecting has yielded more evidence on the use of Ottoman artefacts by outsiders than on the collecting patterns of Ottoman dignitaries themselves.[54]

But art historical studies have yielded information on textile history, decorative metalwork, and "vernacular" architecture, all of which constituted important areas of consumption among the wealthier layers of Ottoman society. In the case of textile history, the historian of consumption may draw upon the growing number of studies concerning rugs and *kilims*.[55] Here is an area where Ottoman and European art history come in close contact with one another. As for the period before the eighteenth century, we possess far more images of rugs on Italian and later Netherlandish paintings than original pieces. Textile history also involves the study of silk fabrics, manufactured in Bursa but equally in Damascus and other places. In addition a few scholars have concerned themselves with the importation of Indian fabrics into the Ottoman Empire and their imitations by local weavers.[56] Museum pieces can be supplemented by the pattern books that occasionally turned up in archives, and of course by written documentation. For the nineteenth century, scholars have tried to link surviving clothes and headgear with the evidence provided by newspaper advertisements and fashion journals.[57] The study of copper vessels and jewelry is less advanced, but may provide the economic historian with important leads in the future: metal goods, being relatively durable, often were collected as a form of savings, so that the study of such holdings links the history of consumption to the broader field of economic history.

During recent years, the study of "vernacular" architecture has progressed considerably, and we now know much more about the living space of Ottoman townsmen than would have been thought possible twenty or thirty years ago. Especially impressive are the studies on cities in the Arab world, such as Cairo, Aleppo, or Damascus, where the wealthier inhabitants built stone houses of great opulence, which have survived much better than the wood or framework constructions typical of Istanbul and much of Anatolia.[58] Scholars dealing with these cities have been able to combine the study of surviving buildings with an analysis of written documents. For upon the occasion of a transfer, either by sale or inheritance, descriptions of the houses concerned were often recorded in the *kadı* court registers. Nelly Hanna's work on seventeenth- and eighteenth-century Cairo, in particular, can arouse the envy of any specialist on urban Anatolia, as the beautiful "fit" between the two categories of documentation which she has been able to secure cannot be duplicated anywhere in the Turkish-speaking regions of the Ottoman Empire.[59] But even the study of written records alone has taught us a great deal about the layout of Ottoman towns, about relationships between neighbors, and about the relative values of the dwellings inhabited by different social groups.[60] This particularly applies to Istanbul, where the surviving records are at times so numerous as to permit the reconstruction of entire urban neighborhoods.[61]

Economic Aspects of Consumption

I will now pass from the overview over what has been done in the past to a list of things which, in my opinion at least, could and should be undertaken in the future. Here our starting point is the level of income of the different socio-political groups making up Ottoman society. Right away, we run into difficulty: in a society in which few people worked for wages or salaries, all we possess with respect to the nonelite consists of some information on wages in the building trade and on the service personnel (cooks, cleaners, and the like) employed by the Ottoman state. Given the paucity of raw data, it is unlikely that we will ever possess series of the kind that could satisfy the requirements of the Committee on Price History, which between the two world wars, inspired so much work on wages in the European context.[62]

But even the few Ottoman wage data available for the prenineteenth-century period have rarely been studied. Therefore the problem can only be introduced in the shape of a rough sketch. When workmen were employed by the central administration, they rarely were paid what they would have received if they had worked for private employers, and inflation resulted in further wage losses.[63] This must have induced some workmen to seek alternative employment. In sixteenth-century Istanbul, nonofficial persons desiring to build sometimes provided an alternative to the sultan's projects.[64] It may in the long run be possible to collect a few wage data for workmen employed by pious foundations on repair projects, and compare them with data contained in the account books documenting state-sponsored construction. But I would not place too much hope in this possibility, since most foundation accounts only give us the overall sums expended on repairs, but tell us nothing about daily wages.

More hopeful seems the case of the menial palace employees, because for these people, wage accounts do survive. However there is the problem of determining which people actually worked and which "wage" recipients were simply enjoying sinecures. Moreover the relevant account books have not been examined at all, and in the palace context, the problem of nonmonetary payments (food, clothing) is particularly relevant. There also survive abundant data for the payment of janissaries. Remarkably enough, even though for ages and ages historians have explained janissary uprisings with the effects of inflation and currency debasement upon their pay, there exists as yet no systematic study of janissary pay registers.[65] But once again, everything conspires to make the task of the historian difficult: for since the later seventeenth century at the very least, many janissaries supplemented their income by economic activity in the crafts and commerce, or by merely "sponging" on merchants and artisans.[66] For this later period—and its beginning will have to be established for every city individually—the pay registers will therefore record only part of the disposable income of many janissaries.

If there is little chance of relating Ottoman wages and prices and thus determining long-term changes in purchasing power, at least there exist a few studies concerning the prices of basic consumer goods such as foodstuffs, building materials, and textiles. However when we use the word "prices" we need to carefully specify what we mean by this term. The Ottoman urban market was tightly controlled, both by the *kadı* and *muhtesip*, and by the craftsmen themselves.[67] For certain large cities such as Istanbul, Bursa, and Edirne, there survive lists of officially administered prices *(narh)*, which list many consumer goods sold in urban shops. But only in the case of a few very large cities can these lists even pretend to be exhaustive. In smaller towns, only a few essential foods, particularly bread and grain, in addition to one or two nonfood commodities were assigned a *narh*.[68] All the goods that do not show up in *narh* lists must therefore have been priced by the guildsmen themselves. Somehow it is difficult to imagine that bargaining is an invention of the nineteenth and twentieth centuries.

Cemal Kafadar has suggested, in my view very convincingly, that administratively determined prices may have been enforced mainly when the Ottoman administration demanded goods and services. Ordinary consumers often may have paid different prices.[69]

In addition there is the vexed question, well known to price historians anywhere, of wholesale and retail prices. Most of the prices known to us are those paid by institutions, especially pious foundations. But foundations often were managed by people high up in the local social hierarchy, who had favors to bestow and moreover bought in quantity. Barring catastrophes, foundation purchases were probably made at the time of year when prices were lowest. Ordinary people bought retail in small quantities, and were therefore gravely affected by seasonal fluctuations that did not touch the larger purchasers. Thus even if in the future we will have constructed wage series for some of the best documented trades, we will still be obliged to relate them to documented prices, which may be much lower than those that wage earners paid in reality. Worst of all, "black market" transactions in times of scarcity, when sellers refused to abide by the prices decreed by provincial authorities, only rarely have been recorded in the quantitative documentation available. Yet qualitative evidence on such periods tells us that "illicit" prices were demanded and paid. We should not fall into the trap of deducing everyday reality from normative texts.

Given the elementary state of our knowledge on the purchasing power of Ottoman townsmen, there exists no real equivalent to the "standard of living controversy" so well known to British historians. Nor do we possess any studies comparing the consumption of Ottoman townsmen with their homologues in other cultures, even in an impressionistic fashion. Halil Inalcık has once suggested that Indian textiles found a ready market in the Ottoman lands because of lower wage levels in India.[70] But imitations of Indian fabrics, manufactured in southeastern Anatolia and Syria, did quite well in both local and international markets, so that the price advantage of the Indian imports cannot have been all that overwhelming.[71] Presumably we will never have very satisfying long-term data on Ottoman real wages and their changing purchasing power. But while some people seem to consider this problem both old-fashioned and insoluble, I think it is basic to everything else we may try to conceptualize. Therefore at least in this case, even imperfect notions are better than no understanding at all.

Social Aspect of Consumption

In most societies, the use of certain items as status markers constitutes one of the most important issues confronting the social historian of consumption. The Ottomans are no exception to this rule. Seventeenth-, eighteenth-, and early nineteenth-century costume books show the robes worn by officials high up in the Ottoman state hierarchy. The European ambassadors who often purchased albums of this kind were at least in part motivated by the practical need to distinguish at first glance the rank of the persons with whom they were dealing. By distributing robes of honor as markers of distinction, the sultans further confirmed the hierarchy of dress.

However robes of honor at least occasionally could be received by people not in official positions. When in the seventeenth century, it became necessary to restore the Ka'aba after it had been destroyed in a flash flood, even the chief building artisans received these decorations, albeit not from the sultan directly, but from the hand of the official in charge of the project.[72] However we do not know how subjects of the sultan not part of the ruling elite used these robes, whether they wore them at special occasions or just kept them stored away in their chests. But costume albums, and their nineteenth-century successors the genre photographs, show that many townsmen could be "placed" in the local social structure on account of their special clothes or headgear. Particularly members of dervish orders wore caps proclaiming their affiliation. In addition to the clothes assigned to different groups by the custom of their guild or dervish order, there were sumptuary laws. Where males were involved, they aimed to make socio-political status hierarchies clearly apparent.

According to the views current among Ottoman officials, the most important difference between Ottoman subjects was doubtlessly their religion. Muslims preceded non-Muslims in official enumerations, and sumptuary laws ordered that differences in religion be made visible, among other things through clothes.[73] Certain colors might be reserved for Muslims, Christians, or Jews, and non-Muslims often were required to wear unobtrusive clothes in dark colors. In some periods, there might be regulations concerning the outward appearance of houses inhabited by non-Muslims. These aimed at making them appear less attractive than those of their Muslim neighbors.[74] Yet one suspects that these rules were broken more often than enforced. In Anatolian towns such as Ankara and Kayseri, by the late seventeenth century, non-Muslims not rarely inhabited expensive dwellings. Given the absence of ghettoes, it is unlikely that prices were driven up simply because large numbers of Christians tried to crowd into a limited space. Moreover in many nineteenth-century provincial towns, non-Muslims tended to adopt amenities imported from Europe more rapidly than their Muslim neighbors. But this situation did not generally lead to public protests that sumptuary laws were being infringed. There must have been many local and regional differences, and the problem is worth further study.

In the case of women, sumptuary laws had a different function, as the major official concern was to make them as "invisible" as possible. However in some cases, the clothes of non-Muslim women, similarly to those worn by men, were regulated in order to set them apart from their Muslim counterparts. Recent work by Madeline Zilfi has shown that in the middle of the eighteenth century, sumptuary laws directed against women were reiterated with a frequency not seen in older periods.[75] This author has suggested that the renewed emphasis on women's seclusion and "invisibility" was due to the fact that, beginning with the "Tulip period," upper-class women, and princesses in particular, had acquired semiofficial roles and a new type of stature.

At present our understanding of the manner in which sumptuary legislation and real life were connected is still rather elementary. Experience from other cultures, in which sumptuary laws have been studied in more detail, suggests that frequent repetition of certain rules may indicate that in real life they were difficult to enforce. But we will need to study *kadı* court registers, hoping to find some examples of people prosecuted for not conforming to sumptuary laws. Such cases were none too frequent, and at present, interpretation can only be tentative.

When the consumption of certain items was linked to high sociopolitical status, it is probable that some people tried to acquire these status symbols even without having previously obtained the relevant positions. This must have been true especially when a status symbol was relatively new and therefore not hedged in by too many prohibitions. Thus in the eighteenth century, wealthy Ottomans were willing to pay respectable sums for tulips and other ornamental plants. One can imagine that wealthy people of modest official status, such as merchants or tax farmers, seized the opportunity to acquire elaborate flower gardens, particularly as there was—at least to my knowledge—no sultan's command that forbade them to do so.

When in the eighteenth century, the ownership of seaside villas on the Bosphorus became a mark of high status, one can imagine similar kinds of competition on the part of wealthy men both in and out of office. Yet in this case, there was a limiting factor—namely, the sultan's dangerously intensive interest in the owners of these villas. The ruler's concern was documented by the order to compile the so-called *bostancıbaşı* registers; a number of them survive and one has recently been published.[76] It is quite probable that possessing a dwelling much more opulent that those of one's peers carried certain risks. At the end of the eighteenth and the beginning of the nineteenth century, a number of unsuccessful wars brought with them serious financial difficulties. In consequence, the old right of the sultan to confiscate the estates of his servitors was exercised much more extensively, and maybe also more brutally, than in the past.[77] Confiscation was even extended to wealthier taxpayers, who as members of the subject population in the "classical" Ottoman Empire, had been immune. In such cases, the Ottoman treasury often claimed that the deceased had been indebted to the fisc; these debts may have been real or else fictitious. Yet the large number of seaside villas enumerated in the *bostancıbaşı* registers shows that the danger of confiscation did not discourage large numbers of wealthy Ottomans from investing in this field.

On a much more modest level, better-off provincial taxpayers in the eighteenth century also favored status markers, which theoretically were reserved to the sultan's servitors. Remarkable is the distribution of silver inlaid arms, which formed the main adornment of a man, jewelry being largely reserved for females. The work of Yvonne Seng on Üsküdar has shown that in the early sixteenth century, silver inlaid arms were in fact owned mainly by members of the ruling group, soldiers in particular.[78] However by the eighteenth century this luxury could be found among the possessions of a modest non-Muslim notable in the outlying province of Kayseri.

Yet consumption goods were more than status markers. To begin with, they were acquired because of the protection against the elements, comfort, and simple esthetic pleasure they afforded their owners, an aspect that scholars obsessed with the social meanings of consumption items often forget. In addition some items may have had memories attached to them, serving as mementoes of dead relatives or of earlier stages in an individual's life. Melek Hanım, the former wife of Tanzimat Grand Vizier Kıbrıslı Mehmed Paşa, once remarked that the memory of their bridal *ceyiz* set out for the admiration of female friends and neighbors was precious to Ottoman ladies even if they were unhappy with their married life.[79]

Although these memoirs must be treated with caution as long as no critical study informs us of the manner in which they were composed, this remark is suggestive and worth following up, for it points to a significant change of mentalities in the past century. Melek Hanım's observation refers to the mid-1850s. In the early 1970s, that is a mere 120 years later, a young Cypriot Turkish woman talked to me about the same custom with extreme revulsion. She felt that it humiliated women by emphasizing the material aspects of marriage, the bride, so to speak, becoming a mere part of the goods to be transferred to her husband. This little observation may warn us of the dangers involved in the search, certainly stimulating and challenging, for the meanings of consumption items to people of the past. Given the small numbers of sources at our disposal, the danger of anachronism is always present.

A Provisional Conclusion

It is the main point of this chapter to show that we know very little, and point to the sources and hypotheses that may allow us to find out more. I have had occasion to note that some of our ignorance is probably due to the limitations of our sources. But at least in my opinion, much more significant is the lack of monographic studies on most aspects of consumption. Given this very provisional character of the present investigation—a conclusion, which after all is supposed to conclude something—seems almost a contradiction in terms. Let us however recapitulate the most salient points, and indicate the directions in which future work can move. To begin with, the history of consumption can serve as a bridge between economic history on the one hand, and social and cultural history on the other. No one can claim that Ottoman economic history has been as well studied as its European or Mughal-Indian counterparts. But in comparison with other branches of Ottoman history, economic history is relatively well known territory. Or at least, this may be claimed of the production (supply) sector; demand has been much less studied. Given the close link between demand and consumption, however, the study of consumption may help us to produce a more balanced understanding even of economic history.

Our knowledge of social and cultural history is much spottier, and this affects our evaluation of consumption. Whenever we attempt to figure out the meanings that Ottomans attached to the consumption of different goods, the danger of anachronism lurks in every nook and cranny. This difficulty is at least partly due to the fact that there has been so little cooperation between the students of the Ottoman Turkish language and literature on the one hand, and historians on the other. Exceptions, such as Fuat Köprülü in the past and more recently Cemal Kafadar, only confirm the general rule. Yet if we want consumption history to be more than a minor branch of economic history, we need to delve into texts in order to find out something about the social context in which individual items were used. Our neglect of the social context in which both production and consumption took place is a deficiency all the more astonishing as most Ottomanist economic historians, more or less explicitly, assume that the rules governing production in a noncapitalist society are fundamentally different from those that determine production under capitalism.[80] This assumption should encourage the study of links between production and consumption, but to date it has not done so.

Fortunately, the study of texts is not the only way leading toward a more refined understanding of what Ottoman consumption may have been. Art history constitutes another avenue. Scholars interested in Ottoman consumption have on the whole had better luck when seeking cooperation with representatives of this discipline. Links between social historians and historians of art have been facilitated by the latters' interest in the "minor" arts, which after all enhanced the esthetic value of items in principle intended for domestic use. Moreover the iconographic interests of certain art historians have led them to ask questions very similar to those asked by social historians. Present-day art historians study the activity of patrons, analyze building accounts, and attempt to find out what impact given types of visual language may have had on the visitor of a mosque or *zaviye*.[81] Especially when dealing with inheritance inventories, we all have much to learn from our colleagues dealing with "vernacular" architecture, metalwork, or jewelry.

Unavoidably the study of Ottoman consumption has a built-in class bias. What we can find out about peasant autoconsumption will always be comparatively limited, even though archaeology may in the future broaden our understanding. But as far as the town dwellers and the elite are concerned, the study of consumption may yet provide a link between different subdisciplines of Ottoman history, while at the same time permitting Ottomanists to engage in a hopefully productive dialogue with their Indianist and Europeanist colleagues. It seems a pity to pass up these opportunities.

Notes

1. I owe this idea to Halil Berktay, University of the Bosphorus, Istanbul. Göçek (1996) reached me too late to be included in this discussion.

2. Dyer (1989), 167.

3. Spufford (1984).

4. Dermigny (1964), Butel (1989).

5. Roche (1989b), 424.

6. Roche (1989b), 321ff.

7. Pardailhé-Golabrun (1988), 332–41.

8. Burnett (1989), 181–88; 255–57.

9. For an example among many, see Lis and Soly (1979), 116–29.

10. Montanari (1994).

11. Schama (1987), 170 and elsewhere; de Vries (1993), 98.

12. Soboul (1970), 425–36; Godechot (1974), 414–15, 432–38.

13. de Vries (1993), 96–97.

14. Stoianovich (1966).

15. Quataert (1994), 881.

16. de Vries (1993), 101.

17. Quataert (1994), unpaginated first page.

18. Evin (1985).

19. Scott (1985), 42–45.

20. Boxandall, tr. Sauerländer (1985), 101; Zilfi (1995).

21. Said (1978).

22. For a curious example from the realm of metalwork, see Melikian Chirvani (1975).

23. Especially relevant are Chaudhuri (1985) and Subrahmanyam (1990).

24. Bayly (1983), 63ff.

25. Kütükoğlu (1983).

26. Bayly (1983), 197ff.

27. Compare for example Arel (1998).

28. Sirman (1988).

29. Akgündüz et al, vol. 1 (1989).

30. Inventories prepared for this reason are not located in the *kadı*'s registers, but in the Başbakanlık Arşivi-Osmanlı Arşivi, Istanbul.

31. İnalcık (1979a).

32. Barkan (1965).

33. Cezar (1977).

34. Faroqhi (1991).

35. Raymond (1973–1974).

36. Establet and Pascual (1994).

37. Papers given at the Congress for the Economic and Social History of Turkey, Heidelberg 1995, and at the AFEMAM Congress, Aix-en-Provence 1996.

38. Sahillioğlu (1983).

39. Faroqhi (to be published).

40. Evliya Çelebi (1314/1896–1897 to 1983).

41. Evliya, ed. Dankoff (1990), 118–19.

42. Kafadar (1989).

43. Barkan (1963), 267–83.

44. Faroqhi (1984), 210ff.

45. Dariusz Kolodziejczyk, at a conference on Ottoman food held at the University of the Bosphorus in the spring of 1996, read a paper on the numerous comments of Polish noblemen concerning the food they were served at the Ottoman court. The papers read at this conference hopefully will soon be published.

46. Feridun Emecen read his paper at the conference mentioned in note 37.

47. Tülay Artan read her paper at the conference mentioned in note 37.

48. Delibaş (1988).

49. Anhegger (1991).

50. Leila Hanoum (1991).

51. Melek Hanım (1996).

52. Gerelyes (1995) and the literature cited in this article.

53. Among this author's numerous works, compare Çeçen (1988).

54. Rogers (1995), 15–25.

55. Ydema (1991) and the literature cited therein.

56. Fukasawa (1987).

57. Stillman and Micklewright (1992) and the literature cited therein.

58. Maury, Raymond, Revault, Zakarya (1983) for Cairo; Abel Nour (1986) and Marcus (1989) for Aleppo.

59. Hanna (1991).

60. Faroqhi (1987).

61. Artan (unpubl. diss., 1988).

62. For an example, see Hamilton (1947), 46ff.

63. Barkan (1972, 1979), vol. 1, 98–99.

64. Barkan (1972, 1979), vol. 2, 292.

65. Explanations of this kind go back to seventeenth-century Ottoman chroniclers and authors of "advice literature."

66. Raymond (1973–1974), vol. 2, 587ff.

67. Kütükoğlu (1983), 12–19.

68. Kütükoğlu (1983), 18–19.

69. Kafadar (unpubl. diss., 1986), 128.

70. İnalcık (1979–1980), 52–54.

71. Fukasawa (1987).

72. Faroqhi (1994), 118.

73. Ahmet Refik (1988d), 47.

74. Stoianovich (1970), 99.

75. Zilfi (1995).

76. Kayra, Üyepazarcı (1992).

77. Cezar (1986), 135.

78. Seng (1991).

79. Melek Hanım (1996), 183.

80. I do not know of a single study that has defended the opposite position.

81. An expert in this kind of work is Gülru Necipoğlu; see among other items Necipoğlu (1986).

3

Toward an *Isolario* of the Ottoman Inheritance Inventory,[1] with Special Reference to Manisa (ca. 1600–1700)[2]

Joyce Hedda Matthews

Isolarii were productions of the early modern era devised with the intent of conveying to Europeans topical and historical lore about newly visited and little known islands—with those in the Aegean sea taking pride of place.[3] Often expressly prepared for presentation to a person of high station, an *isolario* would furnish an outline drawing of the subject island, fringed by markings to indicate the harbors, shoals, and other salient features of the surrounding waters as with a portolan. What distinguished an *isolario* from a portolan was its primary focus on the physical interior of the island. The planal expanse of the island would be densely dotted with verbal descriptions, identifying in detail the character of the island, the natural features of its terrain, such as promontories, rivers and mountains, and its principal resources. For its purpose was not to function as a pilot for the seafaring captain, but rather to offer a learned description of a recently explored island for the special elucidation of an appreciative audience.

The selection of the Ottoman inheritance inventory *(tereke)* as a subject for comparable treatment may at first glance seem to fall short in terms of its potential to divert the reader.[4] Yet, when the present accumulation of knowledge regarding the Ottoman inventory is considered as a whole, we are struck by a close resemblance between these two entities. The paucity of intimate knowledge possessed by contemporaries in the early modern era concerning the physiognomy of the islands in the Aegean is, I believe, a fair match for that possessed by today's scholars regarding the dales and vales of the Ottoman inheritance inventory.

While the counterpart of the Ottoman inventory in Europe and the United States has undergone a fair amount of surveying and exploitation and, on the other hand, despite the fact that those portions of Islamic law on the partitioning of inheritance are readily accessible in the Qur'an and other sources, the Ottoman inventory as an exemplar of the application of these provides a partial explanation of why this class of material may lure the venturesome researcher. Looming above the near horizons of the interested scholar, the Ottoman inventory forms a sizeable and distinct body of material. At the same time, however, its pertinent features remain, from the vantage point of current knowledge, indistinct. These dual injunctions are relatively unknown.[5] The conspicuousness of the inventory in the sea of Ottoman archival records and judicial registers arises from its formal qualities, which also are properties of the Ottoman inheritance inventory—a distinctive and apparently rich repository of information and a largely unfamiliar terrain—make it an ideal subject for an *isolario*. Underlying the present conceit of an *isolario* is the hope that this presentation may prove suggestive of ways in which the treasures of the Ottoman inventory might be opened up to more systematic investigation. This would permit more precise formulations for comparative analyses with Ottoman inventories created in other districts of Anatolia, and territories outside Anatolia, and with inventories produced in non-Ottoman socio-political contexts.

On the Littoral of the Ottoman Inheritance Inventory

The formation of the Ottoman inheritance inventory took place in an Aegean setting—that is to say, western Asia Minor (Anatolia)—some time in the medieval period. Factors of significance in any summary of the character of this milieu include the remnants of the Eastern Roman imperial administration, the Eastern Orthodox ecclesiastical organization, Venetian and Genoese trading colonies, a polyglot populace and, depending on the period, one or more Turkic principalities. (Ultimately, the most successful among these Turco-Islamic principalities was the small, but expanding, polity of the followers of Osman.) These and other elements can still be picked out, but at this remove in time, the original spectrum of colors has lost its vibrancy and been reduced to a simple chiaroscuro.

For instance, when we learn that the Turkish lord and former Byzantine captive, Çaka (Greek, Tazkhas) Bey, whose domain was centered in Izmir and extended north to the Marmara Sea and to the adjacent Aegean islands in the late eleventh century could, reportedly, recite by heart lines of Homer in Greek, we may wonder whether he represented an isolated phenomenon or whether he might have been part of an ongoing shared tradition that extended even up to the time of the founding of the Ottoman state in 1299.[6] Or, for example, it seems evident that only if western Anatolia were viewed as a geopolitical tabula rasa could credence be lent to the account related by an Ottoman chronicler of the late fifteenth century of an incident in which Osman, the founder of the Ottoman dynasty, expresses genuine surprise—and even anger—upon learning that market dues *(bac)* are imposed at a local market.[7] In the end, Osman consents to the imposition of this due, purportedly, after being informed that it was customary among the communities in western Anatolia. The geoeconomic context for this exchange, we should recall, was an active international trading network. Moreover, we should not overlook the fact that this kind of levy (Ar. *hisbe*) had been a long-established and sanctioned practice in Islamic lands.[8]

As intimated by these broad strokes, the medieval Aegean milieu in which the Ottoman state took shape remains, many centuries later, a still wooden diorama and is but one consequence of the present inventing the past.[9] Today, we impress on western Anatolia in the centuries immediately prior to 1299 and the founding of the Ottoman realm, a label reading Byzantine—a label that excludes the various Turkic principalities established there during these same centuries.[10] The succeeding era in this modern time series is called Ottoman, which in its turn, scarcely registers the presence of Greeks (and other ethnic groups), who seem to have continued pursuing a way of life that was familiar to them in this selfsame region. Further, both of these labels sidestep the issue of the Seljuk (1071–1318) legacy in Anatolia.

Future forays into the Ottoman inheritance inventory might prove more profitable if the inventory were approached not as a record exclusively based on Islamic law, but rather as a construction of societal paper-mâche: in effect, a précis of the historic panoply of diverse ethnic groups, languages, and faiths of this peninsula of Asia. (I reject the label "mosaic" to depict the essential character of the Ottoman Empire until such time as it may be convincingly demonstrated that the various individual *tesserae* making up the mosaic underwent no transformation during the Ottoman period.) True, the initial act of creating the Ottoman inventory may be assigned to the injunctions of Islamic law. Nonetheless, let us recall that the Byzantines had also devised a method for the division of inheritance. In theory, the model associated with its impetus might have arisen from this quarter in a manner not dissimilar from that which the chronicler reports the decision by Osman to adopt the indigenous custom of market dues. Confronted with the evidence supplied by a preponderant number of the inheritance inventories in the Manisa court registers in the period under study of what appear to be violations of the spirit of the law, we may readily acknowledge the need to rethink the Ottoman inventory, at least that executed for the ordinary subject in the provinces. In other words, it seems a simpler matter—and a better research strategy—to start with what the existent form itself discloses about its context through an objective examination, rather than initiating a study with the question of why various substantial aspects failed to conform to a model that may no longer survive or possibly never existed. That is why an *isolario,* or what might be called a methodical deconstruction, of the inventory may better assist us in making closer acquaintance with provincial—and, in this instance, Aegean—Ottoman society in the seventeenth century.[11]

Dragoman of the Demesne

Now that we have established a fix on our orientation, we may steady our gaze for a moment on the principal intermediary in the product of the inventory in Manisa: the Ottoman judge or *kadı.* Ordinarily, sources indicate that a judicial official who was expert in such matters *(kassam)* drew up Ottoman inheritance inventories.[12] In Manisa, only in a few instances is there any evidence that such was the case, For this reason, the *kadı* will here be considered as the ultimately responsible functionary.

Though a detailed exposition of the *kadı* and his multifarious roles in Ottoman society would not be wholly out of place in an overview such as this, it would needlessly distract us from the matter at hand. I will confine our treatment to an outline (sufficiently detailed to permit an appreciation of the dynamics involved) of the *kadı*'s training and background, and his task of interpreting for his contemporaries the social drama taking place in the inheritance inventory.

As is known, the foundation of the legal training of an Ottoman judge consisted in the study of Islamic theology and sciences, which was conducted in an institution of higher education known as the *medrese.* (Manisa, itself, boasted six *medreses*.)[13] Regardless of the question of whether or not (and to what the degree and how this state of affairs may have altered over time), the Ottoman sultan was the ruler of a theocracy, it is generally accepted that the judge acted as the deputy of the sultan and as such carried out the primary duty assigned to the Islamic ruler of resolving conflicts among the populace.[14] As the representative of the head of an Islamic state—who ruled by virtue of the legitimacy accorded by the law of Islam—the *kadı* was, thus, a symbol of the Islamic foundation of the state. But the training received by the jurist candidate made him eligible not only to head a local court of Islamic law; but also, to serve as a civil administrator and govern according to the "secular"—edicts by the sultan *(kanun),* which formed an uncodified body of law that both complemented and supplemented Islamic law.[15]

Yet, the name by which the *kadı*'s court was known in the Manisa (and other) registers—*meclis-i şer'i,* (court of shar'ia or Islamic, law)—acknowledged Islam as the essential legitimating element of the state. In the course of executing both sets of duties, the judge possessed essential autonomy. There was no Ottoman court of appeals. Furthermore, the *kadı* could, at his discretion, submit a petition or a complaint on behalf of an Ottoman subject to the supreme body of the imperial chancery *(divan-ı hümayûn)* in Istanbul (or Konstantiniye, as it was then called). Such instruments pertained to public matters previously decided on by the central government or personal disputes over position and property among and by civil or military servants. In this respect, the *kadı* acted as a facilitator, a direct channel for the transmission of messages from the subject to the sultan. But, as a judge, his decisions were not subject to review by the imperial chancery.

By the seventeenth century, the highest religious functionary, the *Şeyhülislâm,* essentially assumed the duty of selecting the judge appointee, whose candidacy was *pro forma* submitted to the *kadı*'s titular superior—one of two military judges *(kadıasker, kazasker)*—for approval. The ranking of the juridico-administrative districts of the *kadı* was based on the estimated gross amount to be garnered each day, and ranged from five hundred *akçes* for the holy cities of Mecca and Medina down to twenty *akçe*s for the least prestigious districts in the seventeenth century. The rank of the judgeship at Manisa had been raised to the highest level of five hundred *akçe*s per day by the late sixteenth century and, reportedly, continued in the seventeenth century.[16]

Yet, from another perspective, the *kadı* served two masters. An appointment to the office of the *kadı* bestowed on its occupant a tax-exempt status, demarcating a dividing line between him and the community he served (i.e., in the sense that the legitimating identity of the state was Islamic). Despite his status as an imperial servant—and, deputy of the sultan—he was also set apart from the overwhelming majority of the highest ranking officials by being, almost without exception, a born Muslim. (In this respect, however, he was like the greater bulk of the population he served, in Manisa, for instance.) As is known, Muslim taxpaying (male) subjects of the empire could change their status and improve their lot by two principal means: performing acts of bravery on campaign in exchange for a land-based stipend, or attending a school of theology with the hope of being awarded an appointment to a position among the ranks of the religious (increasingly bureaucratic) functionaries, including that of a judge. Over the centuries, however, the first possibility had declined in probability while the second had increased. The seventeenth century not only witnessed a great expansion of the members and branches of bureaucracy (also open to *medrese* graduates), but also a phenomenal burgeoning in the number of *kadıs*.[17]

A perusal of the Manisa judicial registers of this period discloses that one connotation of the word *ecnebî* ("alien" or "outsider") was "native-born Muslim Ottoman subject" (specifically, Turks). This startling usage unmistakably informs us that the "other" for the contemporary Ottoman was, in actuality, the inverse of what might have been assumed. An ethos that, evidently, became pronounced around the middle of the fifteenth century with the conquest of Constantinople by the Ottomans and that continued in full strength until at least the middle of the seventeenth century expressed a prejudice against ethnic Turks.[18] We learn that, ironically, the Ottoman "self" was represented by those who were the original outsiders—Christians, primarily from the Balkans, but, in the seventeenth century, primarily from the Caucasus (Georgia, Circassia, and Abkhasia)—imperial slaves, converted to Islam, in the course of being prepared for service. Among the members of this group were the slave staff of the palace and imperial ateliers, imperial viziers, and military governors; it also included the great majority of those who had marital ties with members of the dynasty. But this group excluded the *kadı*. The statutes issued by Sultan Mehmet II (1451–1481) on the protocol to be observed by himself on official holiday receptions omit all mention of the *kadı*.[19] Taking this practice as a reflection of regard, we may also note that a well-informed seventeenth-century observer neglects to mention any *kadıs* being received at similar functions though other dignitaries are noted one by one.[20]

Besides being a Muslim by birth and upbringing—which distinguished him, as we have seen, from the "self"—the *kadı* was looked down upon by his own former classmates. His colleagues in the learned community, ordinarily, viewed his life of study and teaching within the divinity schools and appointments to prominent posts as religious officials more appropriate to their station. From the vantage point of his peers in academia, the office of the *kadı* conferred a lesser status due to the necessity of dealings with the general populace in the marketplace and the figurative hustling for his daily pay.[21] Paradoxically, therefore, the *kadı* as the sole designated deputy of the ruler himself may be, at the same time, perceived as the ultimate outsider. On the one hand, the *kadı* alone represented the symbolic power of the state, which set him apart both from all other members of the tax exempt and the entire taxpaying classes. At the same time, as a born Muslim without connections in the capital or wealth, aspirations of acquiring a post among the higher echelons of the imperial court were quite unrealistic. Hence, he was not, in any real sense, representative of the great majority of the ruling class. As a result, the *kadı* constituted perhaps the ideal judge and determiner of the fate and fortune of Ottoman subjects. Being the true other, the *kadı* could be freed from partiality and carry out his judicial duties with perfect fairness and justice.

The Isolario Proper

The Outlook from Manisa

In our period, the *kadı* of Manisa could be located in the fifteenth-century mosque on the south side of the central marketplace.[22] Preceding the act of his drawing up an inheritance inventory was the unfortunate occurrence of a death within the community. No doubt, in the best of all possible worlds, if our wishes could be granted, the occasion marking the end of our days on earth would resemble the tableau that is limned by those portions of Islamic law pertaining to the division of an estate: ideally, death should arrive at one's door when, at a ripe age, one is found in the bosom of one's happy family, composed of spouse and children (the latter of whom should also be in possession of their majority). As interpreted by the Ottomans, in the event that any one of these conditions was not met, the state could, as was noted previously, step in and act in the deceased—and the community's—best interest, regardless of rank, religious affiliation, or native land; by "community" is here meant the state itself.

Keeping this in mind, the researcher working with such Ottoman records will be on the alert for indicators that 1) the heirs are in their minority; that 2) no heir exists other than the surviving spouse(s); that 3) no heirs are known; that 4) the heirs are for whatever reason some place—known or unknown (*gayb* or *mefhud*, respectively)—beyond the limits of the immediate locale and who must be informed; that 5) the deceased was either an Ottoman subject or a foreigner in transit and that notification of the heirs must be made; or that 6) discord has arisen among the heirs, in all of which cases the reason for intervention by the court as the representative of the community may be denoted by the phrase "upon request" *(talebiyle);* such a request would have been made by a local representative of the state treasury *(emin-i beyt-ül-mal)* except in the final instance when the heirs themselves would apply to the court. No distinction was made by the court in these matters regarding gender, religion, ethnic origin, or native land.

One additional circumstance must be appended to the six listed above: the heirs of an Ottoman non-Muslim (as well as those of a Muslim) subject were free to petition the court to apportion as estate on the basis of Islamic law.[23] Though application to the *kadı*'s court could be made by non-Muslims in cases where the division of the inheritance had given rise to disputes over individual claims, the Ottoman court was, in addition, occasionally utilized by non-Muslims in order to obtain more favorable terms. For example, the share allotted by Islamic law to the wife of a deceased Christian who was an adherent of the Eastern Orthodox church was greater than that provided by ecclesiastical law.[24] The execution of the estates of non-Muslims who had no minor children was, presumably, handled by their respective religious functionaries, whether Jewish, Eastern (Greek) Orthodox, Armenian Orthodox, or other churches. Officially, the right of jurisdiction was granted by the Ottoman state to the supreme heads of the Jewish community *(hahambaşı)* and the Eastern Orthodox and Armenian churches *(patrik)* centered in Istanbul, in the seventeenth century.[25]

Not all instances of voluntary application were explicitly stated as such. This requires the researcher to seek clues in such things as the absence of notice (by name of signifier or the allotment of shares) of surviving children; missing markers for the minority status of any offspring; and the omission of any addenda concerning the appointment of a guardian or a dispute among the heirs over the inheritance. Given the absence of the phrase "upon request," one of the clearest indications that the court was petitioned by the heirs is an inventory wholly or in part composed of a listing of the names of borrowers and the individual amounts of the outstanding loans *(der zimmet)* granted by the deceased. (It must also be presumed that creditors would inform the court when a deceased individual remained in his debt; no information is available about whether a regularized procedure was in effect, other than the fact that notice of these loans had likely been entered in the judicial registers.) Unfortunately, even such evidence by omission as this just cited may be lacking, and other tactics must be employed. The researcher must also take care to identify whether the deceased was of the taxpaying or tax-exempt class, and whether the gross worth of a tax-exempt estate exceeded a certain set amount, which varied over time. In any case, the inheritance inventories of prominent officials whose property had been confiscated by the state, generally, make no appearance in the local *kadı* registers.[26] These records were turned over to the imperial treasury office.[27]

Commonly, the reason for the appearance of an inventory in the local court records—that is, for intervention initiated by the officers of the court—is the question of the age (*el-sagir[e]*, f. and m., or *el-sagireteyn*, pl.) of the children of the deceased.[28] (Again, what was the procedure by which the court was normally informed of such deaths and whether it was officially regularized are unknown, however.[29] Even if no designation of underage status is present, this circumstance can be inferred, as noted above, by the presence of addenda concerning the appointment by the court of a guardian (ordinarily, *vasi tayin eyledi*) or the assignment of an allowance for the care and upkeep of such minors *(nafaka)*. The guardian is not always the surviving parent; a male relative of a deceased father was often selected as a guardian rather than the mother.[30] It is important to note that a married couple who either had no children or no offspring alive at the time of their death were effectively penalized under Islamic law. The sole surviving mate was apportioned merely a share, but never the whole, of the estate. The sole surviving male spouse of a couple without children could be granted a half-share of the estate, while the female counterpart was entitled to only a quarter, with the remainder of the estate was claimed for the state treasury by the local agent.[31]

It is assumed that the funds for child maintenance allowances were provided for by the sale of the property and goods from the estate, particularly when the court fees of an inventory include those for a broker *(dellaliye)*.[32] If no minor children are involved, the inclusion of this fee may also permit the inference that a dispute among the heirs has led to the auctioning of the estate; in Manisa, such goods were auctioned off to the highest bidder in the Sultaniye *suk* or market in the seventeenth century. It is so far unclear whether or not in cases of apparent extreme poverty—for instance, a widow with minor children left only with a couple of assets, like a house (their residence, that is), a donkey and a few odds and ends—such sales were forced; in other words, if the house had to be sold to maintain the family as a unit. It should be emphasized that the children of an ordinary Muslim Ottoman subject who had attained their majority were under no obligation to apply to the court for the division of the estate. (Let me also point out here that the consanguinary heirs of a deceased member of either tax class were, by sultanic decree, members of the same class as the deceased, while the wife partook of the same status as her husband as long as she did not remarry.)

One significant difference between the Ottoman inheritance inventory and that of Europe and the United States is that an estate was defined as the property of the deceased individual alone. Though for tax purposes in the Ottoman state, the "household" *(hane)* was taken as the base—as represented by a male head who was (usually) the owner of a house—at death only that property recognized as belonging to the deceased was supposed to be listed in an inventory. This means that the wife's property, for instance, could not be included in the inventory of a male head of household.[33] One piece of evidence to support a claim that the Ottoman courts had, indeed, observed this precept in practice was revealed by the unexpected occurrence of an item in the inventories of deceased females described in detail, accompanied by an estimate of its monetary value, but which also bore the annotation that the said item was "nonexistent" *(namevcud).*[34] One solution to the puzzle of how goods that were not present could yet be subject to appraisal resides, I believe, in the custom known to have been observed by Ottoman women of having ledgers drawn up identifying the goods that composed their dowry—that is, the movable and unmovable property belonging to the woman at marriage.[35] Such goods were also displayed by the bride at her parent's home, which, ensured the bride, regardless of whether or not she had had a register drawn up, with eyewitnesses as to which goods were her property; such eyewitnesses gave testimony in court in cases of dispute of ownership, such as occurred upon divorce or death.[36] The marginal note that a described item was "nonexistent" may allow us to infer that the court official had simply copied such register entries on the death of the woman, thereby confirming that the wife's goods are indeed regarded as her sole property.[37]

The fact that in such cases nearly all items of the dowry were still extant at the time of the death of their owner may also furnish us with clues as to how to interpret the values attached to goods in the inventories of married females, and, additionally, the place of such goods in the lives of women in Manisa during this period. First, if the appraised value of any item appearing in the dowry registry was simply reproduced in an inheritance inventory, this strongly suggests that these values bore no relation to their market value, particularly if the deceased woman also had grown children. This means that a lapse of some fifteen to twenty years or more had no effect on what the court appraiser would assign to an object or, presumably, what a local purchaser would have been willing to pay at auction. In turn, this raises a very large question about the real meaning of any of the values appearing in an inventory and how—or even whether—any of the values correspond to market prices. In short, a thorough and cautious approach is advised in regard to taking the inventory values at face value.

A parallel area of investigation opened up by this point is the question of the purpose or function of wedding goods in this particular Ottoman community. A working hypothesis might even be formulated that states that wedding goods—regardless of whether they were brought to the marriage by the husband or the wife—should be interpreted as personal capital and not as goods intended for daily use. This was prompted by the presence of a general array of household goods in the inventories of deceased males that often differed very little from those of deceased females. If property is conceived as personal and not joint, and if many of the goods bear no marker in the inventory signifying that their condition is "used" *(müs'temel)*—or "old" (*köhne* or *eski*) or "worn out, threadbare" *(kurade)*—we may be allowed to consider the possibility that such goods (as well as other property) were brought to the marriage by each party for some other purpose than ordinary use.

A modern study of a village in the Manisa area contains an observation in support of such a possibility.[38] Scholars reported that, typically, brightly polished copperware was lined up on shelves in the houses only for display. (In one case, this was underlined by a broad swath of red paint that extended from one end of the assemblage to the other.) The writer reports that, contrary to what is generally assumed, earthenware vessels *(çanak çömlek)* rather than metal served for both cooking and eating purposes. The collection would be taken down once or twice a year to be dusted and polished, and a portion of it would be contributed, when the time came, to the trousseau of any daughter of the household. The practice was observed by both rich and poor, and differed only in the number of pieces. This question is complicated by the fact that the material from which the kitchen wares are made is seldom indicated in the inventories.

Finally, when we focus our attention on the term "used," it would seem natural to assume that personal and household goods should have been in a "used" condition. Yet the term "used" is employed rather infrequently in these inventories. This alone should urge us to investigate whether a custom of not using such goods in daily life was in force. (Alternatively, a better translation of *müstemel* should be sought.) In this light, my earlier supposition that the frequency of "old" *(köhne)* items could serve as an index to the relative age of the owner (never stated) must be reviewed and perhaps discarded. If this new hypothesis proves valid, it appears more likely that the attribution "old" might rather represent an index of poverty. Reframed, our supposition could state that only those in dire straits would have been forced to actually use their wedding goods and that their safekeeping represented their potential utilization as a contingent form of capital or credit instrument.

On a Magnified Scale

Broadly speaking, the inventory constitutes a summary of four main operations executed by the *kadı:* the identification of the deceased and heirs, the listing of assets, the enumeration and deduction of debits, and the apportioning of shares. Closer at hand, the format of the Manisa inventory may be described in the following fashion: the initial section, "introductory protocol," is signaled by a heading and consists of one or more continuous lines that extend the full width of the page (the dimensions of which vary but, on average, measure six inches wide by sixteen inches long).[39] Here, we find the deceased identified by given name and father's name, the place of residence by neighborhood and city (occupation and cause of death are rarely recorded). The immediately succeeding lines contain references to the degree of consanguinity and affinity of the legatees—often supplying their first names and, more rarely, the name of their father—or the title of the treasury agent *(emin-i beytülmal)* (who may not always be identified by name) and the date of the partitioning. Unusually, the introductory protocol is generally concluded by a list of eyewitnesses in the Manisa inventories; in cases where minors are involved, this list alternately follows the addendum indicating the appointment of a guardian.[40]

Occasional notice of the place of residence of an eyewitness as being in the same locale as that of the deceased leaves the question unanswered as to what were the determinants for the composition of this group. Numbering from two to as many as fifteen, the eyewitnesses are listed not in a strict order of social rank, but, nonetheless, possessors of the highest rank—as indicated by prenominal honorifics—are inscribed at the head of the list; these are usually members of the learned class, such as a *medrese* scholar *(müderris)* or a judge. Lending itself to tracking who's who in town, the list of eyewitnesses reveals that the numbers of "the glory of judges" *(fahrül kuzat)* had come to assume a weighty presence by the mid-century mark and serves not only to confirm that the roster of judge-candidates had become swollen as the century wore on, but also to inform us that Manisa was deemed a place as congenial or profitable as the capital to bide one's time until the next posting.

The second section, "context: inventory," consists in the items themselves set forth in a distinctive manner and known in Turkish as a "rose pattern" *(gül dökümü)*; more prosaically, it might be termed a "tier-block."[41] These "roses" present concise notations of the salient properties of the item, which, for movable property, include material, condition, size/quality, color, and value; while for immovable property, reference is made to location and size and other features. The most common order of the listing is 1) structures (houses, shops, watermills); 2) vineyards, trees, and crops (both harvested and standing); 3) livestock (particularly, cattle, camels, with a head count, and even bees); 4) personal and household goods, and stores and produce; and 5) commercial goods. Usually, this listing is concluded by an enumeration of any outstanding loans *(der zimmet)*, with the name of the borrower, place of residence if not in the district center, the amount of interest, if any, and the amount of the original principle or its equivalent in current exchange terms provided. The values assigned may reflect an appraisal or the actual amount for which the item was sold at auction.[42] In addition to or in place of the deduction of a broker's fee *(dellaliye)*, a second indication that a sale took place is heralded by values within a single inventory that are not rounded off as usual. For example, a pot *(tencere)* that usually carries a values of 65 or 70 *akçe*s may bear a value of, say, 63 *akçe*s.

The third section, "personal liabilities," presents an itemization and deduction of the various debts (s. *deyn*, pl. *düyun*) incurred by the deceased or other claims on the estate, bequests *(vasiyet)*, and court fees (*resim* or *harç*). The final section (generally), "partitioning of inheritance shares," specifies the net worth of the estate and the apportioning of shares for each heir. Occurring rarely and only in the mid-seventeenth century, the closing section, "final protocol," consists in simply the name and title of the partitioner of estates of the tax exempt *(kassam-i askerî)*.

Names and Placement of the Deceased

Identification of the deceased in the Ottoman inheritance inventory in Manisa is preeminently characterized by apparent redundancy. The deceased can be assigned membership in different socio-economic, denominational, or administrative groups through utilization of the various identity designators that occur in the first part of the inventory, which denotes, among other things, religious community, gender, and tax status. Even when the given (first) name or that of the father—through whom descent was traced in Ottoman society—is illegible or omitted, the record can nearly always still be assigned to a class by the researcher. This characteristic leads us to propose that it might be possible to establish a positive correlation between the number of signifiers and the social standing of the deceased as ascribed by the community. In the following presentation some of the principal signifiers have been made to accord with the general order of the elements as they occur in the inheritance inventory (the preponderance of which records in Manisa belong to Muslims).

Immediately succeeding what is typically the initial word, or heading, of the inventory—*muhallefat,* or "the inheritance (of)"—is the first identifier applied to the deceased person. In Manisa, when the deceased is a Muslim, this identifier takes the form of the attribute *el-merhum* [the late or deceased] for a male and *el-merhume* for a female and precedes the first name. Other preposition epithets denote ranking within the Muslim religious community and the Ottoman state. Most common is *el-hac,* signifying that the deceased has made the obligatory pilgrimage to Mecca. In the sixteenth century, it has been estimated, five percent of the male Muslims of Manisa had made the pilgrimage.[43] It is, however, important to keep in mind that the connotation of this signifier was restricted to an informal social or religious ranking in the immediate community and had no bearing on one's official status within the community at large. No bureaucratic distinction was extended in regard to tax status between those who had or had not accomplished one of the obligations incumbent on a Muslim of means.[44] Two other religious honorifics, *eş şerif[e]* and *es seyyid[e],* indicate descent from the grandsons of the Prophet through his daughter Fatima and her husband, Ali; the former is reserved for the descendants of Hasan, the elder brother, and the latter from his younger brother Hüseyin, who is regarded as a martyr of the faith by the followers of Ali (for example, Shiites and Alevis). These identity markers, however, granted the possessor exemption from certain taxes despite the official Sunnite identity of the Ottoman state.

Prenominal terms, such as *el-merhum,* that are typically reserved for deceased Muslims, it should be noted, are occasionally applied to deceased non-Muslims, and other de rigueur epithets associated with being a non-Muslim are omitted. Here this occurrence has been interpreted as signifying the ascribed local importance of the deceased. In such instances, when a designator (like *el-merhum*) and the personal name or that of the father (that is, the name is clearly non-Muslim, such as Dimitri or Yorgi) stand in contradiction in terms of religious affiliation, the researcher might, additionally, take into consideration the number and status of the eyewitnesses (ordinarily, the greater the number, the higher the status) and note the gross worth of the estate of the deceased. A correlation might possibly be established among these variables and, thus, illustrate one variety of social cohesion in this Aegean community.

Moving on to the personal names themselves, another instance of breaking down barriers on the basis of religious affiliation occurs in the names chosen by residents of the community of Manisa. It is not uncommon to encounter non-Muslims with names characteristically borne by Muslims.[45] With the exclusion of purely Islamic names, such as Muhammed (Mehmed in Ottoman usage), Ahmed, and Mustafa (both included among the ninety-nine names of God) for males and Zeyneb or Ayşe (the names of two of the wives of the Prophet) for females.[46] Both Muslims and non-Muslims bear secular names in common, like Murad and Karagöz for males and Sultan and Emine for women.[47] Jews and Muslims also share the names of Hebrew prophets and Old Testament figures, with the exceptions of Ilyas (Elijah)—a name more common among Greeks—Nuh (Noah) and Ismail (Ishmael), who replaces Isaac (Ishak) in the sacrifice ordered of Abraham (Ibrahim) in the Qur'an and, naturally, the New Testament name of Isa (Jesus). Other names shared by both groups are Musa (Moses), Davud (David), and Yakub (Jacob). Additional biblical names taken by Muslims in Manisa include Yunus (Jonah), Yusuf (Joseph), and Yahya (John the Baptist)[48] In such instances of the blurring of religious categories, the researcher must then rely on the given redundancies and other signifiers, like the father's name or unmistakable identification tags, like "son of the priest" (papasoğlu) or "son of the rabbi" (hahamoğlu). Additionally, extranomenclature evidence may provide a clue, such as the presence of alcoholic beverages *(hamr)* among the effects of an apparently deceased non-Muslim; however, it should be noted that this is not infallible. Hamr occurs among the possessions of Muslims also.[49]

A point persistently reiterated in the sources when the subject of Ottoman names arises is that the name Abdullah ("slave of God")"—

comparable to the anonym John Doe—denotes a convert to Islam. While this may have long been a common practice in Islamic lands, on the whole it appears to be a generally untrustworthy rule of thumb in Ottoman society. Abdullah was a common name among Ottomans born in Muslim families of all stations in Manisa (and elsewhere in the empire) during this period.

Choices in personal names appear to exhibit regional variance in Anatolia.[50] Names commonly used in Bursa, Edirne, or Ankara in the seventeenth century are seldom encountered in contemporary Manisa and vice versa. For instance, very common among male names in Ankara near the close of the sixteenth century is Bali, alone or in combination with other names. In Manisa Hızır, for instance, exhibits high frequency.[51] The name Bali may originally have been a title in the Bektashi dervish order, and the decreased frequency of occurrence in the Manisa registers raises the possibility that Manisa had a smaller concentration of Bektashi adherents than Ankara at this time. Many of the names appearing in the Manisa registers are the same as the names of the founders of local mosques, such as İlyas (Elijah).[52] Taking these two names alone, one might discover that they were linked to differences in the socio-religious makeup of Ankara and Manisa. For the name Bali is more often associated with Turcomans (in Manisa, at least) and religious syncretism (generally), whereas "İlyas" issues from an "orthodox" scriptural context, both Judeo-Christian and Islamic.

Another influence to take into consideration on the subject of naming is that of the Muslim holy men whose graves and mausoleums are found in and around a settlement. Such saints are often associated with the lodges of dervish orders, with those of Mevlana (Celaleddin Rumi), essentially representing the establishment and, most likely, to be centered within a town, and those associated with heterodoxy, such as Bektashi, situated near the perimeter of the town.[53] Helping to account for the occurrence and frequency of certain names in Manisa, for instance, is the mausoleumof the still popular Karaca Ahmed, a Bektashi saint, which is located near a village formerly known as Horoz (properly Horos, now Muradiye), just southwest of Manisa in the seventeenth century (now, within the municipal limits near the railroad station). It was common in the Ottoman period for the devout to pray at the tombs of Muslim saints in the hope that specific wishes of the petitioner would be fulfilled. Karaca Ahmet was regarded as effective in the granting of wishes for the conception of a child by the childless. To this end, a devout female follower would be required to spend the night alone in the mausoleum with a large, carved wooden phallus bound to her back by a headcloth or sash belonging to the woman. If a male child was the issue of this incubational ordeal, it was named Ahmet, and if a female, it received the name of his mother—Sultan or his wife, Kadıncık or Fatma Ana.[54] Awareness of the possibility that names may be derived from sources like these may provide the researcher with insight into the religious affiliation of a community, or at the very least assist in ascertaining a probable source for the local custom of choosing certain names.

Social norms and expectations and living conditions may, in some cases, also be inferred from the choice of names. For instance, certain personal names might permit the construction of an index of infant mortality. An abundance of masculine Turkish names like Dursun/Tursun ("May he live") or Durmuş ("He has remained alive") were chosen with the aim of preserving the life of the child, the frequency of such names may signify high infant mortality, either in a woman's personal history or in the living memory of a community in a particular habitat.[55] Another method of combating the power of epidemic disease and famine in taking the lives of children can be tested in the ancient custom, widespread in Anatolia and practiced by Jews, Muslims, and Christians, of entering into the symbolic sale of a child.[56] Among the Muslims, Turks are known to have conducted the transaction with the lodge of a dervish order *(tekke)*, a Kurd, or an Armenian. A male child that had been "sold" (to God, that is) was named Satılmış (he has been sold/redeemed) and a female Satı (a sale-redemption).[57] Feminine names among Turkish females exhibit a notable tendency to bestow ambiguity regarding the gender of the bearer. This ambiguity is created by giving male names to females. This may also represent an attempt to bargain with fate by openly declaring that a male child is desired. In the Manisa inventories, it is not unusual to encounter in the registers females named Pasha (General) or Agha (Chief Janissary Officer) or Beşe (Chieftain or Lord), which heightens the importance of the apparent redundancy of identity markers; in fact, if it were not for this redundancy researchers could, occasionally, find it very difficult indeed to determine the gender or isolate the researcher category to which the deceased belonged.

While it is true that the names borne by Muslims, Christians, and Jews are often exclusive to their respective communities, in the Manisa judicial registers, at least, among the postnominal designators, "Christian" forms a false category. Ordinarily, the Islamic signifier for the classification of non-Muslims is *zimmi* (Ar., *dhimmi*)—a class whose population is restricted to Christians and Jews, however. But in the Manisa inventories, when the deceased person happens to be an Armenian, the name of the person and the father is succeeded not by *zimmi*, but rather by the Ottoman lexical counterpart, *Ermeni*. The term *zimmi* was found to be applied exclusively to Greeks (that is, in the seventeenth century, members of the Eastern Orthodox church), who, in Ottoman Turkish generally, and in the Manisa registers, in particular, are otherwise called *Rûm*—that is, Roman—following the Arab practice or identified as one of the *kefere taifesi* (the unbelievers).[58] The name of a deceased Jew *(Yahudi)* is preceded by the term *el-melun* [literally, "accursed"] for male and *el-melune* for female. This term of denigration derives, in my opinion, less from the Qur'an and the experience that the Prophet Muhammed had with the Jewish community in Medina, and more with the common persecution of the Jews in western Anatolia under the Romans and the east Roman (Byzantine) empire.[59] It may also be an index of adoption by the Ottomans of local attitudes. Nonetheless, this is one tradition that tended to die out under the Ottomans. The word *mate[t]* [he/she died] follows the name of a Muslim and *murd[e]* [it died] follows the name of a non-Muslim or a convert.[60] On occasion, the word *muhallefat* may be omitted; in that case the first word will be *mate[t]* followed directly by the first name unaccompanied by the epithet denoting religious adherence.

One group of Manisa inhabitants who appear frequently in the pages of the court registers as residents of the city and environs and yet whose status in the inventories remains indeterminate was the gypsies *(çingâne)*.[61] Gypsies were for administrative purposes treated as a distinct group, neither Muslim nor non-Muslim; but, in the inventories, their identity as a member of this group is unmarked.[62] Though it is not impossible that the word *çingâne* fails to appear in the inventories because gypsies were somehow excluded entirely from the process, this seems quite unlikely, because no distinction was made by the Ottoman *kadı* for any other group or individual. This circumstance urges the researcher to resort to deduction. Noticeable among the inventories are certain deceased individuals who either have names that are unrecongizable as characteristic of any particular religious community or who either have no father's name or the name of Abdullah as the father's name; such features might allow us to identify this anomalous group as gypsies.

Another group which appears quite often in the pages of the judicial registers of Manisa is the Kurds; their ethnic identity is also not distinguished in the inventories. Moreover, their names are, essentially, indistinguishable from those selected by Turkophone Muslims. In short, all Muslims of the Ottoman state, regardless of ethnic group or language, made up one community at death.

A signifier that possessed far greater import to the state than indicators of religious faith was the Arabic word that occurred after the first name of the deceased and denoted the gender of the person as an offspring: *bin* or *ibn* signifies "son [of]" and *bint* or *ibnete* "daughter [of]." (In observing this distinction, Manisa is, so far as known, unique.) The form of this signifier served to mark the deceased as a member of the tax-paying (*bin* and *bint*) or tax-exempt group (*ibn* and *ibnete*), or, alternatively, tax-exempt members of ascribed high status. When the gross worth of the estate was greater than an amount established by sultanic decree, the fees charges for drawing up the inventory would by right belong to the Anatolian military judge (*kazasker* or *kadıasker*) rather than the local *kadı*. If the deceased was a commoner (regardless of occupation or locus of residence) and a Muslim, the signifier was *bin* for males and *bint* for females. The equivalent designation for non-Muslims of *veled* (son [of]) for males and—irregularly—*bint* for females, rather than the counterpart *veledet* was neutral in terms of tax-paying status. This receives support from the fact that it was also commonly used for Muslims in the deeds of Ottoman pious foundations *(vakıf)*. By law, non-Muslims were, with few exceptions, members of the tax-paying class in Islamic states (i.e., they were obligated to pay a per capita tax).[63] Exceptional cases in Manisa were the several non-Muslim (Greek) men in the local militia who performed guard duty *(muhafız)* at the citadel in the sixteenth and seventeenth centuries.[64] In addition, the servants of the imperial palace at Manisa, who were local Greeks, received tax-exempt status in the sixteenth and seventeenth centuries.[65]

Names of occupants and professions usually followed the father's name. These include religious functionaries, like *el-katip* (clerk); *el-hatip* or *el-halife* (leader of prayer on Friday and holy days); *hoca* (preacher or teacher); *müezzin* (caller to prayer); *el-müderris* (head of theological school); tradesmen, such as *helvacı* (maker of *halwah*); *bogasici* (maker of boccassi cloth); imperial slaves, like *yeniçeri* (Janissary); and men of commerce like *tüccar* (merchant). No published work provides a clear understanding of whether or not a hierarchy of the elite can be constructed or what was the nature of organizational ranking in Ottoman society. In other words, it is nearly impossible to attach social meanings to the honorifics and titles that appear in the judicial registers of Manisa in the seventeenth century. Position rather than title appears to have conferred rank, and title was altered to track one's position. This phenomenon can be readily ascertained in encyclopedias, biographical dictionaries, and other reference works on Ottoman history. Personages and officials altered their titles to fit their appointments.[66]

One final example regarding the important subject of names and their significance is the use of *-zâde* or *-zâdeler* (Pers. son or the family of), whose use had been largely confined to the sons of the Ottoman sultan (*şehzade,* lit. son of the shah) prior to the seventeenth century. The increasing frequency of *-zade* is likely associated with both an increase in local power and wealth, and the development of large households with paid clients. Furthermore, an indication—so far unnoted for any other locale—that a man is *tabi,* or a retainer or client, of a named individual—among the names of the eyewitnesses is of particular interest. This identifier also calls to our attention the development of large households in Manisa, noticeable in the seventeenth century. This phenomenon, which culminated in the eighteenth century, was a hallmark of the increasing power of the provincial notables *(ayan),* among whom the Manisa family of Karaosman-zâdeler (or Karaosmanoğulları) was preeminent.

Place Names

The name of the place where the subject of the inventory established residence can assume the same degree of interest and importance for the historian as that of personal names. When the place of residence of the deceased was located in the town of Manisa, the name of the town neighborhood *(mahalle)*—or, rarely, that of the inn *(han)* or bachelor quarters *(odalar)* is cited—otherwise, the name of the village and juridico-administrative subdistrict *(nahiye)* of Manisa or other district in the empire was specified. This is followed by the name of Manisa as the location of the neighborhood or as the judicial district *(kâzâ)* in which the locale was situated, which name may be accompanied by one or more epithets. The town of Manisa is generally assumed to have reached the pinnacle of urban life with the tenure of its final prince-governor, the future Sultan Mehmed III (1595–1603). The epithets selected by the scribes of the Manisa inventories tell a different story. Based on the unusual enhancement of the name of the town of Manisa through epithets, it might be truer to assert that it surpassed its former civic position around the middle of the seventeenth century.

In the inventories dating to the first quarter of the century, the name of Manisa was rarely embellished with honorifics; in this, however, the town exhibited no difference from other leading urban centers, like Edirne, Bursa, Ankara, and Konya. Only very occasionally occurs the epithet of "the city" *(el-mahrusa);* yet even in regard to this action, Manisa was exceptional. Toward the middle years of the century, however, *el-mahrusa* appears invariably and, most commonly, with the additional inscribed flourish of the "well-protected" *(el-mahmiye).* So far as can be determined, this characteristic distinguishes Manisa from all other seats of justice, with the exception of Istanbul. This signifier of civic pride may possibly furnish an index to the prosperity of the town in this period.

The Bereaved

Following the identification of the deceased and the locus of residence occurs a listing of the legal heirs, preceded by the phrase *min el-verâset* (from among the heirs).[67] In addition to any spouse of the deceased, those eligible to be legatees almost exclusively comprise agnatic kin, whose relationship to the deceased is denoted by Arabic signifiers; typically, the personal names of the heirs are also provided. If the death of a married male leaves a pregnant wife, she is described *el-hamel* or *helet-i hamile* ([with] fetus or in a state of pregnancy).[68] Frequently, the name of a child is accompanied by the signifier legitimate (m. *sulbü,* f. *sulbiye,* lit., from one's loins). Because the deceased may not (as was noted above) specify by testamentary disposition which individuals are to inherit (or not to inherit) the estate, the presence of any legatee in an inventory is strictly based on the provisions of Islamic law according to the Hanefi school. In the case of individuals in a wedded state at the time of their death (by far the most common situation), heading the list of heirs is the spouse (occasionally, the mother takes precedence), followed by any children. Under certain conditions, the state as a corporate person and represented by the imperial treasury *(beytülmal)* may also be a designated heir. The following represents a listing, in arbitrary order, of the classes of heirs most commonly encountered:

1. wife *(zeyce)*
2. husband *(zeyc)*
3. daughter *(bint)*
4. son *(ibn)*
5. mother *(ümm)*
6. father *(eb)*
7. full sister *(uht liebeveyn)*
8. full brother *(ah liebeyeyn)*
9. uncle (father's side) *('amm)*
10. imperial treasury *(beytülmal)*

For the sake of completeness, it is appropriate to indicate those classes of individuals ineligible to be awarded the status of legatee under Islamic law. Excluded from consideration are 1) any person who intentionally caused the death of the deceased; 2) any child mothered by the spouse of a deceased male—either during or prior to the marriage—who was not recognized as his own while alive; 3) any non-Muslim, either by birth or apostasy; 4) any slave or a captive in the hands of a foreign power; and finally 5) in the case of a deceased non-Muslim, any subject of a foreign political state (in this context, a non-Ottoman subject).[69] Finally, it should be noted that the institution of child adoption was not recognized under Islamic law, thereby, also denying eligibility to any adopted children.[70]

As one reads through an inheritance inventory, one can easily imagine the scene: upon the arrival of the *kadı* or other court official at the home of the deceased, he would ascertain the particulars of any property possessed by the deceased by means of copies of court records (*hüccets*) in the hands of the family and, possibly, the testimony of witnesses, and jot down their description and value. Upon approaching the house, the *kadı* would ignore for the moment the implements and instruments and products of labor. The tools for land cultivation and conduct of trade, the storage sacks and containers for grain and produce, like barley, chickpeas, and grapes and, perhaps, large earthenware jars for vinegar or pickles; the stone grinder for grain and the three-legged iron *(sacayası)* for the fire built in the courtyard after the harvest and on which were set large and costly copper cauldrons (another index of wealth—their value often exceeding that of a house) for the boiling down of grape juice into molasses *(pekmez)* and the cooking of cracked wheat (bulgur) for winter stores would all be left by the official to the tail end of the inventory. Now, standing in the space in which the occupants took their meals and made their beds, the partitioner would systematically open the trunks and baskets, unfold the cloth bundles *(bohça),* and empty large woven sacks and describe the contents of each in turn. Each of the heirs was noted in turn in the introductory protocol as having been summoned *(med'uv),* as required by law, to act as eyewitnesses themselves to the official reenactment of the dissolution of the bonds that had originally held them together.

Matters of Scale

The norm among the poorer male and female deceased Manisa residents is represented by garments whose individual value nearly equals or exceeds the value of any dwelling or other item of real estate in their possession. Moreover, the description of such garments is comparable and their value is nearly identical to those belonging to individuals with relatively ample means. Commonplace among estates in this category is the occurrence of several fine caftans, or robes, or street coats of silk worked with silver or gold filament, and with a value reckoned at between five and fifteen hundred *akçes*, or *aspers*, which is roughly equivalent to the average valuation of their house. One such robe, if it were interpreted as a wedding costume, would not seem unusual. But two? Or three? Their personal ornaments, such as gold bracelets and earrings, also bear relatively high values. (By contrast, bejeweled tiaras *(istefan)* only appeared among the accessories of more affluent females). In other words, the making of a home in a solitary room, as was common, appears to have been not entirely dictated by a lack of means. The acquisition of a fine robe was, evidently, preferred over the addition of a second room. The question raised by this seeming imbalance is further complicated by a piece of evidence that must be addressed, but whose implications have been—it must be admitted—sidestepped up to this point.

Over the years, the tenure of the designated successor to the imperial throne as prince-governor undoubtedly had led to an increased prominence of Manisa. One measure is the erection of a number of impressive structures. A palace for the princes was built within spacious grounds on the edge of town.[71] The construction of a vast mosque complex with hospice and hospital was undertaken by Hafsa Sultan, the regent mother of prince (şehzâde) Süleyman in the first half of the sixteenth century. And another one, the work of Mimar Sinan, was constructed by Murad III in 1586. And, its judgeship had risen from a middling position in the early years of the sixteenth century to the highest rank in less than seventy-five years.[72] Furthermore, special dispensations had been granted to the town residents in the sixteenth century, exempting them from certain taxes.[73] Even its leather-working industry appears to have been prompted by the princes.

One of the parallels between Manisa and the capital was that, exceptionally, neither city seems to have possessed a sultanic law code *(kanunnâme)* of its own, the issuance of which was traditional upon the conquest and subsequent survey of a territory by the Ottomans.[74] But, perhaps, because Selim (1512–20) felt that his son was in need of guidelines or for some other reason, a decree containing a special penal code *(siyasetnâme)* was issued in 1519 for the Saruhan *sancak* (the military-administrative district whose seat was Manisa) during the tenure of the prince-governor identified as Süleyman Shah (the future Süleyman I, r. 1520–1566).[75] As should be expected, the statutes spell out punishments for violations of public morality (such as adultery) and serious crimes (like theft, arson, and murder). But, the fifteenth of the eighteenth articles is unusual (possibly unique?) and upsets our assumptions about the state of well-being of the inhabitants of Manisa. Without preamble, this article states in toto that the wearing of *new* (emphasis added) clothing is prohibited and anyone who fails to comply is to be banished from the district *(Ve yeni giyenleri yasak edüb ilden süreler).*[76]

This provision brought to mind the observation made by Cissie Fairchilds on a law passed during the French Revolution decreeing that free choice regarding the garments worn by an individual was a basic human right.[77]

> That it might be illegal for certain types of people to wear certain types of clothing offends us, yet this was common in early modern Europe. It was part of a world of consumption now lost to us: a world of scarcity in which clothes were bought third, fourth, or twelfth hand; in which a rich merchant's house might have hundreds of sheets but only six uncomfortable chairs.

Was the Ottoman state in the first quarter of the sixteenth century included in this European world of scarcity? Was the ubiquity of gold embroidered silk apparel a sign that Manisa was no longer experiencing (if it ever had) scarcity? In the course of field research in a village near Manisa some sixty years ago, the discovery was made that the inhabitants shared a common attitude toward the wearing of new clothes: it represented, they explained, unacceptable behavior *(ayıp),* to which they added that the wearing of new clothes was reserved for religious holidays or wedding festivities.[78] Or, should we look for an explanation in the possibility that a shared ethic of simple distaste for display had long existed among the inhabitants?

The evidence of the Manisa inventories is so far inconclusive in regard to this very large question. The frequency of occurrence of tissues worked in threads of precious metals, however, may find yet utility as a more reliable index of wealth (whether relative or absolute) than the gross worth of the estate. A rough and ready yardstick seemed to be that only when the value of the house exceeded the value of a garment of such quality by a multiple of more than one or two could we estimate that the deceased had enjoyed a quality of life somewhat above mere subsistence. A comparable guide to poverty levels consisted in the presence or absence of a vineyard in both male and female estates. In other words, if no vineyard appeared near the head of the listing, one could nearly always assume without looking at the gross worth that the deceased would have very little other property. Other indices of the level of comfort included the frequency of the presence of the stone roller *(loğ)* used for flat roofs made of packed earth, which decreased in frequency over the century, being replaced by tile roofs *(kiremid)*, and the increased presence of a curtain, often of velvet or leather, to be used in summer to close off the hearth *(ocak perdesi)*. This amenity appeared only among those whose means appeared to be moderate and was especially noticeable in the second half of the century.

Still puzzling over the question of scarcity, we might consider the remark made by a European observer in 1838, soon after his arrival in Izmir: "I beheld a whole city of Turks, a very gay scene; but all the people struck me as being disgustingly fat."[79]

Granted that the perception of plumpness is relative (and the possibility occurs to one's mind that the observer may have been accustomed to a "world of scarcity"), nevertheless, this was an era when Ottoman Anatolia was generally reported to be less prosperous than it had been in earlier centuries. And, on the whole, the cupboards of the Manisa inventories do have an air of bareness about them. The *kadı* seems to have been scrupulous, however: a few cups of flour, some handsful of chickpeas or walnuts, or a couple pounds of grapes regularly took their place among the silk gowns and robes. Or we might attribute this lack of plenty to a habit of abstemiousness.

An Ottoman advice book written ca. 1526 contains an anecdote intended to illustrate the naiveté of the peasants; it relates that, one day, a man asked a friend of his, "Which would you choose if you were a lord—a plump chicken or a rich meat dish?" To which his friend replied, "I'd rather eat green onions and pita bread *(balzama)*."[80] Historically, however, a spare diet containing little or no meat was not unusual in the Mediterranean and Aegean region.[81] Roman emperor Septimus Severus, for example, is said to have been representative in his preference for vegetables from his own garden, a drop of wine from time to time, and a general disinterest in even tasting any of the meat dishes set before him.[82] Yet the question continued to nag: a colloquial Ottoman expression that was used as a term of reference for one's wife—*kaşık düşmanı*, literally "spoon enemy"—takes us directly back to the heart of the issue.[83]

Though we may not yet know how often certain vessels may have been filled and with what kind and degree of quality of ingredients, the kitchen wares present an array of differentiation in their types that reflects a specialization of dishes. Flat baking pans *(tepsi)* for savories of filled layers of dough *(börek)* (and a sole occurrence in an inventory of a Greek of a baking pan of the same genre made specially for fish) are distinguished from those for the baked dessert baklava, a construction of thin sheets of dough and an interleaving of nuts or boiled cream, sweetened by a syrup.[84] Serving trays specifically for *halwah/helva,* fruit and coffee, respectively, also made their appearance in roughly half the records. Dual-purpose cooking and serving vessels *(sahan)* for pilau, soup (çorba) and that for legumes, chicken, or meat casseroles or stews *(yahni)* are the most common types of wares. Making a frequent, though not invariable, appearance were the utensils for broiled, roasted, skewered meat (kebab), which might be interpreted as an intrusion into the indigenous vegetable-weighted tradition. Another food preparation that accompanies Turkic pastoral *transhumants* is also found among the stores: *tarhana,* made of yogurt mixed with flour and seasonings and dried and crumbled, easily transported and capable of being stored for long periods; when reconstituted, it is made into a soup. One puzzling aspect of the inventories was the nearly total absence of olive or any other kind of cooking fat. Dairy animals for the production of butter—milking cows, sheep, goats, water buffalo and camel—all occur in the inventories, yet no equipment appears for the making of butter. Two other possible sources of fat (not in the inventories) are suet from the tail of fat-tailed sheep and, as a twentieth-century study of Manisa shows, the fruit of wild pistachio tree called *çitlenbik.*[85] If either were used in the Ottoman period, is their use a taste preference or an economy?

Reckoning Worldly Accounts

Under Islamic law, a Muslim upon dying is quit of his spiritual debts. Obligations regarding mundane debts, however, must still be met. In fact, by law, the corpse of a Muslim who has died while owing any debt in kind is not even permitted to be taken from the home for burial until the creditor has been reimbursed. The first debt acknowledged in the inventory is the obligation of covering the costs of burial expenses *(tekfin ve techniz).*[86] In the broadest sense, the Ottoman inheritance inventory may, perhaps, best be viewed as the state's acting as a proxy for its deceased subjects and taking advantage of a final opportunity to put the worldly affairs of its subjects in good order. Yet it is undeniable that, as a whole, the inventories exhibited a number of anomalies when compared with the letter of the law. Among other points that could be cited, the inventories exhibited an almost total absence of the requisite payment contracted at marriage of the "widow's pension" *(mehr-i müeccel);* a lack of any evidence that husbands paid the obligatory funeral expenses of their wives; and an inexplicable failure to utilize the option of making a bequest, even when this meant that nearly the whole of the estate would be turned over to the state. These are not necessarily "irregularities;" rather, issues such as these make direct statements about Ottoman society that, very likely, made good sense at the time. Our task is to make sense of them today. At a fundamental level, admittedly, lies the so far unanswerable query how representative of Ottoman society are these specimens caught in the inheritance inventory net.

In the seventeenth century, in particular, the perception of the Ottoman judge in regard of his probity was, generally, negative. But, I would be willing to give the judge, Mahmud Efendi, who served in Manisa a good number of years and who wrote the following lines—which may be viewed as his own settling of accounts—the benefit of the doubt:[87]

May God Deem My Earnings Lawful Gain

For the affairs of the court,
For legal matters pertaining to pious foundations and property
And plots of land and their produce,
The registers are at hand and
The leaves of paper have been made ready;

We have adjudicated on the basis of what is fair
And in the light of knowledge, rather than on mere supposition
Or an intent to obstruct justice;

Forgive me, O God, if I have erred,
Grant me great munificence,
Grant me my recompense taken from the abundance,
Honor me with Your Peerless Grace;

O Lord of the Lofty Heavens,
By Your Most Excellent, Most Luminous Divine Light,
Keep your slave, O God, from error in judging cases and suits at law;
I am Mahmud the Cadi, the executor of justice
And the administrator of Sacred Law
In Manisa and its subdistricts.

Notes

1. Extracted from a study in progress on the Aegean community of Manisa in the seventeenth century, this exposition offers a guide to selected byways and vistas opened up by the Ottoman inheritance inventory. The aspects presented are intended to serve as an introduction to the potential for development of the Ottoman inheritance inventory, of which some seven hundred fifty were employed as the primary source. As with contemporary inheritance inventories drawn up in Europe, North America, and elsewhere, Ottoman inventories can furnish an important resource for the scholar in pursuit of the subject of goods and their consumption.

2. Situated in western Anatolia, roughly ten miles as the crow flies, northeast of Izmir (ancient Smyrna) on the Aegean coast, the town of Manisa (Magnesia) was the seat of an Ottoman juridico-administrative district *(kaza)* of the same name. At present, the town is the capital of a province, both of which are called Manisa; the boundaries of the republican province share no identity with those of the Ottoman district. In the seventeenth century, the medium-sized town was sited on a foothill on the north face of Mt. Sipylus (Sipil Dağ, 4,451 feet), overlooking the rich, alluvial plain of the river Gediz (ancient Hermus). Both its situation on the trade route between the terminal points of Izmir—and, ultimately, Europe—and Iran and other points east, which became heavily traveled in the seventeenth century, and its cultivation of cotton, in particular, were sources of prosperity in this period. Engravings of Manisa in the early eighteenth century and a description of seventeenth-century commercial activity in the region can be found in Daniel Goffman (1990), *Izmir and the Levantine World, 1550–1650* (Seattle and London). The Manisa judicial registers *(şer'iye sicilleri)* are deposited in the National Library (Millî Kütüphane) of the republic of Turkey in Ankara.

3. The originator of the genre was Cristoforo Buondelmonti, a Florentine priest resident in Rhodes who traveled in the Aegean 1406–1419. Soucek (1996), 21–22, 32–33.

4. The correct spelling (i.e., transliteration of the Arab script) of this term derived from Arabic is *tereke; tereke* represents modern Turkish spelling and—possibly, Ottoman—pronunciation. Pakalın (1983), 3: 461.

5. On the shares of inheritance specified in the Quran, see el-Enfâl 8: 75, el-Ahzâb 33: 6, en-Nisâ 4: 11–12, 176. Karaman (1985), 158–60.

6. Kurat (1987), 39, 55. See also Anna Komnena (1996), 229–34, passim. The only extant treaty of the fourteenth century between the Ottomans and a Western state was translated for the Genoese from the Greek by a local official of Pera in Constantinople. Fleet (1993), 13. Fleet also notes (p. 33) that a treaty between Beyazid I and Genoa in 1389 is known to have been in Greek. Mehmed II (1451–1481) is reported by Kitsikis to have possessed a command of the language. Kitsikis also quotes a personal letter in Greek of Sultan Beyazid

(1481–1512), sent to the Venetian doge on April 7, 1503. Kitsikis (1996 [1985]), 58–59.

7. Atsız (1992), 25–26.

8. Köprülü (1979), 187–90.

9. Among the pioneers are Speros Vyronis (1971), *The Decline of Medieval Hellenism in Asia Minor and the Process of Islamization from the Eleventh through the Fifteenth Century* (Berkeley); Rudi Lindner (1983), *Nomads and Ottomans in Medieval Anatolia* (Bloomington, IN); Colin Imber (1990), *The Ottoman Empire, 1300–1481* (Istanbul); and Cemal Kafadar (1995), *Between Two Worlds: The Construction of the Ottoman State* (Berkeley and Los Angeles).

10. The name "Byzantine," a by-product of the "rebirth" of Europe, was never employed in reference to their empire of themselves by those whom we today call "the Byzantines." The empire was Roman and the people were Romans. Bastav (1989), v. This terminology was also later adopted by the Ottomans, who called the indigenous Greek-speakers of Anatolia "Romans" *(Rum).* In a piece of verse, Mustafa Ali, a leading sixteenth-century Ottoman scholar, identifies the Ottomans themselves as *"Rûmi"*—that is, neither Ottoman nor Turk, but Roman. Gökyay (1978), 1: 152. Yapp notes that the idea of Europe as a cultural, rather than a strictly geographical entity, gained currency notably in 1684. We cannot help but remark the coincidence of the defeat of the Ottomans at Vienna just the year previous. Yapp (1992), 134, 142–43.

11. Obviously, any reductionist approach to Ottoman society aimed at making a simple tally of which group among its subjects and which traditions contributed what and how much would be of little value. As scholars, we want to know not which Ottoman institution or custom found its origins in which social group or communal body, but rather what are the requisite components for the construction of a model that captures the basis for the selection and the nature of the synthesis of the elements. The question we need to ask is not "Who?" but "How?"

12. For example, Pakalın (1983), 2: 209. The *kassam* for the taxpayers is called *kassam-i beledî* and that for the tax exempt, *kassam-i askerî.*

13. For the sixteenth century, see Emecen (1989a), 90–91, 95, 101, 107. In the account of his visit to Manisa in 1671, Evliya Çelebi neglected to identify any of its *medreses* in his *Seyahatname* (book of travels).

14. The issue of whether the nature of the sultan partook of the divine can be debated. Officially, at least in diplomatic communications, the sultan bore the title of the "Shadow of God on Earth." From a political perspective, some trace the development of the Ottoman state as originating in a theocracy, which evolved into an absolute monarchy. A related position, adopted by the Turkish judge Yaşar Şahin Anıl, in his work on the Ottoman institution

of the *kadı*, is that it was theocratic in character until 1839 and by reason of the dualistic legal system adopted after that time, became semitheocratic. Anıl (1993), 20–21, 34–38. Though it is sometimes alleged that the sultan in the issuance of his decrees took care to conform to Islamic law, this is not quite true. In the first place, Islamic law makes no or almost no provisions concerning land use. In addition, support by religious law for certain legislative decrees was only arbitrarily sought by the sultans. Moreover, even when a religious pronouncement was sought and issued in the form of a *fetva* by the chief mufti or chief jurisconsul (who was, at the same time, the *Şeyhülislâm*, the leading religious functionary of the realm), we should recall that this was a state-appointed position, the tenure of which was, ultimately, at the prerogative of the sultan. God's representative on earth might, nominally, be the *Şeyhülislâm*, but "His Shadow" possessed greater substance.

15. By far the greatest number of entries of the Manisa court registers deal with notarial procedures—for example, the registration of loans, commercial contracts, and notification of the recovery or occurrence of stray livestock; marriage contracts and municipal affairs, such as who has received imperial confirmation of civil and military appointments, oaths of personal surety for newcomers to neighborhoods or guilds, determinations of the highest maximum price for goods and produce sold in the local market, and records of the assessment and collection of taxes.

16. Evliya Çelebi (1938), 85. In 1515, the judgeship of Manisa was ranked at eighty *akçe*s per day as was Izmir; but this was lower than those for other towns in the province *(eyalet)* of Anatolia-Kütahya, 90; Tire, 100; Ankara, 130; and Bursa, 300 *akçe*s per day. Gökçe (1994), 234–35.

17. For a discussion of career possibilities among the learned class in the seventeenth and eighteenth centuries, see Madeline Zilfi (1988), *The Politics of Piety: The Ottoman Ulema in the Postclassical Age (1600–1800)* (Minneapolis), 43–79.

18. For use of the word *ecnebi* in this sense, see, for example, *Kitabi Mesalih*, a contemporary work, in Yücel (1988), 31, 38, 106.

19. Halaçoğlu (1991), 181–82. *Medrese* scholars *(müderris)* were included, however.

20. Withers (1996 [1650]), 133–34.

21. Mustafa Nuri Yılmaz, the head in 1998 of the directorate of religious affairs of the republic of Turkey—and an *imam* (prayer leader) himself—stated in a recent appearance on a television newscast (Channel ATV, January 12, 1998) that the Muslim preachers *(imam)* in the Ottoman period expressed a distaste for carrying out their duties, because of their disdain for the common people.

22. The pious foundation accounts for the *zaviye*-type (with side chamber) mosque include a notice of rent for the court; dated to probably 1599–1600 *(icare-i zemin-i mahkeme-i Şerif-i Çesnigir fi sene 720).* Gökçen (1946), 58, 61.

23. In the opinion of the Hanefi school of law, all the heirs must agree to make the appeal. Aktan (1991), 253. Demirel (Aralık 1990), 946–47, found that 17.4% (out of 1,096 inventories) of Ankara in 1700–1730 belonged to non-Muslims; by contrast, non-Muslim of Damascus made up only 4.3% of a total of 449 inventories in the same period. Establet and Pascual (1994), 38.

24. As a rule, women in the Balkans (including mainland Greece, but excluding certain Aegean islands) inherited nothing except their own dowry and any personal effects of their mother; if there were no sons, the property was turned over to the church. Todorova (1993), 126.

25. Sultan Mehmed II recognized the Greek patriarchate in 1453 and that of the Armenian patriarchate in 1461. Şahin (1980), 38–39.

26. State confiscation of the estates of prominent state servants, whose gross assets were enormous, has not been studied on a systematic basis. This practice is supposed to have constituted an increasingly major source of funds for the state, instituted arbitrarily during the seventeenth century, but systematic starting in the 1770s. Yüksel (1993), 474–75.

27. These are now held by the archive of the Topkapi imperial palace (Topkapı Sarayı Arşivi) and the Ottoman archives under the authority of the Turkish prime minister (Türkiye Cumhuriyeti Başbakanlık Osmanlı Arşivleri), both located in Istanbul.

28. A *fetva* issued in the sixteenth century by the chief mutfi (and *Şeyhülislâm*) Ebussuûd Efendi, clarified the legal issue involved as follows: "the point of law: Does a *kadı* or a court practitioner have the right to come [to the home] and apportion the estate of the deceased, John Doe, for a legatee of high rank? Response: Certainly not; neither of them has any right to do so unless a minor is involved." *("Mes'ele: Zeyd-i müteveffânın verese-i kibâri kismet için, kadı yâ kassam 'elbette varıp kismet ederim' demege kâdir olurlar mı? El-cevap: Aslâ sagîr yok ise olmazlar.")* Düzdağ (1983), 133, number 623.

29. An imperial decree of 1609 (1018 H.), enumerating certain abuses by officials, includes those perpetrated by overzealous judicial officials, who are commanded to henceforth refrain from going on "inspection tours," looking for evidence of newly dug graves and making threats of disinterment in order to extort fees from the heirs. The text in transliteration was first published by Çağatay (1955), 208–14; and in Arabic script by İnalcık ([1965] 1993), 123–33.

30. By law, only the father and his father could act as guardian with full powers *(velâyet)*; otherwise, the powers of any other guardian appointed were restricted to financial matters relating to the minor child *(vesâyet).* Karaman

(1985), 42. Establet and Pascual found that minor children were involved in 69% of all inventories examined from the registers of Damascus of the first quarter of the eighteenth century. Establet and Pascual (1994), 31. The percentage of minor children occurring in the Ankara inventories in the same period was nearly the same—60%. Demirel (Aralık 1990), 951.

31. Aktan (1991), 93, 96. Discussion of the rules of inheritance under Islamic law makes requisite the clarification of terms. First of all, it seems useful to adopt the distinction observed in anthropology, whose prime focus long has been the analysis of kinship and other social relations. It was discovered to be both convenient and necessary to restrict the meaning of the word "inheritance" to the devolution of property and to reserve the term "succession" for the transmission of the rights (or claims) and privileges adhering to the name of the deceased bearer. Stirling (1965), 120. Conforming to this distinction, the word "inheritance" here will denote the sum total or any portion thereof of the property only contained in an inheritance inventory. Moreover, because Islamic law partitions an estate among legatees in a set manner—that is, the estate is entailed—we need to confine the meaning of "bequest" *(vasiyet)* in our context to that one-third portion (and, under certain conditions, more than one-third) over which an individual has the right of free disposal under Islamic law. By this means, we can avoid confusing it with the use of "bequest" in systems where a testatory disposition, or will, is permissible and serves as a synonym for the "inheritance" (or any portion thereof) itself. For the same reason, because the estates contained in Ottoman inventories are entailed, the use of the term "probate" also becomes inapplicable. All Ottoman subjects for whom inheritance inventories were drawn up by the *kadı* died intestate.

32. The *kadı* possessed the authority of public guardian. Anıl (1996), 46.

33. The other side of the coin was that this stipulation had the effect of reducing complications in the event of a divorce, which right, by the declaration of a verbal formula, belonged to the husband alone; the wife could divorce only by petitioning the court and could mean the relinquishment of her financial settlement *(mehr)*.

34. Manisa judicial register *(Şer'iye Sicil)* 112, 228, undated, the preceding inventory on the same page is dated 1658–1659 (1069 H.).

35. Sunguroğlu (Temmuz 1966), 4138–40.

36. Compare the custom of the sultan observed in the seventeenth century of having garments of gold and silver embroidered velvet delivered as gifts to the builders of imperial mosques one day prior to the ceremony (to be attended by the sultan himself and leading personages) to mark the occasion of covering the central dome, when the garments would be hung up on an extended rope for display. Withers (1996), 170–71.

37. We must acknowledge, however, that the problem of inventories of deceased males that include items designated as belonging to that class

of goods—especially clothing—exclusive to women *(zenne)* is in need of explanation.

38. Altıner (1937), 11.

39. Terminology for the sections is adapted from Reychman and Zajoczkowski (1968), 140–49. The comment by Barkan on the difficulties of deciphering the inventories of Edirne can only be strongly seconded on the basis of my experience with those in the Manisa register. Barkan (1993 [1966]), 77.

40. Mention is made by Establet and Pascual (1994), 28, of the occurrence of eyewitnesses (termed "intervenants") for Damascene inventories in the eighteenth century. Eyewitnesses are to be carefully distinguished from the ordinary "witness" *(şahid)* in the legal context. The names of witnesses, whose function is to avow or swear that some event occurred at a past time or that some present statement about facts in the past are true, are inserted in the actual case record or in an appended entry certifying such actions and never under the heading *şud-ül-hal.*

41. Sunguroğlu (Temmuz 1966), 4139.

42. Barkan (19 [1966]), 1.

43. Emecen (1989a), 62, a proportion that he considered "very high." A much higher proportion (26%) of Muslim pilgrims appeared in the inventories of Damascus around 1700 as determined by Establet and Pascual (1994), 41. At Ankara, during the same years, the ratio for pilgrims was 20%. Demirel (Aralık 1990), 947. These figures suggest either that pilgrimages were undertaken more often in the early eighteenth century or that Manisa, in the sixteenth century, was far below the average in this respect. Or that the inventories are not representative. "El-hac" is to be distinguished from "hacı," which may precede (as a nickname) or constitute the given name; though it sometimes implies a greater degree of religious zeal on the parts of the individual, it is unrelated to the actual pilgrimage. Cf. Emecen (1989a), 62.

44. The first three are obligatory for all Muslims: To believe that there is only one God whose name is Allah and that Muhammad was His prophet; to pray five times a day, and to fast in the lunar calendar month of Ramazan (Ar. Ramadan). The other two requirements of giving alms *(zekat)* and making the pilgrimage *(hac)* apply only to those of comfortable means. Hançerlioğlu (1984), 391.

45. One Greek of Manisa who converted to Islam changed his name from Murad, a name commonly taken by Muslims, to Mustafa. Manisa judicial register 46, p. 28, dated March 14–24, 1621 (Evahir Rebiülahir 1030).

46. Kunt (1986), 232, states that the most popular Arabic Muslim names taken by Ottomans are, in order, Mehmed, followed by Mustafa, Ahmed, Ali, Ibrahim, Hasan, and Hüseyin, which comprise more than a third of all the names in the *Sicill-i Osmanî,* the principal Ottoman biographical dictionary.

47. A similar phenomenon was noted in Kayseri and Karaman in the sixteenth century. Jennings (1976), 34, 36.

48. This situation contrasts with the statement by Kunt that the frequency of the choice of biblical names among members of the dynasty and dignitaries associated with the court declined after the fifteenth century. Kunt (1986), 232.

49. For instance, Manisa judicial register 16, p. 350, dated October–November 1601. (Cemaziülevvel 1011).

50. Kunt notes that the distinction between the elite military leaders, who were converts to Islam and who bore Persian names, and the Muslim-born religious dignitaries, who used Islamic names, disappeared around the turn of the seventeenth century, with both groups tending to assume Arabic Muslim names. In his opinion, this indicates that the concluding stage in the Islamization of the empire had been achieved. Kunt (1986), 233.

51. Ongan (1974), 168–210.

52. Ilyas and Hizis were the names of rulers of the earlier Saruhan dynasty.

53. Savaş (1992), 30.

54. Kum (Şubat 1954): 1500–1502. Erol (1992), xxi.

55. Erol (1992), xxiv–xxv, xxxi, 121–23, 395, 431, 76, 395, 399, 431. The many other variations based on the verb *durmak* include, for males, Durak, Durali, Duraman, Duran, Duransel, Duray, Durbaba, Durbâli, Durbeş, Durcihan, Durda, Durdası, Durdemir, Durdu, Durhan, Durpluş and Durun and, for females, Durakadın, and Dursune. The names, "Yaşar" (he will stay alive), Yaşanur, Yaşariye, Yaşatan from the verb *yaşamak* (to live) and Temel, Taştan, Binali, Tokta, and Toktamıd possess a comparable meaning. See also Rásonyi (1988), 22.

56. Erol (1992), xxix, 356. Kum (Şubat 1954), 1502, had the custom explained to him at Afyon by a keeper of the mausoleum where it was practiced. In Judaic tradition, the firstborn was sanctified to God, see Exodus 13: 12–15; and regarding the redemption money for firstborn males, see Numbers 3: 45–51.

57. Erol (1992), 356.

58. One or two instances occurred of both groups being referred to, collectively, as Nasranî, and one assessment list put both groups under the term *zimmiler,* which seems to prove the rule. In terms of community membership, the Armenians were a new group in Manisa in the seventeenth century, and furthermore, appear to have emigrated from Persia; for they are often called simply *Acem* (Persian).

59. After traveling through the Ottoman empire, the Polish Armenian priest, Simeon of Zamosc, went to Rome in 1608, where, he reports with approval, the Vatican required the Jews in Rome to attend Trinity Church on

Saturdays; those who failed to attend were fined and other punishments were imposed. The subject of the sermons delivered in Hebrew concerned the assignment of blame to the Jews regarding the death of Jesus; at the head of each pew stood a guard who would knock them on the head with a rod if they fell asleep or were unwilling to pray. Further, Simeon notes that unlike in Poland and the territories of the Ottoman empire, Jews in Europe were prohibited from being employed in customs offices or serving as tax collection officers and from engaging in trades. They were permitted to make their livelihood in the commercial sector only as dealers in secondhand goods. Andreasyan (1964), 76, 78–79. Statements by Jews who came to Manisa court on May 21, 1663 (12 *Şevval* 1073) in connection with an infringement by builders of a public bath *(hamam)* of the property lines of the Jewish cemetery disclose that their "fathers and grandfathers" had been buried in this cemetery since the time of the "conquest" and that their right to this property had been granted by imperial deeds of trust *(temlikname)*. Gökçen (1950), 41–42. Which "conquest" is being referred to is unclear; it may be that by the Ottomans of Manisa ca. 1412. Emecen (1989a), 22, and not that of Istanbul in 1453. This statement attests to their presence in Manisa earlier than ca. 1500, the earliest date for which evidence is said to be available. Emecen (1997), 30. They numbered around two hundred in the mid-seventeenth century. Emecen (1997), 39.

60. According to Redhouse, this word is usually reserved for reference to the death of animals; however, it appears in *Kitâb-ı Müstetab* to refer to imperial slaves, so it must also have been implied to converts also. Yücel (1988), 4, 11.

61. The Ottoman and Modern Turkish word is apparently derived from the Greek word *atsigani* meaning "the untouchables" *(dokunulmayanlar)*, who are stated to have arrived in Greece in 1322 A.D. Onur (Mayıs 1995), 17.

62. An undated code of statutes pertaining to the Rumelian Turks *(etrâk)* and gypsies states that Muslim gypsies are not to reside with non-Muslims; but, it also states that a tax *(haraç)* (which is assessed only on non-Muslims) of forty *akçe*s is to be collected from "every" gypsy. Onur (Mayıs 1995), 17. For a list of male and female gypsy names, see Altinöz (Mayıs 1995), 24. They were in Ottoman lands by the fifteenth century and, typically, plied the trade of blacksmith. Altinöz (Mayıs 1995), 20. A *fetva* issued concerning the point of law as to whether or not a gypsy (kıptî), though a Muslim, could be considered to possess a status that would make him an appropriate marriage partner (that is, of equivalent status) *(küfüv)* for a girl descended from the elite elicited a response in the negative. ("Müslim olup lâkin kibtî olan Zeyd, sâdât-i kirâmdan Amr"in kızı Hind'e küfüv olurmu? El-cevap: Olmaz.") Yüksel and Savaş (1993), 878. Also in need of study among the inhabitants of Manisa were those termed "Arabs," who may be freed African slaves or Turcomen of Aleppo. Emecen (1989a), 139, believes they are Turcomen.

63. This practice was also observed by the Byzantines for non-Christians with a head tax called *kephaliteion.* Kitsikis (1996), 66.

64. For example, in an entry in Manisa judicial register 95 p. 129, dated January 5, 1649 (19 Zilhicce seman ve hamsin ve elf), a Greek states that because he is an artilleryman at the citadel he is not required to pay a certain tax *(avariz salyanesi)* ("kefere taifesinden Karakass nam zimmi."); his name (or nickname)—Black-Brows—is Turkish, however. The names of the non-Muslims, who are all designated *zimmi* are as follows: Dursun, Cüncor, Gerzi, Kasim, Mihail, and Toma in 1531 and Bazarlu, Gülyan, Karagöz, Kasım, Yorgi, and Yusuf in 1572/1573. Emecen (1989a), 337–39. Note that the names Dursun, Kasım, Mihail, Karagöz, and Yusuf are also chosen by Muslims.

65. Uluçay (1942), 46.

66. One such case, which suggests that the party concerned was experiencing extreme indecision about which rank might wield the greater prestige and utility, involved a man who had succeeded to his father's position as sheikh of a dervish lodge in northeastern Anatolia. After initially being registered as plain Ismail (on three successive occasions), starting in 1691, he became transformed into Ismail Çelebi (Ismail the learned gentleman) in 1698 and, subsequently, became Ali Baba-zâde Ismail Beşe (lord Ismail of the Ali *Baba-zâdes*) in 1700, and then he tried out Ismail Aga (Janissary officer Ismail) twice, before finally settling on Es-Seyyid Eş-Şeyh (the sacred-descendant-of-the-Prophet Sheikh) in 1726. Savaş (1992), 61.

67. The referents for the deceased, the heir, and the inheritance are *müris, varış,* and *miras,* respectively.

68. For *fetva*s confirming that the wife of a deceased male must wait for four months and ten days to elapse to determine whether or not she is carrying the child of her deceased husband before she can legally remarry, see Yüksel and Savaş (1993), 893.

69. Aktan (1991), 59–61.

70. Aktan (1991), 20, 25, 42. Adoption of males by married women for the express purpose of begetting a child *(istibdâ nikâhı)* is known to have been practiced by Arabs in the pre-Islamic era and in ancient Rome. Traces of this practice are retained in Islamic law with the provision for temporary marriage *(mut'a).* Özdemir (Aralık 1990/1991), 997; Ortaylı (1980), 35. Inan indicates that the adoption of a sexual partner was a common mode of action by women in matriarchal exogamous and nomadic societies, including Turkic groups. Awareness of the practice *(döl alma)* can be detected in the Turkic epic *Dede Korkut,* for instance. Inan (1948), 133–37.

71. Illustrated in the sixteenth-century miniature album, *Semâîlnâme-i Ali Osman,* by Talikî-zâde. Emecen (1989a), plate.

72. The top rank was bestowed in 1584. Emecen (1989b), 217.

73. Emecen (1989a), 63.

74. The sultanic statutes *(kanunnâme)* copied into the earliest judicial register of Manisa (covering the years 1529–1546/929–953 H.) lacks the introductory portion, which would allow positive identification, but its contents share similarities with those of the surrounding districts. See Arıkan (1987), 51.

75. Arıkan (1987), 51.

76. Akgündüz (1991), 193.

77. Fairchilds (July 1993), 850. 8 Brumaire was passed on October 29, 1793.

78. Altıner (1938), 10.

79. Fellows (1838), 2.

80. Hengirmen (1983), 168.

81. This tradition has continued to the present in the Izmir (Smyrna) area, which includes Manisa; for types of wild plants used for food and ways of preparing them, see Evelyn Kalças (1980), *Food from the Fields (Edible Wild Plants of Aegean Turkey)*, 2nd edition, (Istanbul, Redhouse Yayınları). On Ottoman diet in general, particularly of the capital in the eighteenth and nineteenth centuries, see Faroqhi (1995), 228–47.

82. Montanari (1995), 24–25.

83. Pakalın (1983), 2:211.

84. The types of baklava for which a Mevlevi sheikh of Edirne gave recipes in the first half of the nineteenth century differ greatly from the kinds made today. There were two kinds, one was *kaymak baklavası*, which had a filling of mashed black-eyed peas (?) *(beyaz börülce)*, milk and eggs, and the other kind had one of melon. Halaçoğlu (1992), 18, 32.

85. Boran (1992 [1945], 239). *Çitlenbik*, or *çitlembik*, is usually translated as terebinth tree *(pistacia terebinthus)* whose products are inedible. Another species is called *buttum (pistacia khinjuk)*, bearing fruit that is edible and used for cooking soap and oil. Baytop (1994), 55, 75, 205.

86. The amount usually deducted—five hundred to a thousand *akçes*—may be compared with (the somewhat higher) market prices in Istanbul in 1640. The cost of a coffin ranged from 20 to 75 *akçes* (for four different sizes), and the fee collected by a digger to dig the grave and cover the coffin was 30 *akçes* while that for the digging of the grave alone, in three different sizes, ranged from 10 to 25 *akçes*. A piece of the lowest quality *(ednâ)* domestic cloth

for a shroud *(beyaz bogası* from Hamid) with a length of 16.75 ft. (7.5 *zira'*) and a width of 2 ft., 2.7 in. (1 *zira'*) cost 100 *akçes*, making a total outlay of roughly 200 *akçes*. Kütükoğlu (1983), 128, 309.

87. Gökçen (Mart 1947), 5. Inscribed in a Manisa judicial register in September/October 1661 (Safer 1072), the following lines of verse by Mahmud Efendi are a translation from the original Arabic into Turkish by Prof. Dr. Ismail E. Erünsal of Marmara University, Istanbul, to whom I would like to express my great appreciation. My translation represents an attempt only to convey the sense of the verses.

4

The Age of Tulips: Confluence and Conflict in Early Modern Consumer Culture (1550–1730)

Ariel Salzmann

Introduction: Modernity's Tulip?

Borrowing a conceit from the eighteenth-century poet Nedim, Ahmed Refik (1881–1937) attached the tulip to one of the Ottoman Empire's most enlightened regimes.[1] His monograph entitled the "Tulip Age" *(Lâle Devri)* documents the cultural achievements and floral preoccupations of Sultan Ahmed III (r. 1703–1730). Under the guidance of the sultan's son-in-law, Grand Vizier Nevşehirili İbrahim Paşa (r. 1718–1730), the state embarked on new policies and programs. Istanbul dispatched diplomats to European capitals, established the first Ottoman language printing press, and promoted commerce and industry. Tulips evoked the ephemeral pleasures and seasonal rhythms of Ottoman public life. In spring, courtiers poured onto the waterways and gardens of the city, especially toward the cottages and pavilions of the Golden Horn where at Kağıthane, a new palace, the "abode of happiness" *(Sa'adabad),* had been constructed on French plans. Nocturnal fetes were illuminated by *çırağan,* tulips beds festooned with colored lanterns.[2]

For early Turkish republican literati the craze for tulips was not only the charming emblem of the old regime. It also served as a cautionary tale of the perils of precocious modernization.[3] After a decade of cultural efflorescence, escalating taxes, the collapse of the Iranian front, and, it would seem, the court's conspicuously westernized practices, provoked an ugly reaction from the capital's pious and poor. Before the insurgency was repressed, the reformist Ibrahim Paşa had been executed and the gardens, pavilions, and palace of the Sa'adabad razed to the ground.

Despite its close association with this episode in Ottoman history, the tulip remains a culturally ambiguous emblem. From the time of Süleyman the Magnificent (d. 1566), cultivation of this flower of West and Central Asian origins had become a celebrated and cross-regional practice.[4] Over the seventeenth century, tulips changed hands between Ottoman poets and Dutch stilllife painters, Mughal gardeners, and French essayists. As the rose before it, tulip bulbs and images reflected a uniquely interlocking "old world" flower culture born of the trade in luxury commodities, global flows of seeds and plants, and scientific investigation.[5] In the early modern period such luxury flowers reflected expanding circuits of commodity exchange, which carried colorful Asian manufactures to European cities.[6]

The Istanbul tulip was itself the product of confluence in early modern consumer markets. The Ottoman plant, as other tulip hybrids that circulated between cities in Asia and Europe, should be considered a "transcultural" commodity.[7] As luxuries, rare flowers long had been traded between states in which confession, occupation, and the rank of individuals and social groups were clearly demarcated and reproduced by visual signs and distinctive behavior—clothing, residence, and ritual.[8] Imported flowers and foral images formed part of an expanding repertoire of the European and Middle Eastern elite's conspicuous consumption, as displayed in festivals, tapestries, formal gardens, poetry, and the patronage of botanical sciences. Flowers and gardens helped elaborate a diplomatic language for political elites who transferred part of their ideological competition from the battlefield to the palace, garden, and parade ground.[9]

In addition to a shared material symbolism, the age of tulips illustrates the conflict brought by early modern consumer culture.[10] The flower's easy entry and circulation demonstrated the quickening pace of commercial exchange and the growing volume of imported mass consumer goods and manufactures. Early modern consumption, both elite and popular, defied the norms that previously had governed material life and the codes of conduct deemed appropriate to various ranks within society.[11] Whether gauged by the rhetorical competition between expanding states, the speculative trading in flower futures, or the gardens that formed part of the conspicuous consumption of elites, tulips highlight conflicts over the circulation of goods and resources, as well as cultural ambivalence toward changing sumptuary standards.[12]

Naming the Tulip

Perhaps the mistaken identification of the tulip's cultural significance derives from the timing of its entry in Mediterranean commerce. Commodification of the tulip occurred in the age of Iberian oceanic exploration. Even Persian vocabularies recognized the flower as a distinctly Eurasian hybrid *(lale-i firengi)*.[13] However, rather than substantiating a Eurocentric pattern of diffusion, its name in European languages and its Caspian and Central Asian provenance alludes to both subtle and substantial ecological and economic continuities following the Mongol invasions of the thirteenth century.[14] More than a simple transfer of plants, flower culture comprehended manufactures, medicinal herbs, perfumes, and design. Long before its acceptance in late medieval Europe, the trade in flowers had found its niche in Indian Ocean cultures through cuisine, ritual, scientific investigation, gardens, and poetics. Borne westward with the *Pax Islamica* after the eighth century, floral commodities and design informed a peculiarly transregional visual vocabulary that defined the "old world" luxury exchange from China to England.[15]

Although the trans-Atlantic conquests would reverse the flow of seeds and plants between East and West, and transform global trade, the Ottoman transmission of the tulip into western markets signaled both the continued flow of Asian flora and the enduring prestige of the Asian commodities, both comestible and manufactured, within European markets. Ottoman rule, encircling the eastern and southern littorals of the Mediterranean by the middle of the sixteenth century, brought this post-Mongol economic order to the very gates of Western Christendom. Architecture and urban planning exemplify the Ottoman environmental vision on its grandest scale. Both a walled fortress and storehouse/treasury of the faithful, the fifteenth-century Topkapı Palace's incorporation of open spaces, flower gardens, and natural vistas, in addition to the prominence of both its kitchens and women's quarters, as Gülru Necipoğlu's research demonstrates, enclosed a model of the imperial state within an earthy paradise.[16] In contrast to Europe's post-Columbian gardens or colonial system, the rebuilding of the former Byzantine capital revealed the resilience of classical forms as well as a distinctly Ottoman sensibility toward cultivated nature.[17] Ignoring the ancient ramparts of the city, by the late seventeenth century this sprawling metropolis of over half a million persons who resided in densely packed urban quarters, garden villages, and elite suburbs resembled the Mughal gardens of northern India: an ecological and ethnic "melting pot" where peoples and plants of conquered and conqueror co-mingled within an as yet unbounded Islamic polity.[18]

La maniera Turchesca Ottoman standards of dress and more generally its commodity culture included a passion for flowering plants.[19] Conveying specific connotation, tulips found their way into Istanbul's bustling flower markets and in its plastic arts along the path of silks and textiles, Islamic mystical symbolism of well-known Persian poets, such as Sa'di (d. 1294) and the portable arts of the Turkish speaking courts.[20] Referring to the dynasty's central Asian roots as well as Persianate concepts of universal monarchy and courtly poetics, the tulip expressed renewal and peace, as well as spiritual turmoil and mystical intoxication, earthy power, and self negation. The tulip's red petals and black stamen served as visual metaphor for the flame, the self-immolation of the seeker in the fire of the divine source, as well as the wine goblet of mystical intoxication. Calligraphers transposed the letters of the Turco-Persian word *lâle* into the spelling of Allah, and that of crescent *(hilal)*. Ottoman ceramic tiles, velvets, brocades, book design, stone carving, and furniture feature stylized tulips alone or intertwined with the rose, carnation, and hyacinth in the well-known *saz* motif.[21]

The name given to this West Asian flower in European langauges sealed a formative connection between power, nature, and manufacture. "Tulip" appears to be a corruption of the Ottoman-Persian word *tülbend*, the name of a west Asian cotton cloth commonly used for and identified with turbans.[22] The first official notice of the plant's passage to central Europe occurred during a period of diplomatic contact with the representatives of the sultan's archenemy, the Habsburg emperor. In 1554 Ambassador Ogier de Busbecq received a tulip as a "gift" and carried it as well as other seeds and bulbs to Vienna.[23] The Western appreciation of the tulip betrays a general fascination with bulbous plants and tubers—including the new world potato—revived interests in botany and horticulture, as well as the tulip's unpredictable changes in coloring (caused by viral "breaking").[24] However, the tulip's circulation among European courts from the middle of the sixteenth century onward did not rely on its botanical features alone. Its prestige was sustained by its association with power and material wealth: the turbaned sultan, the empire's military might and material riches, and the tales of the Ottoman court carried in the writings and drawings of ambassadors, artists, and soldiers.[25] Over the centuries, the repeated gifting of the tulip (called "the queen of flowers" by one French gardener of the seventeenth century and routinely given females names in Persian and Turkish) between two imperial dynasties, in the Persian and Ottoman empires, which did not intermarry, underscores the rich symbolic content of such crosscultural material diplomacy.[26]

Upon the arrival of the first cargos of bulbs from Istanbul in Antwerp in 1561, the tulip had become more than a luxury-gift exchanged between rival states.[27] Marketing as a transcultural commodity permitted, indeed encouraged, variation and adaptation to specific regional and cultural styles. Thus, the wan and delicately pointed petals of the early eighteenth-century Istanbul flower, capturing the form of flowers on Iznik tiles, does not recall either the fuller, naturalistic scarlet tulips of seventeenth-century Mughal painting or the more robust and rounded white tulips tipped with crimson favored by northern Europe's burghers.[28] Yet all shared common genetic roots. Horticulturalists in Europe and Asia avidly sought out seeds and bulbs, and experimented with crossbreeding of plants. Ottoman flower cultivators who once may have relied exclusively on bulbs from the Crimea, began importing seeds and bulbs from European sources by the end of the sixteenth century.[29] Although Muscovy seemed to have derived its initial interests in the plant from west European sources, direct commerical and renewed diplomatic relations with the Safavid Shahs, either through the Persian Gulf after the recapture of Hormuz in 1622 or overland commerce after 1639, explains the role of Iranian cultivars in enhancing all Eurasian tulip stocks.[30]

The cultivation of tulips provided a metaphor for proficiency in territorial rule, while experimentation with its seemingly endless variety of color and form permitted competing states to symbolize moral preeminence on the basis of a commonly recognized and valued natural object.[31] Ottoman tulip historians credit Süleyman the Magnificent's chief justice, Ebusuûd Efendi (d. 1574), author of the formative compilation of imperial statutes and their reconciliation with Islamic law, as one of the earliest private tulip aficionados.[32] In Ottoman lore the multiplicity of the flower's source of origin retraced the empire's perimeters and embodied its parts: Ebusuûd Efendi brought bulbs to the Istanbul from his native city of Bolu in Anatolia. In the sixteenth century, seeds were brought from Bosnia while Sultan Murad IV is said to have retrieved tulips from the caliphal city of Baghdad in 1638 following campaigns which restored the Sunni shrines to imperial guardianship. The prominent portrait of the planting of a gigantic tulip with yellow petals, among other scenes in Lokman's ceremonial treatise and painting album (the *Sûrnâme-yi Hümayun* completed for Murad III [1582]), at a time when Ottoman armies were locked in battle for religious preeminence and territorial control with the neighboring Shi'i state (whose followers recognized their devotion to the *imams* with multipointed red turbans) suggests that contemporary ideology also influenced the selection of the hues of Ottoman flowers.[33]

Hybridity provided European essayists with the opportunity to reinvent the tulip's actual genealogy and thus establish independent claims to the ownership of a treasured but imported flowering plant.[34] But a century after its arrival from Istanbul, Charles La Chesnée Monstereul, one of the first west European experts on the subject and the author of the *La Florist François* (1654), turned the discussion of the tulip's origin into a diatribe on the relative merits of the gardener. Disputing the tulip's Ottoman pedigree, he attributed the plant to classical sources and pointed to its wide diffusion within the Indian Ocean, from Persia to the "Dutch Indies." Ottoman flowers, he told his readers, are so stilted and inferior a breed as to lack "the capacity for transformation or improvement." By contrast, French tulips are proof of a superior gardener who was,

> never satisfied to merely possess the flowers brought from the Indies, but put themselves to the task of understanding their species; [and] judging from resulting variety and color [that their industry has produced] they have indeed discovered the principle of their evolution.[35]

The Floral Intertext of Mass Consumer Society

By the early seventeenth century, tulips had become a transcultural commodity as well as a polyvalent symbol whose cultivation across the Mediterranean and Asia carried with it apocryphal as well as conjunctural meanings and associations. The continued popularity of the tulip in the seventeenth century cannot be separated from the expanding reach of exchange networks and the changing content of commercial interaction between regions and states. Real flowers echoed across an increasingly rich and stratified trade in manufactures and a preindustrial mass consumer market that bore colorful goods and novel designs from East to West.[36] As metanyms for a mass consumer revolution, flowers served as natural representatives as well as sublimated forms of advertising, which refracted a commercialized intertextuality of design found in gardens, and on ceramics and textiles. No longer the privileged possession of a select social group, mass consumption of imported manufactures like luxury flowers challenged the established order of persons and goods, and their regulation by society and the state.

European historians have marveled over the easy adaptation of this exotic flower to the sandy soils of Holland. The banking house of the Fuggers had marketed the Istanbul flower in Germany and the Low Countries in the sixteenth century.[37] Prices of tulips gained steadily in the early seventeenth century, but the growth of the market in rare bulbs and even flower-futures in Amsterdam and Haarlem, which peaked between 1635 and 1637, was unprecedented. Certainly, as Simon Schama concludes, Dutch frenzied speculation over rare tulips and bulbs, expressed changing values of land, simple botanical curiosity as well as a "consumer hunger" for new goods.[38] Yet as a distinctly crosscultural practice, tulip cultivation also situated the Dutch within the old imperialist rivalry. Choice blooms, named for famous admirals, paid homage to the overseas triumphs of its navy, the formation of new trading companies such as the East India Company (1602), and the conclusion of bilateral trade agreements with the Asian states including the Ottoman Empire in 1612.[39]

While the market's crash may have appeared to be an all too fitting punishment for a society that had flaunted Calvinism's codes on acquisition and display, the morality play of Dutch tulip mania, which would be translated into pamphlet, play, engraving, and novel, struck a responsive cord across Europe.[40] Tulip mania allowed ordinary townsmen to appreciate the complex transactions of the long-distance market.[41] In societies straddling agriculture and urban economies, and where cottage industry in textiles among outlying villages competed with urban gardens, the transplantation of foreign flora may have also transmuted the inhibitions against buying "foreign" goods. Yet the unbridled desire for material goods also exposed early capitalism's fundamentally social dilemmas: how to coax open wallets and expand consumer markets while preventing excessive spending and maintaining the sumptuary standards that defined differences in social status.[42]

In an age of transcultural commodities and quickening commercial interaction, Europe's mercantilist policies continued to discipline its merchants and townspeople. Despite tariffs and taxes, the demand for novel sensations and changing purchasing practices forced early modern states to relax or lift import restrictions. By the end of the seventeenth century formerly prohibited goods, such as coffee and tobacco, had become major items of trade and important sources of state revenue across Europe and Asia.[43] Mass consumer products transformed urban life and patterns of social interaction. While the consumption of coffee and tobacco redesigned urban space and public points of encounter, from gardens to coffeehouses, markets, and streets, the consumption of imported cotton textiles and ceramics redefined interior spaces such as manufactories, household decor, tableware, and attire. Flowers provided a particularly apt analogy for the colorful ceramics and cloths that served as the staples of urban households. Colorful, abundant, easy to clean, and inexpensive, cottons expressed fashion and fad: they undermined the acquired social and economic values attached to silk, wool, and linen textiles and affected the fortunes of guildsmen in the traditional manufacturing centers of Europe.[44]

Broadsides and engravings advertised the new consumer culture in Western Europe.[45] Flower commodities and natural imagery were part of a more subliminal transfer of esthetic values, a floral intertext that transcended specific cultural and religious boundaries. Centuries of exchange had provided the main trading partners with a common lexicon of visual idioms and rudimentary syntaxes. The seventeenth-century environmental order represented by gardens was mirrored in commodity oikoumene[46] of floral patterns on porcelain and pottery, embroidered towels, flatwoven and pile carpets, and stamped cotton, as well as in the illuminations of sacred texts. Subtle advertisements for a new consumer culture, flower culture traveled by land as well as by sea. During the second half of the seventeenth century, there was a steady migration of poets and musicians, alongside a traffic in silk, tobacco, coffee, spices, dyestuffs, textiles, across the central Asian "frontier."[47] From Mughal Delhi to Ottoman Sarajevo, poetry connected another world of cultural goods. Transregional poetry schools, such as the "Indian Style" *(Sabk-i Hindi)* of Persian poetry brought a "fresh style" alongside a burgeoning mass consumer culture.[48] Court poets, such as Nedim, who crossed social boundaries to bring popular forms, the *türkü* and *şarkı*, into the courtly repertoire, also popularized elite forms of entertainment and consumerism.[49]

Both East and West elites regarded the flower garden as a particularly suitable setting for refined consumption.[50] A large Safavid ceramic tableau, dating from the first decades of the seventeenth century, depicts a high-ranking Persian lady reclining amid a flower-strewn garden. At her side a European merchant kneels, displaying and, presumably, selling her expensive imported textiles.[51] More than a mere reference to sensual pleasure or domestic pursuits, women's association with the garden demonstrates a "private" consumer agency. According to Lady Wortley Montagu who visited the Ottoman Empire in the first decades of the eighteenth century, removal from the trials of public life left Ottoman elite women free to devote themselves exclusively to consumer practices: "visiting, bathing, or the agreeable amusement of spending money and inventing new fashions."[52]

Perhaps the harem itself, and especially its internal garden complete with kiosks and encircled by tall cypress trees, should be considered, in a twist on Foucault's characterization of the prison, a "totalizing institution" dedicated to consumption.[53] A visitor who witnessed the *çırağan* (tulip beds bedecked with lanterns) parties held at the palace of Esma Sultan (Ahmed III's daughter) toward the middle of the eighteenth century was astounded to witness the harem garden transformed into a nocturnal bazaar for the pleasure of the sultan's sisters, cousins, and nieces. Brimming with rare goods and luxuries provided by merchants on credit, stalls and boutiques lined its perimeters. Women attendants assumed the role of saleswomen.[54]

Let a Thousand Tulips Bloom

Without contesting the critical role of European galleys in transforming the global distribution of goods over the course of the seventeenth century, and the very prominent and public role of European merchants and investors in determining commodity flows, the floral intertext of early modern consumer society illuminates not only the role of Asian and African craftsmen in establishing design standards, but also the hidden powers of consumers—particularly women—in sustaining their esthetic content.[55] At the crossroads of the early consumer revolution, Ottoman townsmen and women were pivotal actors in global trade. Given state policies that encouraged the circulation of luxuries and commercial manufactures to its growing cities,[56] Ottoman townspeople and merchants mediated the flow of manufactures and design between west Asia, Africa, and Europe. They affected the monetary and importation policies of Mediterranean merchants and states.

Given these crosscurrents in the flow of goods, terms like "occidental" and "oriental" fail to qualify a cosmopolitan taste that followed transcultural commodity trends. Thus, we find that later Iznik ceramics adopted European themes. Wealthier households appreciated Chinese and Japanese porcelains, Persian poetry, English broadcloth, and French architectural styles. Anatolian and Syrian manufacturers produced their own import substitutes of South Asia-styled stamped cottons for domestic use and exportation.[57] Always worldly in its pursuit of pleasure, the Ottoman court sought out diverse performance art as well as material goods. Grand Vizier Köprülü Fazıl Ahmet Paşa (1661–1676) requested the Venetian bailo, Giacomo Quirini, to commission a special *commedia dell'arte* for the Ottoman festival of 1675.[58]

Concern for improving trade relations and enhancing commercial revenues may well explain the conspicuous return to gardens and more public style of the Ottoman court at the turn of the century.[59] Extravaganzas of consumption and dramatic enactments of the Ottoman social order, dynastic festivals of this period drew on themes found in religious, urban, and military ceremonies as well as the court rituals of Bursa, Edirne, and Istanbul. It served a multiplicity of cultural, economic, and political ends.[60] Processions of tradesmen and their wares celebrated the producers of the empire's wealth.[61] The circumcisions of hundreds of poor Muslim boys at the palace's expense demonstrated collective religious identities, while the invitation of performance by Sephardic-Jewish dancing troops emphasized the state's embrace of other religious communities.[62] Flowers framed and accompanied these festivities: gardens sculpted of sugar and *nahıls* (towering conical/phallic shaped constructions, bedecked with sugar, colored paper, metal, and wax sculptures in the form of miniature flowers, fruit, animals, and objects) expressed fertility and the shared bounty of a wealthy empire.[63]

The detailed reports of foreign ambassadors and drawings by artists conveyed Ottoman patterns, goods, and consumer practices abroad.[64] Relatively peaceful relations between the Ottoman Empire and West European powers after 1718 provided greater opportunities for interregional exchange and heightened receptivity across the Mediterranean to the adoption of Ottoman styles.[65] Yet it was an acutely "transcultural" consumer culture that allowed travelers and commentators to overcome their parochial tastes and opinions. Lady Montagu draws her reader's attention to details of the vizier's villa that was finished with imported commodities, including the "finest Crystalline glass" from England. Repeatedly noting the Ottoman passion for "oriental porcelain," the consistency of her emphasis on shared tastes in specific goods transcends differences in composition, and suppresses critique over variances in culture and religion.[66]

Although one may question the motives behind this sympathetic portrait of the empire, even the more seasoned and cynical Venetian ambassador Emo, who considered the spectacles to be distractions orchestrated by the grand vizier and suspected the influence of the French ambassador Marquis de Bonnac, still felt compelled to compliment his nemesis for his refined court.[67] Never a European monologue, such a consumeristic ethic conditioned the Ottoman ambassador, Mehmet Çelebi, as well. His high opinion of French Culture owed not to the strange behavior of women or the wonders of mechanical devices, but the successful elaboration of a familiar esthetic, observed in gardens, finely executed textiles, and mimetic depictions in portable and pictorial arts.[68]

Compared to the rustic pleasures of the hunt and the provincial setting of the Mehmed IV's two-week pageant in Edirne (1675), the Ottoman court's return to Istanbul after 1703 permitted a pageantry and conspicuous consumption on an unprecedented scale.[69] The fete, which preceded the circumcision of Ahmet III's four sons in 1720, began officially on September 18 and concluded with a grand parade on October 9, required months of preparation. Recorded in detail by the poet Vehbi, the festival utilized both the archery grounds over the Golden Horn and the city's waterways.[70] The paintings of Levni, sobriquet of Adülcelil Çelebi (d. 1732) for *Sûrname-yi Vehbi*, illustrate the carefully choreographed banquets and parades. The interplay of manufactured nature and urban stages for amusements ranged from a procession of guilds to mock battles and fireworks on the Bosphorus to carnivalesque acts. Awash in fine textiles, Levni's portraits of ministers and religious dignitaries detail the sumptuary style that demarcated rank and position in the eighteenth-century state. Repeated over the century in numerous fetes to celebrate the births, weddings, and circumcisions of Ahmed III's many progeny, the scale of Ottoman pageants rivaled that of royalty in Vienna, St. Petersburg, Naples, and Venice.[71]

Eighteenth-century courtly spectacles were a type of consumer jousting, or "tournament" of values, which established the standards of shared material civilization.[72] Judged on the basis of its scale and variety, noble civilization was also gauged by craftsmanship and details.[73] The Ottoman obsession with flower cultivation, preeminently tulips but also hyacinths, was not, therefore, merely a reinvention of tradition, the sixteenth-century Iznik flower rendered real. It was part of a continuing dialogue with other regimes on the nature of nobility; indeed, taste *(zefk)* defined the proper manners of a noble *(kibar)* estate.

Following the example set by the sultan's own son-in-law, Grand Vizier Damad Ibrahim Paşa (1718–1730), the Istanbul elite contemplated rare blooms, cherished the tulip's endless variety in paint, and celebrated its seasonality in verse.[74] Tulip albums mirror the structure of the state itself, ranking distinguished members of the regime according to their horticultural achievements. Grand Admiral Mustafa Paşa, son-in-law of the grand vizier, is remembered for forty-four new tulip breeds. Although others left more discrete legacies—the steward of the Istanbul market, Süleyman Ağa, cultivated two exceptionally rare bulbs, as did the Mehmed Efendi, Ottoman ambassador to France—

the cultivation of precious and novel bulbs by courtiers and well-known shaykhs defined membership in the Ottoman ruling elite.[75]

Flower culture also represented the spatial interests and defining leisure practices of what Norbert Elias calls a "court society" within the imperial city.[76] Professional gardeners and flower-sellers utilized west European and Asian cultivars to produce hundreds of new varieties over the eighteenth century.[77]

Tulip prices, which began to rise in the last decades of the seventeenth century and peaked in 1726–1727 before state intervention, reflected both the inflated value of treasured rare bulbs and escalating demand for flowers in the elite's palaces and gardens.[78] Flower gardens carved from the urban and suburban landscapes served as settings for courtly distractions. As other court societies, Istanbul's leisure classes drew their income from tax farming. High- and low-ranking officials benefited from the *malikâne* or life lease tax farms, which the grand vizier had reinstated at the outset of his tenure.[79] Benefiting from a steady income from investments on the imperial debt, members of the royal household, administrators, military officers, the *ulema* and literati, appropriated space, time, and taste within the city while demonstrating their noble pedigree to their competitors in Europe and Asia.[80]

The Anti-Tulip Rebellion

Contemporary histories note that on the day of the rebellion, Istanbul's mayor *(kaymakam)* was absent from the city. He had used the occasion of the celebration of *mevlut* (the Prophet's birthday) to oversee the autumn planting of tulip bulbs in his garden along the Dardenelles.[81] With the ministers of the *divan* far from the seat of government and with troop reinforcements long outfitted but still encamped across the Bosphorus, news of the fall of Tabriz to Safavid forces and the high human toll in casualties and captives in September 1730 triggered an uprising in the city's populous inner quarters.

Official court historians did not conceal their disapproval of the regime's negligence, excesses, and moral lapses.[82] However, they do point to the court's refined taste and patronage of the arts as evidence of an overarching social vision. Thus the historian Küçük Çelebizade Ismail Azim Efendi, whose narrative continues the official record of important events begun by Raşid Efendi, cites the tulip mania as a manifestation of the state's unaltered commitment to the redistributive ethic.[83] An example of enlightened self-interest, the pursuit of beauty in the form of flowers transformed the realm into a "paradiselike garden." Tulip mania demonstrated as well the state's power to regulate the economy. When courtiers forwarded a petition to denounce the unscrupulous *(bi-insaf zümresine)* practices of the flower-sellers who had taken advantage of the elite by raising the price of bulbs to that of precious jewels, the state ordered an investigation by the chief steward of flowers *(ser-şükufeciyan)*, Shaiykh Mehmed Lâlezarî. An official inventory of flowers and a price list was issued to the Istanbul judge for enforcement.[84]

Despite the vizier's timely intervention in the luxury flower market, the Istanbul populace might have had reason to suspect Ibrahim Paşa's concern for the urban economy.[85] Antagonism toward the regime did not derive from either the court's "occidental" affectations or its consumption of luxuries. In fact, the city's skilled and unskilled labor depended on court largesse, in the form of services and goods, and found employment in the building of courtly residences and religious institutions. Conditioned by the steady flow of transcultural goods especially from south Asia, artisans including the rebel leader Patrona Halil, a pedlar and part-time soldier, and his companions, a janissary houndsman, a wood seller, a coffee seller, a pickle vendor, and a grocer, might not have felt the impact of imports, much less regarded European luxuries—watches, chairs, binoculars, telescopes, and eyeglasses—as part of some insidious foreign trend.[86] Although attacks upon non-Muslim shops frightened all merchants in the market, the rebels displayed no anti-Christian animus.[87] The insurgents chose the marketplace as one of three meeting sites for its "public" spaces, particularly the coffee and ale *(boza)* houses where they could find sympathetic audiences among fellow artisans, street vendors, and soldiers.[88]

Reports of repeated clashes between nameless malcontents and the *bostancı* (royal "gardeners") who guarded the Sa'adabad gardens during the preceding summer, may, however, provide a better indicator of the points of class friction and the sources of popular discontent.[89] As the population of the city—with the tightly packed inner districts near Aksaray, the Grand Bazaar, Hagia Sophia, and the Golden Horn—hovered well over half a million, contests over space became more acute and involved greater sensitivity to the elite use of land, in addition to the questions of privacy and women's behavior.[90] Perhaps it was the elite's very conspicuous and proprietary use of space that heightened the sense of imbalance and impropriety. While courtiers sequestered lands in various parts of the city for private gardens and villas, courtly festivals and processions functioned as form of "urban renewal" as houses were removed or effaced along the narrow streets of the central city to accommodate the passage of oversized floats and *nahıls*.[91] In the face of cutbacks to the rolls of the janissaries, soaring taxes to pay for the war and critical shortages in the supply of staples,[92] the court's cultivation of flower gardens and even flower "plantations" rather than agriculture or military defense of the empire, must have appeared to be one of the more flagrant abuses of the public weal.[93]

The targets of the crowd's wrath were those who controlled the circulation of goods and people in the city: the guards and financial officers. Wartime policies actually exacerbated the circulation of basic commodities. Prices rose as rural populations fled before armies or existing stocks were diverted to feed troops. The *bostancı*—forerunners of the urban police—patrolled urban road and waterways. They prevented peasants from seeking refuge in the city and stopped those who attempted to smuggle produce into the city's markets by night from Anatolian and Rumelian fields.[94] Chaffing under new fiscal burdens, artisans encountered numerous petty officials and subfarmers who must have multiplied with the reinstatement of life-leases on urban duties.[95] The court's freedom of movement, the continual sultanic and vizierial visits along the city's waterways and from one palace to another, only brought into starker relief the restrictions born by ordinary citizens: at every exit and entry for persons and goods, townsmen confronted the regime's agents, particularly in the person of the widely disliked *voyvoda* of Galata whose jurisdiction reached to the Black Sea.[96]

While palace conspiracies, "class" alliances, personal ambitions, and religious sensitivities certainly played a role in the motivations of actors and alliances, the rebels' actions speak of a broader social bent to restore Istanbul's "moral economy."[97] The leader of the rebellion, Patrona Halil, held a type of anticourt in the coffeehouse. Addressing one another with the term *birader* (brother/comrade), the insurgents recognized their leaders, appointed an official poet, and dictated the chronology of events to a notary of the street.[98] They dismissed the seated Istanbul judge and replaced him with a well-respected legal scholar who could be trusted to fairly dispense opinions as well as enforce price regulations. They demanded that Ahmed III surrender the grand vizier and chief ministers for popular justice. Frustrated by his refusal, the rebels searched the homes and gardens of these officials to carry out the imperial law of expropriation.[99]

Within days, the rebellion forced Ahmed III to abdicate in favor of his nephew. Placating the rebel leadership with offices and titles, the new regime also sought to dissolve the alliance of artisans and janissaries that supported them. Responding to Patrona Halil's demands, the new sultan, Mahmud I, repealed the onerous taxes which had been imposed by the previous regime.[100] He generously distributed the coronation tax among the janissaires, appointed new ministers for the *divan*, and elected new magistrates. Perhaps the most remarkable concession to the rebellion involved the fate of the pleasure gardens and palaces of the Golden Horn, especially the Sa'adabad, a palace which had been constructed after architectural plans for Versailles. Although the demolition of the palace, as other acts of violence against property, is often ascribed to the insurgents, it was an imperial order that sent soldiers to dismantle the "abode of happiness." Courtiers were allowed but three days to raze their own villas to the foundations.[101]

In a striking departure from the previous regime's gay processions to the gardens and palaces, the new sultan and his entourage solemnly prepared for a pilgrimage along the Golden Horn to the tomb of the Prophet's companion Eyüb. Lulled by the regime's solicitude and public acts of contrition, Patrona Halil and his comrades fell into the trap set by the palace. The sultan's guard continued the purge of rebel sympathizers for weeks after the execution of its leadership.[102]

Conclusion: Do Flowers Speak?

The tulip remains an evocative symbol within later Ottoman historiography. Its mythic appeal, reflected in ceramic and textile, continues to sustain a particular memory of the Ottoman Empire's social past.[103] For nineteenth-century intellectuals this spring flower appeared, like the ruins of the Sa'adabad, an exquisitely romantic monument to the transitory nature of wealth, the fragility of despotic rule, and the failed modernization of an "oriental" regime.[104]

Real tulips were, however, ephemeral artifacts of the merging seams of the early modern world.[105] They marked the convergence of commodity circuits and interlocking consumer patterns. Luxury flowers were not the social legacy of a "culture" or a "nation." They defined nobility and privilege in terms of goods and leisure time. They were practices that linked court societies across early modern Europe and Asia. Although separated by a century, tulip manias in Amsterdam and Istanbul demonstrated both the increasingly transcultural nature of commodity culture and the peculiarly integrative symbolic role of flowers—the floral intertext—in bridging mediums and classes of objects, elite and popular tastes, as well as local and long-distance markets. Not the cult of flowers, but the age of mass consumption gave rise to new forms of social conflict and moral controversy as less privileged groups challenged the traditional social use of goods and questioned the state's regulation of expanding urban markets.[106]

As exemplified by Refik's *Lâle Devri*, artistic, sociological and historical accounts of the Ottoman "Tulip Age" often have subsumed such social struggles over economic agency and the distribution of resources within narratives of national character, religious values, and cultural identity.[107] Although this essay takes issue with such interpretations, it does not question the tulip's symbolic place in Ottoman history. Within the poetic canon known by courtier and commoner alike, this flower carried semantically complex and equivocal connotations. The tulip captures mystical quest, self-denial, and spiritual intoxication. Revived at the turn of the century in courtly practices—inner-elite consumer jousting, costly horticultural pastimes, and sensual verse—the tulip's scentless ("soulless") beauty also insinuated abuse and deception.[108] As Azim Efendi's imaginative defense of the tulip regime suggests,[109] the Ottoman elites were aware of this equivocation. Indeed, the outline of the tulip formed by staffs of wheat, found on one of the period's fountains, suggests artistic attempts to graft the elite's devotion to fleeting pleasures with an enduring commitment to popular welfare.[110]

Surely these didactic translations in the state's public arts did not ensure its monopoly over the rich social and philosophical signification of flowers.[111] Within literatures popular and elite, sectarian and transregional, the tulip, especially the highly commodified and hybrid breeds found in flower stalls and courtiers' gardens, was an inferior to the rose. Inviolable and fragrant, the rose was associated with the Prophet Muhammad and his companions. In such company, the tulip all too closely reassembled Ibrahim Paşa's regime: an exquisite facade which masked baseness, carnal desires, and venality. Rather than evidence of religious reaction to reform or an inability to comprehend the nobility's elevated tastes, the 1730 Istanbul rebellion spoke in the "language of flowers." Had not the ordinary soldier and his followers rescued the tarnished soul of a dynasty that had failed to aspire to the purity of the rose?[112]

Notes

This chapter is offered for Dr. Filiz Cağman, director of the Topkapı Sarayı Museum Library. Her help, professionalism, and enthusiasm for both text and image inspired this modest venture. Thanks too are owed to Randy

Martin, Nosha Baqi, Carolle Charles, Donald Quataert, Faruk Tabak, Philip Kennedy, and Robert McChesney for advice and patient hearings of this article in its many varieties. Support for research in Istanbul (1994) was provided by an N.E.H.-American Research Institute Grant, and in London (1997) by the New York University.

1. My copy of Ahmed Refik's *Lâle Devri* is from the 5th printing (1932), although it was originally composed in 1912. Refik draws the allusions to the tulip from Nedim (see Silay [1994], 112–17), as well as his contemporary Yahya Kemal (1884–1958), who popularized the literary association of this progressive regime and the flower. Although Refik may be accused of poetic license, the association between the regime and tulip mania courses through official historiography from the eighteenth-century Azim Efendi to the Tanzimat historian Cevdet Efendi. For cultural achievements of the period, see also the portrait of the period provided by Lewis (1961), 45–53.

2. In addition to Refik (1932), 51ff., see Blunt (1950), Aktepe (1952), (1953), (1954), (1958a); and Melikoff (1967) on tulips in Ottoman history. Lacking extant gardens from this period, despictions of tulip are to be found in paintings of gardens (see Renda [1987]) in flower albums (see Ayverdi [1950] and Baytop [1992]). I thank Tülay Artan for bringing my attention to the latest scholarly efforts on the tulip; see Hezarfen (1995), 300–302; regretfully, I was unable to consult her 1989 dissertation. For other cultural and artistic aspects of the age, see Atıl (1993), 190; Shay (1944), 20; for European depictions of Tulip Age festivities, see Boppe (1989), and Gopin (1994); for a description of the *çırağan*, see Raşid Efendi (1865), 435–36.

3. Compare the processes of cultural and political "modernization" described by Eisenstadt (1966), 36–40; Berkes (1964), 6–7, 51–63; Kurat (1976), 178–220, Mardin (1973); Göçek (1996), 138ff. For other explanations of the Patrona Halil rebellion, see Aktepe, (1958c) and Olson (1974).

4. For an approach to flower "culture" historically, see Goody (1993); for an attempt to situate flower consumption in a crosscultural framework, see my "Ottoman Tulipmania and the Transcultural Matrices of the Early Modern Market (1550–1750)" (unpublished paper.)

5. There is new attention to the trading world before and after 1500; see Abu-Lughod (1989) and Subrahmanyam (1997), as well as studies on geography and ecology, such as Crosby (1972), Watson (1983); Goody (1993); Schama (1995); Foote, Hugill et al. (1994); and Blaut (1993).

6. For the content of this trade see Glamann (1958); Dermigny (1964); Chaudhuri (1978); and Perlin (1983).

7. Appadurai (1986) considers long distance circuits of trade, but not individual commodities, which circulate within them; although the merchants themselves might be rooted in one or more cultures (Curtin [1984]), the goods themselves were transcultural.

8. See Quataert (1997).

9. On luxury generally, see Berry (1994); on the use of display and dress in refashioning monarchy, see Burke (1992) and the use of space, see Rotenberg (1995).

10. See in particular Mukerji (1983), Schama (1985), and essays in Brewer and Porter eds. (1993).

11. See Quataert (1997).

12. Thompson (1991), 1–15.

13. Literally "the European *lale*"; see Melikoff [1967], 346.

14. Ibid., 344–47; see also Harvey (1976) and Tabak (1996) for the post-Mongol ecological and agricultural developments.

15. Flowers form part of a design intertextuality embracing a world from China to England. For Islamic ceramics and its influences and impact see Soustiel (1985); for Islamic carpets—"textile gardens"—in early modern Dutch painting, see Onno (1991).

16. On the flowers and gardens, Necipoğlu (1990), 202.

17. Necipoğlu (1997), 44.

18. Mantran (1962) esp. 41–66; on Mughal gardens, see Wescoat (1990), 106–17. While the association is often made with paradise, the "garden" is also this worldly. The garden figures as part of the "circle of justice." See the Ahlâk-i 'Alâ'i of Kınalızâde 'Ali Çelebi (d. 1572) (1833) iii, 158; for Timurid versions in the "Advise to Alexander" (Herati edition of the *Nasayih-i Iskandar* dating from 829/1425 "the world is a garden for the state to master . . . " (Ms. [f. 12a] cited in Lentz and Lowry [1989], 1).

19. Raby (1982), 82–83; Necipoğlu (1997), 44; Harvey (1976).

20. The sixteenth-century Ottoman poet Nejâtî makes the tulip the emblem of the upstart, "Those tulip-cheeked ones—what they dared do in the garden!/Besides them, the cypress could not sway,/nor the rosebuds open/ They wouldn't let the wild tulip into the/conversation of the rose/Saying it was a stranger from the distant steppes. (Andrews et al. [1997], 41). See also Schimmel (1976); Golombek and Wilber, (1988), 1:174. Soustiel (1985), 134; Schimmel (1976); and Melikoff (1967). On the uses of the tulip in portable arts during the Ottoman period, see *Turquie* (1993) and Petsopoulos (1982).

21. Schimmel (1976), 25. One wonders, in this millennarian century, whether the tulip's scarlet petals might not also have served as a type of floral standard: Istanbul waged war against both the Holy Roman Empire in the West (the red apple of Vienna and Rome) as well as for the hearts and minds of Muslims against the Safavid Islamic challenger in Iran (whose followers wore red turbans). See Fleischer (1990).

22. For the tulip's entry into European history, see Blunt (1950); Melikoff ([1967], 346] claims that its name was not a mistake, but this particular flower or *lale* was actually designated by the name of *tülbend lâlesi.*

23. "We stayed one day in Andrianople and then set out on the last stage of our journey to Constantinople. . . . As we passed through this district we everywhere came across quantities of flowers—narcissi, hyacinth, and tulipans, as the Turks call them. . . . The tulip has little or no scent, but it is admired for its beauty and the variety of its colours. The Turks are very fond of flowers, and though they are otherwise anything but extravagant, they do not hesitate to pay several aspre for a fine blossom. These flowers, although they were gifts, cost me a good deal; for I had always to pay several aspre in return for them:" de Busbecq (1968) i, 24–25.

24. Habsburg court botanist M. Carolus Clusius, professor of botany at Leyden, adapted it and the potato to European soil. Goody (1993), 188.

25. On the influence of the reports by the Venetian *baili,* see Valensi (1987); for the self-projected images of sovereign power in architecture, see Necipoğlu (1990), and the relationship of the harem to that image, Peirce (1993), 153–85.

26. See Ayverdi (1950). Not only were women active in diplomacy (Peirce ([1993], 219–28) but the flower that merited the appellation the "queen of flowers" by the author of the 1674 *Traité des Tulippes* [(1674), 1] may have been an iconic substitute for the exchange of women between imperial; after all, the Habsburgs were the only other state granted the status of an empire by the Ottomans.

27. Blunt (1950), 8.

28. Ibid., 10; Posthumus (1920); Taylor (1995); for reproductions of Ottoman tulip albums, see Ayverdi (1950) and Baytop (1992).

29. Botschantzev (1982), 2; Aktepe (1952), 86–87; Baytop (1992), 2.

30. *Nouveau Traité* (1674), 86; Refik (1932), 45–47.

31. Ibid., 88; for other exchange of flowers taken from the different areas of empire in the sixteenth century, see Ayverdi (1950), 3–7.

32. Two such treatises: the early nineteenth-century physician, Mehmed Aşkî Efendi's *Takvimü'l-kibâr fi mi'yâri' l-ezhar* and the eighteenth-century Mehmed bin Ahmed Efendi, *Netayicü'l-ezhar* (both in Istanbul's Ali Emirî Library, natural history section, nos. 167 and 162 respectively) are utilized by Aktepe (1952), 86–87; see also the *Defter-i Lâlezâr-Ibrahim* written by Reisü'l-Küttab Üçanbarlı Mehmet Efendi (1139/1726) (cited in Baytop [1992], 3). For a list of painting albums, see Ayverdi (1950), 7.

33. *Turquie* (1993), 21.

34. On European classification of plants and the political economy of gardens, see Mukerji (1993), 443; Goody (1993), 184.

35. Monstereul (1654), 17, 20.

36. Mukerji (1983), 166–209.

37. Posthumus (1929), 436; Blunt (1950), 8.

38. Schama (1991), 350–57.

39. Taylor (1995), 6. On Dutch-Ottoman trade agreements and facsimiles of treaties, see de Groot (1975).

40. Posthumus (1929), 436. There were fifty booklets published on the tulipmania in the Netherlands alone; see also Taylor (1995) 13; Schama (1991), 357. Renditions of the Dutch tulip mania were provided by La Bruyère, Dumas, and Charles Mackay (1841/1981).

41. Posthumus (1929), 436.

42. Hirschman (1977), 66; Mukerji (1993), 450–57.

43. Katib Çelebi (1609–1657) writes of these events in the Ottoman Empire in his last work, *The Balance of Truth*; for global trends, see Wills (1993), 141, and Mattee (1995), 27.

44. Mukerji (1983), 294, n. 14; Schneider and Weiner (1989), 10–16.

45. Mukerji (1983), 30–78; see generally, Bermingham and Brewer (1995).

46. Appadurai (1986), 59, n. 11.

47. McChesney (1996), 255–56; Schimmil (1976) 416–17; Aktepe (1952), 93.

48. See Feldman (1997).

49. The "Indian School" included bilingual poets, such as the Azeri Mirza Muhammad Ali Sa'ib of Tabriz (1601–2/d. 1677–1678) (see Rypka [1968], 301–2). For tulips in the seventeenth century, Shalimar Garden of Lahore, see Rehman (1997), 164–65; on Nedim, see Silay (1994), 61, 67, 72–74.

50. See Mukerji (1993).

51. The Metropolitan Museum of Art identifies the merchant as "Portuguese"; however both the dating—which is probably after the recapture of Hormuz—and the lack of specific characteristics determining the "nationality" of the merchant, suggest a more generic interpretation of his "western" identity. (I am grateful to Dr. Susan Babai of Smith College for this personal communication).

52. According to Montagu (Lord Wharnclilffe, ed. [1837] 1, 309) the division of labor between husband and wife was simple: " 'Tis his business to get money, and hers to spend it."

53. Ibid., 272–73.

54. de Tott (1784), 88–91; Artan (1993), 64.

55. In addition to Donald Quataert's pioneering work on this subject, Suraiya Faroqhi has been documenting seventeenth-century households in the empire.

56. Precisely because the Ottomans had their own system of regulating internal trade and interstate commerce, the implications for global flows of commodities must be carefully reconsidered. For Ottoman economic practice, see Genç (1989) and Çızakça (1985); for a provincial model, see Salzmann (1995), 210–54.

57. On Iznik titles, I thank Richard Turnbull who shared this information which was based on his examination of the Metropolitan Museum of New York's collection; for provincial art, see Carsedale, (1977), 330–54; on transcultural consumption and design, see Arel (1988); Göçek (1996); Fukasawa (1987).

58. Nutku (1972) 38.

59. On the uses of the garden for diplomacy, see de Busbecq (1968), 63; Necipoğlu, (1997); compare with Golombek (1988), 142. On the greater public nature of dynasty, see Kuran (1990–91); Atıl (1993), 182; for popular religious festivals, see Faroqhi (1994b), 37–40. Compare comments on other royal spectacles, Cannadine (1987), 4, and generally comments by Norbert Elias (1978); (1982) and (1983).

60. Nutku (1972), 21–22, 44.

61. Ibid. 73–74.

62. On the circumcision of 5,000 poor boys as a gift of the four princes, see Atıl (1993), 184. Jews may have represented both themselves as a non-Muslim group within the empire and generic foreigners (see Nutku [1972], 76, who note that in Mahmud II's festival of 1836, Istanbul Jews followed the end of the guild march dressed in French and Swiss costumes).

63. Nutku (1972), 70; Atıl (1993), 187.

64. One wonders at the influence of the Ottoman multiple capitals on the French construction of Versailles outside Paris. On the reports by the French ambassador to the 1675 fete, see Nuktu (1972) and Renda (1987), 46; on the court of Louis XIV, see Burke (1992), 137–44.

65. Preto (1975), 91.

66. The consistency of these comments in her letters may also reveal an unmediated response to a common material culture and commercialized value system. Montagu ([1837], 315–16) says "Tis true their magnificence is of a

very different taste from ours," calling it an "agreeable confusion," adding that their gardens have "no ornament wanting, except that of statues."

67. Shay (1944), 22–25. Realizing the commercial interests involved in this display of consumption, the Venetian ambassador praises French savvy in influencing trade relations with the empire, saying, "If Mehemet Effendi had brought nothing else from France, Christianity would have no cause to grieve!"

68. Akyavaş (1993), 40–43.

69. Compare Istanbul in the early eighteenth century according to Zilfi (1996) with seventeenth-century London (Fisher [1948], 37–50), Paris and Edo (McClain and Merriman, ed. [1993], 3–41).

70. Atıl (1993), 184.

71. Ibid., 172.

72. Appadurai (1986), 49–50. On the symbolism of sovereignty, see Cannedine (1987); Keller, Lissityzn, and Mann (1938).

73. Both Ahmed III and Ibrahim Paşa was reputed to have exquisite taste. Atil (1993), 182; Unat (1943), 28; compare Elias (1978).

74. For a facsimile one of the period's tulip books dating from 1725 and painted by a certain "Mehmed" (now in the collection of Robert de Belder), Baytop (1992), 17–65.

75. See Aktepe (1952).

76. See Elias (1983); Istanbul should be compared with Edo and Paris, see, for example, McClain and Merriman (1994).

77. Refik (1932), 45–47.

78. Hazerfen (1995); for the order for the 1727–1728, see Refik (1930), 94–97.

79. For two tax-farming letterati, note Qoja Raghib and Hami of Diyarbekir. Gibb (1967) IV:78–79, 92–93.

80. Zilfi (1996), 295.

81. Unat (1943), 28–29; Blunt (1950), 15.

82. Zilfi (1996), 291–94.

83. See n. 1 above.

84. See Aktepe (1958b); (1958c); Unat (1943); *Relation* (1737).

85. See Aktepe (1958a); (1958c).

86. Unat (1943), 28, 33–35; *Revolution* (1937), 26–27; Göçek (1996), 99, 106.

87. Although the sultan is reputed to have called on Christians to come to his aide, the rebels forbade molestation of non-Muslims on pain of death. *Relation* (1737), 27.

88. Unat (1943), 33, 37.

89. On the *bostancıs*, see Pakalın (1993) I: 239. Unat (1943), 29. *Relation* ([1737], 6) puts the problem succintly: "the scarcity of staples, the rise in prices, the misery and lack of commerce which affected the entire country, and the multiplicity and weight of taxes, and the hardships suffered by the troops who had gone to Persia and the frontier which had, it was said, already provoked revolts had caused a general discontent among the people."

90. See Zilfi (1996) and Zarinebaf-Shahr (1998).

91. Atıl (1993), 184.

92. Aktepe (1958a), 9–10; Unat (1943), 27; *Relation* (1737), 5–7.

93. On these gardens, see Cerasi (1994), 217–36.

94. On the encounters between "smugglers" and state, see Isvan (1990–91): 1–27.

95. Salzmann (1995), 142–43; Zilfi (1996), 295; Olson (1978), 197; Aktepe (1958c); on privatization generally, see Salzmann (1993).

96. *Relation* (1737), 26, 46; Shay (1944), 28.

97. Compare with Thompson (1991); note also the symbolism of the annual procession of the guilds described by Evliya Çelebi (cited in Lewis [1962], 120), which ended at the house of the Istanbul judge.

98. The *Abdi* history is a rich source of the symbolic acts of this revolt. See especially Unat (1943), 33–37.

99. *Relation* (1737), 10, 26–27, 46–47; Unat (1943), 26, 35–36.

100. *Relation* (1737), 41–42.

101. Despite contemporary evidence (Unat [1943], 43), the notion that the mob razed the Sa`adabad was current in the second half of the eighteenth century (see Hovhannesyan ([1996], 11).

102. Unat (1943), 45.

103. Baudrillard (1996), 137–38. For crowds along the Golden Horn cheering the gay processions in the vicinity of the Sa`adabad; see Silay (1994). This perspective on the eighteenth century is not so different from the modernist and republican evaluation of its literature. See Victoria Holbrook (1994). We tend to forget modernity's "prehistory." Göçek ([1996], 37–43, 72) sees consumer modernization on differential patterns as a oneway street from Western goods to Eastern minds.

104. Consider the work of Constantin François Chasse-Boeuf Volney (1957–1820), *Les Ruines, ou méditations sur les révolutions des empires* (1791), which was popular among the young Ottomans, and translated as *Harabeler* (Berkes [1978], 563, n. 30).

105. On the numbers of tulips in the eighteenth century, see Aktepe (1952) 90, 113; Refik (1932), 47; Hazarfen (1995), 46; I am grateful to Tülay Artan for providing me with originals of the judge's records (Eyüp Kadı Sicilleri no. 188). From the hundreds—up to perhaps, two thousand—of varieties of tulips in the eighteenth century, but twenty types are current a century later (Abdülaziz Bey [1995], 219–22).

106. The transcultural commodities of the past and their impact on identity formation should be compared with the present paradox of cultural fragmentation in the midst of accelerated globalization. See Barber (1995).

107. The rebels acted out, according to N. Kurat ([1976], 218–19) "deep forces in the Turkish nature, hatred of the infidel, and a habit of satirizing men in power."

108. Nasir-i Khusrau (d. after 1077) chides the court poets of the Seljuks (Meisami [1996], 165): "How long will you go on describing box-trees and tulips . . . with your learning and nobility will you praise one/Who is the source of ignorance and baseness?"

109. See n. 1 above.

110. Aktuğ (1993), 80; Barışta (1993), 27–29, for examples of how the staff of wheat is incorporated into both stilllife and floral relief on a princesses tomb.

111. Here I would take issue with Bourdieu's claim ([1979], 33ff.) that popular classes fail to understand the elite taste because they lack immediate and functional value for them. Compare Calhoun (1983).

112. Melikoff (1967), 355–57; Schimmel (1976), 30–37, who citing Kalim *Tarkibband* (II, v. 5 in Ibid., 31 n. 50), "How can you weigh the color and scent of tulips and rose together? It is a long way from the soulless body [tulip] to the bodyless soul [rose]." On the "purity and corruption" of the janissaries, see Kafadar (1991).

5

Aspects of the Ottoman Elite's Food Consumption: Looking for "Staples," "Luxuries," and "Delicacies" in a Changing Century[1]

Tülay Artan

This is a first attempt at elaborating some qualitative diet definitions for the eighteenth century Ottoman elite in an (ostensibly) material, substance-based, provisions-based kind of way. I try to construct a generalized, all-inclusive notion of "everything edible" to see if we can introduce thinner separations (between staples, luxuries, and delicacies) into that undifferentiated mass. This is my primary concern. But if you change the terms just the slightest bit, it can very well be axially rotated, as it were, into the more explicitly sociological question of using consumption criteria to reconstruct the internal stratification of the Ottoman ruling elite (and then in the long run, perhaps, looking at how this may fit in with other criteria). And while I have highlighted this other aspect in a more introductory paper,[2] here too it is hard to prevent it from framing or partially overlapping with the main argument at every step of the way.

Theoretical Background, Comparative Linkages

Eventually, it could all turn out to be fertile ground. In the first chapter of *Carnival in Romans,*[3] Emmanuel Le Roy Ladurie goes through a methodologically crucial exercise of juxtaposing three different approaches based on ranks or estates, on income and wealth, and on social classes in the Marxist sense, to assess the social structure of a small provincial town in sixteenth-century France, to suggest that they work better in combination (that is, they represent a more comprehensive appropriation of reality). This is more or less my attitude toward consumption: not necessarily to postulate a sharp paradigmatic shift,[4] but simply to see what we can usefully assimilate.

It is possible, of course, that in societies where estates and ranks go hand in hand with material signifiers, the returns to consumption history will actually be greater. It is even possible that the larger the gulf between the elite and the sphere of production, the more illuminating will consumption studies prove to be. But by the same token, neatly demarcating material from sociological signposts (or queries) becomes very difficult to achieve in the case of an estate society, precisely because, to a large extent it turns out to be the political organism's redistributive networks and practices, formally and semiformally institutionalized, reflected in a particular kind of layered documentation, that both attach enormous importance and assign social roles, messages, functions, and definitions to various kinds of agricultural produce in the first place.

Hence, too, it becomes virtually impossible, *pace* Goody, to talk of "cuisine" without "class" or vice versa as has been gradually recognized during the last decade's remarkable explosion in food history. This is generally accepted to have begun with an overwhelmingly anthropological interest, sustained from the 1930s through the 60s into the 70s,[5] giving rise to more refined case studies[6] as well as manifestations of a strong analytical emphasis,[7] while also bringing forth edited collections of research in the latter decade.[8] At the same time, however, alongside social anthropologists, social historians, too, were beginning to come up with broad views overall accounts,[9] and studies of regional or national cuisines were also proliferating.[10] In its turn, this general interest was followed by both a more thematically oriented kind of historical awareness,[11] and a fresh wave of comprehensive efforts at synthesis.[12] In time, this whole, alternately micro-macro process of ground-breaking and field-defining[13] acquired its own unmistakably identity badge: *Food and Foodways*,[14] a journal in the Annales tradition of combining (or arrogating intellectual space from) history, sociology, and anthropology, biology, and the culinary arts. Now research on individual ingredients may be found side by side in its pages with observations on the gendering or empowering functions of food preparation in tribal societies, with close readings of Chinese treatises, and early modern cookbooks in the West, with studies of household accounts of the European nobility, with surveys monitoring the fusion and diffusion of new cuisines or palates, and with cultural explorations into prevailing mentalities about obesity versus emaciation in the contemporary United States of America. Still, there seems to be something of a surviving anomaly: consumption history, despite developing by leaps and bounds on its own, with a few exceptions,[15] has yet to bring food consumption within its scope of vision as witnessed by the near-total absence of the subject from all the massive new volumes that have appeared so far in the series, "Consumption and Culture in the Seventeenth and Eighteenth Centuries."[16]

The Case for an Indigenous "Consumerism" in Ottoman Society

This, though, is exactly where I find myself today: at the juncture of the new history and sociology of food with the new consumption history, more through a series of accidents and typically, barely starting to acknowledge and incorporate the subsphere of food consumption into the Eighteenth Ottoman century. In the context of the rapidly growing interest in Ottoman consumption, as attested to by the 1996 Binghamton conference, this has always been my period of immediate concern. It was also when consumerism was recognized to have appeared as a distinct social phenomenon in Europe. Like so many others, this caused consumerism, too, to be defined in Eurocentric fashion, while consumption in the Ottoman Empire at that time has tended to be viewed mostly from the angle of the increase in Western *imports* like clocks, mirrors, new kinds of textiles, or of an enhanced taste for *foreign* fashions (including tulipmania, the search for privacy, retreat into nature, and fantasies about an "idyllic" countryside all of which, instead of being taken for granted, need to be thoroughly rethought and investigated).

One can think of various possible sources for such externalism: vestiges of an orientalism that persists in regarding Europe as the only possible source of change and dynamisms vis-à-vis an inherently static and stagnant East; the related but not exactly identical mental habit of thinking about the Ottoman "essence" purely in terms of a set of military agrarianate structures (janissaries and *sipahis*, *tahrirs*, *timars*, and *tithes*) whereby all that is urban and commercial comes to be removed to the sphere of the external "relations" of that defterological "essence"—a knowledge of the urban and commercial layers of Ottoman existence that has tended to incorporate relatively more of outsiders' perceptions.

I do not want to get lost in such historiographical debates, and still less would I want to discard a vision of the Ottoman moment of "crisis and change," to quote Suraiya Faroqhi,[17] as fundamentally involving an unequal but combined development kind of response to the onset of the early modern era. I still think, though, that it is important to keep reminding ourselves, first, that the seventeenth and eighteenth centuries were not yet the nineteenth, and second, that urban and rural Ottoman society had its own life and rules of conduct, which ought to be penetrated more thoroughly before or as we bring in any vectors of extraneous impact. Thus for millions of people, not only was a large portion of the Ottoman consumption package(s) probably economically determined, but the political and symbolic aspects, uses, or components of consumption, too, perhaps had to do more with just cultural breaks associated with modernization or westernization, being reproduced all the time in the system's bowels in accordance with indigenous coercion/persuasions requirements.

At least for the imperial metropolis of Istanbul,[18] moreover, I would argue that what might legitimately be defined as a kind of consumerism appears to have assumed an important role in proliferating lifestyles, which in turn served to establish public identities for ranking members of the ruling class. This is very demonstrable for royalty and only slightly less for other highly placed officeholders.

I have commented elsewhere[19] on how, by the eighteenth century, residential architecture along the Bosphorus and the Golden Horn had become a top item in the spending patterns of the Ottoman elite. It was invested with so much significance in terms of a new mode of legitimation and a corresponding set of competitive co-optations or alliances. These required part of the royal family—namely, the sisters and daughters of the sultans—to come out of the historic peninsula and establish their own magnificent households in palatial residences, thereby swarfing their husbands' lesser abodes in order to symbolically thwart the potentially aristocratic ambitions of a new class of dignitaries. It was incumbent on them, at the same time, to keep displaying enough pomp and circumstance through a much more visible, high-profile lifestyle so as to reassure the capital's population in troubled centuries when military victories were no longer forthcoming (so that military charismatic legitimation also ceased to work). So inevitably, there then came the furnishings for that "theater of life," including: luxury textiles, clocks, mirrors, silver and crystal plates, cups and drinking vessels, followed by expensive garments and jewelry, all of which seem to have been acquired in amounts far in excess of generously interpreted maxima for giftgiving or personal use.[20]

Illustrated manuscripts and other books were hoarded as never before, and thesaurized into a proliferation of private libraries.[21] Entertainment expenses in the form of regular salaries for dancers and musicians, and money spent on frequent outings (including carriages) also added up to considerable amounts in household budgets. All these permit us to explore possible necessity vs. luxury packages, as well as "ostentation thresholds" for various subgroups or strata, marking the inevitable elusive boundaries where the private determinants of their consumption shaded into its public determinants.

Past and Future Ways of Studying Food in the Near East and the Ottoman Empire

In this context, what we can ask about food is virtually limitless. "As an item of consumption, food proves exceptionally complex," Brewer and Porter fleetingly acknowledge—partly because it is "simultaneously necessity and luxury" (recognizing which, incidentally, is fundamental to my main theme), partly because of its "extreme emphemerality (once consumed, it disappears totally)," and partly because of "the complex signals associated with eating and obesity."[22] I would add that it is also complicated because it is a question of absolutely universal consumption by an immense diversity of parties—as in the Ottoman case where, under the umbrella of their common but not necessarily unifying subservience, for more than six centuries, to the House of Osman, the hunters, farmers, and fishermen of the Balkans, Asia Minor, and the Middle East, as well as gourmets and army commissariats, travelers, merchants, and wholesale suppliers, Tanzimat reformers, writers on etiquette, and authors of cookbooks, *vakıf* trustees, heads of greater or lesser households *(kapıs)*, their stewards and the people fed at their "door" may all be shown to have represented so many vantage points.

In many ways, too, it has been a "heavy eating" society, not just in the literal sense but also in its ways of surrounding the preparation and consumption of food by layers of rituals and obligations, by sayings and gestures, by order and decorum of eating, including rhythms of ingestion and conversation[23]—even before we get to more sophisticated problems like the share of kitchen expenses in the overall budget of an Ottoman dignitary, or the role played by (spending on) eating and drinking in staking out new social roles—simply questioning what or how they ate can reveal a great deal about the provisioning of the capital,[24] the links it had to constitute between agriculture and trade, the changes that took place in the lifestyle of the Ottoman elite, and the introduction and spread (or rejection and disappearance, as the case may be) on new foodstuffs.

Tomato Tales

Thus at one extreme of simplicity, it is possible to take the red thread of individual products or dishes into a chain or regional (west European, Mediterranean, near Eastern, south Asian) cuisines or palates, and to uncover fascinating "inventions of tradition" in the process. Coffee and tea, corn, tomatoes and potatoes, olives and olive oil, and pepper and cinnamon all have their distinctive tales to tell of how Ottoman eating and drinking culture evolved. Some have been studied, although not exactly in the Ottoman context,[25] while others are shrouded in mystery. The adventure of tomatoes in the Ottoman world, for example, has remained lost to us for a long time.[26] We know that after their arrival in Europe (from South America) toward the very end of the fifteenth century, the Italians developed quite a taste for them by the mid-eighteenth ("apples of love," they and the French called them). In contrast it was the twentieth century before tomatoes really entered the English diet,[27] while Iranians have found very little—and Indians virtually no—use for tomatoes in their traditional cuisine to this day. The Ottomans, however, did embrace them, so much so that, given today's variety of dishes prepared with tomatoes, tomato sauce, or tomato paste, it takes an effort to grasp that things were not always so. But originally and for a long time, it would seem to have been a green variety of tomatoes, called *kavata,*[28] that was involved (while it's hard to believe that the Italians and the French would have named anything green after *amour*[29]). Now the earliest reference to *kavata* that I have come across is at the surprisingly early date of 1694/H./1105–1106, barely two centuries after Columbus, when an account book kept by the imperial kitchens and cellars organization—of which more later—reports an allocation, to the sultan's private apartments in the third courtyard, of 13,350 pieces *(aded)* of them.[30] This might have come to something like a ton—not enough by itself to suggest regular and massive consumption by the (maybe) two to three thousand-strong population of the third courtyard, though still striking, since, to the best of my knowledge, it would be at least another 150 years before tomatoes of any name, kind, or color made their appearance in Ottoman recipes in the mid-nineteenth century.[31] And as *kavata* also crops up on a list of allowances for the young Selim (III) in 1774–1775, when he was being kept in custody in "the cage,"[32] we may conclude that regardless of how far down the social scale these green tomatoes might have percolated by that time, they had not ceased to be considered fit for princes.

Other bits and pieces of potential evidence are circumstantial at best but tantalizing all the same. There is a famous engraving of the second courtyard of the Topkapı Palace by Antoine-Ignace Melling.[33] On the right, directly in front of the row of kitchens with their characteristic domes and chimneys, a few solitary servants are busily picking some round, lumpy kind of produce from low, stubby plants laid out, in a startling mixture of the solemn and the mundane, in the form of two gigantic garden beds on both sides of the pathway leading right up to the Gate of Felicity. They do look like tomatoes.[34] Then comes a personal testimony: in Edirne as late as the second half of the nineteenth century, her great grandmother's generation "used to throw reddening tomatoes away on the grounds that they were rotten," recalls a living, reliable source.[35] This is still widespread Yörük practice.[36])

It is tempting to speculate that because people had grown accustomed to *kavata,* which was always green, even after they had taken to another, relatively new variety of tomato, when the time came for it to turn red they continued to regard it as abnormal. Yet today, no widespread name nor any recipes survive for green tomatoes. *Kavata* itself was grown in small amounts here and there in Thrace, and is an ingredient for some very rare Aegean dishes that only come up at exclusive dinners for gourmet clubs; regular green—in the sense of unripe—tomatoes, on the other hand, are either pickled or go into soups all over Anatolia.

When and how did the double change come—that is, replacing *kavata* by other, reddening varieties, and then accepting the habit of picking and eating them after they had ripened? How much else of what we tend to take for granted is actually of very recent origin? At a recent Istanbul symposium, Stephane Yerasimos surmised, somewhat shockingly for national(ist) mythology, that the best and most expensive carpets had never been a major and prestigious part or a foremost decorative component of traditional Turkish-Muslim domestic life. For centuries after all, the up market product had mostly ornamented mosques and tombs, and perhaps palaces too, while their more modest cousins had been protecting nomads or campaigning soldiers in their tents from the cold and damp earth. In all likelihood it was western orientalism, reimported into the Middle East, that moved quality carpets up to the forefront of household use as prestige objects and status symbols very late in the nineteenth century.[37] And if the switch from green to red tomatoes was similar in inspiration and timing, as indeed suggested by that sudden increase in the frequency of *tomata* or *domates* recipes in cookbooks after their first strong showing in 1844, what other subthresholds of modern acculturation might be lurking in the recesses of the Tanzimat, the Hamidian, or the Young Turks' era?

A Literature of Cultural Rules and Court Organization

But descriptively rich and thought-provoking though such selective narratives might be, they remain episodically superficial beside the more rigorous body of historical studies on Middle Eastern food and cooking pioneered by Maxime Rodinson. In 1949 he undertook a comprehensive medieval survey of, first, compilations of recipes and medical treatises written by or for courtiers, scribes, and savants, and second, books by *belles lettristes* as well as other essays, stories, or poems which featured food imagery, sections or episodes.[38] Rodinson himself went on, in *Encyclopaedia of Islam* "Ghıdha" entry,[39] to provide another overview, this time of the various legal and other regulatory factors, taboos, prohibitions, and socio-religious injunctions, that surrounded and determined the diet of the principal peoples of classical Islam. Illuminating as this was, it does not really allow for variations in diet, cuisine, and food consumption in the subsequent proliferation of Islamic states and empires.[40] In contrast, a 1968 article by Eliyahu Ashtor, though once more based on medieval Arabic sources, may be admitted to have highlighted (at least) the diet of various classes within the same geography and time period.[41] Fundamentally more cognizant of the diversity of historical Islam in this sense, however, have been David Waines (medieval), Halil İnalcık (Ottoman) and John Burton-Page (Mughal) in the individual sections they contributed in 1991.[42] And recently, both Sami Zubaida and Richard Tapper, and Manuela Marin and David Waines have complemented their respective collections of two sets of insightful articles with correspondingly thoughtful reviews of the literature on Middle Eastern food and cooking since Rodinson.[43] Two articles by Bert Fragner,[44] on Iran and Central Asia, have also been drawn within the first (Zubaida and Tapper) volume's coverage, while aspects of food history in Spain and north Africa have been covered by the second volume.[45] And India's share of Islamic cuisine has not been neglected.[46]

Nevertheless, the history of Ottoman eating and drinking, whether in the Islamic, the Middle Eastern, or the Mediterranean context, continues to be a neglected component of cultural history. Thus in 1945, İsmail Hakkı Uzunçarşılı provided a first institutional picture of the imperial kitchens from the royal side—as yet another functional component of the Ottoman state.[47] The late Ömer Lütfi Barkan out of his general interest in the Ottoman "consumption basket," undertook the first studies of the kitchen outlays of the Ottoman royal house.[48] Then typically, it has fallen to Halil İnalcık's lot to develop this line of exploration over the decades.[49]

An alternative avenue, meanwhile, was opened by Süheyl Ünver, a professional of a different discipline working as a knowledgeable but amateur historian who published two separate pamphlets of purportedly historical recipes under the exotic titles of "Fifty Turkish Dishes in History" (1948) and "Dishes from the Reign of the Conqueror" (1952). Upon closer and critical examination these turned out to have been romantically vulgarized and dehistoricized from one of the three eighteenth-century manuscripts (the *Ağdiye Risalesi*) referred to earlier.[50] Since then, however, more scholarly works on food history have been forthcoming from a variety of experts (including folklorists, linguistics, and historians of literature or medicine as well as trained Ottomanists).[51] They have presented ample material from their primary sources on food, and on eating and drinking habits,[52] the esthetics of daily life,[53] and a review of this whole literature.[54]

New Ways of Looking at Imperial Kitchen Registers

I would like to draw attention, at this point, to the enormous potential that, paradoxically, the imperial kitchen registers represent for this kind of research. These are available, of course, primarily as a massive collection of documents, codenamed KK and DBŞM, and carried over into several subcategories,[55] as well as another, almost uninterrupted series of imperial kitchen accounts (for the period from H.1061/1651 to H.1259/1843) within the registers.

Entries are to be found among the MAD collection of the same Prime Ministry Archives.[56] Several of them published, still others synthesized, it is mostly with the administrative and organizational aspects of the flow of supplies to the Ottoman court that they have come to be associated.[57] Thus the imperial kitchens did not simply buy and cook for the imperial palace(s), but together with their subdivision of the imperial cellars under the *matbah emini,* they also allocated, delivered, and distributed, weaving a peculiarity patrimonial relationship between Topkapı on the one hand, and the royal princesses' and some leading dignitaries' subordinated palaces on the other. The very first thing that I myself have done with these registers has been to utilize them in elucidating redistributive patterns and packages.[58]

The imperial kitchen administration recorded (i) its own daily, monthly, or yearly purchases, and what was (ii) periodically delivered to various sections of the old and new palaces, (iii) doled out from its central stores to a string of lesser courts on a regular (daily or monthly) basis, (iv) delivered on special religious occasions (*ramazaniye* and *iftariye*),[59] or (v) for privileged banquets (*ziyafet için*).[60] These registers are actually among the most complete lists we have of Ottoman foodstuffs in an urban, upper-class context. At the same time, other elite households benefiting from such distribution were also undertaking their own independent supply operations, recording them in purchase (*mübayaat*), expenditure (*masarifat*), and account (*muhasebe*) books.[61] In the end, therefore, we have interdependent documentation originating at both the giving and the receiving ends, reflected in the two central and contrasting categories of allocation (*tayinat*) and purchase (*mübayaat*). And at least as far as ingredients are concerned, between them they must be of virtually total, universal coverage.

Exploring a Hierarchy of Diet

It is possible, on this basis, to penetrate the inner world of the Ottoman ruling class's food consumption in systematic and comprehensive fashion. There is enough in the documentation originating from both the imperial kitchens and other high-ranking households to warrant tackling (at least some aspects of) the variety and quality of the elite diet.

Jack Goody remarks:

> A salient feature of the culinary cultures of the major societies of Europe and Asia is their association with hierarchical man. The extreme form of this differentiation is found in the allocation of specific foods to specific roles, offices or classes, swans to royalty in England, honey wine to nobility of Ethiopia.[62]

In turn this suggests that the dietary thresholds between various strata, groups, or subgroups have been marked out in terms of not just quantity but also quality, complexity, and ingredients.[63] Furthermore, the wealth and power messages of food consumption could also be conveyed through a surfeit of servants who performed a variety of household tasks and each of whom had to be fed from the table of the lord.[64] For the Ottomans, which of these or other dimensions can we account for? We know that their socio-political ladder was at the same time a spatial or locational ordering and a scale for redistribution.

Thus, a new and more visibly elaborate hierarchy was gradually stamped on the geography of the capital as certain sites were allocated to particular social groups for their waterfront mansions.[65] The whole process also came to be reflected in what was distributed from the imperial stores: distance from the Topkapı Palace was set in proportion to the rank and status of the elite group settling in each village along the Golden Horn or the Bosphorus. And the amount and variety of the foodstuffs each received from the imperial kitchens were designated to fit a pattern correlated with their place in state protocol.

This, indeed, was when the culinary definition of a new princesshood took final shape in the form of a "full package" that all sisters and daughters of the sultans kept receiving with monotonous regularity over a period of at least one hundred and twenty years (from the 1680s to the end of the eighteenth or the beginning of the nineteenth century).[66] These can be demonstrated to have corresponded to the basic requirements of a satellite court of around one hundred and fifty people.[67] The continuity in question was actually in force for more than two centuries, and not only for the princesses married out of the palace but also for sultans' mothers plus some top bureaucrats.[68] So we certainly have evidence for quantity differentiation. But to what extent was the hierarchy of rank and status also a stratification of diets and culinary practices? Were the items, cooked or uncooked, in the imperial kitchens lists that were cosigned to or reserved for lower/higher tiers within the elite? I already have gone through more than a hundred of these registers and sampled all the various types mentioned above. With some help from cookbooks they can be used, I believe, to probe effectively into the question of the Ottoman elite's socially determined notions of (what were) staples and (what were) luxuries or delicacies within the sphere of perishable household consumption.

Methodology: Systematizing the Information from the Imperial Kitchen Registers

Table 5.1 is an all-inclusive list of every single substance that I have (so far) encountered at least once (but without heed to frequency of occurrence) in the kinds of documentation described above, disregarding group of origin (and hence, flattening out the relative weight of the royal princesses with everybody else), preserving the original nomenclature of the documents, conflating items only if it is absolutely clear that they are identical (as in *francala* and *nan-ı francala,* or *gûşt-ı ganem, lağm-ı ganem,* and *et,* which is always mutton). Each is counted as a separate item even in cases of great terminological similarity if there is the slightest doubt that two or more names may not refer to exactly the same thing (as in *erz* and *erz-i has, pastırma* and *pastırma-ı Kayseri, kaymak* and *kaymak-ı Üsküdari,* or *tuz* and *tuz-i Eflak*). The 210 or more rows obtained in this way are organized into fifteen major groups (labeled A to O to the left of the table).

The twelve column headings, on the other hand, basically refer to what type of documentation these items have been found in, elaborated so as to accommodate new inputs from ongoing work. Thus I systematically have looked at imperial kitchen registers showing allocations (represented by T for *tayinat*) and deliveries by what we might call the chief greengrocer (SP for *ser pazarî*) which arguably constitute the two largest and most fundamental categories of allocation out of the imperial stores—plus purchase, expenditure, and accounting books showing other palaces and household purchases (represented by Mh for *mübayaat*/households) as well as, occasionally, what happened to be found in these palaces' cellars at inventory time (K for *kiler*). In between them are columns 4-5-6 for haphazard deliveries, to trap fleeting references—for example, to "assorted drinks" entered simply as "delivered" (*gönderilen*—hence represented by Dg for deliveries/general—that is, from unspecified sources), to a batch of quail entered as "delivered by the chief gardener" (*bostancıdan gönderilen,* hence represented by Db for deliveries/*bostancıbaşı*), or to a quantity of *kadayıf* entered as "delivered by the chief confectioner" (*helvacıdan gönderilen,* hence delivered by Dh for deliveries/*helvacı*).

To be distinguished from these, on the other hand, are what we may describe as limited allocations from the imperial kitchens for special but periodically or otherwise recurring occasions, such as for banquets (B for *ziyafet için*), or as *iftariye* (I) or *ramazaniye* (R), or for some *mevlid* (column 10 labeled Me).

However, MAp in column 1 stands for the imperial kitchens' own intake or purchases. I have yet to look systematically at these purchase books for the imperial kitchens. I just happen to know that they are there, and likely to be of universal or near-universal coverage, so column 1 has been put in mostly as a precaution. Also, although everything acquired through purchases or allocations may be expected to find its way into the cellar, column 12 should be, but as it stands is not, of universal coverage. This is because not every register or spending includes records of cellar stocks.[69] Both columns 1 and 12 are tautological in a certain sense. In time they may lead to identifying additional items but cannot help with solving problems of redistribution of dietary thresholds;

Table 5.1a

	Types of provision—by groups of food and other supplies	Where encountered in the documentation: Basic allocations		Haphazard deliveries				Limited deliveries for very special occasions					
		MAp	T	SP	Dg	Db	Dh	B	I	R	Me	Mh	K
A. BREAD AND PASTRIES	nan-ı aziz		■									■	■
	nan-ı çakır									■			
	nan-ı çörek									■			
	nan-ı fod(u)la		■										
	nan-ı has		■							■			■
	nan-ı sakız									■			
	nan-ı somun									■			
	Galata somunu											■	
	francala, nan-ı francala											■	■
	kalıp işi has francala											■	
	yağlı simit											■	
	börek											■	
	çörek											■	
B. CEREALS—BEANS—LENTILS—ONIONS—GARLIC	hınta, buğday		■										■
	Mısır buğdayı											■	
	şair [arpa]											■	■
	şariyye [şehriye]											■	■
	dakik, dakik-i has		■										■
	nişasta		■										■
	gendüm göfte (gufte, kufte)		■										
	bulgur												■
	tarhana												■
	erz, pirinç		■									■	■
	erz-i has												■
	nohut		■										■
	leblebi-i şehdane			■									
	mercimek		■										■
	börülce												■
	soğan		■										■
	sarımsak			■									■

Table 5.1b

	Types of provision—by groups of food and other supplies	Where encountered in the documentation: Basic allocations		Haphazard deliveries			Limited deliveries for very special occasions					
		MAp	T	SP	Dg	Db	Dh	B	I	R	Me	Mh	K
C. MEAT—POULTRY—FISH—CURED MEAT—OFFAL	gûşt-ı ganem, lağm-ı ganem, et		■										■
	kuzu		■										■
	toklu		■										■
	kurban											■	
	tavuk, makiyan		■										■
	tavuk-ı Mısrî			■									
	gügercin, kebuter		■										■
	bıldırcın					■							
	beyza, yumurta		■									■	■
	balık-ı mütenevvia												■
	palamud												■
	sucuk		■									■	■
	pastıma		■									■	■
	pastırma-i Kayseri			■									■
	paça		■									■	■
	munbar		■										
	baş-ı ganem											■	
	işkembe-i gav												■

Table 5.1c

	Types of provision—by groups of food and other supplies	Where encountered in the documentation											
		Basic allocations			Haphazard deliveries			Limited deliveries for very special occasions					
		MAp	T	SP	Dg	Db	Dh	B	I	R	Me	Mh	K
D. MILK, CHEESE, AND OTHER MILK PRODUCTS	süd, şir		■										■
	kaymak		■									■	■
	kaymak-ı Usküdarî		■										
	muhallebi											■	
	yoğurt		■									■	■
	kurut		■										
	baharlı kurut								■				
	taze peynir												■
	peynir-i kaşkaval			■					■				■
	peynir-i Çorlu			■									
	peynir-i haseki			■									
	peynir-i tulum			■									
	dil peyniri											■	
	peynir-i Mudurnu												■
E. FATS AND OILS	revgân-ı sade		■										■
	revgân-ı taze		■										
	revgân-ı tere		■										■
	revgân-ı şir, süd yağı		■										■
	revgân-ı zeyt, zeytinyağı		■									■	■
	revgân-ı penbe		■										
	revgân-ı pih		■										
F. SALT AND SPICES	tuz		■									■	■
	tuz-i Eflak												■
	bahar		■										
	darçın, darçın-ı has		■										■
	fülfül, biber-ı siyah		■										■
	kakule		■										■
	karanfil											■	■
	defne											■	
	amber											■	
	misk											■	
	zafiran											■	
	zencefil											■	
	sumak											■	
	asfur											■	

Table 5.1d

	Types of provision—by groups of food and other supplies	Where encountered in the documentation: Basic allocations			Haphazard deliveries			Limited deliveries for very special occasions					
		MAp	T	SP	Dg	Db	Dh	B	I	R	Me	Mh	K
G. SOUR FLAVORINGS	sirke		■									■	■
	taze limon		■									■	■
	âb-ı limon, limon suyu		■									■	■
	turşu											■	
	hıyar turşusu											■	
	kebere											■	
H. SUGAR—OTHER SWEETS—SWEETENERS	sükker, şeker		■										■
	sükker-i minad		■										
	sükker-i reşidi		■										
	sükker-i frengî		■										
	sükker-i kelle								■				
	nebat (nevbet, növbet) şekeri											■	
	pekmez											■	
	asel		■										■
	asel-i gümeç								■				
	asel-i musaffa												■
	asel-i Atina			■									■
	âb-ı gül, âb-ı verd, mai-i verd, gülsuyu		■									■	■
	kadayıf						■						
	şederleme											■	
	ziyafet için elvan şekerler							■					
I. COFFEE, TOBACCO, ETC.	kahve		■									■	■
	tütün, duhan, ıslah duhan, çerkez duhan											■	
	geyik boynuzu											■	
	kudret helvası											■	
J. NONFOOD SUPPLIES	sabun		■										
	sabun-ı helvahane		■										
	sabun-ı Izmir												■
	sabun-ı Trablus												■
	mum		■										
	şem-i asel-i sefid		■										■
	şem-i asel-i zerd		■										
	şem-i revgan												■
	nişadır		■										
	kiler için ecza											■	
	ziyafet günü çarçube kağıdı portakal için							■					

Table 5.1e

	Types of provision —by groups of food and other supplies	Where encountered in the documentation: Basic allocations			Haphazard deliveries			Limited deliveries for very special occasions					
		MAp	T	SP	Dg	Db	Dh	B	I	R	Me	Mh	K
K. OLIVES	zeyt, zeytun			■					■				
	kırma zeytun								■				
	gağlı zeytun												■
	terbiye zeytun								■				
	zeytun-i Girid			■					■				■
L. FRESH FRUIT	dökme meyva											■	
	elma-i miskî, misket elması			■								■	■
	ıslah elma											■	
	emrut			■								■	
	ayva			■									
	ayva çekirdeği											■	
	nar			■									
	tatlı nar											■	
	hurma			■									
	kestane			■								■	
	badam, çağla badam			■									■
	badam-ı huşk			■									
	ceviz											■	
	ceviz-i Rumî			■									
	fındık											■	■
	kaplu fındık			■									
	fındık içi			■									
	incir			■								■	
	unnap			■									
	engür, üzüm			■								■	
	parmak üzümü											■	
	razakı			■									
	Izmir razakı												■
	meviz-i âb			■									
	meviz-i sürh, kızıl üzüm			■									■
	meviz-i siyah			■									
	Izmir siyahı			■									■
	çekirdeksiz üzüm								■				
	koruk												■
	meviz-i mürg, kuşüzümü			■									
	kavun			■									■
	karpuz			■									■
	kiler için kavun karpuz çekirdeği												■

Table 5.1e *(continued)*

	Types of provision—by groups of food and other supplies	Where encountered in the documentation: Basic allocations			Haphazard deliveries			Limited deliveries for very special occasions					
		MAp	T	SP	Dg	Db	Dh	B	I	R	Me	Mh	K
L. FRESH FRUIT (cont.)	turunç			■								■	
	portakal											■	
	kayısı											■	
	kayısı-i Şam			■									■
	kiraz			■								■	
	vişne			■								■	
	kızılcık			■									
	muşmula			■									
	fıstık											■	
	Şam fıstığı											■	
	alû			■									
	alû-i Amasya			■									■
	alû-i taze			■									
	alû-i can			■									
	mürdüm eriği											■	
	bardak eriği											■	
M. SHERBETS AND FRUIT JUICES	şıra												■
	şerbet, eşribe, eşribe-i mütenevvia				■				■			■	■
	gül şerbeti											■	
	kar şerbeti											■	
	vişne şerbeti											■	
	ıslah turunç şerbeti											■	
	enar suyu, nardenk, nardan			■									
	dutlu şerbet			■									
	benefşe şerbeti			■									
N. JAMS, DESSERTS	gülbeşeker											■	■
	üç türlü reçel											■	
	hummaz(iye)											■	
	pelte											■	
	meyve-i huşk			■									

Table 5.1e *(continued)*

	Types of provision —by groups of food and other supplies	Where encountered in the documentation: Basic allocations			Haphazard deliveries			Limited deliveries for very special occasions					
		MAp	T	SP	Dg	Db	Dh	B	I	R	Me	Mh	K
O. VEGETABLES	sebzevat												
	maydanoz												
	kereviz												
	varak-ı asma												
	marul												
	salad, salluta												
	muluhiye												
	bamya												
	kavata												
	kabak, ham												
	badıncan												
	kiler için turşuluk badıcan												
	siyah turp												
	enginar												
	hıyar												
	kiler için turşuluk kebere												
	benefşe												
	sebze-i huşk												

still, they impart completeness to a table that, with the flexibility of introducing more rows or columns as the need arises, is intended to serve above all else as a comprehensive framework for data collection. (And already, everywhere that the 12:K column is more complete than the 11:Mh column, for example, the disparity hints at probable purchases.)

Substantively more significant, of course, is what I have been able to pour into the second, third, and eleventh columns for central allocations (T), for central allocations emanating from the chief greengrocer (SP), and for purchases by households (Mh). On the basis of a relatively satisfactory quantitative sampling, they permit us to formulate a series of tentative questions about, first, what they were eating; second, what entered the redistributive stream; third, what was (essentially, or mostly) purchased, or procured independently of the imperial kitchens; fourth, what gradations, if any, were lurking within the apparent "staples" of (a) bread, (b) meat, and (c) oils and fats; fifth, how variety and qualitative refinement were introduced into the "basic" elite diet; and sixth, how genuine delicacies might ultimately be identified.

What Were "They" Eating?

"They," that is to say not "Ottomans" or "Ottoman society" as a whole—let us remind ourselves—represent only the elite who were part of these redistribution, exchange, and documentation networks. As a first impression, they probably were eating a lot of bread, mutton, and poultry accompanied by the necessary spices, then wheat and rice, beans and lentils, and yoghurt and cheese, I would say, and less of vegetables. Or rather, not less in an absolute sense, but probably not so much vegetable dishes by themselves as meat and vegetables cooked together in the form of stews resembling a ratatouille *(türlü),* along with more meat in *kebab* form, soup, *pilav* and *hoşaf* in large doses.

It is interesting to compare this with some recent summaries of the overall composition or blend of ruling class cuisine in the later Middle Ages,[70] and household accounts of the large number of English lords and gentry,[71] as well as the famous 1512 Northumberland Household Book of the Percys[72]—all of which offer data that can be used to make useful comparisons with the Ottoman case.[73] Allowing for the geographical difference between northwestern Europe and the Mediterranean, for the absence of state-organized redistribution in the former and for the Islamic ban on intoxicating drinks in the latter, there is a rough similarity at least as far as the ingredients are concerned, but more of a contrast, perhaps, in the dishes that result from them. Let us only note for the moment, however, that this does not really negate the idea of a corresponding but nonidentical "grand banqueting cuisine" stage for the Ottomans. I shall be coming back to this.

What Was Distributed, and How?

This, too, is fairly easy, once our main table has been constructed. Looking down its three crucial columns for central allocations (T), for allocations delivered by the chief greengrocer (SP), and for household's purchases (Mh), supplemented with other observations about incidence, allocations in daily or monthly installments from the head of the imperial kitchens (particularly to royal princesses but also to some top dignitaries) may be said to have been especially strong in: group A (three varieties of bread); group B (especially wheat, broken wheat, flour, and rice, followed by chickpeas and lentils); group C (headed by mutton, chicken, and eggs, but also including lamb, pigeons, sausages, pastrami, and some offal or *sakatat*); group D (yogurt more than anything else, with milk and cream lagging far behind); group E (virtually all oils and fats, indeed without any exceptions if *süd yağı* was nothing but a misnomer for *revgan-ı şîr*); group F (salt plus four crucial spices, including of course the *bahar* mixture plus pepper and cinnamon); group G (a very consistent bundle of vinegar, lemon, and lemon juice); group H (again a very consistent bundle of three or four kinds of sugar plus honey, less frequently rosewater); and group J (soap, candles, and beeswax).

Simultaneously channeled through the chief greengrocer, on the other hand, were allocations of more perishable kinds of food that had to have been very recently purchased on the market, notably including, apart from four kinds of cheese in group D and two kinds of olives in group K, a great range of fresh fruit (thirty-odd varieties in group L), but only a few vegetables (group O: no more than three or four varieties recorded).

For the time being, it is also worth keeping an eye on (i) some scattered SP deliveries of famous local or other "brands": king-sized roasted chickpeas (as big as large pearls, or the largest bead in a rosary: *leblebi-i şehdane*), the best kind of pastrami from Kayseri *(pastırma-i Kayseri)*, Athenian honey *(asel-i Atina)*, in conjunction with (ii) a few haphazard deliveries of assorted candies, quail, or sweetpastry *(kadayıf)*, already noted, and (iii) the much more consistent *iftariye* and *ramazaniye* deliveries for the holy month of fasting: four additional kinds of bread, spiced curds, sheep cheese *(kaşkaval peyniri)*, loaf sugar *(kelle şekeri)*, honey-on-the-comb, seedless grapes, and choice olives—again no less than four kinds involved. Here we come across a first subset of items that stand a good chance of being ultimately classified as delicacies.

What Was Not Distributed but Procured Independently?

As already indicated, the distributive and independent procurement principles were not mutually exclusive. In practice, nevertheless, reading the household purchases (Mh) and the cellar inventory (K) columns together where necessary (where a cellar entry could have come only from purchases that "must" have been made but are not independently listed) and checking them against the central allocations (T) and the chief greengrocer's allocations (SP) columns, one can distinguish between areas where the two methods of procurement did and did not overlap.

Thus in group A, out of the three varieties of bread coming in regular daily or monthly installments from the imperial kitchens, only one (with significant name of *nan-ı aziz,* roughly meaning "[our, or one's] daily bread") has so far turned up in our purchase books too, while for the four additional kinds of bread included in *ramazaniye* deliveries, there are no corresponding purchases. For six other kinds of bread or pastries called Galata bread *(Galata somunu),* fine white bread *(francala),* pan-baked white bread *(kalıp işi francala),* ring rolls made with shortening *(yağlı simit),* flaky pastries *(börek),* and sweetened round buns *(çörek)* exactly the opposite is true: there are records of purchases but none of central allocations.

In group B, though "Egyptian wheat" and "the best kind of rice" *(erz-i has)* are suspect, a good case can be made to the effect that barley, vermicelli, boiled and pounded wheat *(bulgur)* and dried curds-and-flour preparation *(tarhana)* were always bought rather than received on the dole.

Groups C, D, E, and K on the other hand look as if they were allocation terrain *par excellence.* Thus in group C, sacrificial beasts, fish, and the remaining two varieties of offal were the only none too significant exceptions to central allocation, while for some items like eggs, sausages, and pastrami, allocations were continually supplemented by purchases. In group D, too, what came from the imperial stores via the *emin* and the chief greengrocer covered most everything except milk and rice pudding *(muhallebi),* uncured cheese, and two other varieties of cheese (*dil* and *Mudurnu*). In group E, as already indicated above, if *süd yağı* was always and everywhere the same as *revgan-ı şîr* we cannot speak of anything that central allocations did not include. And in group K, we have been able to find only one variety of olives (called "oily": *yağlı zeytin*) that appears in cellar stores although it was neither regularly nor specially distributed.

Going back to group F, on the other hand, we come up against another divided situation, four out of eight spices being covered by allocations and the remaining eight of cloves *(karanfil),* sweet bay *(defne),* saffron *(zağfiran),* safflower *(asfur),* ginger *(zencefil),* embergis *(amber),* and musk *(misk)* by purchases only, while salt was both allocated and purchased.

In group G, various kinds of pickles were only purchased; in group H, grape molasses *(pekmez);* in group I, tobacco plus powdered deer antlers and what is translatable as "potency confectionary" (*kudret helvası* and I do not know if anybody might really have expected supposed sweeteners bordering on aphrodisiacs or medication to be distributed).[74] In group J, two kinds of soap (out of four) were left outside the scope of allocation, as were various chemicals.

Among all the finely defined and possibly overlapping varieties of fresh fruit in group L, it is difficult to pick out what was unambiguously left outside the chief greengrocer's rather comprehensive deliveries, though a strong candidate would be oranges, perhaps accompanied by a variety or two of grapes and two kinds of plums. Group M (sherbets and fruits juices) as well as group N (jams and preserves), however, were purchase-dominated, as were most vegetables in group O (to judge by a preponderance of cellar stores).

Just what did all this mean? Some of the items left outside the scope of central allocations, it should be clear, were either cheap and commonplace (barley, boiled and pounded wheat, pickles), or required in house preparation (vermicelli, dried curds and flour preparation, and again pickles), or else had to be bought individually in order to count as a personal act of piety (beasts of sacrifice), or else had to be so fresh (uncured cheese) or were of such irregular supply (fish) as to virtually impossible to allocate regularly under the best of circumstances. In other cases, it seems as if (particularly for princesses) the imperial kitchens undertook to include a few items of each category in a hypothetical notion of a balanced allocation package, while leaving the rest to be procured independently (two out of four varieties of offal, two out of four kinds of soap, etc).

I would like to suggest, however, that among the remaining "purchase only" entries, there are many that constitute a second possible subset along with the *iftariye* and the irregular deliveries noted above—of relatively rarer and dearer items or delicacies. These include some varieties of bread (particularly fine white bread and pan-baked fine bread, as well as, maybe, Galata bread, ring rolls made with shortening, and sweetened round buns—as well as the ordinary milk and rice pudding, long strip cheese, and Mudurnu cheese; four exotic spices; oranges and a few other kinds of fruit; jams, sherbets, and fruit juices; grape molasses, tobacco, and of course sweeteners/aphrodisiacs. Hence this raises the additional question of whether staple to luxury or luxury to delicacy crossover points might not be observable within other groups like meat, oils and fats, or cheese and other milk products.

Bread and Meat in Court and Elite Consumption

It has become a commonplace of the new literature on food that there is nothing innate or natural about notions of necessity versus luxury, rarity, or costliness. They are all socially constructed, and local, regional, or "national" environments, economic processes, class structures, and power configurations, as well as symbolic meanings attributed by rites and rituals. They can all make an enormous difference in the way the same ingredients are culturalized by different societies or by different groups and strata in geographically and climatologically close or similar societies. Thus the French "court" nobility wove its sense of the exceptional around a *haute cuisine* which took part in developing, which was model-setting for the country as a whole—and which was different from English cooking of the time though based on pretty much the same ingredients.[75]

Was All Bread the Same?

In the Ottoman case, perhaps bread, the only "cooked" item in the distribution lists of the imperial kitchens, proved the difference that quality and ingredients can (or could) make. As moderns we might think of bread as perfectly ordinary, and therefore not needing at all to be supplied from the outside (at least not to leading Ottoman dignitaries). It seems, however, that (together with mutton, which I shall be coming to) bread was one of the two main elements in the allocations slated for top dignitaries: virtually everybody got some of them. Moreover, at least after a certain point the amounts received tended to level out and not vary as much as one would expect with regard to rank or status. Finally (the grand vizier and the senior minister of finance excepted), most people got little else—or if they did, either what they received was hardly differentiated, as in the case of snow and ice deliveries to top bureaucrats at the beginning of the eighteenth century,[76] or else a lot of what they received they were expected to pass on to others down the line.[77]

Thus for bread only, while royal princesses of the seventeenth and eighteenth centuries always received eight pairs of *nan-ı has* and twenty pairs of *nan-ı fod(u)la,*[78] almost ten ranks of top bureaucrats from the grand vizier down to the *kazasker-i Rum* received 15-4.5-4.5-4-1-1-1-1-1-pairs of *nan-ı has* to 10-10-10-6-6-6-6-6-6-6 pairs of the more ordinary variety of bread cakes or *nan-ı fod(u)la* from the second half of the seventeenth century onward (see Table 5.2).[79] Even the most humble court dependent came in for at least a single loaf of *fod(u)la.* That bread distribution was so extensive and comprehensive vis-à-vis the sultan's servitors *(kapı kulları),* in particular gives one to think that it was a very valued staple indeed. To all intents and appearances it was, and is, the quintessential staple connoting indispensable sustenance in all Near Eastern religions (echoed in prayers for the Lord to "give us this day our daily bread"[80]). This may have caused it to serve all the more forcefully as a symbol of loyalty and bondage to earthly lordship (as in injunctions "not to betray the door of whose bread one has eaten"[81]).

At the same time, among the various types of bread available, royalty appears to have received a higher proportion of *nan-ı has* to *nan-ı fod(u)la* than dignitaries from the second finance minister down. We have, in other words, a complicated situation involving both a strong group specificity (but not exclusivity) for one product, and a suggestion that more of a particular variety of that product, in terms of both its quality and its name (the best kind of bread: *nan-ı has*) was relatively more emblematic of a higher rank than those of lower status.

At the same time we have already seen that certain kinds of bread

Table 5.2
Bread Distribution

Offices and/or office-holders benefiting from bread distribution	Symbolic bread distribution according to the imperial kitchen registers of 1687, 1688 (pairs of loaves of)		1756–57 (pairs of loaves of)	
	nan-ı has	*nan-ı fod(u)la*	*nan-ı has*	*nan-ı fod(u)la*
sadr-ı âli	15	10	48	—
kaymakam paşa [sadaret kaymakamı]	4.5	10	not cited	not cited
kaptan-ı derya	4.5	10	4	10
defterdar-ı şıkk-ı evvel	4	6	8	40
defterdar-ı şıkk-ı sâni	1	6	1	6
defterdar-ı şıkk-ı sâlis	1	6	1	6
nişancı	1	6	not cited	not cited
şeyhülislâm	not cited	not cited	2	—
kazasker-i Anadolu	1	6	1	6
kazasker-i Rum	1	6	1	6
imam-ı evvel	not cited	not cited	1	6
reisülküttab	not cited	not cited	13	—
kethüda bey [sadaret kethüdası]	not cited	not cited	2	—

were also part of *ramazaniye* or *iftariye* deliveries, and in an interesting way too for while in all other foodstuffs the *ramazaniye* distributions represented only an increase in quantity (more of the same for certain items), as far as bread was concerned they also involved an increase in variety (translating very probably into quality). Thus every day during the month of daily fasting, and fast breaking, our princesses received: 50 additional pairs of *nan-ı has* as well as 33 pairs of *nan-ı sakızlı*, 35 pairs of *nan-ı somun*, 90 pairs of *nan-ı çakır*,[82] and 85 pairs of *nan-ı çörek*, the last four of which were not part of their regular allocations.[83] In addition, at other times as well as during Ramadan, they not only bought from the market the more traditional sounding varieties of Galata bread, flaky pastries, sweetened round buns, and ring rolls made with shortening,[84] as indicated in our discussion of independent purchases above, but also appear to have looked for some new, nontraditional bread.[85] The availability of a great variety of bread is common to many Near Eastern or Mediterranean cultures,[86] and within our broadly constructed category of breads and pastries too, there were (at least) three distinct gradations, it seems, running from the most "basic" and symbolic distributional bread, through an intermediate level of *ramazaniye*, to purchases that (in this particular instance, though not necessarily always) may have represented the highest in taste sophistication.

While there is no real parallel in Turkish historical studies to Steven Kaplan's research on bread consumption in eighteenth century Paris,[87] existing scholarship has tended to concentrate on provisioning or organization of grain transport, milling, and storage, as well as the collection of dies accruing in the process. State regulation occupies center stage. Beyond noting, for example, that the authorities stipulated how all bread and pastries were to be cooked and prepared. Thus as early as some general law codes of the beginning of the sixteenth century, the basis of *çörek* making was defined as "seven *okka*s of fat to one *mudd* of flour."[88]

The product itself, its actual preparation, kinds, availability, or scarcity, and its role in the Ottoman diet or food consumption patterns, probably continue to be regarded as "low history" by a majority of historians. For that same reason, too, arguments of the kind advanced by Piero Camporesi about the possibility of peasants in preindustrial Europe living in a state of almost permanent hallucination, drugged by their hunger or by bread adulterated with hallucinogenic herbs,[89] have yet to be tested in the Ottoman case. Although it is certain that Ottoman bread(s), too, comprised a variety of seeds and herbals, the only concrete clue we have about such secondary ingredients are the *sarcopoterium spinosum L. (abdestbozan otu)* of the *nan-ı çakır*, and the even rarer bread *(nan-ı sakızlı)* in the documents at our disposal.

Historians keep relying on scattered observations by (in most cases) foreigners like Count Marsigli, who is known to have "commented favorably on the nutritional content of the rations provided to common foot soldiers in the Ottoman army."[90] Marsigli's data for the average daily diet of members of the janissary corps, reinterpreted by Murphey in terms of their food values, shows the janissary diet of the seventeenth century to have been composed of daily rations of 100 *dirhems* (832 grams) of bread, 50 *dirhems* (160 grams) of hard tack, 60 *dirhems* (192 grams) of mutton, 25 *dirhems* (80 grams) of butter, and 50 *dirhems* (160 grams) of rice.[91]

Was All Meat the Same?

As previously indicated, the initial impression that we have of meat allocation too, points to such universal or near-universal coverage within the Ottoman elite as to be immediately suggestive of loyalty and bondage. This, again, fits into known cultural traditions: at the huge potlatchlike banquets (*toy* or *şölen*) that they threw in central Asia, it was the Turkish *kaghanate*'s custom to seat each tribal chief always in the same place *(orun)* and to serve to him the same share of mutton *(ülüş)* that was commensurate with the ceremonial recognition of his rank. Centuries later, the custom resurfaces in the form of palace rations, but unlike bread, it now serves to highlight the difference that quantity (rather than quality) could make between the royal vs. the subroyal, or the elite vs. the commoner diet.

In Europe in the Middle Ages this difference was frequently absolute: both eating meat and hunting for it were part and parcel of a closely guarded system of aristocratic privilege, bolstered by villainous gamekeepers trying to keep protein-starved peasants from poaching in forest and chase, as reflected in a Robin Hood-type of literature. "The special characteristic of the aristocratic diet was its emphasis on meat and fish, which were served in large quantities, and in great variety," Dyer laconically notes.[92] In a whole section on "the eating of meat," Norbert Elias is much more graphic: "The relation to meat-eating moves in the medieval world between the following poles," he observes, "in the monasteries an ascetic abstention from all meat eating largely prevails," while "the meat consumption of the lowest class, the peasants, is also frequently extremely limited—not from a spiritual need, a voluntary renunciation with regard to God and the next world, but from shortage." In contrast, "in the secular upper class the consumption of meat is extraordinarily high, compared to the standard of our own times. A tendency prevails to devour quantities of meat that to us seem fantastic."[93]

Even in the seventeenth century, Elias adds, the consumption of a north German court has been calculated to include, for its resident member, "two pounds [of meat] per head per day, in addition to large quantities of venison, birds, and fish." And in another colorful touch, the dead animal or large parts of it, he goes on, are often brought whole to the table. Not only whole fish and whole birds (sometimes with their feathers) but also whole rabbits, lambs, and quarters of veal appear on the table, not to mention the larger venison or the pigs and oxen roasted on the spit, so that "the animal is carved on the table"[94]—prompting Goody, who quotes Elias extensively on all these points, to formulate a felicitous phrase or two of his own about "this carnivorous diet of the rich" and the "the carnivorous nature of the culture of the upper class of medieval society."[95]

Beef vs. Mutton

How different were the Ottomans? First, there is a matter of sheep as against cattle. In medieval Europe "the importance of beef is clear, often exceeding a half of the total of meat consumed, followed by pork and mutton, with game and poultry of least significance," Dyer observes.[96] Given the climate and the vast extent of nomadic pastoralism that not only continued to dominate inner Anatolian space for a long time but also acquired extensions in the Balkans,[97] it is understandable that sheep (and lambs) provided the bulk of the Ottoman meat diet (and served as the *ülüş* meat).[98] Secondly, and notwithstanding the fact that members of the elite in particular were familiar with, and would eat a great variety of game as well as other kinds of flesh or fowl that would thereby appear to have been at least socially defined as delicacies,[99] when it came to basic consumption not only their terminology but their practice too, was less nuanced. While Western usage came to distinguish rather precisely between the animal and its flesh (cow/beef, calf/veal, sheep/mutton, pig/pork, deer/venison), time and again Ottoman documents simply refer to *et* (meat or flesh), though it is safe to conclude (on the basis of many instances, already cited, where *et* and *gûşt-i ganem* or *lağm-ı ganem* are used together and interchangeably) that what they meant was always mutton. As Anthony Greenwood remarks in his study of the wholesale meat contracting *(celepkeşan)* system:

> Furthermore, goat consumption is inextricably mixed with sheep in most Ottoman documentation. The two were sold by the same butchers, although care was to be taken not to mix the meats, and treated as the same category of meat. Beef and chicken, on the other hand, each had their own butchers.[100]

Beef consumption, a large part of which was in the form of cured meats such as *sucuk* (sausages) and *pastırma* (spice-cured beef or pastrami), was not insignificant, but neither was it regarded as a critical part of the diet. So it was only mutton and lamb that was distributed by the *kasabbaşı* to royalty and some top bureaucrats. And thirdly, the way the Ottomans cooked and ate meat was also more "mixed" in other senses: as already noted, most meat dishes were served as stews or on skewers, as a result of which they dipped with their spoons, pieces of bread or fingers into the same large dish, in sharp contrast to the European custom of a central, ceremonial role to a master carver.[101]

Provisioning Istanbul and the Palace

Here, too, the elite's meat consumption was enormous (i) in absolute terms (comparing how much they ate with how much we eat), as well as relative to (ii) the urban lower classes of Istanbul, and (iii) the provinces. There were many ways in which the capital was privileges over the rest of Rumelia and Anatolia. Faroqhi quotes a rescript of H. 1001/1592–1593 ordering a number of *kadı*s in the Balkans to keep local price ceilings low so as to attract more meat into Istanbul, and expressing what we would call a clearly redistributionist patronage argument for this policy "in very blunt terms":

> Istanbul was inhabited by many prominent officials, important *ulema,* illustrious descendants of the Prophet, and other distinguished personages. On the other hand, the author of the rescript in question estimated that most provincial towns contained only a small number of inhabitants worthy of official consideration. For the latter's needs, the slaughtering of four or five sheep a day was deemed sufficient.[102]

The authorities, moreover, tried to ensure whenever possible that all sheep, being more prized, headed for Istanbul, sometimes going so far as to order the provinces to be left to eat goat only.[103] Recently, İnalcık has devoted a whole chapter to "Istanbul and the Imperial

Economy," underlining the enormous problem of "feeding a giant city" though more in terms of wheat than meat, and without distinguishing between the court and the ordinary population.[104] This, on the other hand, is a distinction that Greenwood observes but noting that in either case, per capita consumption of meat is virtually impossible to calculate with any degree of precision, for a variety of reasons, which he discusses at length.[105] He classifies around 50,000 to 55,000 persons as "state-dependents." These include (a) groups fed by the various palace kitchens (Topkapı, Eski Saray, Galata Saray, and from the mid-sixteenth century onward, İbrahim Paşa Sarayı), as well as (b) those supplied by the janissary butchers.

It is, in other words, a two-tiered subsystem in itself. For the former, the Topkapı kitchens alone were feeding around five thousand people every day by the end of the sixteenth century, Greenwood says, while the total number fed from all four might have reached as high as 15,000.[106] For the latter, he thinks that in the wake of efforts to control the swelling of janissary ranks, a seventeenth-century leveling off at around 40,000 "state dependents" (which is actually the 1670 registration figure) is reasonable. Then for the remaining 350,000–400,000 Istanbul inhabitants, he arrives at an average annual consumption of 1,586,000 sheep; allowing for 10 *okka*s or 12.8 kilos of clean flesh per sheep (1 *okka* = 1 *vukıyye* = 1 *kıyye* = 1.28 kilos). He suggests that the mutton supply might therefore have come to 50–58 kilos per head per year.[107] This, he finds, would have been on the same order of magnitude as meat consumption in Paris from the mid-eighteenth to the mid-nineteenth century, which moved between annual averages of 51 to 65 kilos, and higher than that in Rome, which dropped from 38.3 to 21.5 kilos in the course of the seventeenth and eighteenth centuries.[108]

Turning then to the average consumption of Ottoman state dependents: for the janissaries, Greenwood mentions a daily ration of 160 to 190 grams as recorded by Marsigli and other foreign observers.[109] Within the limits given and allowing for either 354 or 365 days to the year, this would have meant an annual mutton ration of 60–70 kilos. In other words, some 180,000 average-sized sheep, Greenwood figures, though in the seventeenth and eighteenth centuries the number of sheep actually supplied to the janissary butchers was approximately half that level at 70,000 to 100,000 animals per year. This discrepancy he attributes to "the fact that for a good part of most years many of the janissaries were not in Istanbul."[110] As for the amount of meat consumed at the imperial palaces, a number of contemporary and modern observations impressionistically agree that this was tremendous. For lamb alone, Barkan cites 1489–1490 figures of about

1,270 tons (costing 12 million *akçes*) for the Topkapı palace and 458 tons for the other three palaces.[111] Seventeenth-century travelers' mixed sheep and lamb estimates (for the Topkapı palace only) vary from slightly over 100,000 to nearly 180,000 sheep per year.[112] Greenwood tabulates his own findings, which indicate the annual sheep consumption of the Topkapı palace kitchens to have risen from 16,379 to 99,120 between the years 1489–1490 and 1669–1670.[113] He argues that the 99,000 level must have been the maximum reached by Topkapı palace consumption, which can be seen to have varied between 72,000 and 96,000 sheep for the rest of the seventeenth and eighteenth centuries.[114] He then adds another 25,000 for the three other palaces, and on the basis of 125,000 sheep for 15,000 palace dependents, he volunteers an annual mutton consumption estimate of around 107 kilos per palace dependent[115]—that is, double his average figure for the nonstate dependent population of the capital.

Collective versus Individual Rations

So how do we get from this notion and measure of "palace consumption" to that of "elite consumption"? This is not easy to disentangle. The nature of palace consumption, which included feasts, sacrificial offerings, gifts, meals for ambassadors and petitioners, distribution of leftovers outside the palace, and even food for the caged lions is such as to make this figure [of 107 kilos] difficult to interpret, warns Greenwood.[116] Some of those 125,000 sheep, in other words, were never transformed into individual consumption. The arithmetic mean may be much less meaningful than the median or the mode. Lumped together in the category of palace dependents fed by the imperial kitchens were a small number of court residents that formed part of the ruling elite (headed of course by the sultan, followed by his "family" and those closest to him) as well as huge numbers of others who were no more than their servants (pages, gatekeepers, halberdiers, sergeants-at-arms, harem attendants). The latter, moreover, had their own finely graduated hierarchy woven in terms of their present ranks and future career prospects, as a result of which certain elements of the palace population were allotted much more than this. The daily mutton ratio of the young trainees in Galata Saray in 1602/1603 was 150 *dirhems* (480 grams) which is the equivalent of 175 kilos a year. This was almost three-fourths again as high as the above average,[117] though neither 107 nor 175 kilos were anything comparable, at first sight, to the 20–30 *kıyye* of mutton that the seventeenth and eighteenth century princesses are known to have regularly received on a daily basis.[118]

In one sense this is a fully legitimate contrast, for in Barkan's "Istanbul Saraylarına ait Muhasebe Defterleri,"[119] not only those princesses that were still living at Topkapı (the *şehzadegân-ı enderun*) but also those who had established their own households (the *şehzadegân-ı birun*[120]), plus some young ones that together with their mothers had been consigned to the old palace after the sultan their father had died, were all explicitly counted as part of the imperial palace(s) network. All of them, in other words, were foremost recipients of allocations from the imperial kitchen, those who were living in their own palaces being entitled to the "full package" cited for princesses above and elsewhere,[121] and those of the new palace or the old palace coming in for sometimes a half, sometimes a fourth as much.[122] This might create the impression that these were all individual rations—or at least suppress any potential question marks and raised eyebrows. But thirty *kıyye* of mutton works out to three sheep per day and 1,062 sheep for a 354-day year, equivalent in clean flesh weight to 10,620 *kıyye/okka,* or 13,593.6 kilos, or slightly more than 13.5 metric tons, while half of that (15 *kıyye* daily) comes to something like 6.8 metric tons, and even the smallest mutton allocation which we have encountered for a royal princess (seven *kıyye* daily) weighs in, so to speak, at 3,172 kilos, or nearly 3,2 metric tons per year. And all this was included in what was being purchased by the imperial kitchens (those 125,000 sheep), which then averaged out as 107 kilos per capita, superficially suggesting a gulf of immense, indeed absurd, proportions between what halberdiers or fighting-fit janissaries, on the one hand, and royal princesses, on the other, were (supposed to be capable of) eating!

Women's Eating Circles as Embryonic Households

Fortunately, however, 13.5 or 6.8 or even 3.2 tons are impossibly huge amounts of mutton and make no sense at all if taken as narrowly individual rations. Instead, I have no choice but to regard them as intended for the entire retinue of a princess, depending on her marital status. Whereupon things suddenly begin to sink into place, since the households of any of these eighteenth-century married princesses appear to be on the order of 130, 150, or 160 (but not 300) people.[123] And 13.5 tons of mutton divided by 150 brings us back to 90.6 kilos per capita per year, or to a quite recognizable daily ration of 256 grams = 80 *dirhems*. This is not only comparable to the janissary ration of 50–60 *dirhems*, but according to Greenwood, was exactly what students at the hospice of the Fatih Mosque were getting in the year 1490.[124] It was, in other words, a quantity that was notionally familiar to the Ottomans, and respectable enough in terms of others (like *ulema* cadets) that it targeted so as to be considered workable for married princesses' households.

And as for those unmarried princesses still residing in the imperial palace, their half- or quarter-quotas, too, are entirely consistent with what we know of life in the harem, which revolved around the foci constituted by the reigning sultan's mother and all the "official" royal consorts), each with her own apartments—this being one reason why the Topkapı harem is architecturally a jumble, a conglomerate of many small pavilions—and her own coterie of female attendants who functioned like a small commune, a cooking-and-eating club on its own. The princesses who were young enough to remain in the palace but old enough to have allocations in their own names would have pooled their resources together with their mother's, placing "orders" each day for so much of what was being kept for them to be taken out of the cellars, to be prepared as desired in the relevant section of the imperial kitchens, and to be served to their joint quarters.[125]

It is safe to conclude, in other words, that the 6.8 or the 3.2 tons of mutton in question were also earmarked for an embryonic household *(kapı halkı)* of smaller dimensions (perhaps comprising 20, 30, or more people) that for the moment was nestling within the imperial harem until its mistress married so that it could clone off into an "independent," full-fledged quasi-royal household. Also fitting into this whole pattern, finally, is the whole approach, already mentioned twice, of cooking meat not separately but in vegetable stews or on skewers, which is what really would have made thirty *kıyye* a day of mutton for the princess serviceable the year round to the 100 to 200 people maintained at her door.

Other Difficulties of Personalizing Court and Elite Consumption

Time for some loose ends and qualifications. First, where did the palace end, anyway—not just for (a) the imperial and royal section of the elite, which was partly inside and among the "palace dependents," and also partly outside, but also for (b) another part of the elite (comprising the top dignitaries) which was basically outside the palace but also benefiting from allocations out of the imperial stores or eating occasionally or frequently at the palace (as meetings of the imperial council)? In all mathematical calculations about average consumption levels, somehow these fuzzy overlaps too have to be accounted for.

And second, if married princesses were using their allocations to feed their own lesser courts, what denominator must we choose in calculating the "average" for all "palace dependents"? By including all the people fed at princesses' doors (their *kapı halkları*) in that global figure, should not we be dividing 125,000 sheep not by 15,000 but by [15,000 + n (150)], n being the number of such "independent" quasi-royal households?

But third, if we do that, should not we also increase the numerator, since the same palace clones were also engaging in purchases on their own, which should also enter any consumption averages? And yet, fourth, was this necessarily true of meat in particular—that is to say, could the seemingly accidental absence of any household purchases (11:Mh) entries so far for mutton and lamb actually indicate an almost 100 percent reliance on imperial kitchen allocations for these crucial components of royal or quasi-royal carnivorousness?

Fifth, how to handle the fact that at least some of those patronized by the married princesses in their quasi-royal households appear to have been receiving allocations from sources that are not clearly identified? Although I have found one instance in which a top dignitary's account books explicitly mention (the cost of) allocations by the *paşa* to some of his top servitors,[126] it is not possible to say with any degree of certainty that that was all they received, or that they did not get anything through other channels—we cannot, in other words, exclude the possibility that some of these top servitors might have been eligible for allocations from the imperial kitchens on their own. But if they were, we cannot simply divide 13,539 kilos by 150 to obtain all too neat a daily ration of 256 grams or 80 *dirhems*; the total intake being larger than just the allocation of the princess or the dignitary in question: either the average, too, would have to go up, or it could be that the secondary recipients (*ağas*, etc.) in question were maintaining their own small "outriding" retinues not covered by the palace payroll. Or else it could be that these allocations were intended to bolster the individual consumption of specific echelons in the palace hierarchy in antiegalitarian fashion—perhaps to the point where this baroque system develops so many tiers and niches and hidden compartments that it becomes meaningless to speak of any averages whatsover? Especially in that case, of course, we would have to know much, much more about the consumption package attached to every single rank post than we do now.

Poultry, Cured Meat, Fish, and Offal

For the moment it is not easy to answer these questions, and arithmetically they may not seem to make such a great difference either, but could do so if more precision is introduced into Ottoman historical statistics. We must build on our mutton consumption figures by bringing other kinds of meat into the picture, and going through the same kind of exercise for each and every one of them while simultaneously looking out for any intrinsic, qualitative differences.

Poultry, for example, immediately leaps to the eye as an important supplement to mutton. Eliyahu Ashtor[127] notes that just the poultry consumption at the sultan's court in Cairo probably came to 500 pieces per day. As for the Ottomans, from the "full package" described above, we know a typical eighteenth-century princess drew 150 chickens per month from the imperial kitchens for her household of (perhaps) 150 people.[128] This may not look like much if you think of it as just one chicken per person per month, but takes on a better appearance if we assume that five times a month, a batch of thirty chickens might have gone into the stew, which (setting a not unreasonable flesh and bones weight of 750 grams per chicken, equal to no more than sixty percent of today's farm broilers) would still come to an additional 250-gram serving per person every six days or so.

Further down the list were cured or dried meats, and offal, for which I have bits and pieces of circumstantial (and occasionally contradictory) evidence. In the first quarter of the seventeenth century, the grand vizier personally supervised the preparation of pastrami in the palace kitchen every year in late autumn, when some 4,000 cows were slaughtered.[129] According to two expenditure registers of December 1719 and January 1722, the following meat items were found in the cellar of the royal residence of Ahmed III's daughter Fatma Sultan: mutton, 1984.5 *kıyye* and 2487.5 *kıyye* respectively; yearling rams, 836 *kıyye* and 725 *kıyye* respectively; chicken, 1,593 and 1,386.5 pieces respectively. These were enormous amounts, ranging from 66 to 83 times the standard daily allowance for mutton, and from almost eleven to more than nine times the standard monthly allowance for chicken, the meaning of which we are just beginning to explore. But in any case, also listed (in 1722 only) were 413 pigeons and an unspecified quantity of miscellaneous fish, as well as an insignificant amount (5 *kıyye* each) of sausages and pastrami in both registers.[130]

Curious, too, is the absence of any reference to offal, since Fatma Sultan's husband, the grand vizier (Damad) Nevşehirli İbrahim Paşa, is known to have been fond of trotters *(paça)*, repeatedly ordering them from Süleymaniye (on three successive days at one point).[131] Still, this vaguely fits a general pattern. I have no records for the game or game birds consumed at the imperial as well as the lesser quasi-royal courts, although they could have held a place of importance on the palace menu.[132] Pigeons occasionally are listed for the reigning sultan. Fish, too, rarely come up in either the imperial kitchen registers or books of private accounts.[133] Offal, on the other hand—including trotters, tripe, gut sausages, and sheep's heads—often do, and sometimes even became part of regular allocations. A case in point are monthly deliveries to the future Selim III in 1774/1775, which appear more varied than the standard *tayinat* for our eighteenth-century princesses, comprising, in addition to a variety of fruit, also lambs, yearling rams *(toklu),* ox tripe *(işkembe-i gav),* gut sausages *(mumbar)* and trotters *(paça)* for both *ruz-i Kasım:* August-November 1774, and *ruz-ı Hızır,* May–August 1775.[134] In that same summer of 1775 he also appears to have received some bonito, probably to be salted and pickled (as *lakerda*) since it was paired with a delivery of Wallachian salt; this is very rare indeed in my registers.

Eddies of Terminal Redistribution

A certain amount of wastage is inherent in any consumption process, and it would be useful to be able to calculate Ottoman wastage ratios. Greenwood's 50–58 kilo average for Istanbul's nonstate dependent population lumps the rich together with the poor, of course, and the latter's meat consumption is difficult to calculate. But actually, at least some of the huge amounts of meat appearing to have been "consumed" at the imperial and other courts must have percolated down to the poor. The Ottomans frowned upon throwing food away, with the corollary that sitting down to betters' or higher-ups' leftovers was considered no dishonor—facilitated, of course, by their entire manner of eating, in the context of which these were not really "individualized" leftovers on personal plates, but simply what still remained in the large service containers they all dipped into. The Western tradition developed so that once the food on the table had been shared out to members of the party, it became shameful and disgusting, indeed unthinkable, to reuse it except as garbage. Not so with the Ottomans, so, when a foreign ambassador and his retinue were received and feasted in the imperial council hall, all the gatekeepers, constable, or sergeants-at-arms took care of what was left behind.

It was, in other words, the physical chewing and swallowing of food that consummated, or was identical to, the process of sharing out and individual appropriation. Short of that bodily internalization the meal on the trays or service containers, could also be returned to the kitchens in the same way, to be wiped out there by the kitchen attendants or else to find its way back into some common pot or cauldron (*kazan*, which still carries communal overtones in modern Turkish) for recycling or further redistribution. Thus might intraelite crossovers or handdowns dovetailed into a series of crossover or handdown points between the elite as a whole and the people as a whole. And such handdowns did not have to comprise leftovers in the strict sense, but could begin with potential excess. We know some of the regular allocations from the imperial kitchens to have been directly and immediately passed on by its first recipients to the soup kitchens of various imperial complexes or dervish lodges.[135] One minister of finance in the late eighteenth century had been receiving a daily allowance of 27 *kıyye* of meat and 7 *kıyye* of sausages.[136] Instead of keeping all the mutton for himself, however, he was sending on nine *kıyye* daily to the Tekke-i Mevlevihane-i Galata, 3 *kıyye* daily to the Tekke-i Murteza Efendi at Eyüp, and 5 *kıyye* daily to the Tekke-i Kasım Paşa.[137] And other top, middling, or lesser members of the elite had their own smaller and smaller intersecting circles of secondary patronage,[138] culminating, in all likelihood, in "terminal redistribution"—to coin a phrase—on the scale of a small street or neighborhood.

Olive Oil: The Political and Fiscal Dynamics of Induced Demand

Throughout history, the coastal areas of the Mediterranean have served as a melting pot for movements out of a tri-continental hinterland, though not without opposition. Georges Duby, for example, has generalized about the Germanic tribes' diet of butter, meat, and onions *versus* the Roman staples of wheat, olive oil, and wine as two contrasting "modes of consumption."[139] Strabo related how disgusted the Romans of Aelius Gallus were to find clarified butter instead of olive oil used in cooking in the Hidjaz,[140] that is to say, the preference for olive oil in some subregions of the Mediterranean (southern Spain, southern Italy and Greece) did not extend to the Middle East. This is supported by Zubaida and Tapper, who remain quite skeptical about assumptions concerning the Mediterraneanness of, and hence the supposedly widespread use of olive oil in, the Middle East, noting that "oil (whether olive or other) was confined largely to vegetable cookery (though not when cooked with meat). It was sometimes used as a flavoring or a dressing added to complex dishes which were started with animal fats. It is only in recent years that cooking habits with respect to fats have changed. These changes are the product of global influences in technology and trade as well as in health ideologies," they go on to argue.[141]

This appears to have been the Ottoman pattern, too, even in the capital and into the last century or so of empire, and the ethno-cultural reasons behind it are not hard to understand. It was through encircling and intersecting zones of Latin (crusading), Byzantine, or Italian (Venetian and Genoese) control in the Aegean that the Turcoman principalities of Anatolia made contact with the sea and the culture of its littoral zone.[142] They carved out a political space but at the same time continuing to work through old economic networks,[143] and learned from them, as embodied in a wholesale takeover of fish names from Greek and of nautical terms from first Greek and then Italian,[144] with culinary tastes and practices probably following in their wake. Thus for a long time the Turcomans were obviously not great fish eaters (as indicated in the previous sections on meat consumption). The predilection of a new urban classes around the Black Sea, Aegean, and Mediterranean seaboards for fried fish accompanied by green salads and anisette is a distinctly modern phenomenon of the kind mentioned by Zubaida and Tapper that has flourished particularly in cosmopolitan centers of crosscultural interaction like Istanbul/Constantinople and Izmir/Smyrna. Then, too, like the Germans with whom they had once shared the world of the Eurasian steppes,[145] they had the pastoralist's strong preference for milk products. As a result, butterfats *(sadeyağ, taze yağ, tereyağ)* were highly favored in the Ottoman palace, in the rest of Istanbul, and elsewhere in the interior. Meat, rice, and pastries were always cooked in butter (at least by those who could afford it), the alternative being not olive oil but animal fat (*iç yağı*, preferably from sheep tails.[146]

But of course this does not imply that commoners in general had no use for olive oil whatsoever,[147] or that the court might not have had its own distinct preferences. Here the geographical omnipresence of olive trees stands out as possibly a factor in itself, for while few regions seem to have used olive oil in significant quantities, it is also the case that the use of olive oil cannot be assumed to have been limited to only those parts of greater Syria, Tunisia, and the archipelago where it is known to have been produced in some abundance. In fact, olive trees grew everywhere in the wide frost-free rainfall zones of the Mediterranean. If people domesticated and took care of them, one may well suppose that eventually they must have had some use for the harvest (even if this included lighting and soap-making along with cooking).[148] Then there are various trade networks to consider. Thus İnalcık, who lets drop a tantalizing remark about olives and olive oil being "a basic stuff for the masses,"[149] provides evidence to show that Istanbul's intake was "principally from Edremid and Mytilene, the nearest supply areas. Olives and olive also came from the rich groves of the valley near Athens."[150] France and England (with their culinary demand as well as increasing industrial uses for olive oil[151]) competed with the Ottoman capital as well as other Mediterranean customers for the output from these and other leading areas. England, for example, was importing olive oil in the sixteenth century from the Greek islands mostly under Venetian control. Later, in the seventeenth century, it imported from the ports of Modon and Coron, which were in Ottoman hands.[152] But in the 1620s, the olive oil for the palace too was brought in from Modon and Coron, while the sultan's special share was procured from Kandiye/Iraklion in Crete, which was still Venetian.[153]

By the 1690s, olive oil in Tunisia had become a profitable export item; olive plantations were extended and the value of land with olive trees on it increased considerably. Tunisia, however, exported its olive oil to France.[154] Olive oil from the archipelago was increasing in importance as an export item in the eighteenth century.[155] At the same time olives have been grown in, and olive oil supplied from, some rather unexpected places. Thus a late seventeenth-century imperial kitchen register shows that olive oil was brought to the imperial cellars from Sarıyol (a district of Florina) in the Balkans, and from Ankara, Bursa, and Kayseri in Anatolia.[156]

McGowan has pointed to an interesting dynamic in this regard:

> In some remote villages, and out-of-the-way neighbourhoods of the capital city [there were] occasional attempts to hide new workshops, so as to escape the controls of the state and some craft associations. (Thus not all migration was toward the cities.) The disincentives of agriculture under Ottoman rule pushed some villagers, especially in the hilly regions, to develop products, such as yarn, dyestuffs, and olive oil, which they might process and either sell locally or to agents of a wider trade.[157]

Crete: Trade Diversion through Conquest?

Looming large in this context is the final conquest of Crete, a major production center for olives and olive oil (as well as for wine and raisins), by the Ottomans in 1669.[158] Crete had long been a way station for Venetian merchant convoys engaged in the luxury trade with the Muslim ports of the eastern Mediterranean, but also had vast quantities of its own products to export.[159] Functioning as "a veritable breadbasket" for Venice in the fifteenth century, the island increasingly had replaced wheat fields to export more and more *malvasia* (or malmsey) wine as well as olive oil over the next hundred years or so. This seems to have attracted the attention of the Ottomans who were always hungry for tax revenues,[160] already in the second half of the sixteenth century.[161] Events snowballed into the Ottoman-Venetian war of 1570–1573 over Cyprus, during and after which Crete became so short of grain that the Venetians went back in the seventeenth century to encouraging wheat cultivation at the expense of viticulture (but not olives).[162] Meanwhile Ottoman Istanbul, as well as the Levant, remained an enormous market for Cretan products. Istanbul was the most common port of destination after Venice, accounting for 14 percent of all departures.[163] Overall, forty percent went to Venice, but in some years the gap was narrower, as in 1611, when "21 boats left the harbor of Kandiye for Venice, another 14 departed for Istanbul, two each for Alexandria and Syria and one to Izmir."[164] Cretan trade with the Ottoman capital continued in importance over 1636–1640, but after war broke out in June 1645,[165] Istanbul was no more among the destinations for Kandiye ships.[166]

After the conquest was completed with the surrender of Kandiye, commerce presumably should have resumed, Greene suggests, along the three old circuits of (i) the international transit trade in luxuries, (ii) the provisioning of the colonial capital, and (iii) the local trade with nearby ports.[167] But now, Istanbul and not Venice was the colonial capital. But to what extent, if any, did this involve a trade diversion from the Adriatic to the Bosphorus? "The links with Venice must have weakened," Greene hypothesizes,[168] but at the same time, the Greek islands of Kos, Samos, Chios, Mytilene, and Lemnos, remained most important to Istanbul's provisioning system in the second half of the eighteenth century, Mantran has argued.[169] By implication "Crete's principal orientation was to Egypt, although trade with Istanbul was by no means rare," Greene concurs.[170]

There was, however, yet another dramatic shift, this time not only from wheat but from also wine to olive oil, and a corresponding explosion in exports of Cretan olive oil,[171] neither of which were missed by the Ottomans. "By 1715, Crete's brief role as a wheat exporter was over."[172] Meanwhile, the turn toward olive oil production that had already begun under the Venetians[173] was gathering force:

> Fed by growing European demand, this secondary export [to wine] under the Venetians had become the premier export of the Ottoman Crete by the early eighteenth century. Between the years 1700 and 1721, the French exported an average of 92,000 *mistat* of olive oil per year, which accounted for about a third of Crete's total production. By way of contrast, about 50,000 *mistat* of wine left the island every year, and even smaller amounts of raisins.[174]

This was a response to market conditions more than anything else. Masson had already noted that French commerce in Crete was dominated almost entirely by olive oil because it was in such strong demand by the soap-making industries of Marseilles and Toulon.[175] While Greene may be right in criticizing Baladie for an excessive "focus on . . . international trade with the West," thereby "ignor[ing] Crete's role in the eastern Mediterranean,"[176] it is important to recognize that this is probably the result of Baladie's sole reliance on the French archives—which "over-document," the olive oil trade in Chania.

From Tax-Farming Olive Oil to Cooking with It in the Palace

The way Istanbul took stock of this resurgence in the olive oil trade may have triggered a complex chain of events culminating in a shift of culinary tastes in the imperial capital. In striking contrast to the early modern turning of European commercial demand away from luxuries toward such industrial raw materials[177] as were needed to develop production within the limits of a mercantilistically defined "national economy,"[178] the Ottomans continued in their fiscalist ways, "interested only in those products whose value was great enough that a tax would be lucrative."[179] They were ruling over an old fashioned "extensive" empire, dependent on squeezing out and concentrating tiny bits of surplus from innumerable low-productivity peasant households spread over vast expanses of territory, in conjunction with which "wealth was expected to derive from new tax sources in the lands annexed by conquest, not by intensive methods such as maximizing the income from agriculture, industries and commerce through new technologies."[180]

Late in the seventeenth century, moreover, one would expect that "the official and more traditional sources of royal patronage had largely been exhausted [or had] dried up."[181] Hence in 1669, the Ottomans had "high hopes for the riches to be garnered from Crete," regarding it, in Evliya's words, as "a second Egypt,"[182] the resources of which they hastened to impound in their tax-farm *(mukataa)* units. This was also a time when all modern states-in-the-making were finding their traditional finances enormously strained by the new technologies and modes of organization collectively known as "the military revolution."[183] For the Ottomans in particular the seventeenth century dragged out as a series of high-cost, low gain conflicts,[184] including their 24-year effort to conquer Crete. Soon after this, they were left utterly drained and starved of cash. In 1695, they switched from short-term *(iltizam)* to life-farming *(malikâne),* whereby they both tried to get a fuller count of their resources and perhaps to bring them under tighter dynastic control by interpolating royal princesses at the top of chains of subcontracting stretching out from the capital into some of the richest core provinces of the empire.[185]

So it comes as no surprise that by 1718, a *ferman* should be sent to the governor in Kandiye imposing a tax of three *akçe*s on every *okka* of olive oil exported, which meant an extra 22 percent to be paid by the exporter. The rescript was very clear about the cast of mind that prevailed in Istanbul:

> Because of the bounteous production of olive oil in the provinces and villages of Crete, Ottoman and foreign merchants purchase it in great quantity. Despite their being able to buy olive oil all over the island, when they load it at Kandiye, Souda, Chania, Rethymnon and the other islands, they pay only a small customs tax, just as is done with other products, and nothing more for the public treasury. While these merchants make a great profit, the income of Crete according to the latest survey—does not cover her expenses . . . If a tax for the Public Treasury is levied on the great amount of olive oil exported from the harbors of Crete, there will be a great benefit to the Public Treasury . . . It is understood that because this tax will not burden the indigenous population, it will not be a source of unhappiness for them while the Public Treasury will benefit.[186]

As the eighteenth century wore on, "the demand for Cretan olive oil in other parts of the empire began to grow, and [from 1723] the development of a local soap industry increased the demand still further."[187] And inevitably, we find Cretan *mukataa*s for soap dues *(resm-i sabun)* as well as olive oil dues *(resm-i revgâ-ı zeyd)* added to the tax-farms and revenue grants of leading women of the royal house (like Esma the Younger, Beyhan, Hibetullah Sultan, and maybe others, too) by the end of the eighteenth and the beginning of the nineteenth century.[188]

Evidence for the Shift: Princesses' Rations, Gifts, Spot Purchases

What was the impact on demand for the products involved in trade, taxation, revenue sharing, or tax farming? If there was a switch, it must have been relative, and not in the form of a sudden jump, for Cretan olives and olive oil appear to have been favored in the Ottoman capital even before the conquest. Thus, as indicated in Table 5.1 (see 5.1:5a, section K) they are frequently singled out in the available documentation as Cretan olives *(zeytun-i Girid)* or Cretan olive oil *(revgân-ı zeyt-i Girid)*. And (at least later in the eighteenth century) we find Cretan olives set in a jar cut in Venetian style *(kâse-i Venedik kavanos)* for Beyhan Sultan (b. 1765-d. 1824), figuring among the delicacies reserved for selective *iftariye* distribution. For another, with all the detail provided by Baudier some forty years before the conquest about olive oil for the palace,[189] it is difficult to imagine that he was talking not of the best kind of cooking oil but only of unrefined oil for lighting purposes.

Still, as far as bulk use at the court(s) is concerned, at this stage olive oil must be admitted to be running (at best) fourth behind butter, cottonseed oil, and even sesame oil.[190] Table 5.3a reproduces just the rows for oils and fats from tables for the seventeenth- and eighteenth-century princesses that I have published elsewhere.[191] Thus back in the sixteenth century, from the very incomplete data that we have for imperial kitchen allocations to the married princesses named Şehzade, Şah (d. 1572), and Mihrümah (1522–1578), it looks as if, after an initial mention of animal fat (*iç yağı* or *revgân-ı pih*), larger but irregular amounts of butterfat make their appearance.[192] Second, these butterfat rations stabilized at the level of a standard 100 *kıyye* per month (= 128 kilos) for a late seventeenth–early eighteenth-century quartet of Rukiye (d. 1696), Gevherhan (1642–1694), Beyhan (1645–1700), and Hatice (d. 1743).[193] Third, this becomes the standard amount regularly received over almost 150 years by ten more married princesses from Safiye (1696–1778) to Hibetullah (1788–1841).[194] At the same time, three other late sixteenth–early seventeenth-century princesses (Gevherhan b. 1544, Ayşe d. 1605, Fatma of unknown lifespan) appear to have received a distinctly smaller cottonseed oil *(revgân-ı penbe)* ration of 10 *kıyye* per month.[195] But this cannot be documented to have been continued for the immediately following Rukiye-Gevherhan-Beyhan-Hatice foursome,

Table 5.3a
Food Allocations

Types of provisions	Evidence on food allocations for 16th- and 17th-century princesses, showing an early pattern as well as late 17th-century regularization									
	Şehzade ?	Şah ?–1572	Mihrümah 1522–78	Gevherhan 1544–?	Ayşe ?–1605	Fatma ?	Rukiye ?–1696	Gevherhan 1642–94	Beyhan 1645–1700	Hatice ?–1743
monthly if not, otherwise indicated; or else given as *yearly* (broken down into monthly)										
revgân-ı sade (s), or revgân-ı pih (p), or revgân-ı penbe (pb)	110 kıyye p = 9.2/mo	292 kıyye s = 24.3/mo	2160 kıyye s (Kefe) = 180/mo	10 kıyye pb	10 kıyye pb	10 kıyye pb	100 kıyye s	100 kıyye s	100 kıyye s	100 kıyye s
revgân-ı şir (ş) or revgân-ı zeyt (z)							9 kıyye ş	9 kıyye ş	9 kkıyye ş	9 kıyye ş

Source: For the first six columns (Şehzade, Şah, Mihrümah, Gevherhan, Ayşe, Fatma), Ömer Lütfi Barkan, "Istanbul Saralarına ait Muhasebe Defterleri," *Belgeler*, Cilt 12, Sayı: 13 (1979).

For the last four columns (Rukiye, Gevherhan, Beyhan, Hatice), Başbakanlık Arşivi: KK7237 (1687), KK7238 (1688), KK7289 (1694/5), and KK7241 (1703).

Table 5.3b
Princess Benefited

Types of provisions	18th-century princesses benefiting from a very clearly standardized ritual redistribution										
	Fatma 1704–33	Safiye 1696–1778	Zeynep ?–1774	Saliha 1715–78	Ayşe 1715–75	Esma the Elder 1726–88	Şah 1761–1802	Beyhan 1765–1824	Hatice 1768–1822	Esma the Younger 1778–1848	Hibetullah 1788–1841
monthly											
revgân-ı sade		100 kıyye	100 kıyye	100 kıyye	100 kıyye	100 kıyye	100 kıyye	100 kıyye	100 kıyye	100 kıyye	100 kıyye
revgân-ı şir or revgân-ı zeyt		9 kıyye	9 kıyye	9 kıyye	9 kıyye	9 kıyye	9 kıyye	9 kıyye	9 kıyye		

Source: Başbakanlık Arşivi DBŞM.MTE 11202, 11204, 11291, 11451, 11574, 11745, 11761. For the shift from *revgân-ı şir* to *revgân-ı zeyt*, see 11202, 11204, and 11451 in particular.

each of whom turn out to have been provided with 9 *kıyye*s of sesame oil *(revgân-ı şîr)*.[196]

The turn of the century, however, brings a difference. From Safiye (born in 1696, that is to say, almost thirty years after the fall of Kandiye) onward, along with 100 *kıyye* of butterfat all married princesses start receiving 9 *kıyye*s of olive oil (rather than the same amount of sesame oil).[197] We are now facing a continuity of 128 kilos of butterfat plus 11.52 kilos of olive oil as the standard oils and fats complement of the full "princesshood package." But thereby, too, the movement from cottonseed oil through sesame oil to olive oil becomes more marked, with a strong indication that given the similarity of the quantities involved, these 10 *kıyye* of cottonseed oil, 9 *kıyye* of sesame oil, and finally 9 *kıyye* of olive oil (and though it does not fit into the same category of liquid oil, perhaps even that much earlier 9.2 *kıyye* per month of animal fat?) must all have been intended as frying rations. It is hard not to associate this with greater access to Cretan olive oil.

Secondly, in the context of the patronage relationships inevitably arising between royal princesses in Istanbul and the gentry, and notables of the localities where they had their revenue districts,[198] it seems that the former habitually received supplies of all kinds as gifts from the latter. And they included olive oil, as in 1795, when Esma the Younger's steward ordered a consignment of 1,019 *kıyye* of clarified butter from the gentry *(beyzade*s) of İzdin, plus 80 *kıyye* of olive oil from Edremid to be turned over to her ladyship's kitchen.[199]

Thirdly, there are bits and pieces of evidence that this was also happening between Crete and Istanbul. That is to say, at least some of those eighteenth-century princesses with Cretan *mukataas* (including most probably Beyhan Sultan over the years 1776–1802) were receiving special, additional consignments of quality olives, olive oil, and soap from the three main centers of Chania (Hanya), Kandiye (Candia/Iraklion), and Resimo (Rethymnon).[200] Fourthly, many such households were also engaging in spot purchases of olive oil from the market, as reflected in a large number of small, irregularly kept slips or receipts, which nevertheless hint at significant price variations for (presumably) different kinds of qualities of olive oil.[201]

Olive Oil and the Sea

The overall impression is one of increased availability and use of olive oil—mostly, I might add, for fish dishes. This is where cookbooks come in, and one has to have some idea of how to handle them. Mennell, who has provided a very useful overview of Italian, French, and English cookbooks from the Middle Ages onward, has two critical dichotomies to offer in this regard.

First, he questions in each case whether it was written by a practicing cook for fellow practitioners, or else as a record of high fashion by and for a literate elite who only vicariously commanded operations in the kitchen. Second, he cites Elizabeth David's conclusion that "there was typically a lag of up to four decades between changes in practice occurring in the English kitchen and their appearance in the cookery books." And yet in other cases, he goes on to counterpose, "especially in eighteenth-century France, some of the books appear to represent the very latest culinary fashions or even to run ahead of them."[202]

In the Ottoman case, this second kind of phenomenon begins to manifest itself in an acculturation context after the onset of full-fledged westernization and from the 1870s, when cookbooks suddenly begin to abound in ultra-French recipes that could not possibly have reflected previous Ottoman practice. Before that, however, the very few menus, recipes, or cookbooks that have survived from the late eighteenth into the mid-nineteenth[203] probably reflect the first kind of traditional, lagged on-hands development (though as we shall see, not to the total exclusion of experiments).

Furthermore, recent studies have shown that these were all variations of an original, the famous *Ağdiye Risalesi,* dateable again to the eighteenth century.[204] So in two other eighteenth-century cookbooks that are assumed to be among the earliest but still later than the *Ağdiye Risalesi,*[205] when almost all the recipes involving olive oil turn out to be seafood, including: fish soup, baked scallops *(tarak külbastısı),* a stew of blennies, and scorpion-fish stewed *(papas yahnisi),* mackerel stew *(uskumru yahnisi),* sardines, pickled fish *(balık turşusu),* and caviar salad, this is likely to reflect past practice (though just how far past remains unclear). In those early cookbooks that have come down to our day, the only exceptions to this overwhelmingly marine use of olive oil are egg plant pilav *(badlıncanı pilav)* and lettuce salad *(marul salatası).* And like fish dishes, vegetable recipes in these early cookbooks too are few and far between. In the eighteenth century *Ağdiye Risalesi,* for example, only four vegetable dishes are listed (with clarified butter explicitly indicated as the cooking medium for two of them). Meanwhile, in an 1827 list of the trades and crafts in Ankara, "fish-and-olive-mongers" constitute a single group,[206] attesting to an enduring, and very strong, association between olive oil and the sea. But whether the emergence of an enhanced taste for olive oil after the conquest of Crete might have also meant a rise in fish cooking and consumption, at least by the elite or the court, so that the cookbooks in question were actually capturing a relatively recent (maybe a Mennellian 30–50 years old) development, is for the moment an open question.

Refining the "Grand Banqueting Cuisine" of the Ottoman Ruling Class

It is time, perhaps, to return to my initial course of inquiry about the nature of the Ottoman "elite diet," which must acquire its "elite" appellation not in a vacuum but relative to what the rest of society was eating. Other kinds of elite practice, certainly, were not lacking. Just as in medieval English or Italian Renaissance courts, in the Ottoman world too, members of the ruling class engaged in food exchanges among themselves, dispensed with largesse vis-à-vis commoners, and ran huge households, which placed great emphasis on preparing and serving food, as well as on its distribution, cooked or raw, among equals and the less fortunate.

"Elite Diet" versus Haute Cuisine

As I have already noted, however, the quality of the food itself is a different matter, and the vast inequalities of wealth and power implicit in all of the above do not necessarily say anything directly about how much better, or rather how differently, they were eating from the lower classes. More specifically, was the upper end of the Ottoman scale held by what could genuinely be called an haute cuisine with its expert cooks, special dishes and waiter service, accompanied by the elaboration of rules of etiquette and hospitality, of the kind that eventually developed in ancient Egypt, imperial Rome, and medieval China and India (at the beginning of the Christian era)[207]? Not every ruling class diet or set of culinary practices is (or grows into) an *haute cuisine* in this sense, and a central question for Jack Goody is "why a differentiated *haute cuisine* has not emerged for Africa, as it has in other parts of the world."[208] He contrasts the relatively undifferentiated cooking cultures of sub-Saharan African with those of the class differentiated historical civilizations of China, India, the Near East, and Europe. In the former, where a limited and localized range of ingredients was used, there was little cultural differentiation between rich and poor. The rich just ate more of the same.

In the end, Goody's argument is that specific forms of high cooking for the upper classes, as distinct from the staples of common people, develop under conditions of diversity of ingredients (based on more advanced agriculture and trade), and a sizeable class of relatively prosperous and adventurous eaters who adopt an esthetic attitude to food. How far were these conditions satisfied in, and how differentiated in the direction of a full-fledged *haute cuisine,* were the royal or the elite diet(s) of, the premodern, prewesternization Ottoman Empire?

Pilavs Galore

With or without some fish dishes cooked in olive oil, and despite a considerable amount of variation in quality, complexity, and ingredients, the food of the Ottoman court as well as of the people at large from the sixteenth to the eighteenth centuries remained largely typical of a society of pastoral origins now living on agricultural and animal products. I have already suggested, after a first look at the information from the imperial kitchen registers, that along with ratatouillelike stews, they were also eating a lot of grilled or skewered meat plus soup, rice, and cold, sweet fruit-stew *(hoşaf)* in large doses. This is borne out by what they were feasting on: an apparent abundance of dishes that upon closer scrutiny turn out to be just so many variants of a very limited range of basic ideas. In the folk memory world of Nasreddin Hoca, let us remember, *pilav* and *hoşaf* (in large quantities, or course) are the stuff that feasts are made of, and to judge by Evliya Çelebi's description of the banquets in Bitlis in 1655/1656 real-life feasts were not much different:

> Two hundred silver platters, full of culinary delights, ornamented the *meydan,* their delicate odors perfuming the brains of those attending. There were numerous kinds of *pilav*s and soups but the *pilav*s of partridge and pomegranate and various juicy and well-cooked *kebab*s were incredible.[209]

H. Reindl-Kiel has shown that a comparable variety of *pilav*s were also featured at mid-seventeenth century banquets in the Topkapı Palace: plain, with pepper and onions; with currants; with squash (or pumpkins?) and honey; with mulberries; with cracked grain, sweetened with sugar; Persian style, with red grapes; with boiled and pounded wheat; with fried meat; with ground meat.[210] A contemporary source for the magnificence of Ahmed III's reign is the *Surname-i Vehbi*[211] where the miniatures depicting the seemingly endless banqueting of the 1720 circumcision festival bear witness to the same succession of rice, chicken and meat stews, and skewers, though it is very interesting to note that fish are also being served to large numbers of people.[212] Official meals at the palace on the occasion of ambassadorial receptions or meetings of the imperial council turn up similarly uninspiring, nonadventurous menus.[213]

There is a further point. We have (i) a number of account books recording the monthly purchases of cellar stores of the grand vizier Damad İbrahim Paşa that were intended for distribution among the members of his household.[214] And we have as well as (ii) two other registers that record the purchases and contents of the cellar of his wife Fatma Sultan's royal residence.[215] Meanwhile (iii) five more documents record their outer and inner apartments together—in other words, the kitchens of both İbrahim Paşa and Fatma Sultan.[216] Some of these, moreover, coincide in terms of their time coverage: one each from (ii) and (iii) for the period 14 December 1719 to 11 January 1720, and one each from all three groups for the period 19 January to 16 February 1722. And collectively, they turn out to contain information on the distribution of "our daily bread," mutton, quality rice, clarified butter, coffee, and tallow among the members of the grand vizier's household. Notwithstanding doubts, referred to earlier, about whether some of these might have been sent down from the imperial cellars, the grand vizieral household clearly was a replica of the royal court, and foodstuffs allocated to/or procured for the servitors of a servitor of the sultan (to echo Metin Kunt's problematic of *kulların kulları*[217]) covered basically the same types that the *kapı* holding servitor-of-the-first-rank himself had access to. Once more, such practices make it very difficult to analyze the distribution pattern for the ruling elite as a whole.[218] At the same time they suggest very strongly that at this stage, and at least within the elite, one rank simply ate (or rather, received) more than another.

From Quantity to Quality in Europe

One way or the other, all this is strikingly reminiscent of Mennell's idea, mentioned earlier, that in Europe there was a medieval aristocrat stage of "a grand banqueting cuisine," which emphasized meat consumption in the form of grills and roasts "to which the various savoury and sweet made dishes provided contrast and relief"[219] though with relatively little attention to preparation and differentiated taste. Also, hierarchical differences in what people ate remained more striking than geographical ones, and the lack of both quality and localism was reflected in an absence of cookbooks (since it was not yet considered important to be able to reproduce a specific, narrowly defined and described dish in different places).[220] As a corollary eating in quantity really was distinctive. Mennell remarks that in the sixteenth and seventeenth centuries,

> there were many who seem to have been noted more for their capacity than for the refinement of their taste. Cathérine de'Medici was celebrated for her appetite and frequent indigestion. Diarists at the court of Louis XIV have left graphic accounts of the great king's prodigious consumption. Nor does he appear to have been untypical of his court. The Princess Palatine often describes the overeating of the French nobility.[221]

Then, however, there took place a gradual "civilising of appetite," which "appears to have been partly related to the increasing security, regularity, reliability, and variety of food supplies." There was, first, a sheer physical constraint:

> By the sixteenth or the seventeenth centuries, for the nobility to eat quantitatively more than they did would have been physically impossible. That was one reason for increasing demands made upon the skill of the cook in making food more palatable."[222]

"[T]he psychological basis for the elaboration of cooking in an age of plenty,"[223]

> when just as the civilising of appetite was entangled with several other strands of the civilising process, including the transformation of the table manners, so the improvement of food supplies was only the strand in a complex of developments within the social figuration which together exerted a compelling force over the way people behaved. The increased security of food supplies was made possible by the extension of trade, the progressive division of labour in a growing commercial economy, and also by the process of state-formation and internal pacification. Even a small improvement was enough to enable a small powerful minority to distinguish themselves from the lower ranks of the society by the sheer quantities they are and the regularity by which they ate them.[224]

Cookbooks, too, became popular as part of the same process(es), and by the seventeenth century a number of them were attesting to several departures from medieval cookery. As a result, "what now came to distinguish the aristocratic table was not only the abundance and riches of dishes, but their delicacy."[225] And while "extreme gluttony appears to have become the exception" by the mid-eighteenth century[226]:

> The skills of cooks . . . could be applied to stimulating the sated appetites of the glutton, but also to invention and elaboration of an endless variety of ever more refined and delicate dishes; when the possibilities of quantitative consumption for the expression of social superiority had been exhausted, the qualitative possibilities were inexhaustible.[227]

The Built-in Conservatism of the Imperial Kitchen Registers

The Ottomans had something comparable if not identical.[228] The eighteenth century catches them in a similar kind of transition, where several of the "appetite civilising" factors cited by Mennell (such as sated gluttony, pacification, or the search for qualitative expressions of social superiority) might very well have been internally operational apart from, or before, the onset of western influence. At this point, it becomes important to recognize that different, even contradictory time frames are likely to be embodied in the relatively static versus the relatively dynamic components of our documentation. Thus what emanated from the imperial kitchen probably represents a very conservative kind of record. It orginated in the relatively remote past in response to a complicated matrix of power and taste requirements and it then changed only slowly out of sheer bureaucratic inertia, so that we may suspect their *ad hoc* allocation packages to have been derived mostly, if not entirely, from a certain idea of the elite diet as defined much earlier, probably in the sixteenth century. The imperial kitchen registers, in other words, likely extended the culinary memory of the classical age, so-called, into the eighteenth century, admitting modifications (as with the seventeenth-century systematization of the full "princesshood package," or the replacement of sesame oil with olive oil as the main frying medium), but remaining not easily and immediately adjustable.

This, though, is precisely what one would expect elite household's stewards to be capable of in the marketplace, taking snap decisions in the face of novelties, and reflecting these *post hoc* in their daily, weekly, or monthly purchases, expenditures or accounts. Of course there were overlaps, as already noted. To repeat: many expensive items were regularly or irregularly supplemented by market purchases. The former did not exclude strong candidates for luxury definition (at least in quantitative terms) or even a few outright delicacies, while the latter clearly covered apparent staples.[229] Even bread straddled the line: both allocated and purchased, certainly a staple for most of the population most of the time, but at least some varieties of it figuring as a delicacy in other situations.

Among what were bought on the market for Esma the Younger, for example, were coffee, unitemized groceries, and snow and ice.[230] Beyhan Sultan's men appear to have shopped for quality flour, various kinds of bread, eggs, cheese, lemons, olive oil, and yoghurt.[231] Most of these were also covered by deliveries from the imperial kitchens to both princesses. In an undated document for Beyhan in particular, while we find (1) all the standard items in standard quantities under "state allocations,"[232] (2) another line qualifies past purchases as "what was bought when our lady was alive, many female slaves were being kept, and great the demands that had to be met, though there is no need for them now."[233] This introduces (3) another list of goods as "what is being presently turned over to the kitchen on a daily basis."[234] here again, many items from list (1) are also included in (2) and (3), though in considerably smaller quantities, except for meat, which appears to have duplicated the state allowance.[235]

At the same time we obtain a fascinating glimpse into the rigidity allocations versus the flexible adjustment, the expansion and contradiction of a royal household's "own" economy in response to the life-rhythms of patronage. In short, then, we cannot simply regard the state's standard deliveries as an index to what the Ottomans regarded as staples, thereby also defining delicacies as what elite kitchens were purchasing on the market. And yet, the possibility of particularly the latter kind of association should not be dismissed out of hand. The daily, monthly, or annual account books of the Ottoman great are not easy to work with: for one thing, they are even less systematic than the imperial kitchen registers. Because there appears to have been just one outlet for all the various compartments of a segmented household to place their orders with, purchases of all kinds of goods like furnishings, animals to be sacrificed, wigs, slippers, food, drink, Qu'ranic fascicules, and medicine boxes all end up being lumped together in the records kept by that single contact with the marketplace. Hence, too, there seems to be no pattern at all to the way they recorded food purchases. Finally, there is a very major problem of frequently leaving quantities, weights, numbers, quality, or unit prices unspecified. Even then, however, such purchase or expenditure books are better than the imperial kitchen registers in providing clues to the quality of the Ottoman diet, since it is possible to form some connections, at least, between certain dishes and all the various ingredients simultaneously being bought.

More importantly, the entire set of structures and practices underlying and giving rise to these books of purchases and accounts must have been much more likely a vehicle for (a) the search for delicacies relative to a certain threshold of basic taste or diet, and (b) innovation and transformation beyond that threshold.

An Era that Sought for Delicacies among Individual Items of Final Consumption

To start with the first of these questions, where should we look for delicacies, and in what form, at this level of taste and diet corresponding to the historical moment embodied in the eighteenth-century imperial kitchen registers, in the midst of this "grand banqueting" style of pomp and display on the table that may have prevailed through the reign of Ahmed III? We now have better context, I think, for turning to look not just at elements of what elite households were buying on their own, but also at the columns in Table 5.1a–e for purchases by the chief greengrocer (SP), for "haphazard deliveries," and for "limited deliveries on special occasions."

The case for the second of these categories would seem to be self-evident. Why should the keeper of the palace gardens send on some quail or the chief confectioner some sweet pastry, if they could not thereby hope to specially please their patrons? For the first, it is important to note that as in *iftariye* listings, what we may take to be the best fruit, vegetables,[236] dairy products, or honey are always identified by their place or origin. Thus at the higher echelons of taste, we have not just regular white cheese, but those qualified as long strip cheese; as sheep cheese; as being from Çorlu or Mudurnu; as the *peynir-i haseki* that sounds like "the favorite cheese" or "cheese fit for the royal consort," but which I have not been really able to identify or define. Olives, too, are described as broken, cured, Cretan, or from Kalamata. Most spending on thick cream comes with the source attached.[237] Annual deliveries of lemon juice from Kos[238] or mint pickles from Cairo[239] are also entered, separately, explicitly, perhaps lovingly. As for the third and last group for "special occasions," among them the *ramazaniye* deliveries loom quantitatively larger than the *iftariye*. The latter, in contrast, seem to have come with a definite emphasis on the trappings as well as the locally defined contents of precious packages.[240]

What really helps at this point is that we have detailed evidence on, and can speak of both similarities and differences in, what was distributed on these occasions to (a) two leading princesses, and (b) lesser members of their households. For the month of Ramadan in 1792, we know Esma Sultan the Younger, her mother and her husband to have *each* received as *iftariye:*

2 Saxon goblets *(Saksonya bardak)*

8 gilded English goblets *(yaldızlı İngiliz bardak)*

2 jars full of a dish flavored with sorrel *(rumex)*, rhubarb *(rheum)*, or other acid herbs *(hummaz kavanos)*

4 gilded bowls filled with assorted drinks *(eşribe-i mütenevvia yaldızlı kâse)*

4 gilded bowls filled with assorted jams *(reçel-i mütenevvia yaldızı kâse)*

3 boxes full of honey on the comb *(asel-i gümeç kutusu)*

2 Venetian style jars full of precious olives *(elmas zeytun Venedikkâri kavanos)*

2 Venetian style jars full of broken olives *(kırma zeytun Venedikkârri kavanos)*

2 Venetian style jars full of cured olives *(terbiye zeytun Venedikkâri kavanos)*

3 baskets filled with pastrami *(bastırma)*

3 baskets filled with sheep cheese *(kaşkaval)*

6 baskets full of various kind of vermicelli (pasta?) *(şeyriyye-i mütenevvia)*

3 baskets of spiced curds *(baharlı kurut)*[241]

But that same document also lists the *iftariye* allocations that were distributed to member of Esma's household. And now, while the types of food remain basically the same, they are enumerated in a very ordinary, matter-of-fact way: sugar for all the marmalades and the various drinks; rhubarb; various olives; sheep cheese; Athenian honey; cured meats; curds and assorted vermicelli.[242]

At around the same time, the relationship between the *iftariye* allocations for Beyhan Sultan and her retinue was of parallel construction. Thus the royal lady received:

9 gilded bowls *(elmastaş kâse)* full of various drinks

2 jars cut in Venetian style *kâse-i Venedik kavanos* full of quality Cretan olives

15 *kile*s of quality *kaşkaval* cheese

3 baskets of quality long-strip cheese *(dil peyniri)*

12 *kile*s of sugar

Simultaneously, members of her close retinue were treated to: sugar, sherbets, olives, *razakı* grapes, raisins, figs, Amasya plums, pastrami, sausages, cheese (generic: *peynir*) and various marmalades.[243] So in both cases, the most obvious difference between what household members or retinues and their mistresses received consisted of all those quality grades or origins, plus the wrappings or packagings for her ladyship that were described in detail. And it was this aspect or dimension of conspicuous consumption more than any other that appears to have fascinated James Dallaway, the chaplain and physician of the British Embassy in Istanbul, when he visited the Beyhan Sultan's palace at Arnavudköy. In a room built over the water so that it was possible to fish through a trap door in the middle of the floor, he says, what was served as compliments of coffee, conserves, and perfume was a truly magificent exhibition. The cups and spoons were of gold studded with diamonds, and a confection of exquisite flavor was offered, called the conserve of rubies, as well from the richness of other ingredients like pounded rubies that were part of the composition.[244]

But of course if they were pounding rubies into confectionary, those entries for "payment for gold"[245] or "the cost of gold leaf"[246] that keeps turning up in the imperial kitchen registers could also point to that ultimate culinary ostentation that does not necessarily have anything to do with taste as such: the art of cooking with gold.[247]

Increased Public Visibility—Greater Reliance on the Market

Turning to elite household purchases on the market, what immediately strikes the eye is the continuing search for quality among fresh fruits in terms of either improved strains or particular kinds of local produce, accompanied by a selective taste for a few dishes probably prepared by specific vendors or cook shops. Thus, Esma the Younger ask for melons and flaky pastries.[248] Beyhan Sultan asks for sweets, pickles, and fruit, in addition to all their bulkier purchases. Greater detail is to be found in an account book purporting to record all of Damad İbrahim Paşa's expenditures month by month for the year 1723.[249] Frequently bought for the grand vizier, it seems, were chestnuts, nuts, and pistachios; improved *(ıslah)* apples, melons, and watermelons; and then other types of fruit that, improved or not, would have to figure heavily on our list of delicacies: pears, sweet pomegranates, grapes, quinces, cherries, and oranges. The last in particular, bought from a rather vague *karşu* (the opposite shore?),[250] must have been quite a rarity for them to go to the trouble of wrapping them singly in expensive *çarçube* paper (which was the thin, transparent but durable kind used in window panes). In contrast, relatively few vegetables are mentioned: mallows, artichokes, eggplants, and tomatoes.

The difference between fruits and vegetables, of course, is that the former are (mostly) consumed whole and fresh, while the latter are intermediate goods. Is this yet another sign that there (still) was no premium on made, prepared, cooked dishes as delicacies? Perhaps all the more interesting in this regard are the even rarer hints that some ingredients are needed not in themselves but for finished or semi-finished dishes: apples and walnuts for something called *elmalıklar* (which is not easy to interpret since fruit bowls were not called by that name, but could well be *elmasiyeler*, cooked desert), and eggs for pasta *(pastacılar için yumurta)* in the Italian or modern Turkish sense. As for sweet and sour flavorings, while clotted cream, sherbet, and various kinds of jam too, were frequently bought on the market, pickles (watermelons, eggplants, and capers) were prepared at home. Some of the many items obtained on the market were sent on to the various palaces or palatial residences of the grand vizier located at different points: Saadabad, Vefa Bahçesi, Hasan Efendi Yalısı (Bebek), and Tırnakçı Yalısı (Kuruçeşme). Finally, as with flaky pastries for Esma the Younger, İbrahim Paşa appears to have repeatedly sent out for trotters from some shop(s) in the vicinity of the Süleymaniye complex.

So they did not feel that absolutely no street food was better or fit for them. In Ottoman society a household's status was marked socially, in part, by its degree of independence from the commercial cooked food establishments of the market, which catered more to the needs of other sections of the population.[251]

The data at this point are flimsily anecdotal. But could it be that such proudly self-sufficient domestic isolation was more characteristic of all-subsuming "official space" of the late fifteenth and sixteenth centuries, while reinscription of both the royal house and a growing and proliferating class of dignitaries into an increasingly vibrant and diversified Istanbul "public space" went hand in hand with their opening up for cooked food too, to the civil society institution of the market?

Some Concluding Remarks: Structure and Process at the Dawn of the New Era

And finally, how to generalize about this? To repeat, first: clearly there is something that we can identify as the culinary legacy of the classical age. Inherent in this usage, of course, are the dangers of distortion. I do not want to suggest for a moment that sixteenth-century practices somehow constituted "golden" norms, from which all subsequent movement was decay, degeneration, or decline. (A rather different view of change and development actually is implied, I would say, by the kind of analytical narrative that I have tried to sketch.) Furthermore, allowance has to be made for the possibility that we ourselves have ended up with exaggerated impressions of the uniformity and longevity of that legacy as a result of the predominance of "monumental time,"[252] frozen into the imperial kitchen registers, over the lower-down and more flexible "social time" reflected in the private, considerably more fragmented documentation.

Still, by the sixteenth century there existed an Ottoman kind of "grand banqueting cuisine" not a passive structure fitting quite closely into all the rest, but an active one, considerably helping to signify, symbolize, and reproduce the extensively redistributionist patterns and culture of that society as a whole. And secondly, the available evidence warrants the inference that what counted as delicacies for the *longue durée* of the Ottoman "grand banqueting cuisine" were not made dishes (or their ingredients) but individual items of final consumption, mostly locality-specific, and—not unlike individual human beings' personal wrappings of *kaftans*, furs, or headgear—coming in containers commensurate with the recipient's ranks or status. This is borne out by (i) what they prized most among the chief greengrocer's deliveries; (ii) the way the special *iftariye* allocations in particular were presented, especially to royal princesses and then also, less discriminatingly, to members of their retinues or households; and (iii) what quasiroyal or subroyal courts kept their eyes open for in the market. And of course, this approach to refinement is strongly consistent with what one would expect of times when quality and taste differentiation in the Mennellian sense had not yet gathered force.

More directly, if all or most of the foregoing is true, what kind of consumption world was this? As in production, so in the sphere of consumption, it was an "extensive" rather than "intensive" mode or lifestyle. More specifically, it was one in which luxury or conspicuous consumption (for example in mutton) was measured, not by a surfeit of what was placed on the table per eater (then to be partially or largely, but in any case demonstratively, thrown away), but—to repeat and paraphrase what Goody has noted about an alternative channel for culinary wealth and power messages[253]—by a surfeit of servitors fed, in calculated and standardized fashion, at the door of the lord, or rather, at a series of doors unfolding and proliferating outward from the imperial court. For the sultan and in turn the other great men of the empire, handing out food to people outside their own staff(s) in the narrow sense constituted perhaps the main form of distributing largesse and displaying munificence. That led[254] to eating, and eating up, on a massively socialized scale. So much so that once anybody became attached to the palace, there was hardly any (further) need to (keep) work(ing) for a living.

Without slipping into essentialism it is still worth considering the implications of the contrast between this sort of behavior and the kind of every man for himself ethic that accompanied the development of a possessive, acquisitive kind of individualism in western Europe. On all these points, as I suggested at the outset, instead of throwing up radically new concepts, consumption history begins to converge and fruitfully interact with elements of existing approaches or paradigms. This, then, was the general picture around the end of the seventeenth or the beginning of the eighteenth century, the background against which they looked for the fresh, the crystal-encased, or the not easily available. Of course it was not static. I have tried to show that the "classical" diet of the Ottoman elite was not strictly limited to the regularly allocated items, including goslings, pigeons, ducks, and fish along with mutton and chicken, and displaying a familiarity with most of the fruits and vegetables that we know today, such as balsam shoots, cucumbers, eggplants, gourd, or coriander. Yet for a long time, they do not appear to have done much with all these ingredients, so that their prepared dishes were rather similar as between the court and elsewhere.[255] It is considerably restricted in variety compared with the present.

Early in the eighteenth century, however, signs of change are visible along at least three main axes or dimensions (apart from the barest hint of an enhanced awareness of the market possibilities for cooked food, already noted): (1) parallel to the increased use of olive oil, the expansion not only of seafood but also of vegetable dishes; (2) the appearance of improvisation and experimentation over made dishes, often developed by amateurs from among the dignitaries, which the elite were increasingly enthusiastic to sample and to circulate into fashions; and (3) the emergence of a new kind of sociability initially around (sometimes original forms of) desert, accompanied by what was simultaneously a new phase introduced into the eating process as such, and a discrete social phenomenon arrogating its own spaces—namely coffee and sugar consumption.

But these are enormous topics in themselves, especially the first one—the secret history of vegetables in Turkish cuisine, the material on which I have had to set apart for another article. Suffice it to say for the moment, though, that given the current fame of Turkish cuisine as being very long on desserts and pastries, it cannot be insignificant that under "pastries," an eighteenth-century cookbook should have recorded all of the following as novel *(nevzuhur)* recipes: small balls of sweet carbonated batter, deep fried in very hot oil *(lokum),* the similar *lalanga* (plain and with a cheesy batter), also the similar *lokum* (not what we know as Turkish delights, but once more fried batter: plain, with eggs, or sweetened), cheese-and-flour pudding *(peynir höşmerisi),* and various flaky pastries with fillings of squash, leeks, onions, chicken, mastic, and thick cream *(kabak-pırasa-süt-sakız-soğan-tavuk böreği).* Some of these are deceptively named or confusingly repetitive, while others seem to hint at a marked rise of Balkan influence, especially in terms of the *lalanga*s, cheesy batters and the chicken or vegetable *börek* fillings.

But what is most interesting is the implication that a lot of our present standards of taste might have at most two hundred years behind them. This is also when İbrahim Paşa calls for "eggs for pasta makers," and there are other signs of experimentation, too, in the reign of Ahmed III. These include a reference to *akıtma,* a kind of crépe, which was created explicitly for the sultan in Edirne,[256] a dessert that came to be called *Nuriye* after the favorite of the local *kadı* who concocted it,[257] (and two other meat dishes named after its inventor Teşrifatî Naim Efendi[258]) seemingly pointing to the opening of a new era of innovation by upper-class literati, as described by Mennell, at the same time that cookbooks are beginning to come out into the open.

"It is perhaps not far fetched to see in cookery, a transition in style parallel to that in architecture, from the classicized baroque of France under Louis XIV to the rococo of the age of Louis XV, the elimination of excess and the cultivation of delicacy," writes Mennell.[259] For the Ottomans, it is not surprising, but absorbing nevertheless, that before the takeover of *alla franca* cooking from the mid-nineteenth century onward, when the elite opted for distinguishing itself from the ordinary folk by the partial adoption of the cuisine of prestigious foreign civilizations, in food as in so many other things it should have been the eighteenth century to witness the onset of indigenous (not to say isolated) transformations.

Glossary of Food and Other Ottoman Historical Terms

âb	water
> âb-ı gül	—rose-water: same as *âb-ı verd, gülâb, gülsuyu, mai-i verd*
> âb-ı limon	—lemon juice: same as *limon suyu*
> âb-ı verd	—rose-water: same as *âb-ı gül, gülâb, gülsuyu, mai-i verd*
aded	piece, number, head-count
ağa(s)	(in this context) leading male servants, heads of the various departments of a great household
ağnam	sheep: pl. of *ganem*
> ağnam-ı toklu	yearling rams: pl. of *toklu*
ahu	antelope, antelope-meat
akıtma	a kind of crêpe
alû	plum(s): same as *erik*
> alû-i Amasya	—Amasya plums: same as *Amasya eriği*
> alû-i can	—a variety of green plum: same as *caneriği*
> alû-i taze	—fresh plums
> Amasya eriği	—Amasya plums: same as *âlu-i Amasya*
amber	ambergris
armut	pear(s): same as *emrut*
arpa	barley: same as *şair*
arslanhane	the lion-house of the Ottoman palace
asel	honey
> asel-i Atina	—Athenian honey
> asel-i gümeç	—honey on the comb
> asel-i musaffa	—clear-strained honey
asfur	safflower, bastard saffron
ayva	quince(s)
> ayva çekirdeği	—quince seeds
badem	almonds
> badem-i huşk	—dried almonds
badıncan	eggplant: modern Turkish *patlıcan*
> turşuluk badıncan (kiler için)	—eggplants for pickling (for cellar storage)
> badıncanlı pilav	—eggplant pilav: modern Turkish *patlıcanlı pilav*
bahar	a standard blend of assorted spices
baharlı kurut	spiced and dried curds
balık	fish
> balık turşusu	—pickled fish
> balık-ı mütenevvia	—assorted fish
bamya	okra
bastırma	same as *pastırma*

baş, baş-ı ganem	(sheep's or lamb's) heads, grilled or broiled, served whole
bat	geese or ducks
benefşe	violet(s)
> benefşe şerbeti	—sherbet made of violets
beyza	egg(s): same as *yumurta*
bıldırcın	quail
biber	pepper: same as *fülfül* or *karabiber*
birun	literally, (belonging to the) outer or exterior; the "outer" apartments, intended for official or public business, and hence generally more accessible, of an Ottoman palace or palatial residence
bostancı(başı)	the chief keeper of the palace gardens
börek	flaky pastries with cheese, meat, or other kinds of filling
> kabak böreği	—with a squash or zucchini filling
> pırasa böreği	—with a leek filling
> sakız böreği	—with a mastic filling
> süt böreği	—(a dessert) with a sweet, thick-cream filling
> tavuk böreği	—with a chicken filling
börülce	black-eyed beans
buğday	wheat: same as *hınta*
bulgur	boiled and pounded wheat
bumbar	gut sausages: same as *munbar* or *mumbar*
buzcubaşı	head of the snow-and-ice procurement section of the imperial kitchen
celepkeşan	drovers or cattle-dealers quasi-forcibly contracted into supplying meat wholesale to the capital
ceviz	walnut(s)
> ceviz-i Rumî	—literally: Rumelian walnuts
çağla badem	green almonds eaten in the shell
çakır	sarcopoterium spinosum L. *(abdestbozan otu)*, used in making *nan-ı çakır*
çarçube kağıdı	a thin, transparent but durable kind of paper used in window panes, and for wrapping oranges
çerkez duhan	Circassian tobacco
çörek	(usually sweetened) round cakes or buns
dakik	flour
> dakik-i has	—quality flour
darçın	cinnamon
> darçın-ı has	quality cinnamon

DBŞM	short for *Bâb-ı Defterî Baş Muhasebe Kalemi:* the central accounting division of the imperial chancery; the name of a major collection of documents, also comprising long series of imperial kitchen registers, in the prime ministry archives in Istanbul
defne	sweet bay, laurel
defter	register, book of records
defterdar	finance minister
> defterdar-ı şıkk-ı evvel	—senior finance minister
> defterdar-ı şıkk-ı sani	—second finance minister
dil peyniri	long-strip cheese; same as *peynir-i dil*
dirhem	(Ottoman standard =) 3.207 grams
domates	tomato(es): in standard modern Turkish pronunciation
> domates dolması	—stuffed tomatoes
> domates garnitürü	—garnished tomatoes
> domates kurusu	—dried tomatoes
> domates pilakisi	—cold stew of tomatoes in olive oil
> domates salatası	—tomato salad
> domates salçası	—tomato paste
> domatesin tepsi musakkası	—large-tray tomato stew with meat
> domatesli makarna	—pasta with tomatoes
> domatesli midye pilakisi	—cold stew of mussels in olive oil, with tomatoes
> domatesli pilav	—tomato pilav
> domatesli yahni	—tomato stew
> etli kırmızı ve yeşil domates dolması	—red and green tomatoes stuffed with meat
> midyeli domates dolması	—tomatoes stuffed with mussels
dökme meyva	assorted fruits (?)
duhan	tobacco: same as *tütün;* also see *çerkez duhan* and *ıslah duhan*
dut	mulberry
> dutlı serbet	—mulberry sherbet
ebegümeci	mallow(s)
ecza (kiler için)	chemicals (for the cellar)
ekmekçibaşı	chief baker: head of the breads department of the imperial kitchens
elma	apple(s)
> elma-ı miskî	—musky apples: same as *misket elması*
elmalık	literally: apple-holder, apple orchard; but contextual meaning unclear

elmasiye	fruit jelly: a cooked dessert made with apples
elmastaş kâse	crystal bowl
emanet	literally: (placing under) trust or trusteeship: the Ottomans' way of running their relatively most centralized institutions under appointed, salaried officials (as distinct from remuneration through fiefs or tax-farming)
emin	literally: trusts or trustee: the top salaried official in charge of any institution that the Ottomans wanted to keep the tightest tabs on (including the imperial kitchens)
emrut	pear(s): same as *armut*
enar suyu	pomegranate juice: same as *nardan, nardenk*
enderun	literally: (belonging to the) inner or interior; the "inner" private apartments of an Ottoman palace, larger than but comprising and surrounding the women's quarters
enderun-i darüssaade	the Third Court(yard), also called the court of the male pages, of the Topkapı Palace: entered through the Gate of Felicity, and except for the Imperial Audience Hall just inside that gate, generally held inaccessible to anybody outside the sultan's own household, including the top dignitaries of the empire.
enginar	artichoke(s)
engür	grape(s): same as *üzüm*
erik	plum(s): same as *alû*
> Amasya eriği	—Amasya plums: same as *alû-i Amasya*
> bardak eriği	—a large, apricot-shaped variety of plum
> mürdüm eriği	—damson plum
erz	rice
> erz-i has	—fine rice, quality rice
eşribe	drinks
> eşribe-i mütenevvia	—assorted drinks
et	literally meat, flesh; in the context of Ottoman records having to do with food: always mutton
fındık	hazelnut(s)
> fındık içi	—hazelnut kernels, shelled hazelnuts
fıstık	pistachio(es)
francala	fine white bread (literally: French- or Frankish-style); same as *nan-ı francala*
fülfül	pepper: same as *biber* or *karabiber*
Galata somunu	literally: Galata bread
ganem	sheep

gendümgufte	(or *göfte* or *kufte*) broken wheat
geyik boynuzu	(powdered) deer antlers
gıda	food, foodstuff
gönderilen	literally: sent on, or delivered; an entry in allocation recipients' records for haphazard deliveries from unspecified sources
> gönderilen	—an entry in allocation recipients' records for (bostancıbaşıdan) deliveries from the chief keeper of the palace gardens
> gönderilen	—an entry in allocation recipients' records for (helvacıdan) haphazard deliveries from the chief confectioner
guşt	meat, flesh
> guşt-ı ganem	—mutton
gügercin	pigeon(s): same as *kebuter*
gül	rose
> gül reçeli	—rose jam
> gül şerbeti	—rose sherbet
> gülâb	—rosewater: same as *âb-ı gül, âb-ı verd, gülsuyu, mai-i verd*
> gülbeşeker	—rose jam: same as *gül reçeli*
> gülsuyu	—rosewater: same as *âb-ı gül, âb-ı verd, gülsuyu, mai-i verd*
harem	women's quarters, off-limits in principle to any adult, virile male other than the head of the household
haseki(s)	official royal consort(s) of the sultan
> haseki kadın	—a royal consort who has mothered a daughter
> haseki sultan	—a royal consort who has mothered a son
hınta	wheat: same as *buğday*
hıyar	cucumber(s)
> hıyar turşusu	—pickled cucumbers
hoşaf	(originally *hoşab*: "delightful water") sweetened fruit-stew, cooked with dried fruits and then eaten cold, immersed in its own plentiful juice
hummaz	red-colored sugar, used for making maternity sherbet
hummaziye	a dish flavored with sorrel *(rumex)*, rhubarb *(rheum)* or other acid herbs
hurma	date(s)
ıslah	improvement; an improved strain (used for produce)
> ıslah duhan	—improved tobacco
> ıslah elma	—improved apples
> ıslah turunç şerbeti	—sherbet made of improved bitter oranges

iç yağı	animal fat, sheep's tail fat: same as *revgân-ı pih*
iftar	the fast-breaking meal taken at sundown during the holy fasting month of Ramadan
iftariye	special allocations from the imperial kitchens designated as being for the evening's fast-breaking dinner during Ramadan
iltizam	tax-farm(ing), usually short-term
imarat	hospice, soup-kitchen
incir	fig(s)
işkembe	tripe
> işkembe-i gav	—ox-tripe
kabak	squash, zucchini; also gourd, pumpkin
kadayıf	a kind of sweet pastry
kakule	cardamom
kalıp işi has francala	best quality pan-baked white bread
kapı	literally "door" or "gate": the residence, corresponding to the rank and post, or an Ottoman dignitary, in its capacity of serving as the source of employment and livelihood for members of his extended household
kapı(sı) halkı	all the people in the service, hence eating at the "door," of an Ottoman dignitary; i.e., members of his extended household
kapıkul(lar)u/ı	servitor(s) of the sultan
kaplu fındık	unshelled hazelnuts
kar şerbeti	sherbet obtained by pouring syrup, molasses, or honey over snow
karabiber	pepper: same as *biber* or *fülfül*
karanfil	clove(s)
karpuz	watermelon(s)
kasabbaşı	chief butcher: head of the meats department under the imperial kitchens administration
kâse	bowl
kâse-i Venedik	
kavanos	jar cut in Venetian style
kaşkaval peyniri	sheep cheese, kashkaval cheese
kavanos	jar
kavata	a green, hard, and bitter variety of tomato
> etli kavata dolması	—kavatas stuffed with meat
> kavata turşusu	—pickled kavatas
> kavatanın kuşhane musakkası	—kavata stew with meat in small casseroles
kavun	melon(s)

kavun karpuz çekirdeği (kiler için)	melon and watermelon seeds (to be stored in the cellar)
kayısı	apricot(s)
> kayısı-i Şam	—Damascene apricots
kaymak	clotted cream
> kaymak-ı Üsküdarî	—(fine, or the best) clotted cream from Scutari/ Üsküdar
kazasker-i Rum	chief military judge for Rumelia
kebab	meat grilled before an open fire, in large hunks on a rotating spit, or on smaller individual skewers
kebere	caper(s)
> kebere (kapari) turşusu	—pickled capers
> turşuluk kebere (kiler için)	—capers for pickling (for cellar storage)
kebuter	pigeon(s): same as *gügercin*
kelle şekeri	loaf sugar: same as *sükker-i kelle*
kereviz	celery
> kereviz kökü	—celery root(s)
kestane	chestnut(s)
kızılcık	cornelian cherries, dogwood
kile	(standard) 20 *okka*s = 25.659 kgs; (in Istanbul, c. 1500) 24.215 kgs
kiler	cellar, pantry, store-room
> kiler-i âmire	—the imperial cellars, not parallel to but under the imperial kitchens
kiraz	cherries
KK	short for *Kämil Kepeci (Tasnifi)*: a collection of documents, classified by and hence named after Kâmil Kapeci, that constitutes a major component of the prime ministry archives in Istanbul
kiyye	(= *vukiyye* = *okka*) = 1.128 kgs
koruk	sour grapes
kudret helvası	literally: potency confectionery
kurban	beast(s) of sacrifice
kurut	dried curds
kuyûd-ı mühimmat	registers of important entries: a major collection of the prime ministry archives subsumed under MAD defterleri
kuzu	lamb
lağm	meat, flesh (more correctly *lahim*)
lağm-ı ganem	mutton (more correctly *lahm-ı ganem* or *lahim-i ganem*)

lakerda	salted and pickled fish (bonito)
lalanga	a pancake or crêpe of Balkan origin
leblebi-i şehdane	king-size roasted chickpeas (literally: as big as large pearls, or the largest bead in a rosary)
limon suyu	lemon juice: same as *âb-ı limon*
lisan-ı sevr	borage
lokma	small balls of sweet batter, deep-fried in very hot oil
MAD	short for *Maliyeden Müdevver Defterler*: registers turned over from the finance ministry, a major collection in the prime ministry archives
mai-i verd	rosewater: same as *âb-ı gül, âb-ı verd, gülâb, gülsuyu*
makiyan	chicken, poultry: same as *tavuk*
malikâne	life-farm, the life-farming system
marul	lettuce
> marul salatası	—lettuce salad
masarifat	spending, expenditure
> masarifat defter(ler)i	—any book(s) or register(s) of expenditures
matbah	(modern Turkish *mutfak*) kitchen(s), including, in organizational and therefore in conceptual terms, all subunits and spaces integral to the process of preparing and serving food
> matbah emini	—the head or chief administrator of the imperial kitchens
> matbah-ı âmire	—the imperial kitchens, comprising various departments and sections under the *matbah emini*, including the imperial cellars or storerooms, as well as all that in an accounting sense was considered to be a part thereof
> matbah-ı âmire defteri	—(pl. *defterleri*) any book(s) or register(s) kept by or under the imperial kitchens administration
maydanoz	parsley
mercimek	lentils
mevlid	religious rite in memory of a deceased person, involving the chanting of Süleyman Çelebi's Nativity Poem, where guests are also served sherbet
meyve-i huşk	dried fruits
Mısır buğdayı	Egyptian wheat
misk	musk
misket elması	musky apples: same as *elma-ı miskî*
mistat	(for wine) 9–12 *okka*s (for olive oil) 10 *okka*s
mudd	(standard) = 20 *kile*s = 513.160 kgs

muhallebi	milk and rice pudding
muhasebe	accounts, accounting
> muhasebe defteri	—book or register of accounts (for a specified period)
	an Ottoman revenue-district that could be exploited under any one of the *emanet, timar* or *iltizam* systems
muluhiye	marshmallow(s)
mum	candle(s)
mumbar	gut sausages: same as *bumbar* or *munbar*
munbar	gut sausages: same as *bumbar* or *mumbar*
muşmula	medlar(s)
mübayaat	purchases
> mübayaat defter(ler)i	—any book(s) or register(s) of purchases
nan	bread
> nan-ı aziz	—literally: "dear bread" or "cherished bread", or the same expression that would be used for saying "our daily bread"
> nan-ı çakır	—bread with *çakır* (q.v.)
> nan-ı çörek	—bread made of *çörek* dough
> nan-ı fod(u)la	—breadcake(s)
> nan-ı francala	—fine white bread, same as *francala*
> nan-ı has	—best bread, quality bread
> nan-ı sakızlı	—mastic bread
> nan-ı somun	—bread loaf
nane turşusu	mint pickles
nar	pomegranate(s)
> nardan	—pomegranate juice: same as *enar suyu, nardenk*
> nardenk (or nardeng)	—pomegranate juice: same as *enar suyu, nardan*
nişadır	salamoniac, ammonia
nişasta	starch
nohut	chickpea(s)
nuriye, sütlü nuriye	a kind of *baklava* made extra-soft by being soaked in milk, and with a more creamy filling
okka	(= *kiyye* = *vukiyye*) = 1.28 kgs
orun	ceremonial seat assigned to each tribal chief or nobleman at a Central Asian feast or banquet in symbolic recognition of his status or rank
paça	sheep's feet, trotters
palamut	bonito
palaz-ı müri	young fowl (duck, goose, or pigeon)

papas yahnisi	a mixed stew of blennies and scorpion-fish
pastırma	(convenient to render as) pastrami: spice-cured meat, actually darker, leaner, and tougher than Western pastrami
> pastırma-i Kayseri	—*pastırma* from Kayseri (= quality *pastırma*, the best kind of *pastırma*)
pekmez	grape molasses
peksimet emini	head of the biscuits division of the imperial kitchens
pelte	jello
peynir	cheese, usually plain white cheese
>peynir höşmerisi	—cheese-and-flour pudding: a sweet dessert made with unsalted, fresh cheese mixed with flour and sugar (or honey)
> peynir lalangası	—*lalanga* with a cheesy batter
> peynir lokması	—*lokma* with a cheesy batter
> peynir-i Çorlu	—(quality) cheese from Çorlu
> peynir-i dil	—cheese drawn out or coming apart in long strips
> peynir-i haseki	—literally: the favorite's cheese, or cheese fit for the royal consort
> peynir-i Mudurnu	—(quality) cheese from Mudurnu
> peynir-i tulum	—a dry kind of cheese cured inside an animal skin
pilav	the standard Ottoman-Turkish rice dish, translatable as boiled rice, but with the proviso that the rice is stir-fried in butter (and other ingredients, as the case may be) before adding water
> ab-şule	—(unidentified)
> amber	—with ambergris
> avşila	—(unidentified)
> badam	—with almonds
> büryan	—with roasted meats on top
> çilav	—plain boiled rice
> dane-i Acem, meviz-i sürh	—Persian style, with red grapes
> dane-i bulgur	—with boiled and pounded wheat
> dane-i dutlı	—with mulberries
> dane-i fülfül maa piyaz	—with pepper and onions
> dane-i kabak maa asel	—with squash and honey
> dane-i kavurma	—with fried meat
> dane-i kırma, sükker	—with cracked grain and sugar
> dane-i kıymalı	—with ground meat
> dane-i meviz-i mürg	—with currants
> dane-i sade	—plain
> dûd	—with mulberries
> fıstık	—with pistachioes
> gülnar	—with pomegranates

> hoşik	—(unidentified)
> kırma badem	—with crushed almonds
> kişniş	—with raisins
> kûfte	—with meat balls
> kûkû	—(unidentifed)
> kübeybe	—(unidentifed)
> maverd	—with rosewater
> müzafer	—with saffron
> rümman	—with pomegranates
> sanevber	—with pine-nuts
> sarımsak	—with garlic
> şille	—plain boiled and soft
> ud	—with aloes
portakal	orange(s)
rakı	Turkish anise drink, the same as the Lebanese *arak*
ramazaniye	special allocations from the imperial kitchens designated as being for/in the name of the Islamic month of fasting
reçel	jam, marmalade
> reçel-i mütenevvia	—assorted jams or marmalades
resm-i revgân-ı zeyd	olive oil dues
resm-i sabun	soap dues
revgân	oil
> revgân-ı penbe	—cottonseed oil
> revgân-ı pih	—animal fat: same as *iç yağı*
> revgân-ı sade	—clarified butter: same as *sade yağ*
> revgân-ı şir	—sesame seed oil: same as *süd yağı*
> revgân-ı zeyd	—olive oil
> revgân-ı zeyd maa zeyd	—olive oil with olives in it
> revgân-ı zeyd-i Girid	—Cretan olive oil
sabun	soap
> sabun-ı helvahane	—soap produced in the palace confectionary shop
> sabun-ı İzmir	—İzmir/Smyrna soap
> sabun-ı Trablus	—Tripolitan (Syrian) soap
sade yağ	clarified butter: same as *revgân-ı sade*
sakatat	offal
sakız	mastic
Saksonya bardak	Saxon(y) goblet(s)
salad, salluta	green salad
sarımsak	garlic

sebze	vegetable
> sebze-i huşk	—dried vegetable(s)
> sebzevat	—vegetables (pl.)
semizotu	purslane
ser pazarî	chief greengrocer, in charge of deliveries of fresh fruit and vegetables from the imperial kitchens to all beneficiaries of redistribution
simit	ring rolls
sipahi	a rank-and-file member of the Ottoman territorial cavalry, holding the lowest kind of ordinary military benefice or *timar*
sirke	vinegar
siyah turp	black radish(es)
soğan	(dry) onion(s)
sucuk	sausage(s)
sultanan-ı birun	same as *şehzadegân-ı birun*
sultanan-ı enderun	Same as *şehzadegân-ı enderun*
sumak	sumac
süd yağı	sesame seed oil: same as *revgân-ı şir*
sükker, şeker	sugar
> nebat, nevbet, or nöbet şekeri	—cane sugar (?)
> sükker-i frengî	—French (Western) sugar
> sükker-i kelle	—loaf sugar: same as *kelle şekeri*
> sükker-i minar	—(unidentified)
> sükker-i reşidî	—sugar from Rosetta/el Reşid in the Nile delta
şair	barley: same as *arpa*
şariyye, şehriyye	vermicelli
> şariyye-i mütenevvia	—assorted vermicelli (or: assorted pasta)
şamfıstığı	pistachio nuts
şehzadegân	plural term covering, according to context, not only sons but also daughters of sultans
> şehzadegân-ı birun	—married daughters of sultans who have therefore moved "out" of the (*harem* of the) imperial palace
> şehzadegân-ı enderun	—unmarried daughters of sultans who are still living "in" the (*harem* of the) imperial palace
şeker	sugar: same as *sükker*
şekerleme	candies, confectionery
şem-i asel-i sefid	white beeswax
şem-i asel-i zerd	yellow beeswax
şem-i revgân	tallow
şerbet	sherbet, a sweet fruit drink
şıra	grape juice

şir	sesame seed(s)
şölen	ceremonial feast or banquet (also see *toy*)
tahrir	a land-and-population survey, held in newly conquered provinces, as well as at intervals of a few decades thereafter, for tax assessment purposes
tarak	scallop(s)
> tarak külbastısı	—baked scallops
tarhana	preparation of dried curds and flour
tava ekmeği	the modern name for pan-baked bread
tavuk	chicken: same as *makiyan*
tavuk-ı Mısrî	turkey
tayinat	ration, allocation; what was allocated from the imperial kitchens to any royal or elite household
taze limon	fresh lemons
taze peynir	fresh (uncured) cheese
taze yağ	fresh clarified butter
tere yağ	butter
timar	the lowest rank of Ottoman military benefices, being considered sufficient for the upkeep of an ordinary cavalryman and a few accompanying men-at-arms
toklu	yearling ram: sing. of *ağnam-ı toklu*
tomata	tomato(es)—in Ottoman-Rumelian or Rumelian immigrant speech
toy	ceremonial feast or banquet (also see *şölen*)
turaç	francolin(s)
turşu	pickles
turunç	bitter orange, Sevilla orange
tuz	salt
> tuz-i Eflâk	—Wallachian salt, salt from Wallachia
türlü	ratatouille; stew of assorted vegetables
tütün	tobacco: same as *duhan;* also see *çerkez duhan* and *islah duhan*
unnap	jujube(es)
uskumru	mackerel
> uskumru dolması	—stuffed mackerel
> uskumru yahnisi	—mackerel stew
üç türlü reçel	three varieties of jam
ülüş	share of mutton assigned to each tribal chief or nobleman at a Central Asian feast or banquet in symbolic recognition of his rank; hence also: lot, share, sharing

üzüm	grape(s): same as *engür*
> çekirdeksiz üzüm	—seedless grapes
> İzmir razakı	—*razakı* (q.v.) of İzmir/Smyrna
> İzmir siyahı	—a variety of black grapes from İzmir/Smyrna
> kızıl üzüm	—red grapes: same as *meviz-i sürh*
> koruk	—sour grapes
> kuşüzümü	—currants: same as *meviz-i mürg*
> meviz-i âb	—(unidentified)
> meviz-i mürg	—currants: same as *kuşüzümü*
> meviz-i sürh	—red grapes: same as *meviz-i sürh*
> parmak üzümü	—a long kind of grape
> razakı	—large white grapes with seeds
vakıf	a pious endowment, comprising properties and/or their income streams assigned, through a formal deed considered to be inviolable under Islamic holy law, to the upkeep of some kind of religious or other public institution
valide (sultan)	the mother of the reigning sultan, who was in the position of ruling over the harem quarters of the (new) imperial (Topkapı) palace, and who would be moved from the new to the old (Beyazıd) palace if and when her son died or was deposed (hence also returning to the Topkapı if and when he happened to be reinstalled)
varak-ı asma	vine leaves
Venedikkâri kavanos	Venetian-style jar(s)
vişne	sour cherries or Morello cherries
> vişne şerbeti	—sour (Morello) cherry sherbet
vukiyye	(= *kiyye* = *okka*) = 1.28 kgs
yağ(lar)	(generic) fat(s) and oil(s)
yağlı simit	ring rolls made with shortening
yaldızlı İngiliz bardak	gilded English goblet(s)
yaldızlı kâse	gilded bowl(s)
yoğurt	yoghurt
yumurta	egg(s): same as *beyza*
zafiran	saffron
zencefil	ginger
zerde	rice pudding with saffron
zeytin, zeytun	olive(s)
> elmas zeytun	—best quality olives (?)
> kalamata zeytun	—*kalamata* olives
> kırma zeytun	—broken olives

> terbiye zeytun	—cured olives
> yağlı zeytun	—literally: oily olives (?)
> zeytun-i Girid	—Cretan olives
ziyafet	feast, banquet
> ziyafet için	—literally, "for a banquet": designation for certain kinds of special, one-off deliveries from (any section of) the imperial kitchens
> ziyafet için elvan şekerler	—assorted candies for a banquet

Notes

1. Department of Archival Research, Faculty of Letters, Istanbul University. The spadework for this paper was financed in large part by a research support grant for 1996 awarded by ARIT (the American Research Institute in Turkey), where I was able, thanks to the director, Dr. Anthony Greenwood, and the entire staff of the Istanbul branch, to take pleasant refuge. The actual writing, on the other hand, extended into a Fulbright fellowship at Harvard. Prof. Günay Kut and Mr. Turgut Kut, who have themselves been working on Ottoman food and cookbooks for a long time now, were kind enough to read an earlier draft and to offer some corrections, as well as together with Dr. Filiz Çağman of the Topkapı Palace Museum, a number of fruitful suggestions in response to my endless queries. All of these I have tried to indicate wherever appropriate. Ditto for Cemal Kafadar, who saw a later version, and along with providing much needed moral support, also gave generously of his own insights into the small-scale loci and practices of sociability in Ottoman Istanbul. Meanwhile, Halil Berktay has been sharing my ever-growing enthusiasm for consumption (including food) history, and apart from puzzling things out together, has also helped by volunteering information. So he has to go undercited, while the responsibility for all views ultimately expressed, as well as for any persisting mistakes, remains entirely my own.

2. Artan (forthcoming c).

3. Le Roy Ladurie (1981), 23–29.

4. As in Mann (1986, 1993); for another attempt at classifying types of power, see Wolf (1990), cited in Mintz (1996), 28–32. For an applied approach to power virtually as an independent variable, see McNeill (1982), which situates itself within the burgeoning military revolution literature to be referred to later (see note 183, below).

5. As represented by Richards' (1932, 1939) pioneering studies, which were followed by a growing body of research by social anthropologists including, most notably, Lévi-Strauss (1966, 1970, 1973, 1978) and Douglas (1971, 1976–77, 1977), as well as Douglas and Nikod (1974).

6. A typical example of which is Appadurai (1981).

7. As represented by Goody (1982). For critiques of Goody's book (as well as for his reply), see the *Symposium Review on Cooking, Cuisine and Class* (1989).

8. See, for example, Arnott ed. (1975); Fitzgerald ed. (1976); Chang ed. (1977); Jerome et al, eds. (1980); Farb and Armelagos eds. (1980); Fenton and Owen eds. (1981); Khare and Rao eds. (1986); Fenton and Kisbán eds. (1986); Teuteberg ed. (1992); Geissler and Oddy eds. (1993). Although the field has (gradually) been penetrated by some degree of pluralism in choice of subject, still dominant are studies on Europe in the Middle Ages. Otherwise, China is pretty much the only non-European culture whose eating and drinking habits have been studied in rather satisfactory fashion. Chang's 1977 edition of *Food in Chinese Culture* introducing many, perhaps most, of the issues that were later to be taken up at length with respect to other cultures, has remained for twenty years the most comprehensive treatment of Chinese food history, joined halfway through by Anderson (1988).

9. Tannahill (1988)[1973].

10. Thus purely for England, there have been: Wilson (1976); Johnson (1977); Burnett (1979)[1966]; Freeman (1989); Drummond and Wilbraham (1994)[1939]; Wilson ed. (1994), and many others.

11. As represented by Barkas (1975); Henish (1994)[1976]; Camporesi (1993); Simoons (1994).

12. Thus Toussaint-Samat (1992)[1987], for example, has more comprehensively covered a great(er) variety of foodstuffs. At the same time, and along with a number of popular accounts such as Pool's (1993) or more thematical undertakings such as Grimm's (1996), nowadays hardly a day passes without fresh histories of regional or national (British, French, Italian, Chinese, or Indian) cuisines and quite a few historical recipe books too, coming to light, while the explosion of interest in the field over the past decade has been evidenced also by conferences, study groups, or even exhibitions, such as the one organized by Theophano (1996).

13. For the emergence of a new historical sociology of food, also see Elias (1969) and (1982)[1978]; Murcott ed. (1983); Bourdieu (1984)[1979] and (1977)[1973]; Forster and Ranum eds. (1975) and (1979); Flandrin and Montanari eds. (1996). Particularly revealing and stimulating, at least for me, have been Revel (1982)[1979]; Goody (1982); Mennell (1996)[1985]; Mintz (1985, 1996); Flandrin (1981, 1983a, 1983b, 1992, 1996); Flandrin and Hyman (1986); and Montanari (1994), all of which may be said to have redefined the studies on European food history by drawing history, sociology, and anthropology closer together in more tightly theorized matrices. And then there are numerous studies on demography, malnutrition, hunger, and famine to try and keep

track of! The history of specific food products, such as spices, herbals, culinary poisons, etc. will be referred to in subsequent footnotes.

14. Co-edited by Maurice Aymard, Jean-Louis Flandrin, and Steven L. Kaplan, the first volume appeared in 1985. Later, Claude Grignon too joined the editorial board.

15. Notably Dyer (1989), Shammas (1990).

16. Quite dramatically reflective of all this new historical interest in consumption are Brewer and Porter eds. (1993); Bermingham and Brewer eds. (1995); Brewer and Staves eds. (1996). Nevertheless, Mintz's contribution to the first volume, on "The Changing Roles of Food in the Studies of Consumption," is the only study on food that they incorporate. Meanwhile the general title for the series has also been coopted for an all-inclusive bibliographical compilation that does have a separate section on food and diet: Brewer ed. (1991). For an example of attempts at reinterpreting long-established *topoi* (such as the Renaissance) from a consumption perspective, see Jardine (1996).

17. See the title of her recent chapter: Faroqhi (1994c), in İnalcık with Quataert eds. (1994).

18. A whole literature exists on the all-too-special nature of this case. See more in footnote 24, below. Again, most recently, see İnalcık (1994), 179–87, on the problem of feeding a gigantic city in late medieval or early modern times.

19. Artan (1993).

20. Artan (1995a, b); for a comparison also see Artan (forthcoming a).

21. Artan (forthcoming b).

22. In Brewer and Porter eds. (1993), 5.

23. See Artan (forthcoming c).

24. Notwithstanding a general awareness of just how important this question is, most research to date has tended to concentrate only on grain provisioning. On the internal grain trade in the sixteenth century, see Güçer (1949–50, 1954, 1964). For grain provisioning in the eighteenth and nineteenth centuries, when the state was playing a considerably larger role in provisioning the city by directly purchasing and setting up a grain reserve, see again Güçer (1949–1950), as well as Cezar (1978); Faroqhi (1979–80); Güran (1984–85); Alexandra-Dersca Bulgaru (1958). For more general views of Istanbul's food supplies in the sixteenth century, see two more articles by Alexandra-Dersca Bulgaru (1969) and (1983); Emecen (1989). For documentation, see Ahmed Refik, (1988a, b, c, d) and idem (H.1332/1913); also Abdurrahman Şeref (H.1336/1917). Most of this material has been summarized in Murphey (1988). For meat supply, see Cvetkova (1976); Cezar (1981); Greenwood (1988). For other foodstuffs, see Mantran (1962) and Faroqhi (1994).

25. A notable exception is the treatment of maize: Stoianovich (1951, 1966); otherwise, for coffee, we have Hattox (1985). Cf. Salaman (1985)[1949] for potatoes, and Mintz (1993) for coffee, tea, and sugar as the real luxuries in/of England in the early modern era.

26. For the history of tomatoes, in addition to general historical accounts of foodstuffs, see Corbett, (1930); Grewe (1987) 82–83; Smith (1992), 1–2; and Smith (1994).

27. Tannahill (1988)[1973], 206–7. Also see an experiment in exchanging French and English schoolchildren as narrated by Mennell (1996)[1985].

28. Redhouse (1890), 1478: "a green and very bitter variety of solanum pseudo-lycopersicon"; Şemsettin Sami (H.1318/1900), 1086: *acı ve sertçe bir cins tomata ki başlıca turşusu yapılır."*

29. These, in turn, would appear to have been at least golden or orange-colored, to judge by Tannahill's suggestion of a Moor > Mori > Amor(i) line of emendation: Tannahill (1988)[1973], 206. A botanist and medical doctor, Joseph Pitton de Tournefort (1656–1708), who traveled through the Ottoman lands at the end of the seventeenth century, recording and publishing his observations of herbs and plants, fruit and vegetables, does mention *lycopersicon* (and calls them love apples), but not *solanum pseudo-lycopersicon* in his *The Compleat Herbal* (1717–1730).

30. Transcribed by Tarım (1987). In the same original document, Başbakanlık Arşivi KK 7289 (1694–95), there is mention of other Third Courtyard deliveries of 63,000 *aded* okra *(bamya)* or 63,000 *aded* walnuts *(ceviz-i Rumî).* Though this does sound strange, it seems they actually sat down and counted the contents of the deliveries in question, albeit roughly (to judge by the round numbers involved).

31. Of course, a time lag between the actual use of a certain dish and its appearance in a cookery manuscript should be commonly assumed; see Mennel (1996)[1985], 65. Still, it seems significant that there is no mention of tomatoes of any kind or color in the earliest Ottoman recipe books that we have from the eighteenth century (the three manuscripts that are referred to as *Ağdiye Risalesi, Yemek Risalesi* and *Ali Eşref Dede Risalesi* in the secondary literature; see below, note 50). Then toward the middle of the nineteenth century, Mehmed Kâmil's *Melceü't-Tabbâhîn,* the first Ottoman cookery book to be published (H.1260/1844), suddenly includes a tomato stew *(domatesli yahni),* stuffed tomatoes *(domates dolması),* tomato pilav *(domates pilavı),* and a tomato salad *(domates salatası).* And from that time onward we encounter an increasing number of tomato dishes. My hypothesis is that the actual culinary popularization of the tomato occurred in the first half and was reflected in the cookbooks of the second half of the nineteenth century. Also significant, perhaps, in this regard is that a late nineteenth-century cookbook by Ayşe Fahriye (H.1300/1882), in presenting a few *kavata* recipes for the first (and last) time,

also makes a clear distinction between *kavata,* as in a *kavata* stew with meat in small casseroles *(kavatanın kuşhane musakkası); kavatas* stuffed with meat *(etli kavata dolması),* and pickled *kavatas (kavata turşusu),* on the one hand, and *domates* on the other, as in more than ten separate dishes, including tomato stew *(domatesli yahni),* tomatoes stuffed with mussels *(midyeli domates dolması),* a large-tray tomato stew with meat *(domatesin tepsi musakkası),* red and green tomatoes stuffed with meat *(etli kırmızı ve yeşil domates dolması),* garnished tomatoes *(domates garnitürü),* a cold stew of mussels in olive oil with tomatoes *(domatesli midye pilakisi),* a cold stew of tomatoes in olive oil *(domates pilakisi),* pasta with tomatoes *(domatesli makarna),* tomato pilav *(domatesli pilav),* tomato salad *(domates salatası),* dried tomatoes *(domates kurusu)* and tomato paste *(domates salçası).* As already indicated, there is no further mention of *kavata* in later cookbooks, and neither does it appear in a most helpful dictionary of plant names by Bedevian (1936). None of this undercuts my hypothesis, advanced in the main text, that the switch from *kavata* to *domates* was well under way before published cookbooks, which therefore would have mostly codified the victory of the tomato, while only Ayşe Fahriye's may be said to have preserved a distant memory of the earlier coexistence of *domates* with *kavata.*

32. Başbakanlık Arşivi DBŞM. MTE 11333 (1774–75).

33. Melling (1819).

34. Much less likely are bulbous roots like onions or potatoes, which they would have had to dig for—and in any case, potatoes began to be planted only in 1842, says Turgut Kut, pers. comm. For the produce of royal gardens in the sixteenth century, see G. Necipoğlu (1997).

35. Pers. comm. from Dr. Filiz Çağman, whose grandmother, Makbule Öğütmen, was still relating in the early 1980s how *her* grandmother had told her that they had "used to eat only green tomatoes in Edirne." This is roughly dateable to the 1890s.

36. Again: Turgut Kut, pers. comm.

37. Yerasimos (forthcoming).

38. Rodinson (1949). Waines and Marin (1994) list numerous studies preceding Rodinson which, however, were devoted to medieval Arabic cuisine only.

39. Rodinson (1965).

40. Also, as noted by Zubaida and Tapper, while scholars such as Waines (1989, 1994), Heine (1982, 1988), Marin (1994), Perry (1988), and a few others have continued to work on medieval Arabic cuisine, "there is no equivalent cluster of scholarly work on the food of the early modern and modern periods in Middle East history. Rodinson devotes a few pages of his survey to cookbooks appearing in Turkey, Egypt, and Syria in the nineteenth and early twentieth centuries. Some of these are particularly their native food cultures,

and partly because they give accounts and adaptations of European foods." See Zubaida and Tapper eds. (1994), 4, 5.

41. Ashtor (1975)[1968].

42. Waines, İnalcık, Burton-Page (1991), 807–15.

43. Marin and Waines eds. (1994) and Zubaida and Tapper eds. (1994). Both volumes originated from conferences, Xàtiva (1991) and London (1992) respectively.

44. Fragner (1994a, b).

45. Rosselló-Bordoy (1994); Rubiera Mata (1994); Gardia (1994); Diouri (1994).

46. For the most up-to-date sample, see Achaya (1994).

47. Uzunçarşılı (1945).

48. Barkan (1962–63a, b, c); idem (1971); idem (1979). All of these studies were based on documents from İstanbul Belediyesi Kütüphanesi, Muallim Cevdet no. 0.91; Başbakanlık Arşivi KK 7270 and MAD 1954.

49. See note 42 above; Inalcık's section covers pp. 809–15.

50. Respectively: *Tarihte 50 Türk Yemeği*, and *Fatih Devri Yemekleri.* Also misleading is the title of another book by Ünver which represents a nineteenth-century fire map as a map of waterways belonging to the reign of Bayezid II (1481–1512): *Fatihin Oğlu Bayezid'in Su Yolu Haritası Dolayısıyla 140 Sene Önceki İstanbul*, Istanbul, 1945. Nevertheless, with this as well as through his (1941, 1953) studies of food distribution through pious foundations, Ünver may be admitted to have created an interest in the question of historical recipes as such. For historical recipes published since then, see Sefercioğlu (1985); Günay Kut (1984, 1986, 1987a, 1987b, 1988); Halıcı (1992). For general bibliographical information on printed Ottoman cookbooks, see Turgut Kut (1985, 1990).

51. Koşay and Ülkücan (1961); Koşay (1982); Genç (1982a); Köymen (1982); Cunbur (1982); Paviot (1991); Reindl-Kiel (1995); Terzioğlu (1992). Specifically for protocol and menus, see Kütükoğlu (1995); Genç (1982b); for table manners, see Cunbur (1990); Gökyay (1978, 1985). For the relationship between food history and the history of literature, see Gökyay (1987). For the relationship between food history and the history of medicine, see Sarı (1982); Erdemir (1991); Özakbaş (1996).

52. See, in particular, Kafadar (forthcoming a). I am grateful to Cemal Kafadar for allowing me to consult his transliteration of a particular *hakaretname* or "Guide to Bad Manners" that he has been preparing for publication. For a study of a different version of the same manuscript, see Develi (1997).

53. Faroqhi (1995).

54. Günay Kut (1996).

55. KK stands for the Kâmil Kepeci classification of the prime ministry archives; DBŞM stands for the central accounting office of the imperial chancery *(Bâb-ı Defterî Baş Muhasebe Kalemi)*, and MAD is short for documents transferred from the ministry of finance *(Maliyeden Müdevver)*. Included therein are the *kuyud-ı mühimmat*, i.e., the registers of important entries, so-called.—The imperial kitchen registers themselves are of various kinds: some are arranged by individual recipients but others by groups; some pertain to special arrangements for various banquets or other forms of temporary distribution; some show the accounts and allocations of the *matbah emini* himself, and others the accounts and allocations of related offices like those of the *ekmekçibaşı* (dealing with bread), the *kasabbaşı* (dealing with meat), the *buzcubaşı* (dealing with snow and ice for cooling and preserving), the *peksimet emini* (dealing with biscuits), and the *ser pazarî* (dealing mostly with fresh fruits and vegetables).

56. Bostan (1995).

57. It is worth noting that Uzunçarşılı's, Barkan's and İnalcık's archival documents on the imperial kitchen come from the Kâmil Kepeci classification mentioned in note 55, above, which in the interval 7270–7388 lists some 100 registers for the period in question.

58. Artan (forthcoming c).

59. Literally: what was distributed "for the holy month of fasting" in general, and what was designated more closely as being distributed "for the evening's fast-breaking dinner" in particular. For the customs relating to these, see Günay Kut (1996).

60. For types of produce or allocation by groups of commodities, see note 55, above.

61. I myself have located a few more at the İstanbul Büyükşehir Belediyesi Atatürk Kütüphanesi Muallim Cevdet Manuscript Collection: MC B.19 (an account book for a certain Nasuh Paşa, dated H.925–1022); MC B.12 (another account book, dated H.1183); MC B.11 (an account book for the imperial palaces during the reign of Osman III); MC B.14 (an account book for Hafız Ali Paşa, dated H.1227).

62. Goody (1982), 99.

63. Goody, *loc cit.* For an attempt in the direction of defining, and differentiating between, the concepts of elite diet, cuisine, and *haute cuisine,* see Freeman (1977), 144, who suggests that as against ordinary traditions of cooking, the development of a cuisine implies (1) the use of many ingredients (including some which are not naturally produced in a given locality); (2) no exclusive reliance on a single tradition but selecting from, amalgamating, and organizing the best of several traditions; (3) the presence or emergence of a sizeable corps of critical, adventuresome eaters, not bound by the tastes of their native region and willing to try unfamiliar food.

64. Cf. Goody (1982), 374–75, quoting the observation of a nineteenth-century traveler, d'Abbadie, in Ethiopia: "A Lord of even mediocre importance names his seneschal, his provost, his guards, a foreman of domestics, a chief baker, a butler, a squire, and various captains and pages; then he sets up a hierarchy often in ridiculous proportion to his position."

65. Artan (1989).

66. Artan (forthcoming c).

67. Artan (forthcoming c and d).

68. Artan (forthcoming c).

69. A notable exception, which I intend to go into as a separate study, is evidence on the cellar stocks at the royal residence of Fatma Sultan, Ahmed III's daughter given in marriage to Nevşehirli İbrahim Paşa: Başbakanlık Arşivi DBŞM. MTE 10975 (14 December 1719, 11 January 1720) and Cevdet Saray 3972 (19 January, 16 February 1722); see note 130, below.

70. Mertes (1988), 108.

71. Dyer (1989), 63; see also Dyer (1983).

72. Mennell (1996)[1985], 56.

73. Mennell (1996)[1985], 40, 45.

74. For *kudret helvası (manna querina)* also see Günay Kut (1985), 182.

75. Mennell (1996)[1985], 127–33.

76. Artan (forthcoming c), based on Başbakanlık Arşivi MAD 7398, MAD 1827, MAD 5356 (all dated 1703).

77. Artan (forthcoming c).

78. Artan (forthcoming c), based on Başbakanlık Arşivi DBŞM. MTE 11161 (1756–57); MTE 11451 (1784–1803); MTE 11202 (1771–?); MTE 11204 (1758–1775); MT 11291 (1769); MTE 11574 (1807); MTE 11745 (nd); MTE 11761 (nd).

79. Artan (forthcoming c), based on Başbakanlık Arşivi KK 7237 (1687) and KK 7238 (1688), as well as DBŞM. MTE 11161 (1756–57).

80. Once more it is interesting to note, in this connection, that the name for one variety of Ottoman bread entering our lists, *nan-ı aziz,* literally "[our] dear [or cherished] bread," is close in meaning to "our [or one's] daily bread."

81. In Turkish: *ekmeğini yediğin kapıya hiyanet etmemek.*

82. While standard dictionaries identify *çakır dikeni* as burdock *(arctium tomentosum),* also known as *dulavrat otu* (synon. *cappatomentosa*) whose dried roots *(radix Lappae)* were used in the treatment of gout (*nikris* or *damla hastalığı*), the *çakır* that went into the making of *nan-ı çakır* appears to have been the plant

that was also known as *abdestbozan otu (sarcopoterium spinosum L.)*; a close relative is known as *boğa dikeni* or *deve dikeni eryngium carupertre L.)*. Once more I am grateful to Turgut Kut for providing me with this information.

83. For all of the above, concerning exceptional varieties of bread distributed either as *ramazaniye* and/or *iftariye* during the holy month of fasting, see: DBŞM. MTE 11161 (1756–57).

84. Topkapı Sarayı Arşivi D. 247/120 (1809).

85. Topkapı Sarayı Arşivi E. 247/132 (nd).

86. Ancient sources already record a great variety of bread. In the *Onomasticon* of Amenope, for example, forty items starting with flour, and in the Papyrus Harris thirty forms of bread and cake are to be found, while Athanaeus enumerates seventy-two different types of bread made in Greece. The *Onomasticon* of Amenope (twentieth dynasty, c. 1000 B.C.), is a document which purported to include the name of everything that existed in the world, and most of these entries have a determinative, says Goody, that shows them to be kinds of pastry, bread, or cake made from cereals. The Papyrus Harris is dated to c. 1200 B.C. The work of Athanaeus, a native of the Egyptian town of Naucratis, dated to A.D. 200, is our earliest surviving culinary treatise. For all these, see Goody (1982), 100, 103.

87. The only exception is Balta (1994). For bread in the Middle Eastern context, see Waines (1987). For comparison, see Kaplan (1976, 1984, 1996).

88. Pulaha and Yücel eds. (1988), 35ff.

89. Camporesi (1989)[1980].

90. Cited Murphey (1988), 242.

91. Murphey (1988), 242, claims that "in the Ottoman empire there was a clear awareness of the direct correlation between the diet and the productivity of workers or the stamina and forcefulness of enlisted soldiers." He goes on to argue that "the consistent successes of the Ottomans in battle during the sixteenth century had been linked with quantity and quality of army provisioning even more closely than with tactical innovation or modern artillery." He then tries to estimate the caloric value of these rations, as well as their cost according to the price regulations of 1640. Also see İnalcık (1994), Index entries on rice.

92. Dyer (1989), 58.

93. Elias (1978), 118.

94. Elias (1978), 118—leading into a whole discussion of carving. The carving at the table of a lord (as distinct from cooking in the kitchen) played a very prominent part in the life of princely courts where (when the lord was not doing it himself) the office of the carver was reckoned as among the most honorable.

95. Goody (1982), 138–39.

96. Dyer (1989), 60.

97. See, in this connection, İnalcık (1994), 37–41 ("Nomads and the Economy"); 158–162 ("The Rural Landscape and the Settlement of Nomads"); and 271–311 ("The Black Sea and Eastern Europe"). For the extension of nomadic pastoralism into suitable terrain northwest of the Black Sea, and the importance this region then acquired for Istanbul's meat supplies in particular, also see Index references to Dobruja and Varna.

98. For the preference for mutton in the Middle East see Ashtor (1975), 145–47; Faroqhi (1984), ch. 9 (including map). But for a preference for mutton over beef (by the middle classes) in England, too, in the nineteenth century, see Freeman (1989), 194–95.

99. Thus a list of edible meats in the *Tabiât-name*, a medical treatise in verse composed for Umur Bey of the House of Aydın in the first half of the fourteenth century (of which more below), includes, in addition to the familiar mutton, beef, hens, and chicken, and pigeons: horse-meat, camel-meat, antelope-meat *(ahû)*, francolins *(turaç)*, hares, water-fowl (*bat*: ducks and/or geese), various bird *kebabs* as well as doves, quail, and sparrows listed separately, plus brains, trotters, and bone marrow.

100. Greenwood (1988), 8. The author adds that where he has run across figures distinguishing between sheep and goats, the proportion of goat flesh has been small, generally less than ten percent.

101. Elias (1978), 118; Goody (1982), 139ff.

102. Faroqhi (1984), 222 and note 6.

103. Greenwood (1988), 8.

104. İnalcık (1994), 179–87.

105. This, in turn, is brought further down by Yerasimos (1994) to as low as 200,000.

106. Greenwood (1988), 11–12. A discrepancy crops up at this point: he first gives 10,000 for all four, but then goes on to make his final calculation (see below) on the basis of 15,000 overall. So initially, he must have meant 10,000 for the other three (though this does seem very high).

107. Greenwood (1988), 15.

108. Greenwood (1988), 17.

109. See notes 90–91 above, as well as Greenwood (1988), 15.

110. Greenwood (1988), 15.

111. İnalcık after Barkan (1962–63 c).

112. Seventeenth-century travelers' estimates of Topkapı palace consumption include Baudier (1632): 200 sheep and 100 lambs a day, or 106,200 per year; and Tavernier (1675): 500 sheep a day, or 177,000 a year. Both are quoted in Eremya Çelebi Kömürciyan (1988) (1952), 112–16. A mid-seventeenth-century Ottoman source, the descriptive *Kavanin-i Osmaniyye* utilized by Greenwood (1988), 15, mentions 300 sheep per day, or, as with Baudier, 106,200 sheep per year.

113. Greenwood (1988), 13.

114. Greenwood (1988), 13 and Appendix F on "State-dependents' Mutton Consumption," 285–87.

115. Greenwood (1988), 14 and note 13.

116. Greenwood (1988), 14.

117. Greenwood (1988), 14 note 3.

118. See the documentary evidence set out in note 78, above.

119. Barkan (1979); see Greenwood's (1988) sources for Table 1.

120. I must emphasize that there is no error here: the Ottoman chancery actually used the word *şehzade(gân)* to designate not only princes but also princesses, as often becomes clear from the context; also see Barkan (1979).

121. Artan (forthcoming c).

122. In 1574 Mihrümah Sultan received 720 heads of sheep for the whole year, which comes to 20.33 *kıyye*s (or approximately 26 kilos). Lesser princesses in the eighteenth century received 15 or 7 *kiyye*s per day. So far I have been unable to find many references to sultans' mothers', princes', or top bureaucrats' standardized meat allocations. The only exceptions are two chief butchers' *(kasapbaşı)* registers where daily meat allocations for a long list of princesses and dignitaries, including the royal prince *(şehzade-i şehriyarî)*, the sultan's former son-in-law *(damad-ı esbak)*, the head of the royal mint *(emin-i darphane)*, the chief steward of the palace *(vekilharç ağa)*, the chief keeper of poultry *(ser makiyan)*, the accountant for the royal equerries *(defter[dar]-ı rikab)*, the chief *kadı* of Istanbul *(kadı-ı Istanbul)*, the grand vizier's deputy for Istanbul *(kaymakam)*, the city prefect for Istanbul *(şehremini)*, etc., are recorded: Başbakanlık Arşivi DBŞM. MTE 11975 (27 May–24 June 1770), distribution in Ramadan of 1760, see DBŞM. KSB 11981 (17 April–16 May 1760).

123. Artan (forthcoming c.)

124. Greenwood (1988), 14 note 13.

125. Necipoğlu (1991), 69–72; for food symbolism, see especially pp. 19, 55, 61, 71–72.

126. As presented and discussed in Artan (forthcoming d).

127. Ashtor (1975), 146.

128. Artan (forthcoming c); Artan and Berktay (forthcoming).

129. Baudier (1626), 158. This makes interesting comparison with the perennial autumn slaughter in England: Dyer (1989).

130. See Artan (forthcoming d): based on Başbakanlık Arşivi DBŞM. MTE 10975 (14 December 1719–11 January 1720) and Cevdet Saray 3972 (19 January–16 February 1722)—the two account books, already referred to in note 69 above (in the course of the discussion on the 12:K column of Table 5.1.

131. This is from an annual purchase register for the grand vizier: Başbakanlık Arşivi MAD 19771 (1723–24).

132. See note 99, above.

133. A rare example of fish transactions is found in the 19 January–16 February 1722 account book for Fatma Sultan (see notes 69 and 130 above), where an unspecified amount of fish is listed as having cost 1,200 *akçes*. Likewise, one of the monthly registers corresponding to the same period records a single entry, for Damad İbrahim Paşa, of fish worth 6,000 *akçes*: Başbakanlık Arşivi Cevdet Dahiliye 6612. Also, there was a flourishing fishing sector and a certain market for dried fish, which one might expect to have been Greek-dominated. For a fishery (or weir: *dalyan*) register, see Başbakanlık Arşivi KK 7451 (H.1191/1777). But a seventeenth-century traveler notes that fish were not allowed into the palace: Baudier (1626), 133–136. It seems that fish were enjoyed as a delicacy at Istanbul's brethren tables, comprising petty shop-keepers and artisans *(esnaf)*, middling members of the military-administrative class, and tradesmen like spice-vendors, grocers, bakers, book-binders, quilt-makers, and others. Thus in the diary (dated 27 August 1661–13 July 1665), of a dervish—studied both by Gökyay and Kafadar—we come across several references to fish. In addition to listing the participants at dinner parties by name and assigning numbers to each name showing precisely how many brethren there were, Seyyid Hasan catalogued the menus too, and enumerated each item indicating the order in which each dish was served: Gökyay (1985), 132; Kafadar (1989), 142–143. Gökyay concludes that fish did not figure very highly in these brethren tables, which brought members of the elite and the lesser elite together. But dishes like grey mullet soup or (generic) fish soup, stuffed mackerel, stuffed red mullet, or (generic) stuffed fish, deep-fried red mullet, blue fish, and aterina would seem to reflect no lack of sophistication in seafood, although they do occur less frequently than the skewered meats, stews, stuffed vegetables, *böreks* and *pilavs* that made up the bulk of these banquets. On the other hand, royal banquets honoring foreign embassies seem to have more frequently included fish in the menus. A practice that we do not know much about is that of allocating food to embassies too, out of the imperial kitchens. But for a record of the fresh fish, salted fish, cod, and olive oil included in the allocations slated for the embassies of

Muscovy and Prussia, see Başbakanlık Arşivi KK 7312 (1756–57); also see Itzkowitz and Mote (1970), 27–31.

134. Selim III, Başbakanlık Arşivi DBŞM. MTE 11333 (1774–75). For *ruz-ı Kasım* and *ruz-ı Hızır,* see Redhouse (1890).

135. Başbakanlık Arşivi, DBŞM. MTE 11161 (1756–57).

136. Başbakanlık Arşivi, DBŞM. 1716 (1746–47).

137. Başbakanlık Arşivi, DBŞM. MTE 11451 (1784–1803); the sheikh of the Tekke-i Kasımpaşa appears to have received regular favors from Damad Ibrahim Paşa: Başbakanlık Arşivi MAD 4885 (1723–1726).

138. Artan (forthcoming c). We know, for example, that some of the middling bureaucrats and *ulema* received 5 *kıyye*s of mutton daily and that most of the lesser state dependents too, were given meat in varying quantities according to their rank. As already indicated, moreover, we cannot, at this point, a prioristically exclude the possibility that some members of the grand vizieral households—for some of which we have complete lists of individual allocations though from unspecified sources—might have been directly benefiting from imperial kitchen handouts.

139. Duby (1974), 17–21.

140. Rodinson (1965), 1057.

141. Zubaida and Tapper eds. (1994), 43. At the same time, however, they seem to imply that the Ottoman Empire was to some extent acting like a framework, an umbrella of adoption, systematization and hence of dissemination for new tastes.

142. This is an important theme that seems to have emerged from especially the first two early Ottoman papers read at "The Ottomans and the Sea" conference, Cambridge, 29–30 March 1996: Elizabeth Zachariadou, "Monks and Sailors under the Ottoman Sultans"; Catherine Otten, "Relations between the Aegean Islands and the Turks in the Fourteenth and Fifteenth Centuries." Pers. comm. Halil Berktay.

143. As an example, see İnalcık (1994), 37–38 on the development of carpet production in the hands of Turcoman nomads settling in the mountains and valleys of the Aegean hinterland.

144. For numerous examples, see Kahane and Tietze (1958); for more popular reading about fish names, see Alan Davidson (1981).

145. A point made strongly by Musset (1975).

146. Zubaida (1994), 42–43.

147. Zubaida and Tapper eds. (1994), 23–24. Their perception of a very limited use for olive oil in present-day Turkey seems to me to have been

based on inadequate observation or historical analysis. For olive oil in the larger Ottoman Empire, see, for example, Doumani (1995); for the way it entered into international trade as a major commodity, see numerous references vis-à-vis particular regions and trade routes in İnalcık's (1994) trade chapters, 179–379.

148. For olive groves and related sectors in Palestine, for example, see Singer (1994).

149. İnalcık (1994), 187.

150. İnalcık (1994), 187, as well as Table 1: 36, 180–81. For the Syrian olive groves, also see pp. 157 and 164, as well as Faroqhi (1994), 501 in the same volume.

151. Michael Fontenay, in a paper, "Le commerce des Occidentaux dans les éschelles du Levant vers la fin du XVIIe siècle" that he read at the 4–9 July 1994 Symposium in Tours on *Chrétiens et Mussulman à la Renaissance,* noted that by 1687–1688, what Western merchants were buying up in the Easter Mediterranean were basically local raw materials including olive oil for soapmaking; this new orientation away from the traditionally consumption-oriented trade in luxuries of the Middle Ages was a decisive moment, he argued, in the (further) development of capitalism in the West and the consequent peripheralization of the Eastern Mediterranean.

152. Hakluyt cited by Braudel, and later by Faroqhi (1994), 364, 370–71, 377.

153. Baudier (1626), 133–36.

154. Faroqhi (1994), 509–10.

155. McGowan (1994), 727.

156. Başbakanlık Arşivi KK 7289 (1684–1685).

157. McGowan (1994), 697.

158. The long war in Crete began in June 1645 and ended in September 1669. For the Ottoman land regime in Crete, see Greene (1993), 74–88; for tax revenue and the new provincial elite, see *ibid.,* 90–97.

159. Greene (1993), 24–26. "Travelers to Crete invariably marvelled at the variety and abundance of the crops that the rich soil of the island produced," says Greene, going on to cite the Dutch mercenary John Struys's 1656 description of the grapes of Crete.

160. On fiscalism, see İnalcık (1970); Genç (1975); İnalcık (1994), 44ff. citing van Klaveren.

161. İnalcık (1994), 212ff.

162. Greene (1993), 26–30.

163. Greene (1993), 33–34: Cretan merchants brought citrus juices to the Ottoman capital and came back with dried fish and caviar.

164. Greene (1993), 33.

165. Greene (1993), 35–43.

166. Greene (1993), 38.

167. Greene (1993), 85.

168. Greene (1993), 221.

169. Mantran (1962), 490.

170. Greene (1993), 183.

171. Greene (1993), 190–200.

172. Greene (1993), 196.

173. John Mocenigo cited by Greene (1993), 197.

174. Stoianovich and Baladie cited by Greene (1993), 197, notes 84, 85, 86. A *mistat* was initially used by the Venetians, and then also by the Ottomans who retained preconquest practice, to measure both wine and olive oil. A *mistat* of olive oil was worth 10 *okkas*, a *mistat* of wine between 9 and 12 *okkas*, depending on the place: Greene (1993), 227, note 55.

175. Green (1993), 197–98, note 88 (citing Masson): "Indeed, the French consuls in Crete were fond of saying that without the French demand for olive oil, the island would be ruined."

176. Greene (1993), 184.

177. See note 151 above (on Fontenay); also see Greene (1993), 217: "The French in Crete concerned themselves with the export of raw materials, particularly olive oil since it was so vital to their soap-making industry."

178. For the failure of the fiscalist and provisionalist Ottoman "welfare state" to develop some such notion (and hence to defend itself or the economic space under its control against the mercantilist West's predatory practices), see İnalcık (1994), 44–54, 188–217.

179. Greene (1993), 217.

180. İnalcık (1994), 51.

181. From R. G. Asch's preliminary paper submitted to the Fiesole workshop, "Court as an Economic Institution," cited in Artan and Berktay (forthcoming).

182. Heywood writing on Kandiye in the *Encyclopaedia of Islam*, cited by Greene, (1993), 184.

183. From among a rapidly growing literature, see, as some useful landmarks or summaries: McNeill (1982); Parker (1988); Black (1991); Downing (1992).

184. Thematized in the opening section of Cezar (1986).

185. Artan (1993), 198.

186. Greene (1993), 198.

187. Greene (1993), 198.

188. Artan (1993), 70–72.

189. See note 153, above.

190. Yet another candidate might have been almond oil. But while almonds, often raised side by side with olives, do show up in imperial kitchen allocations and despite their rarity appear to have been used in numerous dishes, almond oil is somehow never mentioned.

191. Artan (forthcoming c).

192. Artan (forthcoming c). The relevant documents are İstanbul Belediyesi Kütüphanesi, Muallim Cevdet Manuscript Collection MC 0.91; Başbakanlık Arşivi KK 7270 and MAD 1954 in Barkan (1979).

193. Artan (forthcoming c). The relevant documents are Başbakanlık Arşivi KK 7237 (1687); KK 7238 (1688) and KK 7241 (1703).

194. Artan (forthcoming c). For the relevant documents, see note 78 above.

195. Artan (forthcoming c). The relevant document is Başbakanlık Arşivi KK 7289 (1694–95).

196. See note 190 above. For this shift from *revgân-ı zeyt*, see Başbakanlık Arşivi DBŞM. MTE 11202, 11204 and 11451 in particular. At an earlier stage in my research I was puzzled by the term *süd yağı*, which seemed to alternate with *revgân-ı şîr* in my documentation. Believing that the two could not possibly be the same, I was deluded into hypothesizing that they must have been using (allocating) butterfat in alternation with sesame oil. Now, however, I am most grateful to Prof. H. Sahillioğlu for informing me that the two were indeed the same thing (i.e., sesame oil), and that *süd yağı* was nothing but a scribal misnomer resulting from the increasing colloquial use of *süd* for *şîr*, based on the double meaning of *şîr* (both milk and sesame) in the first place. There was a marked tendency toward linguistic Turkicization in the eighteenth century, and when confronted with something like *revgân-ı şîr* some simplifying scribes would be tempted to put down *süd yağı* without stopping to think as to whether it might be the other *şîr* or not. This is the same process that is reflected in the (unambiguous) evolution of rosewater from *mai-i verd* to *ab-ı verd, ab-ı gül,* and finally to *gül suyu.*

197. Başbakanlık Arşivi DBŞM: MTE 11202 (1758–1760); MTE 11204 (1758–1775); MTE 11451 (1783–1803).

198. See Artan (1993, 1996) for examples of such patronage networks.

199. Topkapı Sarayı Arşivi D. 3219 (1794–1795).

200. See three registers of purchases for Beyhan Sultan: Topkapı Sarayı Arşivi D. 874 (1777–1783); D. 842 (1788–1799); D. 3017 (1793–1821).

201. Thus in the winter of 1719, while Fatma Sultan bought 102 *kıyye*s of (one kind of) olive oil for 28 *guruş*, on another occasion she paid almost twice as much for only 11 *kıyye*s of (presumably another kind of) olive oil. It is tempting to assume that this more expensive stuff was intended to be used at the table. In yet another transaction, moreover, she paid 36 *guruş* for 15 *kıyye*s of oil with olives in it: see the aforementioned register of Fatma Sultan, Başbakanlık Arşivi DBŞM. MTE 10975 (14 December 1719–11 January 1720). For different qualities of olives and olive oil, also see Başbakanlık Arşivi KK 7289 (1694–95) as well as Beyhan Sultan's account book, Topkapı Sarayı Arşivi D. 874 (1777–1783).

202. Mennell (1996)[1985], 65.

203. For a recent overview of the materials for the history of food in the Ottoman world, once more see Günay Kut (1996).

204. For two overviews of this literature, see T. Kut (1985, 1990).

205. Sefercioğlu (1985); Halıcı (1992).

206. McGowan (1994), 698.

207. Goody (1982), 115, based on Prakesh, *Food and Drinks in Ancient India* (1961), 100.

208. Goody (1982).

209. Dankoff (1990), 116–17. Dankoff has been able to find explanatory names or equivalents for most but not all of the pilavs enumerated by Evliya Çelebi for this banquet, coming up with the following varieties: with saffron *(muzaffer)*, plain boil rice *(çilav)*, with roasted meats on top *(büryan)*, with mulberries *(dûd)*, plain boiled and soft *(sille)*, with pomegranates *(rümman)*, with aloes *(ud)*, with ambergis *(amber)*, with meat balls *(kûfte)*, with pistachios *(fıstık)*, with crushed almonds *(kırma badem)*, and with raisins *(kişniş)*; it is not clear, however, what *ab-şule, kûkû, maştaba, kiji* or *lakise* refer to. At a later banquet thrown by the Khanım Sultan too, Evliya accounts for more than twenty different kinds of *pilav*, all distinctly named and described, including some that appear for the first time, and of these Dankoff (1990), 308–9, can identify the ones with pomegranate *(gülnar)*, with garlic *(sarımsak)*, with rosewater *(maverd)*, with almonds *(badam)*, and with pine-nuts *(sanevber)*, but not *kübeybe* or *hoşik* or *avşıla*.

210. Reindl-Kiel (forthcoming).

211. See Koçu (1939) and Atıl (1969). Another *surname* for that same festival of 1720 too provides very little culinary detail, simply mentioning rice, rice pudding with saffron, sherbet, coffee, and rosewater as being served to dignitaries' retinues; see Kızıltan (1987).

212. Earlier examples of banquet scenes are found in sixteenth-century manuscripts such as the *Nusretname* (Topkapı Sarayı Kütüphanesi, H. 1365, Nusretname, fol 134b); *Kitab-ı Gencine-i Feth-i Gence* (Topkapı Sarayı Kütüphanesi R.1296, fol 48b), *Tarih-i Feth-i Yemen* (İstanbul Üniversitesi Kütüphanesi T.6045, fols 453a and 557a), *Surname-i Hümayun* (Topkapı Sarayı Kütüphanesi H.1344, fol 27a), *Hünername* (Topkapı Sarayı Kütüphanesi H.1524, fol 120a), and *Şehinşahname* (Topkapı Sarayı Kütüphanesi B.200, fol 48a). Thus in the *Nusretname* of 1584, a miniature depicting a banquet thrown by Lala Mustafa Paşa during his eastern campaign shows fish bones littering the long spread on the ground that they were eating on.

213. Reindl-Kiel (forthcoming); Kolodzicjezyk (forthcoming).

214. Başbakanlık Arşivi: (1) Cevdet Dahiliye 8838 (17 August–14 September 1719); (2) DBŞM: 1395 (15 October–13 November 1719); (3) DBŞM 1405 (14 November–13 December 1719); (4) DBŞM MTE 10981 (24 August–22 September 1720); (5) Cevdet Dahiliye 4594 (4 October–1 November 1720); (6) Cevdet Dahiliye 9405 (28 April–27 May 1721); (7) Cevdet Dahiliye 6611 (19 January–16 February 1722); (8) MAD 19771 (2 September 1723–20 September 1724); (9) MAD 4885 (1133–1139); (10) Cevdet Dahiliye 8789 (11 August–8 September 1725); (11) MAD 1736/pp. 480–481 (29 September 1729–28 September 1730).

215. Previously mentioned in the section on "Poultry, cured meat, fish and offal," these are Başbakanlık Arşivi Cevdet Saray 3972 (19 January–16 February 1722) and DBŞM. MTE 10975 (14 December 1719–11 January 1720).

216. Başbakanlık Arşivi: (1) Cevdet Dahiliye 6053 (14 December 1719–11 January 20); (2) Cevdet Dahiliye 7266 (12 January 1720–10 February 1720); (3) Cevdet Dahiliye 6187 (22 October–20 November 1721); (4) Cevdet Dahiliye 6612 (17 February–18 March 1722); (5) Cevdet Dahiliye 6024 (16 March–14 April 1724).

217. Kunt (1975).

218. This was first noted in a previous section on "Other difficulties of personalizing court and elite consumption." For a comparison with a mid-eighteenth-century Scottish household, see Robertson (1987), 49–79.

219. Mennell (1996)[1985], 51.

220. Mennell (1996)[1985], 40, 45.

221. Mennell (1996)[1985], 31.

222. Mennell (1996)[1985], 32.

223. Mennell (1996)[1985], 33.

224. Mennell (1996)[1985], 32.

225. Mennell (1996)[1985], 73.

226. Mennell (1996)[1985], 31; Sabban (1986), 161–96.

227. Mennell (1996)[1985], 33. The author goes on to explore in detail the links between the growing arts of the cook, developing conceptions of refined taste, and changing patterns of social contest (of the elite): Mennell (1996)[1985], 127–33.

228. There are many other questions suggested by reading Mennell. Was it, for example, the same kind of socially generalized overeating that stories of Ottoman gluttony (or nicknames like *Semiz*) referred to? And what was their perception not only of taste, but also of health, obesity, good looks etc.? Did they, as in the rest of Europe, consider a healthy stoutness to be prestigious? These are all possible, though for the moment only the questions can be posed. But then, that is what comparative history is for.

229. Başbakanlık Arşivi: DBŞM: MTE 11161 (1756–57); MTE 11279 (1775); MTE 11451 (1778); MTE 11574 (1807); plus Topkapı Sarayı Arşivi D.5483 (1792–1798).

230. Topkapı Sarayı Arşivi E. 247/120 (1809).

231. Topkapı Sarayı Arşivi D. 874 (1776–1784); D. 842 (1790, 1793–1795, 1797–1799), D. 3017 (nd).

232. In the original: *taraf-ı mirîden tahsis buyurulan tayinat.*

233. In the original: *cevari çok ve itah çok iken validemiz hayatta iken mübayaa olunandır; şimdi iktiza etmiyor.*

234. In the original: *matbah için yevmiye verilen zahire beyan olunur.*

235. Topkapı Sarayı Arşivi E. 316/339 (nd).

236. Başbakanlık Arşivi DBŞM. MTE 11054 (1738), DBŞM. MTE 11062 (1739).

237. Başbakanlık Arşivi KK 7308 (1736).

238. Başbakanlık Arşivi KK 7314 (1765).

239. Başbakanlık Arşivi KK 7314 (1765).

240. For definitions, refer to note 59, above.

241. Topkapı Sarayı Arşivi D. 5483.

242. Topkapı Sarayı Arşivi D. 5483. *Hummaz* was a kind of red-colored sugar used for sweetening the warm maternity sherbet offered to visitors after childbirth, while *hummaziye* was a dish flavored with sorrel *(rumex)*, rhubarb *(rheum)* or other acid herbs; here it must be the dish rather than the sugar that was involved. For rhubarb, see Foust (1992)[1928]. *Kurut* is a kind of dry yoghurt. It was considered a rarity; see Köymen (1982), 18–19 after Kaşgarlı Mahmud, *Divani-Lügat-it-türk*; see Dankoff and Kelly eds. 1982–85; also see Genç (1982b), 63. *Şehriyye*, literally vermicelli, seems to have referred to various kinds of pasta in practice.

243. Topkapı Sarayı Arşivi E. 316/336.

244. Dallaway (1797).

245. In the original: *bedel-i altun*.

246. In the original: *bahâ-i altun varak*.

247. For *bedel-i altun* see: Başbakanlık Arşivi DBŞM. MTE 11745 (nd) and DBŞM. MTE 11761 (nd); for *bahâ-i altun varak* in a kitchen register, see: Cevdet Dahiliye 6053 (14 December 1719–11 January 1720). For the culinary use of gold, see Tezcan (1995), 275. In Sarı's (1982) study of a particular undated register ascribed to the sixteenth century (Topkapı Sarayı Arşivi D. 9599), which deals with suiting the qualities of food to the season and the condition of the human body—the idea behind which was the theory of humors that constituted the basis for all medical practice—we encounter the use of gold in food for health purposes.

248. Topkapı Sarayı Arşivi E. 247/120 (1809).

249. Başbakanlık Arşivi MAD 19771 (1723–24). It has been very fruitful to compare this register, which I am preparing for publication, with an account book of a yeoman/tradesman family from south Lancashire in England; see Weatherill ed. (1990).

250. What is actually cited in the relevant documents is a rather vague *karşu* that we should be careful not to identify as the other side of the Bosphorus. This would be anachronistic. Indeed there is evidence from other contexts that *karşu* was their way of referring to the other side of the Golden Horn, as in nineteenth-century references to Pera newspapers as *karşu gazeteleri*. This firmly establishes their vantage point as one anchored in the historical peninsula.

251. İnalcık (1991), 808.

252. See, for example, Herzfeld (1991), 4–16 and *passim*; for observations about the way the grand estate surveys *(polyptyques)* of the early ninth century in Carolingian France froze the "already antiquated" reality of the manorial system into a "static" description, see Duby (1974), 83–97.

253. See note 64, above.

254. Artan (1995b).

255. Unfortunately, for the period in question we do not have menus like the one for the private dinner given at St James's palace by Queen Anne on 19 December 1705, which consisted of: Oleo, Pigeons, Sirloin of Beef Rost, Venison, Chyne of Mutton, Turkey, Snipes, Ducks, Partridge. "That seems to be a large meal for a large lady," muses Mennell, "but there is little to suggest any very elaborate or refined cookery." He considers the dinner served to King George I at St James's on 1 July 1721 to be distinguished by nothing more than an increased use of "garbled French": Pottage Profitrole Pullet, Beeff Hotch Pott, Fricandoes white, Chickens and pease, Chyne of Lamb, Capons Enfans, Squobbs fricassy [young pigeons]: see Mennell (1996)[1985], 124–25. Records of royal receptions are more fruitful in terms of making sense of ingredients: Başbakanlık Arşivi DBŞM. MTE 10983 (1724); MTE 11081 (1741); MTE 11279 (1775); Cevdet Saray 3335 (1854).

256. Sefercioğlu (1985), 8–9.

257. Sefercioğlu (1985), 20–21.

258. A *kebab* and a meat stew: Sefercioğlu (1985), 44 and 64–65.

259. Mennell (1996)[1985], 80.

6

The Transition to Mass Fashion System Dress in the Later Ottoman Empire

Charlotte Jirousek

The word "fashion" is sometimes taken to mean simply change in style driven by changes in tastes. Fashion is typically discussed in terms of esthetics and visual appearance, or perhaps as a social/psychological phenomenon in which dress is the visual expression of cultural norms in a particular time or place. However, clothing—fashionable or otherwise—is also a complex system that involves economic as well as social and esthetic factors. Textile manufacture and trade were certainly important—indeed crucial—sectors of the Ottoman economy as they were of the global economy. Clothing is the most significant end use for textiles. Patterns of consumption for clothing alter over time in large part as a reflection of changes in production, marketing, and income as well as changes in the socio/cultural environment. Fashion change cannot be fully understood unless economic as well as esthetic and social factors are considered.

This study looks at the changing character of dress in Ottoman society between 1600 and 1920, using a socio-economic model to analyze change from "traditional" to "mass fashion system" dress as will be defined below. During this period the rate of change of dress gradually accelerated from the slow and subtle alterations typical of traditional dress to the rapid pace characteristic of mass fashion system dress. Since mass fashion system dress did not significantly affect rural dress patterns until after the Ottoman period, this discussion will center mainly on alterations in dress that occurred among urban populations, primarily in Istanbul.[1] Nonetheless this process of change in the economic and cultural meaning of dress surely also had impact on

Ottoman society at large as the developments of the seventeenth to nineteenth centuries continued to unfold.

The Mass Fashion System Model

In a recent paper I examined the process by which dress forms changed in a twentieth-century Turkish village.[2] In that study I expanded on a model developed by Jean Hamilton that described a "mass fashion system" to account for the transition from "dress" to "mass fashion dress" in eighteenth-century Scotland. Hamilton suggested that her model might also apply to times and places outside the European context:

> There is no such thing as mass fashion without a mass manufacturing system, one with the capacity to produce and distribute goods to a viable consuming population with a willingness and ability to participate in it. . . . There is no such thing as fashion marketing without . . . the expectation of relatively rapidly replaced style changes, accepted by most people for a limited time. *Mass fashion, therefore, requires . . . effective means of large-scale production, distribution, and communication.*[3]

Alan Hunt also defined fashion as based in a production and consumption system in which both producer and consumer view frequent change as a defining factor. He also stresses its importance as a concept not to be taken lightly:

> While common sense responses to the phenomenon of fashion often tend to view it as volatile and unstable, marked by idiosyncratic vagaries and irrational fads, the interests of both historians and sociologists have been stimulated by the fact that despite its superficially erratic features its true significance only emerges when it is perceived that it is a classically "social" phenomenon. Fashion exhibits long-term trends . . . that are not amenable to explanation pitched at the level of individual choice.[4]

Fashion is a major and visible object of consumption, and as such can be a useful means of discovering the mechanisms of demand and supply in the context of economic and social history.

One problem with the term "fashion" has been the tendency to apply it from a Euro-American frame of reference. Often European clothing forms and esthetics are linked to ideas of fashion. Yet the economic conditions needed to generate a mass fashion system do not necessarily require that the forms of dress adopted be drawn from the European esthetic. Fashion systems as defined in Hamilton's model can be observed in cultures where European clothing forms are not a major factor. West African dress is a particularly clear example where there are distinctively African and also decidedly seasonal changes in form, color, and pattern in dress stimulated by the industry and fashion leaders in the society, followed assiduously by consumers.[5] All the same, in many places mass fashion arrived in European clothes, no doubt due to the European origins of the mass production technologies and capitalist production systems that accompanied it. Events in the Ottoman Empire tended to lead toward the introduction of European forms of dress as this transition to mass fashion system dress occurred. Yet there is something to be said for trying to describe the fashion phenomenon in a framework that is more inclusive and less culturally centered.

The central feature of the model proposed is that the mass fashion system is a creation of the textile and apparel industry. Industry promotion of planned obsolescence and frequent change in dress has created an inflated demand for textiles and clothing.[6] The vanities of fashion are a product of, but also a driving force in, the economic expansion of the textile industry and all the industries that flow from it. Dress is also, to be sure, an expression of particular time and place, not to mention the roles and status of the individual wearer. However, once the economic and social conditions necessary for mass fashion were in place, the culture as well as the economy will have changed, and with it the form and meaning of dress.

"Traditional Dress"

Hamilton's model concentrated on the emergence of a mass fashion system, but I also wanted to look at the clothing system that would precede the mass fashion system, and consider the transition from one to the other. Although the term "traditional" needs to be approached with caution, as it is subject to many interpretations, it seemed the best descriptor for premass fashion dress.[7] I defined the earlier traditional dress system as "an expression of traditional behavior that identifies the individual in terms of local norms for class, ethnicity, and gender."[8] Tradition is "a long established and generally accepted custom or method of procedure having almost the force of law."[9] *Tradition limits change, but does not exclude it.* It should be self-evident that no human activity is completely static. Traditional systems are never completely fixed and unchanging, although change is usually slow. Roles are rigidly defined by the traditional community, with relatively few choices left to the individual, and this is reflected in dress. Traditional forms of dress may change when new inputs occur, although the changes are usually limited.

In fact, the only thing about traditional culture that is static might be the *perception* that tradition is static. Traditional dress is continually reinvented. As new ideas or materials enter the culture, the perceptions shift to encompass the new elements, but maintain the illusion that the society is stable and unchanging in its essentials.[10] New materials and even garments may be incorporated into a traditional dress system in this way. In some instances, this reinvention may be a quite self-conscious attempt to preserve the perception of a static concept of tradition. A good example of this may be seen in the creation of *folklor* dress following the establishment of the Turkish republic. As part of the effort to establish a Turkish national identity, folk dance festivals were encouraged. Provincial or regional dance teams created their costumes by selecting the most theatrical elements of festive village costume in their region. The costumes used are in fact an amalgam of rural dress that does not represent any actual Turkish community past or present.[11] The costumes have continued to change, furthermore, as many of the handmade textiles and accessories have become unavailable. Yet these costumes are now enshrined as the essence of traditional dress in Turkey, in the heart of a society that has in fact lost many of its "traditional" characteristics. Tradition thus provides the illusion of stability in situations where the community wishes to look to the past for affirmation of community values.

Traditional modes may begin to give way to more fluid modes when a traditional system no longer meets the needs of a significant proportion of the community. As transition occurs from a traditional to a mass fashion system of dress, hybridization of clothing forms may occur which combine features of the disappearing and emerging dress styles.

There is also a tendency to equate the adjective "traditional" with folk costume and not with the costume of more sophisticated civilizations. The intention in this discussion is to make the case for viewing the premass fashion mode of dress as a traditional form, whether the example is of European dress or Ottoman dress, urban or rural, providing that the circumstances and the clothing features meet the definition offered here.

Dress has been defined as "the total arrangement of all outwardly detectable modifications of the body itself and all material objects added to it."[12] In traditional communities, if change occurs in dress, the changes are more likely to be in the form of new materials or accessories rather than fundamental garment forms. Hunt points out that a significant distinguishing characteristic of traditional dress is the lack of gender differentiation between the basic male and female garment forms (although accessories, materials, and colors do identify gender distinctions.) This is in contrast with the highly gender-specific garment forms characteristic of mass fashion dress.[13] This description does apply to the traditional Ottoman dress matrix, in which the basic garment vocabulary for men and women was the same, with distinguishing materials, shaping, and accessories used to mark gender and status.

The Origins of the Mass Fashion System in Europe

It is generally accepted that a fashion system first began to develop in Europe in the fifteenth century.[14] The Duke of Burgundy, whose wealth in large part depended on the textile industry and international trade in textiles, required members of his court to alter their attire for special occasions. Courtiers were expected to conform to standards of dress that changed periodically. It became apparent that this form of conspicuous consumption had the dual effect of establishing elite status through dress, and of providing a steady market for the luxury textile industry. In the seventeenth century under the policies of Louis XIV and his minister of finance, Colbert, the mass fashion system came into its own as a tool of the state.[15] The requirements of court dress were established by the example of the king and his court. The center of power was at Versailles, and those who wished to participate in power needed to reside there, not on the provincial estates where individual power had been maintained in the past. Participation in court life required elaborate dress that needed to be changed for every event. In addition, seasonal changes in styles were decreed. The extravagant requirements of maintaining a court wardrobe and suitable household served to encumber the wealth of noblemen who might otherwise invest in political adventures against the crown. It also served to grease the wheels of the state-owned textile industries, enriching the royal coffers. In this period we also see the first fashion publications depicting seasonal alterations in dress.[16]

So vanity, ambition, and the profit motive combined to create planned obsolescence in dress, the beginnings of a true fashion system. In the late seventeenth century this system mainly involved the elite, but gradually the enticements of fashion would spread as income and access to fashion ideas and goods increased. By the eighteenth century dress alone in France might qualify one to participate in court life. Madame de Pompadour is a famous example of a person of bourgeois birth who rose to high position based in large part on her educated taste in dress and other matters.[17] By the nineteenth century and the rise of the industrial revolution, the textile and fashion industries catered to a growing middle class. The success of the great couturiers, beginning with Charles Worth, depend on their ability to set continually changing standards of dress that created a incessantly renewed market for their product.[18]

The Emergence of Mass Fashion in the Ottoman Empire

In the Ottoman world, dress evolved toward mass fashion from the relatively stable traditional forms seen in the sixteenth and seventeenth century. The rate of change began to accelerate in the eighteenth century. By the nineteenth century it burgeoned into a mass fashion system of dress. This evolution corresponded to alterations in economic and social conditions necessary for the emergence of a mass fashion system, as described above. Throughout the Ottoman era dress expressed the highly defined roles of Ottoman society. Its importance in this regard would continue into the twentieth century. Although clothing was viewed as an important marker of status, and a necessity for comfort and modesty, the utility of fashion as fuel for the industrial engines apparently was not recognized since other priorities drove Ottoman economic policy, as will be discussed below.

Moral proscriptions against luxurious dress tended to disarm any tendency to systematically exploit the vanities of fashion as a market incentive at a time when mass fashion was taking hold in Europe. The Quranic admonitions to modesty and simplicity in dress contradicted desires for display and luxury.[19] For example, in 1759–1760 an edict forbade women from wearing "extravagant clothing" in the public markets.[20] There is a clear suggestion that luxurious and unsuitable dress is a moral failure that threatens society.

It has been noted that in Europe religious leaders also spoke against luxurious dress, but the comparison with the Chinese proscriptions against dress is not an exact one. The relationship of Christianity to capitalism and mercantilism was quite different from that of the ulema to the quite different economic policies of the Ottoman system.[21] Many bishops and cardinals dressed as extravagantly as any duke or king. Sumptuary laws in Europe in the seventeenth century and later were secular in nature, not religious. By the seventeenth century in Europe, sumptuary legislation was declining, and virtually disappeared thereafter. Hunt has suggested that although in no period was European sumptuary law congruent with accepted practices, it was important as an early response of a feudal system to the appearance of modernism, and declined with the establishment of a commercial bourgeoisie and a capitalist market economy.[22] He describes a progression from an emphasis on moral views of the social order, to class struggle issues, to economic management He also points out that in fact all three elements interact in any given period. The issues of social control as reflected in sumptuary law relate to the congruence between formal sanctions (law and religious decree), informal sanctions (social pressures), and internalization of the sanction. The progression Hunt describes for European sumptuary legislation may in fact also describe the progression that occurred in the Ottoman Empire. However, the concurrent events in the two regions differed.

For urban Ottoman dress, a period of transition began in the eighteenth century that mirrored developments in many areas of Ottoman society. Changes in trade, production, and income distribution began to bring about new consumption patterns that appear to correspond to the "industrious revolution" described by deVries for eighteenth-century England. He asserts that "this industrious revolution emanating to a substantial degree from the aspirations of the family, preceded and prepared the way for the Industrial Revolution."[23] These family aspirations became incentives to transfer household resources from self-sufficient production to production aimed at the generation of disposable income. In the eighteenth century the beginnings of a commercial bourgeoisie also began to emerge, generating goods, income, and an increasing taste for consumer goods. Although new textiles and other luxuries became available to increasingly broad sectors of society, the fundamental traditional forms of dress continued.[24] The use of new textiles and accessories, including imported items, altered the vocabulary of dress somewhat during this period, but for the most part did not alter the classic sartorial canon of unfitted layered coats, vests, shirt, and *şalvar* completed by headcoverings. However, the introduction of European goods into Ottoman consumption patterns in this period seems to have been more in the area of *objet* for one's environment; clocks, textiles for interior use, boxes, furnishings, and collectibles that could be displayed in the home. It may be that such items satisfied a growing taste for (and ability to acquire) exotic goods in a way that was less personal than clothing. Since clothing is a statement of identity, adoption of foreign clothing forms is likely to occur after other foreign artifacts (and ideas) are accepted. In any case, the eighteenth century remained a period of mixed influences, with goods from domestic and Eastern, often Indian, sources remaining important.

Even more drastic alterations in dress occurred during the nineteenth century as Ottoman society continued to experience other kinds of change. By the end of the nineteenth century Ottoman economic and social institutions were in a state of flux, and traditional roles more fluid. As industrialization occurred, it began to generate increasing quantities of consumer goods, and a population that could afford them. For a variety of reasons to be discussed below, industrialization of fashion in the Ottoman Empire led to the acceptance of European clothing forms. The beginnings of a mass fashion system could be seen. The introduction of European fashion forms began discreetly, but as other western goods and ideas were accepted among the elite, dress too began to include items from the European fashion vocabulary. This tendency was greatly accelerated by the adoption of European garments as bureaucratic dress by Sultan Mahmud II. The social and political implications of this introduction of western styles have been widely discussed.[25] However, there were also economic factors that affected clothing choices.

The diffusion of new clothing forms corresponded to changes predicted by Hamilton for the establishment of a mass fashion system; that is, changing availability of materials, the rise of a middle class with disposable income, and increasing access to new ideas and distribution systems. As these factors came together in the nineteenth century, mass fashion emerged as the pattern of dress behavior among urban elites.

Four factors will be used to discuss the process of change from traditional to mass fashion system dress by which clothing choices are made. These factors are *rate of change, change in social mobility, causes of change,* and *changes in materials used.*

Rate of Change

Traditional dress, in contrast to mass fashion system dress, changes only very slowly. Traditional cultures are not static, but change must overcome the resistance of powerful and ubiquitous cultural sanctions. The dress of traditional cultures may retain its characteristics in part because external influences are avoided. This avoidance may be a result of environmental factors that limit contact, or it may be a matter of choice. For example, religious views may discourage acceptance of new ideas, and certainly did in Ottoman society. Especially before 1700, European goods, including dress, did not capture the attention of most Muslim consumers in the Ottoman Empire. There may be exceptions to this, but the evidence for it is not apparent. Images of sixteenth- and seventeenth-century Ottoman dress, whatever the source, or the ethnicity of the Ottoman citizen depicted, retain Ottoman features that vary little from earlier periods (Illustrations 1–3 and 5–7). Most Ottoman citizens were not exposed to Europeans or European products in significant quantities in this period. Travel by Europeans in the Ottoman Empire was closely regulated. Early European visitors to Ottoman lands frequently cautioned against wearing European dress while traveling to avoid offending Muslim sensibilities.[26] Henry Blount, writing of his visit to Constantinople in 1634, mentions that he was only able to give up Ottoman dress for his "Christian habit" when he moved from the Islamic section of the city to the home of an English resident of Galata, the district populated by foreign residents. He also tells us that "the chief time I had to view [the city] was my first two days, when I lodged in the Hane of Mehmet Basha," before his move to an Englishman's home and his reversion to European dress.[27] So even if an Ottoman citizen encountered a European, he was unlikely to encounter his clothes. In the sixteenth century, Izmir (Smyrna) was sheltered from contact with non-Ottomans, although as its commercial importance changed in the seventeenth century, this would change.[28] By the later seventeenth century Izmir could be described as a place where Europeans could be relatively relaxed in their attire and lifestyle, and even cultivate local friendships. However "in other parts of the Empire the Franks adopted Turkish robes and turbans in the hope of passing in the street as Turks; here [in Izmir] they wore the loose robes for comfort, but winter or summer kept hats on their heads to advertise their alien status."[29] The English Levant Company factors did bring their wives with them by the 1650s, but thereafter the presence of European women was discouraged by the company.[30] Thus until the end of the seventeenth century the opportunity to observe European forms of dress remained very limited. Also, during this period, the European imports into the Ottoman market tended to be woolen broadcloth or the coarser wool fabric known as kersey, plain fabrics suitable for use in the customary dress of the Ottomans.[31] However, relatively few luxury goods related to dress seem to be noted until after 1700, when it is known that specialty silk patterns were being produced in Lyons for the Ottoman market.[32]

Only as trade and diplomatic contacts increased in the eighteenth century and thereafter did European fashions and goods begin to seriously impinge on Ottoman tastes. Therefore when innovations in materials or form occurred in Ottoman dress during this period, they were more likely to be drawn from trade with other parts of the Islamic world, or from established trade routes with the East.

Yet new materials, accessories, or even garments might be introduced from time to time and be absorbed into the traditional dress esthetic. Çağman[33] relates that periodic changes in style did occur in Ottoman dress throughout the early period, as particular textiles, accessories or arrangements of garments became popular. Cotton textiles from India were significant as imports,[34] as were textiles from Persia and other Islamic centers. As indicated earlier, some European textiles also were imported from the early days of the Ottoman era. By the beginning of the eighteenth century French silks were being designed specifically for Ottoman tastes. Accessories and fabrics could be incorporated into established forms in dress and interiors. Imported cloth also served as prototypes for Ottoman textile production.

These new materials did not result in major variations from the established Ottoman *forms* of dress, however. The very gradual evolution of Ottoman dress prior to the nineteenth century cannot compare to the rapid, planned obsolescence typical of mass fashion system dress thereafter. For the most part it appears that the mandated forms of dress for the various religious communities and occupations remained in force prior to the reforms of Mahmud II. However, those with the income and the inclination began to take liberties within the Ottoman dress esthetic during the eighteenth century. By the time Julia Pardoe was writing her travel memoirs in 1835, she was able to report that European accessories were being worn by Ottoman women.[35] Nonetheless, the basic Ottoman esthetic of a variety of layered coats, vests, and jackets over shirt *(gömlek)* and baggy pants *(şalvar)*, with sashes and mandated headgear was maintained by most classes until late in the nineteenth century and even beyond.[36] The effect was one of modesty and bulk that revealed little of the body. The essential garments and layered arrangement of forms were essentially the same for both men and women, though gender was usually distinguished by the choices of materials and cut, and certainly by the choices of accessories and headgear. The male and female clothing depicted in Illustrations 1 and 5 demonstrate this lack of gender differentiation in traditional Ottoman dress. The layering of garments is similar, and only the headgear clearly defines male and female.

Although Ottoman dress forms did vary in detail over time, a

Illustrations 1–4. The fundamental esthetic of Ottoman dress is derived from its Central Asian nomadic roots, stressing layering of garments, modesty, and bulk. The ensemble for either men or women begins with shirt *(gömlek)* and loose trousers *(şalvar)*. Over this multiple layers of vests, jackets, and coats in various forms *(yelek, cebken, kaftan, antari)* are worn with multiple sashes, creating a bulky silhouette, topped by distinctive headgear. The more layers, the more luxurious the costume. In this series of images dating from the late fifteenth century to the late eighteenth century, the fundamental garment forms remain very much the same, although there are alterations in the headgear of most sultans. Mandated headgear of other ranks remained generally unchanged after 1600. All ensembles include several layers of long coats, the outermost edged with fur, and with sleeves of underlayers exposed. Hanging sleeves are also a shared feature in all periods, though not shown on the partial figures.

1. *Mehmed II, c. 1480.* Collection of Topkapı Museum, Istanbul.

2. *Mehmed III, 1596.* Collection of Ullstein Textarchiv und Bibliothek, Berlin.

3. *Mehmed IV, c. 1648–1687.*

4. *Selim III, 1789–1807.* Collection of Bodleian Library, Oxford.

Illustrations 5–9. Ottoman women's dress. The form of women's dress in the early Ottoman context followed the same esthetic as that of men. The primary difference was in the headgear. In some instances the cut of the *antari* was nearly indistinguishable from that of men. However, though the vocabulary of forms remained constant, the cut of women's coats significantly altered in the eighteenth century, signaling the beginnings of a movement toward the sexual dimorphism characteristic of mass fashion system dress.

5. *Women musicians at the Sultan's gathering, ca. 1460.* The closed, high necklined, layered *kaftan* of the women (lower left) are very similar to those worn by some of the men. However, the women wear scarves and a headband, and two of the women wear tall pointed hats. Collection of Topkapı Museum, Istanbul.

6. *A group of women, late sixteenth century.* This image, from a European album, shows dress very similar to that seen in the previous example dating from more than a century earlier. The caps worn beneath the veils are flatter and lower, but the characteristic headbands and scarves are still in evidence. One woman is shown without her *kaftan* in a sleeveless quilted vest over a long chemise, like that seen under the *kaftan* of the other women. Similar short jackets (with sleeves) are seen in both earlier and later periods. The neckline is slightly lower, but buttoned and filled by the high neckline of the chemise. Collection of Osterreichische Nationalbibliothek, Vienna.

7. *Women in a garden, ca. 1603–1618.* The dress of these women, about fifty years later than is shown in Illustration 6, is very similar to the previous example, except that the hats worn are smaller. Also the *kaftan* is unbuttoned at the throat, revealing the chemise *(gömlek)* beneath. Collection of Milli Kütüphane, Ankara.

8. *Woman winding her headscarf, 1720–1725.* A century later the unbuttoned higher neckline has become a deep, open neckline that creates a deep decolletage. The chemise is still buttoned at the throat, but the fabric is very transparent and the single button does not close the slit front. The *antarı* is very tight across the breast, as can be seen from the gaps between the buttons. The *antarı* is also open below the waist to reveal the transparent chemise, the jacket, and the trousers *(şalvar),* all of which are garments worn by women in earlier periods. The split sleeves of the jacket and the chemise emerge from the shorter sleeve of the *antarı.* Other paintings by Levni depict variations on these styles, but all include the classic Ottoman vocabulary of layered jackets and coats over chemise and trousers. Signed Levni. Collection of Topkapı Museum, Istanbul.

9. *A woman from Istanbul, 1793.* The *antarı* visible under her fur-lined *kaftan* is buttoned tightly across the torso, but leaves the breasts uncovered except for the sheer fabric of the chemise, which also can be seen emerging from the sleeves of the *antarı*. Her large elaborate headdress *(hotoz)* is characteristic of this period, as are the small delicate patterns seen in the textiles and the sumptuous variety of materials used, suggesting both wealth and availability of a wide variety of goods. Nonetheless, all of the structural components of the ensemble were in use in earlier periods. Collection of Istanbul University Library.

comparison of costume images from the fifteenth century through the end of the eighteenth century shows a remarkable similarity of form (Illustrations 1–4). The cut of Ottoman official garments changed very little between 1550 and 1800.[37] Official headgear also stabilized after 1600, although most sultans did alter their turbans.[38] The consistency is great enough so that an observer from the court of Mehmed II (1451–1481) would have been able to identify the status of many citizens should he have been transported to the Istanbul of Murad III (1574–1595), Ahmed II (1691–1695), or even of Selim III (1789–1807).

For women's dress fewer early examples are available, but what there is suggests that for women, consistency of form with some variation in detail holds through the seventeenth century, although greater variation appears in eighteenth century dress. The basic ensemble of the Ottoman lady involved the trousers *(şalvar)*, long chemise *(gömlek)*, and a hip length jacket or vest, below which the skirt of the chemise might extend to the ankles. Over this would be worn the outer coat *(antari)*, with short sleeves, exposing the sleeve of the jacket underneath. The *antari* was buttoned up the front in the formal situations typically depicted in fourteenth- and fifteenth-century painting, but might be removed at home (Illustration 5). Another looser coat might be worn over the entire ensemble. By the sixteenth century, the buttoned *antari* has developed a neckline that was a little lower (Illustration 6). After the sixteenth century the closed and buttoned *antari* was depicted more commonly as being left unbuttoned at the throat, exposing a high-necked, closed chemise (Illustration 7).[39] Occasionally the neckline might be cut somewhat lower. Also panels were added to the sides of the *antari* below the waist to add fullness. Apart from variations in headgear, however, the essential form and arrangement of the garments remained the same. Thereafter however, some more noticeable changes in the form appeared if not the basic assemblage of garments for women's dress. By the early eighteenth century the *antari* and vest or jacket changed in cut, with the neckline becoming wide and deep to expose a rather open, and also very transparent, chemise and deep decolletage (Illustration 8). The upper part of the *antari* was now tightly buttoned around the body—not as loosely fitted as in previous periods—while it was not buttoned at all below the waist, exposing the jacket, chemise, and trousers beneath. By the end of the eighteenth century the headgear, consisting of tall, expansive hats and turbans, became extremely large (Illustration 9). Both the tightly buttoned upper coat and the large headgear were features that strongly resembled the silhouette (though not the tailoring) of European women's bodices and headgear in this period. Since there are known to have been *Turquerie* features in European dress in the late eighteenth century, it is difficult to clearly attribute a direction of influence for every characteristic, although the new fitted *antari* with its low neckline is very suggestive of this much older feature of European women's dress. However, the basic vocabulary of Ottoman dress—layered coats over chemise and trousers—remains in force, and the essentially Ottoman character is clearly identifiable.

Given the relative isolation of rural communities, these alterations could not have been expected to spread at all quickly beyond the urban elites. Unfortunately very little information is available regarding variations in rural dress in the Ottoman era, although it can be assumed that regional and ethnic identity in dress was more important than urban styles for most of the population. However, a few examples of regional dress can be found in travelers' chronicles. These examples probably represent provincial townsmen, not peasants. They show distinctive local features, although examples are too few for meaningful comparisons over time. For the indigenous population of rural Anatolia, however, the process of change from traditional to mass fashion dress would not really have much impact until after the establishment of the Turkish republic.[40]

The alterations in Ottoman dress over time were relatively minor when compared with the more drastic rate of change seen in contemporaneous European fashions, induced by mass fashion factors already in operation. To begin with, the basic esthetic form of western European dress is quite different from that of Turkish dress. The essential feature is that the clothing reveals the contours of the body. Tailoring—the use of curved seams and darts to achieve individual fit—is a distinctly European invention of the fourteenth century.[41] For men, the legs are displayed in hose or (later) in tailored trousers. For women the legs are modestly enveloped in long skirts, but the upper body garment is closely fitted, and the neck, head, and face may be exposed. Yet within these general esthetic limitations we see changes so dramatic that our time traveler from the fifteenth century would be hard put to identify the nationality, much less the rank or occupation of the examples shown here (Illustrations 10–13).

The rate of change in Ottoman dress accelerated once the transition to a mass fashion system began. Alterations in dress became more frequent in the eighteenth century. Imported goods from the East continued to be important, and European goods also became increasingly significant. Both Ottoman elites and minorities, who dominated commercial relations with Europeans, began to acquire and wear

Illustrations 10–13. European dress has been characterized by an esthetic that stresses body contours. Although the ideal body silhouette has varied, and has been altered by padding and other devices in many periods, clothing is shaped to follow the body, particularly for men. Women's dress is similarly fitted above the waist, although long skirts cover the legs until the twentieth century. However, within this esthetic, a great deal of variation occurred between the late fifteenth and beginning of the nineteenth centuries.

10. *Young gentlemen, Flemish, ca. 1460.* The one piece doublet with its short peplum/skirt features broad, padded shoulders and a narrow waist. The legs, covered only by hose, terminate in long pointed shoes. A tall hat is worn.

11. *St. Megrin (School of Clouet), France, ca. 1581–1582.* The padded and slashed doublet features the full "peascod" belly and sleeves, with the waist dropping to a point above the separate, balloonlike slops and hose. The curled hair is decorated with jewels and a small soft hat, and the face is framed by a closed ruff collar unique to this period. Courtesy of Photo Flammarion.

12. *Fashionable gentleman (Bonnart), 1693–1695.* The silhouette is funnellike, and the doublet has given way to shirt, lace cravat, waistcoat, coat, and knee breeches. A full wig is worn, and it is curled so high that the tricorne hat required for fashionable court dress must be carried rather than worn. High heeled shoes are also worn. Bibliothèque Nationale, Paris, Cabinet des Estampes.

13. *Parisian gentleman 1808.* Lace and brocade have been replaced by sober wool and linen. The modern European men's suit is clearly recognizable, as is the top hat. Bibliothèque Nationale, Paris, Cabinet des Estampes.

14. *A coffeehouse, ca. 1890–1895.* Most of this group of men wears traditional Ottoman dress, except for the man in the center, who wears a European-style suit. Istanbul Fransız Kültür Merkezi.

European textiles and accessories, if not actual garments.[42] Gifts of European goods to Muslims were also factors in the diffusion of new products. The presence of increasing numbers of Europeans was in itself a significant means of diffusing European fashion ideas.

In the nineteenth century the rate of change increased. The Tanzimat edicts opened the way for substantial change by proposing alterations in dress that corresponded to westernizing institutional reforms. However, the reforms imposed by the Tanzimat initially did not reach beyond the imperial household and the military and civil bureaucracies. Candid photographs and street scenes from the mid-nineteenth century demonstrate that for many urban citizens the traditional *şalvar, kaftan,* and turban remained the standard apparel (see Illustration 14). Acceptance of the new fashions was far from universal, and reflected the strong traditional sanctions that opposed the reforms.

Even when foreign modes of dress were adopted, this did not necessarily signify adoption of the values the new clothing was intended to signify. Instead, items of dress may have been merely appropriated into the traditional esthetic and concept of the function of dress. The new forms were redefined as markers of traditionally defined class and status. The fez, for example, was initially a symbol of reform imported from North Africa.[43] It became in due course a substitute for the older turban, *börk*, and other mandated headgear, and therefore ultimately a replacement symbol of Ottoman/Muslim traditionalism.[44] It remained in use for a century, essentially without change, adopted into the traditional bureaucratic dress code, so that by the time of the republican revolution, it had become a symbol of reactionary traditionalism, not of reform. Yet by the latter nineteenth century among some urban elites it was possible to observe alteration rates in fashion that corresponded to those seen in European cities as these groups adopted mass fashion dress habits.[45] However, for most of the population, the dress forms, if not the materials, remained in the traditional mode well into the twentieth century.

A more recent example of this process of change is men's village dress, which also incorporated new forms that came to carry traditional meanings. In the twentieth century, rural dress forms converted from the Ottoman baggy pants, vest, and jacket (*şalvar, yelek,* and *cebken*)[46] to European suits, also characterized by pants, vest, and jacket. During the 1920s major historical events brought about a new paradigm, just as the Tanzimat reforms had a century earlier. The new republic encouraged westernization in dress that corresponded to the modernizing, westernizing reforms being promoted in other aspects of society. Industrialization of textile production also encouraged the use of newer materials and discouraged the production and use of traditional materials. Yet the changes in rural Turkish dress occurred initially without significant changes in the traditional rural culture that adopted the new dress.[47] As a result, the garment forms adopted became static in form, and were reinterpreted as an expression of village culture. The suits worn by Turkish villagers as late as the 1960s and 1970s were still cut in the pattern of the sack coat fashionable in Europe and America before World War I. The suit was worn, not as formal attire, but rather for field work or any other purpose, in lieu of the Ottoman era layered *cebken, yelek,* and *şalvar.* Thus the "fashionable" European suit became a new static element in the traditional dress vocabulary. It was incorporated into the traditional rural dress esthetic as a nonfashion form through the process of cultural authentication.[48] The European suit thus worn certainly was not evidence that there was acceptance of European of mass fashion ideas—not to mention other European values. Any Turkish man wearing a suit in this manner, cut in this style, was instantly identifiable as a villager. The rate of change in dress began to accelerate in the 1970s and 1980s as the economic and social conditions that permit a mass fashion system reached rural Turkey.

Changes in Social Mobility

Historically fashion is an elite behavior that gradually spread to other segments of society. Various theories of fashion diffusion have developed that describe this process. The hierarchical nature of many societies before the twentieth century means that the "trickle down" model generally provides the most appropriate description. In this model fashions are set by "fashion leaders," usually the ruling family or other important or popular figures. Fashion ideas are then disseminated gradually from class to class, moving from the top to the bottom of the social ladder. As societies become more pluralistic, other patterns of fashion diffusion apply.[49] Because of the hierarchical patterns that operate in the historical context, it is inevitable that fashion examples used must be drawn from elites. In the case of Ottoman fashion history, the information, particularly the visual information, is very limited for even bourgeois patterns of dress (much less peasant dress) prior to the nineteenth century. This makes it very difficult to identify comparable examples across time. Therefore many of the examples to be shown and discussed will be limited to elite dress, although where possible, information about a broader population will be included.

If social mobility is restricted, dress patterns also tend to be fairly rigid, and reflect the narrowly defined roles within the society. Thus dress forms remain essentially traditional. This describes Ottoman society and dress prior to the seventeenth century, when on the whole the political structure of the empire was fairly stable, social mobility was limited for most, and class, status, and roles were relatively clearly defined.[50] Shortly after the conquest of Constantinople, Mehmed II established regulations that stipulated dress for all ranks and categories of Ottoman subjects.[51] Sultan Süleyman the Lawgiver subsequently expanded these laws. A sumptuary law of 1568 very specifically delineates the dress of a minority male: gray outer coat, a sash, the use of a certain cloth woven of silk and cotton of a designated value, a specified headgear made from Denizli muslin, and black, flat-topped, unlined shoes.[52] For minority women, the required dress was to be made of Bursa cotton, a striped silk and cotton weave fabric *(alaca)* in red and yellow only, head wraps, and blue *şalvar.* Subsequently shoe colors were stated more specifically: Jews and Armenians were to wear black and purple, and Greeks red. Yellow was reserved for the shoes of Muslims.

It appears that sumptuary laws in the early Ottoman Empire reinforced a relatively stable system, and the dress codes were generally obeyed. Social control theories propose that in fact formal sanctions such as law only succeed when they correspond to the informal sanctions of community expectations and the deeper sanctions of internalized values.[53] That is, there is a tacit social contract by which the governed accept (or don't accept) the justice of the system that defines their lives. If attitudes in society at large come to be in conflict with the formally sanctioned policies of government, laws become very difficult to enforce.

Quataert has noted the apparent paucity of sumptuary legislation from the sixteenth century, when Sultan Süleyman the Lawgiver expanded the dress code, until the beginning of the eighteenth century, when signs of social and economic transformations appeared.[54] If in fact there were few such laws promulgated in this period, it might suggest that the existing laws were being obeyed, and that the social categories they defined were congruent with community expectations. When we look at the actual record of clothing as represented in artworks and as surviving artifacts, we find that indeed the forms and even many of the details remained very consistent throughout this period, suggesting a reasonable degree of stability in clothing norms. Quataert further suggests that an incentive for complying with sumptuary regulations was that these edicts protected the rights and privileges of group members. Dress codes were therefore generally viewed as beneficial, so long as members accepted the fundamental socio-political structure of Ottoman society.

Wealth is often used to display social prestige. Wherever economic and social conditions permit, most individuals will try to dress in ways perceived to enhance their prestige. Hunt terms such sartorial behavior as "vicarious consumption."[55] He suggests that vicarious consumption confers prestige on the wearer through the borrowing of dress forms from high status individual or classes, and that much of sumptuary law is an attempt to manage vicarious consumption. If a given society permits greater social mobility, it is likely that dress will vary more within a given social group. However, even when roles and dress forms are rigidly defined, those who can afford to do so will still seek out luxuries within the limitations of their system. This inevitably acts as a pressure against the established sumptuary order. As a state enjoined to uphold Quranic values, the Istanbul regime from time to time passed sumptuary laws that discouraged the wearing of clothing woven with silk, gold, or silver thread.[56] Even when economic justifications were given in such edicts, the moral outrage is palpable:

> It is the duty of the azim and the padishah and the vezirs to make known the appropriate clothing for each group of people and make certain each wears that clothing. . . . In putting on airs and being prodigal by eliminating distinctions, the common rabble become like the wise . . . this is insulting, scornful.[57]

However, luxuries were widely embraced by those who could afford them in spite of such prohibitions. Not only do we have the evidence of repeated sumptuary edicts in later periods and descriptions of dress, we also have the evidence of surviving examples of richly embellished garments.

By 1700 many political, economic, and social factors had begun to erode the stability of Ottoman institutions. Dress codes became defensive attempts to shore up crumbing social barriers, but often failed to do so. This constraining mode more closely resembled the intention—and the lack of success—characteristic of European sumptuary laws in the sixteenth and seventeenth centuries and earlier. In Europe dress codes were almost always initiated as a defensive response to emerging pressures for change, and therefore were inherently difficult to enforce.[58] The incongruity of the informal sanctions of community values with the formal sanctions of law made such legislation futile. When the social contract of Ottoman society began to dissolve, the Ottoman dress codes also became ineffective, even though sumptuary regulations were periodically restated.

Before 1700, then, the social structure was reflected in dress forms that essentially were traditional. All the same, there were subtle alterations over time in the traditional dress ensemble and there were alterations in the society; stable does not mean static. However, as the economic, social, and political alterations of the eighteenth and nineteenth century occurred, the stability of Ottoman society began to alter. This would open the way for movement toward a mass fashion system that would correspond to a relatively greater array of life choices and social mobility. Flexibility and multiplicity of choice in dress typical of a mass fashion system is generally a reflection of flexibility in social roles. This relative freedom is associated with industrialization as well as greater individual choice in dress.[59] It also allows the option of adopting dress associated with other groups.

As these changes began to be felt, trade and contact with Europeans was a significant factor. The minorities within the Ottoman Empire had the greatest contact with the growing European communities in eighteenth-century Ottoman cities. Therefore these were among the first to adopt European dress forms, and were also the subject of decrees that forbade such dress.[60] As minority communities began to dissent from the Ottoman system, and as they achieved greater independence economically through their relations with the growing European trade communities in the Ottoman Empire, this increase in mobility and social options was expressed in departures from the mandated forms of dress.

In a study of inheritance registers containing mention of western goods, Göçek noted that between 1700 and 1820, the elites were the most likely to list such goods, and the likelihood remained constant. However, throughout the period the proportion of subjects listing western goods steadily increased. She reasons that there were a rising number of subjects who had achieved the necessary level of disposable income, and access to distribution of goods.[61] That is, a bourgeois class was emerging that could become consumers of imported luxury goods (either European or from other sources). The stimulus of fashion diffusion from elites may have engendered new demand for fashionable attire and luxuries. This demand could provide the necessary motivation to shift households from self-sufficiency production to income-generating production, so that cash would be available to purchase status goods. This would be in keeping with the "industrious revolution" concept proposed by deVries.[62]

Economic and Political Factors that Govern the Change Process

Occasionally major changes in traditional dress systems may occur which reflect major, even traumatic, events that change the broader environment and experience of the traditional community. The Tanzimat reforms introduced new forms of dress along with new governmental, military, and educational institutions. However, the imposed forms of dress initially were merely a substitution for older forms, and as such did not necessarily represent adoption of mass fashion values. Rather, the new coat, trousers, and fez became a new uniform for the male elite, replacing the mandated clothing of earlier periods. This can be seen, in portraits and photographs, in the way these garments are worn. Gradually the clothing forms began to alter in accordance with the seasonal dictates of mass fashion consumption for a significant proportion of the elite. As men began to conform to European fashion forms promoted by the state, women began to experiment with European fashion forms as well. By the 1850s it is possible to find portraits of Ottoman gentlemen who are clearly being dressed by the finest European (or European-trained) tailors. The earliest photographs showing Ottoman women in European dress date to the late 1870s and 1880s. By the last quarter of the century, European fashion forms and attitudes had been adopted by many of the new commercial and bureaucratic bourgeoisie.

It was not enough to mandate new styles to create a "European"-style fashion system; other factors were necessary. This is not to suggest that the Tanzimat reforms had no bearing on the emergence of mass fashion, though indeed the intentions of the dress reform were quite removed from any concern about the future of the textile and apparel industry. These reforms sanctioned change and opened the door to new choices, including European ideas about dress as well as other matters. The social and economic changes that would follow included a number of innovations not anticipated in the original vision of reform.

In the context of the mass fashion system, industrial production is dependent on the mass marketing of fashion and the planned obsolescence of styles, encouraged by fashion leaders such as members of elite classes. A consumer base with disposable income and access to fashion information and goods are also essential. Göçek has suggested that the beginnings of this consumer base can be seen in eighteenth-century records as both demand for goods and income rose. Eighteenth-century costume illustrations depicted more changes in detail for both men's and women's dress, but these minor variations still tended to run the course of a generation, and were typically associated with the accession of a new sultan.

Additional factors inhibited the early development of economic conditions needed to build a true mass fashion system in the Ottoman world. The particular evolution of industrialism in the Ottoman Empire impeded the development of access to both the goods and disposable income necessary for a mass fashion system.

> Western states [in the eighteenth century] drew on new sources of power generated by parts of society which were allowed to keep part of their wealth and to enjoy the protections of developing codes of law. Under the Ottoman system, neither the towns nor anyone in them could expect the kind of security from interference which would encourage the technical experimentation and study of nature, which were among springs of growing power in the West.[63]

By the late eighteenth century the trend toward export of raw materials rather than finished cloth to European markets also created supply problems for the Ottoman textile industry. There was in addition the continuing government policy of channeling industrial production to serve the needs of the state.[64] Among the many goods considered strategic, hence controlled, were textiles. Therefore traditional systems of production remained in force, impeding innovation and growth. The creation of both goods and the disposable income necessary for mass fashion production had to wait until market factors and industrial production permitted. Following the destruction of the Janissaries in 1826, the guild monopolies that provided strategic goods such as textiles (and previously under the protection of the janissary bureaucracy) also fell to new laissez faire economic policies. The Anglo-Turkish convention of 1838 and the Tanzimat decree of 1839 formally established a policy of free trade and removed the longstanding protections on domestic manufactures. Ottoman producers now had to compete with European industrialized production to supply the new uniforms mandated for the military and bureaucratic elite.[65] This breakdown of the old production institutions would create both turmoil and opportunity for the Ottoman textile industry.

Throughout the nineteenth century there were both great increases in textile imports from Europe, but also great alterations in the domestic textile industry as it struggled to compete and adapt to the rapidly changing circumstances. Although Quataert does conclude that the presumed decline of Ottoman domestic textile manufactures has been greatly exaggerated, he also points out many reasons why Ottoman producers found it difficult to compete with European cloth, dyes, and yarn.[66] The importance of price, and the need to reduce quality to meet price was not well understood, nor was the growing taste for European fashions that required different types of cloth. Shortages of raw materials were caused by both internal and external events. The British government lifted its ban on the export of textile machinery in 1841, but it was not until the end of the nineteenth century that mechanized spinning and weaving factories began to appear.[67] Some manufacturers were unwilling or unable to adopt new technologies, in part because of the existing guilds and networks. Therefore European goods were a burgeoning factor in Ottoman fashion in the nineteenth century, although Ottoman manufacturing continued to develop new modes of production and to provide goods that could not be provided by foreign producers.

Changing in Materials Used in Dress

It is sometimes suggested that traditional dress is a product of a self-sufficient economy in which the members of the community produce essential goods such as textiles and clothing. Nonetheless it is possible for either pre- or postindustrial materials to be part of traditional dress. Handmade garments and accessories may use postindustrial materials. Some industrially woven textiles were used by rural villagers in the Ottoman era.[68] A rare photograph taken around 1885 shows a peasant woman wearing a quilted coat that appears to be made of such a printed fabric (Illustration 15). The way in which garments are worn, and the manner in which these forms adhere to traditional standards, is more important to their traditional character than is the source of the materials. However, it could be argued that the inclusion of industrially produced materials in traditional dress signals the beginning of a transition from traditional to mass fashion modes of production, however gradual. Since industrially made goods must be purchased with cash, its availability and access to markets must be occurring in these communities. These simple transactions with the wider world portend other expanded connections to come.

On the other hand, mass fashion dress is generally made of industrially produced materials, assembled by industrial mass production methods. Historically, assembly might include more handwork than today, but nonetheless, mass fashion clothing is produced by ateliers, workshops, or factories, to be purchased for cash, as opposed to individualized family production or custom work by local tailors that might be part of a community barter system. The rise of ready-to-wear clothing is a significant feature of the mass fashion system. As mass fashion and ready-to-wear systems take hold, garment forms, materials, and embellishment are modified in order to make production more cost effective. As a result, mass fashion clothing is less elaborately finished than traditional clothing.[69] Mass fashion clothing may be homemade, but when this is done the goal is to imitate industrially generated fashions. The development of sizing systems and the publication of printed patterns also contributed to the dissemination of fashion ideas.[70] The fashion industry also actively promotes and encourages changes in styles in order to increase sales.

15. *Peasant women, ca. 1885.* The standing woman wears a jacket made of a printed textile, presumably cotton. The crouching woman's apron is also a print. Istanbul Fransız Kültür Merkezi.

These changes must be sufficiently different so that older garments cannot be merely rearranged to meet the new ideal. The cut of garments must be altered so that the fashion consumer must acquire a new wardrobe to achieve the desired look. It may be possible to distinguish between the ensemble of an Ottoman citizen of the sixteenth and seventeenth century because new materials may be introduced, and assembly and accessories (notably headgear) may give a somewhat different silhouette. However if the individual garments are laid out, as they are in the galleries of Topkapi, it is often very difficult to identify with certainty the date of the individual *kaftan, antari,* or *şalvar.* Indeed, since documentation is often unreliable, the dating of many of these garments is very uncertain, because the fundamental forms and even materials remained in use for long periods of time.[71]

Moreover, the basic garment forms worn by both men and women are also very similar in the Turkish traditional clothing esthetic. Even though accessories and cut distinguish the sexes, the fundamental set of garments worn—*şalvar, gömlek,* and layered coats and jackets—are essentially the same. Hunt has noted that European prefashion system dress was also quite gender-neutral in form, with tunics and draped mantles as the basic forms worn by both men and women as late as the mid-fourteenth century.[72] However, as the fashion industry began to take form, a marked sexual dimorphism emerged. The forms of clothing took on very gender-specific characteristics.[73] The beginnings of sexual dimorphism in Ottoman dress can be seen in the changes that occur in eighteenth century women's dress (Illustrations 8 and 9). This transition from gender-neutral to gender-specific forms seems to have appeared with mass fashion system dress whenever it has occurred. Sex sells, and selling clothing is selling attractiveness—a very ancient marketing truth, indeed.

In the nineteenth century Ottoman economic policies moved from the old approach of centralized control through free trade, to a protected national economy by World War I.[74] During this period the Ottoman economy also experienced the dislocation brought about by competition with the early Industrial Revolution in Europe. This stimulus contributed to a restructuring of manufacturing and the subsequent growth of the Ottoman textile industry, including textile production for the domestic market, particularly after 1870. At the same time, importation of European and American cloth continued to rise. Therefore by the last quarter of the nineteenth century the infrastructure necessary for mass fashion production was in place, ready to supply the expanded commercial and bureaucratic bourgeoisie (Illustration 16). These groups were available as consumers, equipped with cash, and able to receive fashion information and goods. By the end of the nineteenth century, the shops of Pera were providing the latest fashions in ready-to-wear to Muslims as well as non-Muslims.[75]

Conclusions

Confusion about the meaning of the term "fashion" has occasionally led scholars to misconstrue the implications of fashion change in many different contexts. Since change occurs in any human society, it is necessary to consider the context of change before determining its significance. A mass fashion system is a result of economic factors relating to the development of the textile industry. To have a true fashion system, there must be substantial means of production, an effective distribution system that includes the ability to disseminate rapidly changing fashion ideal, and a mass consumer public that has both the income and the social mobility to support such a system. Of course, many social and cultural factors contribute to the nourishment of this economic model.

Change in dress forms can also occur in traditional societies from time to time as new materials or forms are accepted or imposed. However, in traditional systems of dress change tends to come slowly. New forms are usually incorporated into preexisting notions of the function of dress and the established dress esthetic. Once the fashion system forms have been appropriated into a traditional system, they cease to follow the dictates of rapid mass fashion changes. Although infusions of new forms and materials did occur from time to time throughout the Ottoman era, the simple fact of change proves only that Ottoman society was a living organism. Dress in stable traditional societies, as in all living communities, does change and evolve, though it does so at a different rate and possibly for different reasons than it does in more fluid industrial societies. As the transition to a mass fashion system occurs, however, forms of dress will begin to alter more rapidly, reflecting the more fluid state of economic and social conditions. This transitional process can be seen in the eighteenth century, and the rate of change accelerated in the early nineteenth century as a consumer class with disposable income developed, and fashion materials became more readily available.

Dress forms borrowed from the European fashion system were imposed in the early nineteenth century as part of the reforms of Mahmud II. Yet Ottoman dress remained essentially traditional in

16. *An Ottoman official and his family in Aleppo, ca. 1915.*
Photo Courtesy Quartet Books, Limited.

character until the economic and social alterations of the later nineteenth century created the necessary conditions for development of a true mass fashion system. Even then, this phenomenon was generally limited to an urban elite until after the establishment of the Turkish republic brought both dress reform and changing economic patterns to the general population. The expansion of the mass fashion system has occurred gradually throughout the twentieth century, and by the 1990s has begun to affect rural populations. As availability of materials, a consumer economy, and improved means of distribution developed, there was also an increase in social mobility and rate of change in dress.

These changes in turn corresponded to other changes in political, social, and economic structures. Hunt points out that since "in a distinctive way fashion straddles the realms of production, consumption, and culture [it] provides an opening that needs to be developed."[76] The esthetics of dress is an expression of personal and communal identity as well as economic factors. In the last quarter of the twentieth century, the resurgence of the religious right has been reflected in a resurgence in conservative and traditional dress, reflecting the pluralistic quality of modern Turkish society. However, even within these subcultures mass fashion principles are operating; there are styles, fads, and seasonal alterations in style for the urban religious conservative just as there are for the secular sophisticate. It is just that one group is participating in a different esthetic model than the other. Mass fashion dress thus continues to be a reflection of cultural values, and a significant measure of change when examined in proper context.

The comparison between Ottoman and European experiences with the evolution of a mass fashion system deserves further study. The mass fashion system model, initially developed to describe a European evolutionary process, also has been useful in understanding this aspect of consumption behavior in the Ottoman context. Furthermore, it is a model that avoids many of the pitfalls that can be associated with a discussion of fashion change outside the Euro-American context. It is easy to simply discuss fashion in terms of the European garments adopted rather than the socio-economic forces that led to the changes, but fashion is structured by broader issues such as distribution patterns, social mobility, and communications. Variables in the economic and political environments point out the extent to which the success of sumptuary legislation is a function of the social contract that binds a society. In Europe, it has generally been held that sumptuary law was inevitably doomed to fail; yet for significant periods of time sumptuary regulation was apparently an effective part of the mechanisms of social control in Ottoman society. The degree to which the society agrees to the social contract codified in law would seem to make the difference. Once that social contract came into question, Ottoman sumptuary law became as ineffective as that previously seen in Europe. Yet the Ottoman experience of more than two centuries in which there was at least the *perception* that dress codes worked to "create" social order has led to a shared belief that what one wears matters intensely as an expression of morality, group identity, and suitable behavior. Therefore when reform was attempted in the 1820s and the 1920s, clothing was perceived to be a major implement for building the changes in values that were devised. Even at the end of the twentieth century, Turks wax passionate over issues of dress and appearance, as they seek to either reanimate Islamic values through symbols of dress—headscarves and beads—that arise from Ottoman era concepts of proper dress; or they seek to reanimate the secular principles promoted by Mustafa Kemal through an adherence to European forms of dress. Paradoxically European dress is still embraced, even though the current thinking may be that for Turkish modernism, a Euro-American model may not be the best or only option. But in this case, it is the most obvious alternative with which to oppose the sartorial symbols of the religious right. However, the language of clothes, like all nonverbal signal systems, reaches us at a level outside reason. And in Turkey, the language of dress has an emotional power that is often hard for westerners to grasp, perhaps because for Europeans and Americans there is no shared historic perception of dress as a successful tool of social control.

Another issue that needs further examination is the degree to which Ottoman dress has affected the development of European fashion. This is a subject that has only been touched upon in a very limited way.[77] Although this subject has not been explored fully, it is a topic that deserves more attention. The evolution of dress described in this essay is only one side of a far more complex interchange of ideas about dress in which its materials, forms, and their meanings have undergone many permutations. Dress can be a useful vehicle through which to examine the interchange of goods, ideas, and values across the East-West divide that was not, truly, such a divide as sometimes has been presented. The frequent preoccupation with the westernizing features of modernization in the non-Euro-American world has caused us to ignore the other side of the equation of exchange and influence.

For those who have not previously considered fashion as a serious topic of study, it is easy to dismiss it as the self-indulgent pastime of a privileged few. Understanding the economic processes that govern fashion should take us beyond the frivolities of individual taste and vanity, while helping us remember that vanity has been a not insignificant motivation in human affairs. By looking at fashion as an economic system that has wide influence, we may gain useful insight into the ongoing processes of supply and demand that govern consumption behavior.

Notes

1. Furthermore, beyond Istanbul, throughout this study the data will be drawn primarily from the Anatolian context.

2. Jirousek (1997), 203–15.

3. Hamilton (1990), 45.

4. Hunt (1996), 44.

5. Heath (1992), 20–21.

6. Nystrom (1928), 328.

7. Horner, 1990. This thesis offers a useful and extensive analysis of the idea of tradition, a term that has been used in ways that are far from respectful. All the same, the idea of tradition is one that many embrace with pride, and when carefully defined, it can be a much more flexible and universal descriptor of dress, at least, than are other commonly used terms such as ethnic or regional—both of which create difficulties in the Ottoman context.

8. Jirousek (1997), 205.

9. *Oxford English Dictionary* (1989), 3372.

10. Hobsbawm and Ranger (1983).

11. Özel (1992), 43–44.

12. Roach and Musa, 1980.

13. Hunt (1996), 45.

14. Batterberry (1982), 87–88.

15. Roche (1989).

16. Boucher (1987), 270.

17. (Davenport (1965), 681; Sweetman (1988) 44–45. There is also a rather

interesting story in connection with the meeting of Mme de Pompadour and the King, arranged to occur at a costume ball. A print depicting this occasion shows a number of guests dressed in Turkish attire, complete with exaggeratedly large Turkish headgear. The king was said to have dropped his handkerchief at the feet of his new favorite, after the manner ascribed to the Turkish sultan in selecting his favorite. All of this exemplifies the European fascination with *Turquerie,* an issue I discuss elsewhere. Jirousek (1995), 22.

18. Milbank (1985), 22–26.

19. Göçek (1996), 38.

20. Şem'dâni-zâde (1976–1981), 36.

21. Hughes (1983). The evidence for the church speaking out against dress was not consistent, nor was the church, especially after 1600, since church and state in Europe were increasingly less unified. By this period religious pronouncements were not papal bulls or other formal edicts with any force of law. Christian polemics against dress mainly took the form of sermons and essays intended to persuade. Such essays have been generally taken as evidence that people were doing the opposite of what religious leaders railed against.

22. Hunt (1996), 29–34.

23. deVries (1994), 256.

24. Scarce (1988), 13–31; Çağman (1993), 256–57.

25. See Baker (1986), 72–85; Micklewright (1987), 33–43; Koçu (1969); Göçek (1996); Scarce (1980), 144–167; Çağman (1993), 256–58; Şeni (1995), 25–40.

26. Tavernier (1678), 47; deBusbecq, (1633), 150.

27. Blout (1636), 26

28. Goffman (1990), 10–14.

29. Anderson (1989), 6.

30. Anderson (1989), 7.

31. Skilliter (1977), 150; Goffman (1990), 108; Anderson (1989), 290.

32. Evans (1988), 28–31.

33. Çağman (1994), 256–58.

34. Faroqhi in Quataert, ed. (1994), 14. The imported Indian cloth also spawned an industry producing *indiennes* around Aleppo and in eastern Anatolia in the seventeenth century and thereafter. These textiles were also exported to France in the eighteenth century.

35. Cited in Micklewright (1987), 34.

36. Scarce (1987), 81.

37. Tezcan (1986), 26.

38. Kumbaracılar (no date).

39. Since trustworthy images of women's dress are not abundant, interpretation of the visual evidence must be done cautiously. For example, are the unbuttoned, lowered necklines seen in the seventeenth and (a few times) sixteenth centuries a change in fashion, or is it that the conventions of Islamic painting discouraged such informal depictions in earlier periods? There is at least one example of a closed front *antari* with a moderately deep round neckline Çağman (1993). Certainly the depictions of women in some seventeenth- and certainly in eighteenth-century paintings have an erotic flavor absent in earlier works. In any case, the garment forms remain fairly similar in the sixteenth and seventeenth centuries.

40. Jirousek (1997).

41. Russell (1983), 145; Payne, Winakor, and Farrell-Beck (1992), 2–4.

42. Göçek (1996), 99.

43. Baker (1986), 74–76; Koçu (1967), 113–14. There are slightly conflicting accounts of the origin of the fez. Koçu states that the idea of a fez was introduced to Mahmud II by Mehmed Husrev Pasha, admiral of the Mediterranean fleet, who first introduced it for use by his sailors. According to Baker, however, the acceptance of the new headgear was argued from the precedent that the army of Muhammad Ali, governor of Egypt, was already wearing it. However, in either case it is north African in origin, and introduced by a successful military officer with a taste for European military methods. There also seems to be agreement that the fez was initially manufactured in Tunis for the Ottoman army, although fez factories were soon established in Istanbul and other Anatolian locations.

44. Baker (1986); Quataert (1997).

45. Micklewright (1987), 40–41.

46. Koçu, (1967), 51, 215, 242.

47. Jirousek (1997).

48. Eicher and Erekosima (1980).

49. Davis (1992), 108–15.

50. Karpat (1973), 2; Gerber (1988), 213.

51. Kinross (1977), 142–43.

52. Göçek (1996), p. 34; 156, nn. 58, 59.

53. Scull and Cohen 91983), 6.

54. Quataert (1997).

55. Hunt (1996), 51. Hunt borrows this term from Thorsten Veblen (1979) *Theory of the Leisure Class,* New York: Penguin Books, but turns it to his own uses in his model of sumptuary patterns in Europe.

56. Göçek (1996), 38.

57. Şem'dâni-zâde (1976–1981), 36.

58. Sutton (1991), 255; Hughes (1983), 69–70 and 99. Hughes also points out, however, that sumptuary edicts could serve other ends than legal enforcement in Italian cities, where the moral stance taken by the act of legislation was viewed as an end in itself. Circumstances no doubt differed in Ottoman society, and more research is needed before we can claim to understand the full meaning of these laws.

59. Lang and Lang, 1965.

60. Göçek (1996), 93.

61. Göçek (1996), 98–107.

62. deVries (1994).

63. McGowan in İnalcık with Quataert (1994).

64. Genç in Quataert, ed. (1994), 60.

65. Quataert (1993), 4–7.

66. Quataert (1993), 162–65.

67. Quataert (1993), 40, 90, 118, 162.

68. Garnett (1891), 429.

69. Nystrom (1928), 328.

70. Kidwell (1974), 101–11.

71. Tezcan and Delibaş (1986), 27–28.

72. Boucher (1987), 191.

73. Hunt (1996), 45.

74. İnalcık with Quataert (1994), 762–63.

75. Micklewright (1987), 41.

76. Hunt (1996), 76.

77. Jirousek (1996), 22–33; Baines (1981).

7

Cheap and Easy: The Creation of Consumer Culture in Late Ottoman Society

Elizabeth B. Frierson

Ottoman Economies in the Age of Capital

In her edited volume, *The Sex of Things: Gender and Consumption in Historical Perspective,* Victoria de Grazia raises a number of questions about male-female patterns of consumption, and differentiations between male and female in the discourses of consumption which can be applied usefully to Ottoman historiography of the nineteenth century. In introducing her contributors' work, she problematizes categories such as commodification, capital, and the public sphere, and the paired notions of a male wage-earner and a female wage-spender. At the same time, she invites challenges from precisely such work as is presented in our volume, and I suspect she does so intentionally, by framing it within what she calls a "Euro-American model," and pointing to ways in which her volume will challenge that model.[1] Still, her definition of consumer society for the purposes of the volume shows just how profound a challenge our work might bring to Western historiography:

> This concept [consumer society] is intended here to identify the emergence of a peculiar type of market society, the Western capitalist system of exchange, and especially to probe the ever more identifiable *modern* aspect of its development. This modernity lies first in carrying out acts of consumption within capitalist exchange networks and then in the organization of institutions, resources, and values around ever larger flows

> and accumulations of commodities. It also lies in the transformation of goods from being relatively static symbols around which hierarchies were ordered to being more directly constitutive of class, social status, and personal identity.[2]

Such transformations in Ottoman semiotics of hierarchy and status were delineated over twenty years ago by Şerif Mardin, and others have built on his analyses to portray the growing inherence of identity in goods.[3] He showed, however, that an intertwining of hierarchy and status in the Ottoman case is not specifically modern, but more precisely has changed its terms and signs over time. Also, what is most modern about the development of market society in the Ottoman nineteenth and early twentieth centuries is quite different from de Grazia's use of the term. At the level of state politics, the Hamidian public sphere showed a marked rhetorical resistance to "carrying out acts of consumption within capitalist exchange networks." Ministers of state, provincial governors, and state and municipal bureaucrats of Sultan Abdul Hamid II (1876–1909) presided over, and at times intervened directly in, dramatic changes in commerce and manufactures, and the expansion of each of these spheres reshaped Ottoman society at all levels.

A recent trend in efforts to capture social responses and cultural changes within a historical perspective draws on photographs, records of commercial life, work life in the new factories, and changing home industries, and on print sources such as the inexpensive commercial press and schoolbooks.[4] In the Abdul Hamid era, then, de Grazia's "capitalist exchange networks" were seen both as an intrusion from the West and as something to be adapted and domesticated. In Illustration 1, we have an example of a long-running advertisement for Singer sewing machines, dating from the point when Singer began marketing machines to the home consumer and small workshop owner. The advertisement indicates the domestic setting for its portable machine and ornate ironwork table by resting the latest model on top of a Turkish-style rug. Were such rugs in fact features of households that used Singer sewing machines? The advertiser apparently thought so. Here we can bring into analytical play the ways that Michel de Certeau highlighted responses by consumers to consumer society, and complicate our understanding of the reception of consumer values by shoppers. De Certeau's intent was to break through the perception that consumers were passive receivers of market imperatives, acting as obedient consumers of capital goods. Instead, the processes by which consumers choose and use the goods they buy are actions that explicitly

Illustration 1

destabilize ideas of market dominance. One of de Certeau's interpreters put the intention of this notion succinctly:

> With the category of tactics, de Certeau extracts consumption from theories of mass society and repositions it as a form of resistance. Consumption is no longer victimization by the culture industry or irrational conformity to mass society, but a play of heterogeneity, a disruptive intervention in the smooth operations of the system.[5]

This facet of de Certeau's work can provide insight into the other precisely modern and non-Western aspect of late Ottoman consumer markets: a modernized but not entirely Westernized commercial sphere was turned by various actors to Ottoman loyalist purposes, and later to the service of explicitly nationalist agendas. In other words, Ottoman consumer agendas came to have specifically anti-Western, buy-local, and ultimately buy-Turk imperatives. Furthermore, through the medium of the cheap, illustrated press, these imperatives, often originating in state policy, were adopted, internalized, and refined by advertisers, readers, and shoppers into techniques of resistance to western manufactured goods.

Though conclusions to such questions lie far beyond the scope of the present paper, it is also worth positing that flows and accumulations of commodities in the variants of statist capitalism which policy makers tried out in the Abdul Hamid (1876–1909) and Young Turk (1908–1923) eras also may show norms very different from those suggested by de Grazia. The years from 1911 to 1922 with wartime economies from conflicts in the Balkans, World War I, and the Turkish War of Independence will be especially important in tracing the development of a nationalist economy that might be at odds with this paradigm. If our work on Ottoman consumer society in this volume and further studies turns up more such discontinuities with the Euro-American model, then we will be in a position to argue forcefully for disaggregating the categories "Western" and "modern" and remixing them in a more analytically productive way.

In this essay I hope to add new evidence from Hamidian press advertising to our current debates, which frequently invoke questions of colonial versus noncolonial relationships and structures in the Ottomans' politics and in their shifting positions in the world economy. I find these questions productive and also an accurate reflection of many of the concerns expressed by late Ottoman writers and readers in the popular press. Still, I am uncomfortable with the primacy this formulation places on the penetration of capital and subsequent responses to the West, and continue to search my sources for ways to stretch our questions to include experiences and attitudes that do not comfortably fit within such a model. Elsewhere I have discussed the compound of production, consumption, display politics, and fashion which inflected much of Hamidian discourse about clothes and shopping, arguing that display and spectatorship contained subversive elements with respect to Western culture.[6] Shoppers and strollers, and those who chronicled and policed them, used selection, adaptation, and display of consumer goods to convey both admiration of, and hostility and resistance toward, Western fashion and consumer culture. Here I present a more detailed study of one factor in these encounters, late Ottoman merchandising and responses by shoppers in the cheap, illustrated press.

Media and Markets

From the 1890s, the inexpensive, illustrated press for women became a forum for discussion among the new professional and skilled working women who had graduated from the Hamidian schools, especially the industrial arts schools and the normal school or teacher training college. The women's cheap, illustrated press constituted a public sphere that was distinctly Ottoman in its formation first of maternal and wifely ideals, then in its continual debate on more complicated questions forming around women at work and women in public life, largely framed in terms of reinventing tradition and selective modernization. The productions of editors, writers, advertisers, and responsive readers highlight social transactions and state-society interactions that roughly parallel changes in the economic spheres as state officials intervened, and entrepreneurs, bankers, and workers responded, to increase the competitiveness of Ottoman manufactures in a rapidly changing world economy.

The press' role expanded as editors endorsed products and professionals, as writers, explained principles of education, health, nutrition, fashion, and esthetics, and as advertisers promoted their goods in keeping with the pedantic tone set by these journals (see Illustration 2). Readers in turn wrote letters to endorse places of business or to protest high prices, and they fiercely debated moral-freighted products such as the corset. In the last two decades of the Hamidian era, these endorsements, promotions, and protests increasingly centered around Ottoman manufacturers and retailers, as well as Ottoman professionals in medicine and pharmaceuticals, as a venue for loyalist expenditures. After the mid-1890s, editors moved away from endorsing Ottoman manufacturers, retailers, and professionals, which implied support of all Ottoman subjects regardless of ethnic, confessional, or protonational identity, and toward endorsing specifically Muslim places of business and consultation. This striking change in rhetoric and options is highlighted by a contrast with two constants in the language of advertisers throughout this transformation: the cheapness of their products and the ease with which they could be purchased either with cash or on credit.[7]

Hamidian-era advertisers informed readers of their locations, hours, and available goods and services in a variety of ways. Large

Illustration 2. Advertisement for a women's clothing store.

concerns, such as Ottoman pharmaceutical and cosmetic companies, featured ornately calligraphed product and price information in full-page advertisements, while others used illustrations of their goods, especially accessories such as gloves or fans, or educational, such as primary readers. Fashion advertisements for clothes usually featured these as if they were fanned out on a counter, or on a model, but the human in the clothes rarely appeared in the Hamidian era, unless the person depicted was clearly a Westerner. Pattern and how-to sections as well as news from the latest collections were full of pirated, imitated, and original illustrations of Parisian or British or American women of style, but advertisers, by contrast to editors, generally shunned full-body portrayals of their models.

In a rare break with this trend, in February 1897, Haïm Mazza and Sons advertised their main department store to the readers of *The Ladies' Own Gazette (Hanımlara Mahsûs Gazete)* with a lavish illustration of ladies shopping at their fabric and pattern counter (see Illustration 3). In this advertisement, we see one facet of the Ottoman urban marketplace: minority merchants selling the finest of dry goods to upper-class women dressed in a range of *allafranga* fashion, one of them accompanied by a man whose frock coat and fez also presented a norm for the modern Ottoman male.[8] The depiction of one woman who is veiled in a continental style accords with other evidence that Ottoman women of the upper class, Muslim as well as non-Muslim, were venturing outside their homes to see for themselves the array of goods imported by the merchants of Galata and Pera.[9]

Haïm Mazza and Sons either lost their prime spot in the magazine or pulled the advertisement of their own accord within a week of its first appearance, however. With the signal exception of satire, I have not yet seen another such illustration of a veiled woman shopping in a modern dry-goods store in the Ottoman-language press of this era.[10] Perhaps Haïm Mazza and Sons were too bold in featuring even this slim evocation of Ottoman women in their advertisements, or perhaps the loyalist editors of *Hanımlara Mahsûs Gazete* preferred not to showcase a posh Jewish establishment among their exhortations to Muslim progress and civilization, as much as it might accord with a multiethnic Ottomanist view also featured in such publications. I will return to both of these possibilities, but first I want to highlight a few elements of the language used in this advertisement.

In the first two lines, in almost the same breath, Haïm Mazza and Sons touted the high quality of their silk fabrics and their low prices, claiming that their goods were of such a low price as to admit no competition or, in the slang of the 1990s, they would not be undersold: *reqabet qabul edemiyecek derecede haqiqi ehven fiat ile furuht ettiğimiz . . . i'lan olunur.* They also emphasized through repetition that their goods were imported; in addition to silks, they carried velvets, prints, embroidered fabrics, *çarşaf*s in the latest fashion, or *son moda çarşaflık,* as well as fabrics and other goods for families. They reiterated their claim of the lowest prices available, and also offered wholesale prices to customers who paid cash for fabrics bought in meter lots: *metro ile reqabet*

Illustration 3

qabul eyitmez derecede gayet ucuz satıldığı ve her güne mubay 'at peşin aqçe ile icra olunduğu i 'lan olunur.

Some advertisers offered more complicated terms of purchase in their advertisements, though whether this argues for a more sophisticated consumer or for an increasing familiarity with credit purchase, is unclear. Quataert has discussed credit arrangements that factory workers could make with retailers, as when one worker's purchase would be backed by a guarantee that his co-workers would finish out the payments if he was unable to do so.[11] The Singer Sewing Machine Company marketed its products both to home and factory producers, and offered credit arrangements that would have affected many homes at all levels of society, from sweatshop owner through factory owners to *konak* households with private seamstresses and tailors.[12]

Advertisers exploited this environment of buying on credit in the 1890s, and developed a competitive rhetoric of increasing sophistication in the early 1900s. The Herdjai Store in the Covered Market offered its pure silver and gold chains, jewelry made with pearls and precious gems, walking sticks and watches (of the most exquisite quality at the cheapest prices possible) on terms of five percent of the purchase price paid per week. Shoppers paying with cash received a five percent discount. The owners would take used jewelry in good repair as a pledge or pawn of ten percent for those paying cash, and fifteen percent for those paying on credit.[13] Other types of inducements were used to lure customers. The Petit Lyons store in Galata offered more down-market goods than the Herdjai store, specifically fake diamonds as a defense against the extravagant expenditures necessary for "civilized people in our era," suggesting that the color and appearance of their paste diamonds would persuade any shopper against spending "excessive amounts" on the real thing.[14] Nikolai Pappadapolous sold his pure olive oil with an imperial license and a registered trademark, in amounts ranging from one bottle up through large tins, and offered a rebate of 100 lira to any customer who could find a more pure or better-tasting olive oil.[15]

The locations of these stores in the traditional shopping districts of the city, such as Stamboul, the Covered Bazaar, and Galata, suggest the range of shopping venues available for consumer goods, despite imperial decrees, forbidding Muslim women from shopping in Christian stores. The press took on a hortatory role in the same vein as the decrees at the turn of the century, and they were joined by their readers in this effort. Belkis Hanım from the wealthy suburb of Bebek wrote to *Hanımlara Mahsûs Gazete* in December 1899 to describe in glowing terms her first visit to a new store, *Haşmet ve Rıf'at Mağazası,* in a traditionally Muslim market at the opposite end of the Galata Bridge from the mainly Christian shopping districts. The high quality of the silk and wool fabrics came third on her list of reasons to shop there. First was the treatment she received, the description of which evokes operetta in its extremity of praise:

> The cleanliness, good nature, and organization in this store is magnificent, and the courteous treatment and honorable behavior truly dazzle the eyes. . . . Truly, with such refined dealings together with the zeal and endeavor which they are exerting on behalf of the ladies of our nation, Haşmet and Rif'at Efendis'

> store is a sure witness of . . . the elevation and progress which have been shown in the Empire in a short span of time.

Second, she was delighted by the low prices, half of what she would have been compelled to pay in the European district of Beyoğlu for similar or for shoddy goods, while Haşmet and Rıf'at Efendis imported the latest and finest of European goods. Her tone was unreservedly triumphant at having found a Muslim store selling first-quality goods at a lower price than in the European shopping district. This was not a new departure for Belkis Hanım, though, because she was driven to search out Haşmet and Rıf'at Efendis' store in the first place because her former Muslim dry-goods merchant, Emin Yahya Efendi, had closed his business.[16]

It is of course possible that Belkis Hanım was providing free advertising for a business that was close to heart for more personal, economic reasons. Whatever her motivation, her recommendations were picked up by Bedriye Hanım, who wrote a few weeks later from Çamlıca to confirm and add an explicitly political point to Belkis Hanım's recommendations. After reading Belkis Hanım's description, she went to the Haşmet and Rıf'at Store herself, along with a young bride-to-be who was shopping for her trousseau. Bedriye Hanım was also full of praise for the variety of quality goods, and the honorable and courteous service provided, but she was even more emphatic in her hopes for what the store represented for Ottoman Muslims. In addition to the "magnificence" of the store which had to be seen to be believed, she also was "proud of the degree of progress of Ottoman places of business. God willing, in the future a day will come when the merchandise sold in such stores of ours will consist only of Ottoman goods." But pity Emin Yahya Efendi, whose store Bedriye Hanım dismissed as "not having been all that elegant anyway," as she pronounced the new store better than the old.[17]

The writers' references to "our gazette" make it appear initially that they were staff writers, but both Belkis Hanım and Bedriye Hanım used this phrase while making it clear that they were in fact subscribers to the magazine, using it as a clearing house for information. To further confuse matters, their descriptions were not that different from those used by the editors of the magazine for promoting Muslim professionals and enterprises. Advertisers also came to adopt the language of endorsement and recommendation to bring customers to their shops and offices. Both readers and advertisers used new journalistic turns of phrase and vocabulary to give themselves the authority and the protection held by editors in loyalist serials such as *Hanımlara Mahsûs Gazete.*

Professional Services

Pharmacists, dentists, and doctors of various specialties became part of the advertising scene fairly rapidly, first as editors' announcements or recommendations in the early days of the cheap press. By the 1890s, they routinely took out their own advertisements, and followed the editorial endorsement practice of describing in detail their Ottoman or Western degrees, their honors, and their honorable characters. In his advertisements, Dr Hafız Hilmi described in excruciating detail his expertise in the most dangerous and intricate of obstetric and gynecological complications. Dr Şükr Ahmet explained his ophthalmic experiments and surgeries in similar detail, making these advertisements a sort of scientizing infomercial.[18] Editors continued to weigh in with their own opinions. In a series on Muslim pharmacies which celebrated "the honesty and uprightness" of their proprietors, editors gave the pharmacist Ahmed Nüzhet Bey a glowing testimonial. In Nüzhet Bey's case, his years of studying for both a medical and a pharmaceutical diploma were singled out for praise. Most striking of all, Nüzhet Bey apparently considered "the welfare of the state as his primary duty, on the one hand, by coming to the aid of the sick, on the other by complying with the state's lowering of pharmaceutical prices and therefore earning thousands of lira for the state treasury by hindering those pharmacists in the Mısır Çarşısı who profit illegally from the hoarding of goods."[19] In the same issue, a ritual circumciser who had inherited his father's business through apprenticeship rather than medical training was recommended similarly for his skill, and especially for his speed and skill to those parents wishing "not to cause distress" to their children.[20]

By contrast, the announcement of a Greek pharmacist's "Ottoman pharmacy" seems somewhat subdued, giving Lefter Efendi credit for "refined dealings" with his customers and nothing else by way of praise. The editors recommend the pharmacy, in relatively terse phrasing, to those in need *(erbab-i ihtiyacat)* for its practice of having physicians with various specialties on hand for consultation.[21] What lifted members of the modernizing professional service classes above their peers, then, was not necessarily Western training. More important were such qualities as being Muslim and serving "the welfare of the state." In the loyalist press, however, this avoidance of a powerful endorsement was as close as discussions of doctors and pharmacists came to the blatantly patriotic tone of discussions about clothes and other consumer goods. Details about medical fees were also oddly absent in the price-conscious advertising world of the late Hamidian press.

Nutrition products, today's health foods, also seemed immune to concerns about low prices and competition, as in graham crackers or pure gluten bread, or baby food and supplements.[22] These goods, like imported beauty products, were marketed to an elite section of the reading public, those who could afford to experiment with nontraditional remedies for common illnesses, and who were inclined to believe in the efficacy of western science.

In families of all social levels, anything promising to improve a child's chances of good health was probably given greater priority in household budgets than were clothes and household furnishings. For these and other reasons, providers of medical services felt no need to draw customers with promises of cheap prices and easy payment. The discussion of the pharmacist Nüzhet Bey's compliance with state regulation of pharmaceutical prices also raises the question of setting and policing the prices of imported goods. Perhaps health products, as is often the case today, were subjected to higher import duties or were under tighter controls that made them impossible to sell profitably at discounted prices.

Blurred Boundaries

Finally, who precisely was promoting a set of goods or services may not always have been clear to readers, as both editors' endorsements and advertisements mixed freely in the end pages of most magazines. While doctors' advertisements tended to be boxed off from the rest of the text, their language was often hard to distinguish from the prose of a scientific writer discussing a new mode of treatment, and even harder to distinguish from editors' endorsements, as both endorsements and advertisements were generally in the forms of announcements.

An announcement typically would follow the form of one used to promote a new midwife's practice, which reported one Fahime Hanım's training and career as a midwife at the imperial medical school with enthusiasm. The editors of *The Ladies' Own Gazette* boasted of her prize-winning results in qualifying exams, stressed her aid to needy women, and offered their administrative offices as a place of referral for expectant mothers seeking to contact her.[23] Raşide Hanım's bridal shop near the Bayezid complex, near a traditionally Muslim shopping district, was more soberly promoted in December 1900 for her "appropriate" fashions at low prices: blouses, jackets, skirts, bridal gowns, dresses, and overcoats, as well as jewelry and supplies for banquets.[24] A small typesetter's note in the corner of the block of prose taken up by the discussion of this store was the only indication that this, unlike the notice about Fahime Hanım, was an advertisement and not an editors' endorsement.

These scant boundaries between endorsements, advertisements, and readers' shopping advice indicate that as state protectionist policies bore fruit in the forms of Ottoman manufacturers, and as educational reforms brought more Ottoman professionals into their respective fields, editors became increasingly forthright in their efforts to create an Ottoman consumer ethic among their readers. Letters to the editor and responses to individual articles about the corset or Western-style suggest further that readers were actively participating in this formation of new patriotic loyalties and anti-Western, ultimately anti-Christian and anti-Greek, anti-Armenian practices.[25] In the years immediately prior to the Young Turk revolution of 1908, exiled opposition writers as well joined in the growing antiminority bias in the marketplace. This is one of the many continuities in Ottoman practices between the Hamidian and Young Turk eras. While some opponents of the Hamidian regime protested the massacres of Armenians by Kurdish irregular, others found the escalation of hostiles suited to their efforts to create a purely Muslim, and eventually a purely Turkish, Ottoman identity. By 1905 anti-Armenian consumer ideologies were fashioned into a plan of the rightwing of Young Turk ideology, as opposition thinkers attempted in their own way to tailor "modernization into an Islamic jacket,"[26] here in a call for a boycott of Armenian goods:

> Why should we bow before these Armenians, who make of us a laughingstock though we never deserve it? The fortunes that they have made, the arts that they have grasped, are all generated from the fact that they have lived at our expense. Let's display zeal, let's roll up our sleeves. Do not have any kind of relationship with the Armenians; then the number of our merchants and artisans will increase as a natural consequence.[27]

These attitudes gained force after the revolution and the continuing conflict with European powers and their favored minorities. By 1911 in the Young Turk era, the editors of *Kadın (Woman)* completely merged the endorsement and advertisement formats to urge their readers to perform a national service—shopping at the Nejidler Store:

> To our honored readers . . .
>
> In order not to be overwhelmed or deceived by the deep torrents of Istanbul trade; if you wish to make a visit that is

> pleasant, elegant, graceful, and good-natured . . . if you would both encourage an Ottoman place of business and also be of service to our nation then, dear readers, we sincerely recommend that you visit the Nejidler Store, next to the Qomanto Han, for inexpensive, elegant, sound, and beautiful *çarşafs*, fabric for clothes, laces, cords, and ribbons, and so forth, all of these things inexpensive to an astonishing degree, our hope being that Ottoman money would stay in the Ottoman state.[28]

Contraindications and Conclusions

I have presented here a progressive narrative, showing first, a move away from imports and toward local manufactures, and second, a move toward buy-Ottoman and then to buy-Muslim promotions in the late-Hamidian press. It should nonetheless be stated that these are broad trends which in no way imply a clear transition from one mode of advertising or shopping to another as the century turned. Memoirs of the era describe pedlar women who were still making the rounds with their *bohçalar,* suggesting that as with the jobber in Western retailing, old forms of distribution continued within the evolution of new forms of merchandising.[29] In addition, as Illustrations 4 and 5 from 1903 and 1904 show, advertisers in Muslim magazines continued to embellish their prose with lettering in Armenian, Greek, Latin, and even faux Japanese. This would suggest strongly that foreign merchandise had lost neither its appeal nor its profitability across the board. Farmer's almanacs giving the dates for neighborhood markets may also have been used by pedlars whose goods reached sectors of society largely distinct from those touched by the print media.[30]

Finally, of course, I have been able to present only a sample of the very extensive Hamidian women's press in Ottoman Turkish, leaving aside not only the less successful women's magazines but also the family press, professional journals, serials in other languages, children's and men's magazines, and a host of other venues for print communication about commerce. Comparisons with these other branches of the cheap, illustrated press will allow Ottomanists to answer de Grazia's and others' theories of consumption, gender, and capital more fully. If my reading of the women's press is any indication, further evidence on commercial life and consumer values in this era will turn up as many contradictions as continuities. Such ambiguities bolster the sense that at least in its capital city, Ottoman society was neither classically

Illustration 4

Illustration 5

colonial nor entirely autonomous in its economic discourse of selective Westernization, civilization, and modernity. The evidentiary trends outlined above suggest a consumer culture that consistently prized good value and ready money, and that flexed with some agility around new forms of credit, new products, and questions of esthetics. Further, we can see in broad strokes how patriotism came increasingly to play a role in opinion-makers', promotion of goods. In response to the exhortations of editors and advertisers, consumers in turn developed strategies and tactics along the lines set out by de Certeau. These strategies are seen in bold relief in the Young Turks' economic policies, and we are beginning to see the documentation of similar attitudes among Hamidian policymakers. Further research into the processes of advertising and documentation of Ottoman consumption patterns will allow us to refine our understanding of the points at which Western goods were accepted wholeheartedly, rejected as thoroughly, and when they were accepted only insofar as they could be turned to ends resistant to western capital and political domination.

Notes

1. de Grazia (1996), 5.

2. de Grazia (1996), 4.

3. Mardin (1974); Toprak (1982).

4. I use the term "popular press" to refer to the cheap, illustrated weeklies and dailies which proliferated in the Hamidian era. While we do not yet know how many people could read or afford even the cheap serials, I have argued in my dissertation and elsewhere from evidence of rising school enrollments, internal evidence in the magazines, from the change in writers from elite housewives to schoolteachers and professional journalists, and from changing styles of writing, advertising, and reader response, that from the 1890s forward these serials reached a wider audience and addressed concerns beyond those peculiar to an elite readership. See Frierson (1996) and Frierson (1995b).

5. Poster (1997), 124.

6. Frierson (1995a).

7. For this essay I have drawn my examples, unless noted otherwise, from *Hanımlara Mahsûs Gazete* or *The Ladies' Own Gazette,* the women's magazine for which state sponsorship and toleration are most easily proved due to its longevity and content.

8. *Hanımlara Mahsûs Gazete* 100 (18 February 1897), 3.

9. Mustafa Asım quoted a Frenchwoman resident in Salonica describing the Istanbul twopiece *çarşaf* and *peçe* as revealing and highly ornamented with braids and laces, and thus out of keeping with Islam, not all that different, in fact from Parisian *pèlerines* and *voilettes*. *"Çarşaflar ve peçeler," Hanımlara Mahsûs Gazete* 89–291 (13 December 1900), 3–4. He may have been giving her account more credence than it merited, though, in order to foward his own rhetorical agenda against *allafranga* street fashions on Muslim women.

10. See Palmira Brummett, research on satire in the late Ottoman period.

11. Quataert (1993), 56–57.

12. Ibid., 56. See also Tezcan (1992).

13. *Hanımlara Mahsûs Gazete* 1 (15 March 1904), 20.

14. Ibid.

15. Ibid.

16. Belkis Hanım, *Hanımlara Mahsûs Gazete*, 239–37 (30 November 1899), 3–4.

17. Bedriye Hanım, *Hanımlara Mahsûs Gazete*, 243–41 (28 December 1899), 3.

18. *"Doktor Hafiz Hilmi, ebe ve kadın hastalıkları tabib-i husûsi—tedavi-yi cedid," Hanımlara Mahsûs Gazete* 7 (9 April 1903), 98; on Dr. Ahmet, *Hanımlara Mahsûs Gazete* 1 (15 March 1904), 20.

19. *"Islâm Eczahaneleri ve Ahmed Nûzhet Bey," Hanımlara Mahsûs Gazete* 1 (19 March 1904), 10–11.

20. *"Sünnetci Mahmud Efendi,"* ibid.

21. *"Eczane-yi osmani," Hanımlara Mahsûs Gazete* 241–43 (28 December 1899), 6.

22. *"Halis gluten ekmeği," Hanımlara Mahsûs Gazete* 1 (19 March 1904), 14.

23. *Hanımlara Mahsûs Gazete* No. 151 (3 March 1898), 4.

24. *Hanımlara Mahsûs Gazete* 289–91 (13 December 1900), 6.

25. See Frierson (1995a) for an elaboration of this point. Nicole van Os forwarded similar arguments for the Young Turk era into her paper on national fashion at the Koç University conference on women in the Ottoman world, September 1996.

26. Hanioğlu (1995), 8.

27. Ulug, *"Ermeniler"* ("Armenians"), *Türk* 11, 21 October 1905 (published in Cairo). Cited in Şükrü Hanioğlu, *The Young Turk Revolution of 1908*, forthcoming.

28. *Kadın* (10 Temmuz 1327/23 July 1911), p. 13. This announcement appeared weekly for several weeks.

29. Porter and Livesay (1971), 52–53, 214–27.

30. There are many such almanacs in library collections, usually without the name of a publisher. They generally sold for 1 *guruş* from the 1290s forward and covered lunar and solar years.

8

Personal, Public, and Political (Re)Constructions: Photographs and Consumption

Nancy C. Micklewright

This study of photographs has two goals: first, to suggest a framework of analysis for photographs from the Ottoman Empire within the context of consumption studies; and second, to examine aspects of Ottoman photography within that framework.[1] I have gathered materials for the construction of this analytical framework from: consumption studies done primarily in a European or North American historical context; anthropologists working on the social role of objects; art historical models for the analysis of objects in a social context; studies of photo history from different contexts; and historians of the Ottoman Empire who have looked at aspects of economic and social life.[2] The photographs on which this study is based are those that have been published in the various studies of Ottoman photography or history,[3] as well as those collected into albums primarily during the reign of Sultan Abdul Hamid II, now in the Istanbul University Library.[4]

Photographs occupy an intriguing position in consumption studies, and indeed in the material world of economic activity.[5] On the one hand, their relatively modest cost places them at the bottom of a scale of relative economic value, especially compared to such conspicuously expensive items as villas/*yalıs*, elaborate dresses, furniture in the European mode, jewelry, and other similarly costly objects which are sometimes used as an index of Ottoman consumer practices. From the point of view of consumer cost, photographs are more similar to ephemeral goods such as food or drink, lower-priced goods, whose use nonetheless may reflect important changes in consumption practices. Yet far from being regarded as ephemeral, photographs are valued precisely because of their ability to capture a moment and preserve it. The modestly priced photograph, accessible to many levels of society, is saved and circulated long after *yalıs* have burned down or been sold, dresses worn out and old furniture discarded. In this way, the photograph is more similar to other art products, part of whose value lies in the expectation of their long postproduction life and circulation.

It is not my task here to define consumption studies,[6] but it is useful to consider what we may hope to gain by studying Ottoman photography from the point of view of consumption. In economic history generally, the focus of study often falls on production, and on aspects of production such as supply and demand, considered on a large-scale basis. While art historical studies may often concentrate on issues of patronage, this is generally in an elite context, since that level of society commissions the works of art which have been valued enough to be saved over the years. Directing our attention to consumption will perhaps allow a recognition of consumer agency (in contexts not generally described as patronage), as well as a foregrounding of the household, or other small groups, as a unit of economic action.

A number of the writers involved in such projects argue for the importance of reexamining the basic assumptions which underlie our thinking about why patterns of consumption change. Particularly useful is the idea that goods would be desired for their own sake and not because of attached prestige. This challenges perhaps the most basic assumption of all—that people adopt new fashions, new art, new furnishings for their houses because they want to be like those higher up on the social ladder—in other words, emulative consumption.[7] In a European context, being higher up on the social ladder is generally a matter of wealth and social position. This concept has influenced the common assumption that the new goods, which came from Europe, were adopted because Ottomans wanted to be more like Europeans. While this is still a possibility worth examining, the idea that Ottomans adopted some new goods, including photographs, because of their intrinsic merits, should also be examined.

Two articles that are especially useful in thinking about photography in the Ottoman context are Jean-Christophe Agnew's work in the 1993 book on consumption edited by Brewer and Porter, and one by Igor Kopytoff, in the well known 1986 volume edited by Arjun Appadurai, *The Social Life of Things*.[8] Each author is careful to embed the study of objects, and of consumption, in a social context that is complex as well as historically and culturally specific. Kopytoff talks about what he calls the cultural biography of things, looking at objects as a "culturally constructed entity, endowed with culturally specific meanings, classified and reclassified into culturally constituted categories."[9] So for photographs, we might ask what were the culturally specific meanings of family portraits for the Ottomans, especially in a culture which did not have a very extensive tradition of portraiture? How did these meanings change during the decades that the Ottomans were adopting photography for their own use? How did the meanings of the photographs themselves change as they passed from one person to another? Into what categories were photographs placed?

Agnew refers to the work of a number of other scholars who examined working-class and immigrant patterns of consumption in the United States, who suggest that in these contexts, goods were often incorporated into alternative systems of meaning; that there could be oppositional or negotiated readings of meaning, and that meanings exist on different levels, in unstable relationship with each other. This series of ideas, too, is very helpful for beginning to look at what photography meant in an Ottoman context.

Photographs demand study from a variety of viewpoints: as examples of technical skill, as pieces of art, as personal possessions, as goods which have economic value in a market. But as objects which produce and carry meaning, photographs are in many ways much more complex and difficult to deconstruct than, for example, ceramics or textiles. I regard them not necessarily as documents of a reality, but as texts which require careful analysis. They are part of the construction of a normative social reality which involves class, gender, ethnic, and professional identities and claims to identities. Before looking specifically at photographs in the Ottoman Empire, it is worth taking a bit of time to lay out some of the challenges which photographs present, to problematize our look at the Ottoman material.

Because of their perceived ability to reproduce an image of reality, photographs since the announcement of the first techniques in 1839, always have been valued, on an explicit or implicit level, for their truthfulness. Despite the fact that the possibilities for the manipulation of the photographic image are virtually unlimited, people continue to believe in the reality of what is presented in a photograph. In contemporary photography, artists can play with this quality of the photograph, creating blatantly unbelievable images to get our attention, as (to cite only one example) in the work of the American photographer William Wegman who poses his dogs, dressed in human clothing, in human settings.

In an Ottoman context, the creation of a particular photographic reality can be more difficult to unravel, especially at a distance of a

Figure 1. Photographer unknown. Favorites of the Harem, ca. 1900. Half of a stereo view marketed by Underwood and Underwood. Collection unknown.

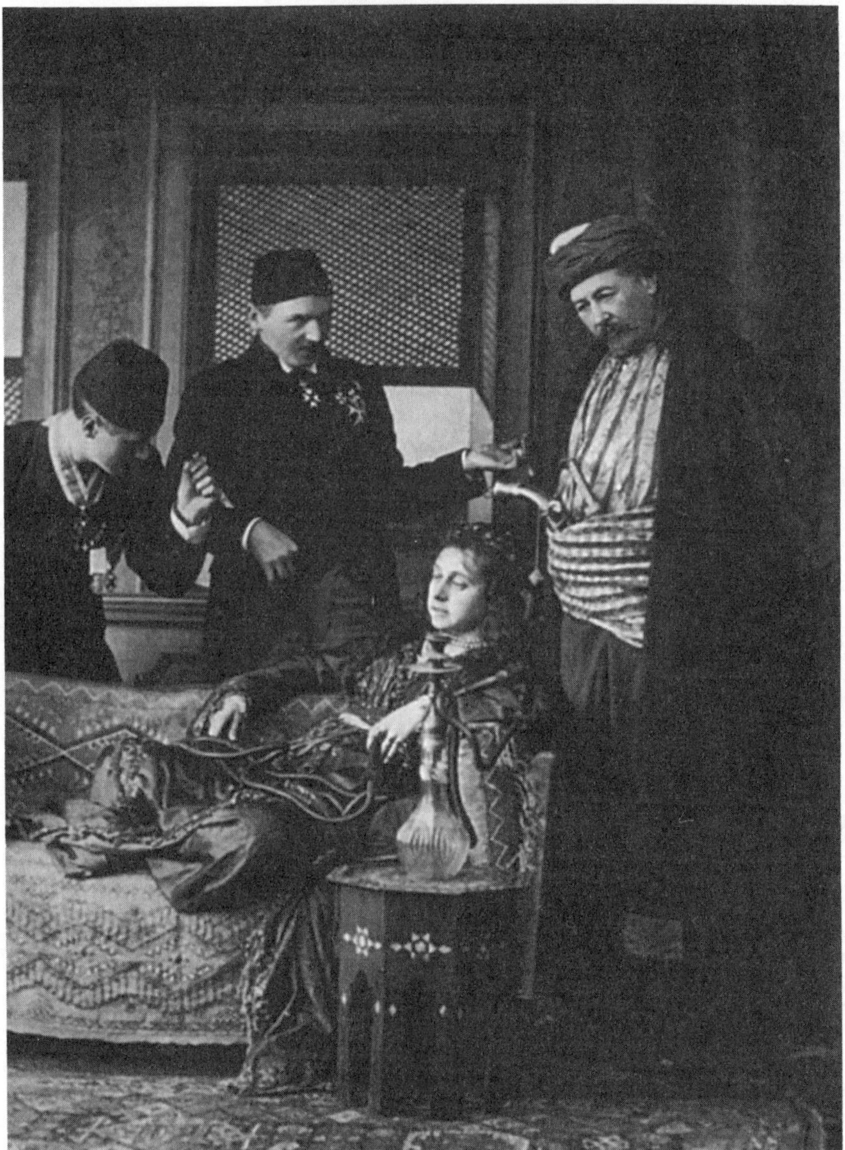

Figure 2. Berggren. Christmas Eve, 1885. Wet collodion negative/albumen print. Original in The Zorn Collection, Mora, Sweden.

Figure 3. Photographer unknown. Wedding of Ashalouys Zelvayan and Arshak Tashdjian, Mersin, 1920. Techniques unknown. Private collection, London.

century or more. The view of a harem shown in Figure 1, marketed by Underwood and Underwood[10] in about 1900 is immediately identifiable as a fabrication, but what about the cozy scene illustrated in Figure 2? Is that an Ottoman family at home? Can we use the photograph to learn about contemporary dress or interior furnishings? In fact, we know from various sources that the subjects in the photograph are four Swedes, a well-known painter and his wife, and a member of the Swedish legislature and his son, who had visited the Istanbul studio of the Swedish photographer G. Berggren, on Christmas Eve of 1885 in order to have themselves photographed in Turkish costume.[11] Dressing in local costume for the purpose of having a souvenir photograph made was a popular activity for European tourists in the Middle East (numbers of such photographs have survived), and it is only one of many circumstances which complicate our reading of historical photographs.

As scholars seeking to understand aspects of the Ottoman Empire, we would like to be able to read meaning from the huge corpus of photographs which appear to record the last century of the empire. However, despite the apparent clarity and straightforward presentation of information, reading meanings from, or understanding a photograph, is not a simple exercise. As an example, consider the wedding photograph in Figure 3, already published in Sarah Graham-Brown's book *Images of Women*.[12] In many ways it resembles wedding photographs produced by commercial photographers in Europe and North America, in the stance of the subjects, their wedding attire, romantic studio backdrop and their isolation from other family members. Because of these formal similarities, it is easy to assume other similarities, to read meaning into this image and imagine the same social circumstances that we would assume for newly married couples photographed in London or New York at about the same time. In fact, this couple, who married in Mersin in 1920, probably had not met before their wedding, which was arranged between the groom and the bride's father. The couple wears contemporary western dress, but other, less visible, aspects of their marriage, as well as their larger social realities, would have been completely different than the circumstances of a couple photographed at the same time in London. Without access to this kind of information, generally only provided by a relative or written documentation accompanying an image, understanding the social relationships pictured in a photograph is extremely difficult. The photograph illustrated here thus provides good evidence of fashion history, but its value for social history is a bit more problematic.

Turning now from the general to the more specific, what do we know about Ottoman photography? When the invention of the daguerreotype was announced by the French government in August 1839, the faster and more accurate recording of the Egyptian antiquities was one of the specific benefits of the new technology mentioned in the official document, and in fact it was only a few months later that daguerreotype artists reached various parts of the Ottoman Empire. The invention itself was announced in Istanbul in the newspaper *Takvim-i Vekayi* on October 28, 1839 (19 Ş 1255).[13] Soon afterward, photographers set themselves up in business in Pera—Albert Smith, a British tourist, reports having his portrait made by a daguerreotypist in 1849.[14] The Crimean War, the first war to be reported photographically, brought the photographer Robert Fenton to the Ottoman Empire,[15] and increased attention to the work of James Robertson, chief engraver of the Ottoman mint, who also opened a photographic studio in Pera in the mid 1850s.[16] Robertson's views of Istanbul were sold to tourists, exhibited in London and Paris, and marketed in various forms.

The burgeoning tourist market, both at home and abroad, was the primary driving force behind the numbers of photographers who set themselves up in business in major Ottoman cities. Before the development of the first Brownie camera, marketed by Kodak in the 1880s, tourists documented their travels by purchasing the work of commercial photographers, either as single images or in albums. The travel guides of the day directed tourists to the best shops for different kinds of photographs. By the end of the century, commercial directories from Istanbul were listing the names of sixty-five photographers active in the city, most with businesses in Pera.[17] These photographers produced thousands of pictures of the people and places which survive today in public and private collections in Turkey, Europe, and North America—more photographs than we will ever be able to study.

Like any other document, a photograph is more useful when it is accompanied by information such as a name, date, or location of the subject or name of photographer. Unfortunately, the vast majority of photographs reach us with none of that. With the exception of a few major figures, photographers came and went, often buying and selling signed glass negatives among themselves as their business fortunes waxed and waned. It is extraordinarily difficult to construct a history of Ottoman photography out of the bits and pieces of information that remain. Scholars working in this area have managed so far to produce several monographs on specific photographers, James Robertson, G. Berggren, and Ali Sami, shorter articles on individual photographers, and volumes which reproduce historical photographs, often arranged around particular subjects.[18] In addition, the albums assembled under the direction of Abdul Hamid and presented to the governments of Great Britain and the United States were the subject of a special issue of the *Journal of Turkish Studies* in 1988. By far the most ambitious work in the area of Ottoman photography is Engin Çizgen's *Photography in the Ottoman Empire,* published in 1987. This book is full of the names and images of photographers who were active in the Ottoman Empire, and is an incredible compilation of information. Unfortunately the book contains no footnotes or other documentation, so it is difficult to use this work as a starting place for additional research. A recent publication highlights an extensive body of photographs, formerly in a private collection, now at the J. Paul Getty Museum: *Images D'Empire, aux origines de la photographie en Turquie/Türkiye'de fotoğrafin öncüleri,* with text by Nazar Ölçer and Engin Çizgen, published by the French Cultural Center in Istanbul. Finally, in terms of the publication of Ottoman photography, there are a number of works in which photographs with Ottoman subjects play an important role, although they are not the primary focus, for example, Zeynep Çelik's 1986 work, *The Remaking of Istanbul,* and Sarah Graham-Brown's book, *Images of Women,* published in 1988.

So far, most work on Ottoman photography has been concentrated on certain specific goals: identifying individual photographers and documenting their careers, identifying the subjects of various photographs, and looking at the photographs as evidence of European interest in the empire and reconstructing how photography was used by outsiders: tourists, artists, publishers, missionaries, government officials, and others. As an example of the challenges posed by this sort of endeavor, look at Figure 4. We know nothing about the circumstances surrounding the production of this image. Who is the woman pictured, who took the photograph, for whom, and when? There are a seemingly infinite number of photographs about which similar questions could be asked but not answered. Considering the endless numbers of photographs for which we have incomplete information, it is not surprising that researchers so far have been occupied in attempting to answer at least some of the questions.

What we have not looked at, and what is much more important from the point of view of consumption, is how photographs were used by the Ottomans themselves. In order to understand how Ottomans, at least in Istanbul, used photographs, it would be useful to know when they began to visit the commercial photographers' studios in Pera, and the sorts of photographs they bought. Additionally, knowing when

Figure 4. Photographer unknown. Studio portrait, late nineteenth century. Techniques unknown. Collection of the author.

they began taking their own pictures, and the situations outside the studio when Ottomans had contact with photography would give us further insight into how the Ottomans had contact with photography. Finally, their interaction with photography should tell us something about consumption patterns in the last decades of the nineteenth century.

For most people in Europe and North America in the 1840s and 1850s, the most exciting application of the new photographic technology was for portraiture. No longer the sole prerogative of the wealthy, portraiture became accessible to the expanding middle classes. The *carte de visite,* a playing card sized piece of cardboard with a photograph mounted on it, became a standard format for inexpensive photographic portraits in the 1850s. By the 1860s, spurred on by the example of Queen Victoria herself, the collecting of these portraits and their subsequent assembling into albums had become a craze in both Britain and North America. The albums were designed to allow the insertion of *cartes de visite,* and for display in a parlor or sitting room. A slightly larger version of the *carte de visite,* called the cabinet card, was introduced in the late 1860s. Both sizes remained in use in some areas until World War I. In response to the development of photographic portrait formats, such as the *carte de visite* and others, as well as the enormous increase in numbers of people who had access to portraiture, the role of the portrait in a European or North American social context began to change. Early photographic portraits adopted the conventions of painted portraits, in the pose of the sitter, the formal setting and the carefully chosen objects to indicate learning or social position. Their use was similar to the portrait miniatures they replaced: small, formal portraits of family members to be carefully displayed in an appropriate context, such as a formal sitting room table. Over time, both the format of photographic portraits and their use became much less fixed, with a breaking down of specific conventions of representation, and an increase in the ways portraiture is used, to commemorate important social events such as marriage, to maintain ties between far-flung friends or family members, and so on.

In the Ottoman context, portraiture in the time before photography has been mostly limited to the quasi-official portraits of the sultans painted to illustrate Ottoman histories and genealogies, and to painted portraits of high-ranking advisors or viziers, as for example, the well-known portrait of Barbaros Hayrettin Paşa, the sixteenth-century admiral (Figure 5). The similarities in format and style of these portraits indicate the existence of certain artistic conventions for the painted representation of the sitter, as well as a limited use of the portraits.[19]

Figure 5. Nigâri. Admiral Barbaros Hayrettin Paşa, ca. 1560. Topkapı Palace Museum, H.2134.

Renda and others who have studied this genre of Ottoman painting see the distinctive stylistic conventions which developed for Ottoman portraits as a blending of European and Ottoman painting styles, evidence that even in what is commonly regarded as a "Golden Age" in Ottoman art, artists of the Ottoman court were not working in isolation, but were exposed to and interacting with European painting in an active fashion.

With the decline of the Ottoman court system of painting in the mid to late-eighteenth century, the influence of the European genre of portraiture seems to increase. Although evidence about painting for this transitional period in Ottoman art (roughly 1750–1860) is very scanty, a few examples of painted portrait miniatures survive which are similar to those found in Europe during the same years.[20] With the development of oil painting in the Ottoman capital in the last decades of the nineteenth century, we see the creation of numerous painted portraits of both men and women. Similar to what we might find in the oeuvres of Europeans or North American artists of the same period, these Ottoman portraits are done in different styles, with their sitters posed in various positions and settings, in varying degrees of formality. While these painted portraits would have been commissioned by relatively wealthy patrons of the artists and intended to be displayed in private homes, the numbers of photographic portraits that exist from the same decades indicate that portraiture was understood to function in a variety of social contexts.

Certainly Ottomans were interested in having their portraits made, and visited the commercial photography studios for this reason. A June 1845 advertisement written in Ottoman and placed by the Italian photographer Carlo Naya to proclaim his skill at portraiture indicates that at least one commercial photographer considered Ottomans to be potential clients.[21] It is clear from Naya's advertisement that the modest cost of a photographic portrait (in this case, a daguerreotype) was considered to be one of its selling points. "The cost varies from 60 *kuruş* to 100 *kuruş*. If pictures of several people are taken at the same time the price can be reduced."[22] Indeed, published portraits demonstrate the accessibility of photography. While there are certainly many portraits of the wealthy elite of Ottoman society, such as the beautiful picture of Fehime Sultan, the elegantly dressed daughter of Murat V, probably taken shortly before her wedding[23] (Figure 6), we can also find numerous depictions of Ottomans of other social classes. Figure 7, for example, shows a woman dressed for the street, photographed with her face uncovered. The fact that she is photographed at the studio and not in her own home,

Figure 6. Photographer unknown. Fehime Sultan, late nineteenth century. Techniques unknown. Topkapı Sarayı Museum, 17/435.

Figure 7. Photographer unknown (possibly Ali Sami) Standing woman, ca. 1898. Techniques unknown. Collection of the author.

as well as details of her *çarşaf,* clothing, and modest jewelry seem to indicate a person of more limited means than Fehime Sultan.

Several decades after the establishment of the commercial studios in Istanbul, photographic technology began to be more widespread and accessible to amateur enthusiasts. Local photographers had been at first primarily Greek or Armenian, but Muslims also began learning how to take pictures. The first Muslim photographers received their training as part of a military education and then went to work for the palace or other parts of the government, beginning at about the time of the accession of Abdul Hamid.[24] Commercial studios owned by Muslim photographers did not become numerous until into the twentieth century. However, despite the absence of Muslim commercial photography studios, with the spread of technology and the availability of photographic supplies, Muslim photographers could take pictures of their family and home life, and thus determine, at least to some extent, the manner in which they presented themselves photographically. The work of one such photographer, Ali Sami, demonstrates that he and his family, at least, used photographs to record themselves in a range of situations and roles. Figure 8 shows members

Figure 9. Ali Sami's daughter, Muhlise, 1907. Glass negative; modern print. Collection of Engin Çizgen.

of Ali Sami's family at home, with four different newspapers visible. They are informally grouped, wearing everyday clothes, photographed in one of the rooms of their house. Figure 9, in contrast, is a full-length portrait of Muhlise, one of Ali Sami's daughters. Posed against a painted backdrop, she wears an elaborate formal gown and meets our eye with a serious expression.[25] Presenting different images of themselves to the viewer, and taken to record different moments in the family's life, these two photographs reveal the degree to which some Ottomans were able to interact with the medium of photography.

There are other aspects of Ottoman photo history which should also be mentioned in the context of consumption—for example, the commercial aspects of the technology which began to be used at the end of the century, as it was elsewhere, for the illustration of books and periodicals. Another technical application of photography quick to be adopted in the Ottoman empire was the use of X-ray images in medicine.

An important category of the use of photography in the Ottoman context, what might be called the explicitly political, is demonstrated in the state collections of photographs assembled under Abdul Hamid, a near-mythic figure in Ottoman photo history, at whose behest thousands of photographs were assembled from all over the empire for his perusal.[26] The photograph albums assembled for him contain approximately 34,879 photographs,[27] on every possible subject: views of the people and buildings of different parts of the empire, views of official ceremonies such as the opening of railroads or civic events; portraits of Ottoman officials, hospitals, ships, weapons manufactured both abroad and within the empire, new Ottoman factories, palaces both Ottoman and foreign, the major monuments and works of art of Europe and Japan, catalogues of goods, imperial horses, and so on. There are a number of interesting stories in the literature about exactly what Abdul Hamid did with his visual archive, a body of material which would appear to lend itself very well to the kind of analysis of photography as a means of surveillance in the service of the state, which has been carried out for nineteenth-century photography in England and North America by John Tagg and others.[28] In those more limited contexts, local governments or police departments used photography as a means of constructing albums of criminal "types." The images in the album then served both to identify specific individuals who had been arrested before, or to allow the identification of suspected criminals based on their physical resemblance to the types constructed in the albums. Photography thus became a tool used by the state as a means of constructing and imposing a social identity on those under its control. In fact there are seven albums in the Abdul Hamid collection which contain about 1,462 images of people, labeled variously "capital offenders" or "criminals" *I'damlık Suçlular* or *Mücrimin Resimleri*.[29] Keeping track of this element of Ottoman society was obviously important, at least at some periods. (Although these albums present a large number of people, the photographs appear to have been taken all at the same time, thus indicating perhaps a specific campaign to document prisoners, but not necessarily an ongoing project of criminal documentation.) It is not clear how these photographs would have been used, although one album, *Album Criminel du Royaume de Serbie* (91340), certainly suggests that its intent was to aid local police in identifying who might have traveled to Istanbul from elsewhere.

One related use of the Abdul Hamid photo archive was the compilation of two large series of albums, for presentation to the British and American governments. These collections of photographs (the set in the Library of Congress contains 1,819 images) reveal the careful construction of a view of the Ottoman Empire, emphasizing its modernity, beauty, and the importance of its ancient monuments. As the photograph of school children shown in Figure 10 demonstrates, Ottoman subjects appear in a variety of identities (students, hospital inhabitants, and military personnel being the most common), and always as loyal subjects of the ruler. Intended to communicate on a government-to-government level, the albums confirm that Abdul Hamid and his advisors were perfectly aware of the subtleties of photographs as a means of communication, and comfortable with the use of those qualities of photography.

However a more extensive use of photography as a means of communicating information emerges from the larger body of images within the collection as a whole. These albums are generally described as being the means by which a ruler who did not often leave his palace precincts was able to be informed about events and circumstances in his far-flung empire. They thus served to inform him of a myriad of topics: what European cities looked like, for example, including the interiors of many European palaces, as well as the major monuments of European architectural and art history. Japan was also of interest, as was Moscow. There are thousands of pictures of various parts of the empire, many commercial views such as tourists would have purchased, but others which seem to have been taken specifically to present a view of a town or region to the palace. These albums often open with a formal portrait of the local Ottoman official, followed by photographs of buildings of note, especially new

Figure 10. Abdullah Frères. Students at the Emirgan Middle School, before 1893 (albumen print). Abdul Hamid albums, Library of Congress, Album #9544.11, neg. 81304.

government buildings, the mosque, and anything of engineering interest, such as a new bridge, factory, water system, or train. The album may include school children, the surrounding countryside, and views of the town's streets. Other photographs taken for the sultan recorded opening ceremonies of new buildings, state occasions, important military ceremonies, and other events of which he must have wanted to have been informed. There are several albums which present local police officials, standing at attention in groups of two or three in front of their buildings, with ground plans of the buildings attached to the photograph. Just as the Ottoman Empire was "packaged" for presentation to the American and British government by the Ottomans, it was also "packaged" for presentation to the sultan by those responsible for sending him photographs of themselves and their official domains.

The collection includes thousands of individual portraits in a *carte de visite* format: Ottoman officials at all levels of rank, princes and princesses of the royal family, members of European royal families, notables of both the Ottoman empire and Europe, criminals, prisoners of war, Native Americans from the United States, and many who have not so far been identified. It is clear from the photographs themselves that Ottomans of various ranks were frequent visitors to the commercial photographers of Istanbul, and that Abdul Hamid at least participated in the enthusiasm for collecting *cartes de visite* which swept Europe and North America. While many of the portraits are assembled like a catalogue of officials, accompanied by notes providing their names, ranks, and perhaps other details, and thus had a governmental function, others are more similar to the albums assembled elsewhere of famous people, rulers, and acquaintances.

Many of the images in the Abdul Hamid collections reveal the involvement of photographic subjects at the direction of the photographer, and express little desire on the part of the subjects to be photographed. Soldiers, school students, hospital patients and others would have had little choice about their presence in the photographs taken at the behest of the sultan. However, there are numerous other

Figure 11. Photographer unknown. Graduating class of the National College, Kharpert, 1909–1910. Techniques unknown. Bibliothèque Nubar de l'UGAB

photographs which indicate that the subjects understood and exploited the evidentiary quality of photography. The many photographs of sports teams, graduating classes from academies all over the empire (as shown in Figure 11), musical bands, and groups of local notables all demonstrate that Ottomans from different areas and different social classes wished to document aspects of their social identities through photography. Furthermore, although a large number of the photographs collected by Abdul Hamid indicate a desire to keep a photographic eye on his subjects, other groups within the empire similarly documented many of their own activities, understanding in the same way as the government did the value of photography for the (re)construction of events.[30]

Other perspectives on the people and events of the empire appear in the hundreds of postcards and stereoviews which were produced by commercial photographers. Taken either by local commercial photographers or those traveling on assignment from larger firms such as Underwood and Underwood, these images privilege a certain view of the empire, often concentrating on traditional modes of production and lifestyles with little concern for accuracy. As tourists began to carry their own simple cameras and produce their own souvenir photographs in the last decades of the nineteenth century, the postcard gradually replaced the larger format albumen print of earlier decades which had been the staple of the commercial photographer's tourist business.

Stereo views, photographs produced to appear three-dimensional when viewed through a special apparatus, played in late nineteenth century middle-class life in North America a role similar to television today, as a primary means of family entertainment. The stereoviews were marketed in sets, arranged according to topic or region. Both postcards and stereo views were significant vehicles for the communication of visual images and stereotypes in popular culture, and to some extent functioned on a global basis, in the sense that the consumers for whom these goods were initially intended, the tourists and residents of Europe and North America, sent postcards from all over the world and purchased stereoviews of every possible location and subject. What is much less clear at this point is the role that these images played in the culture they purported to display. That is, did Ottomans send postcards of men sitting at a coffeehouse to one another, or purchase stereo views of harem women? Or perhaps they were interested in looking at Niagara Falls, one of the most popular stereoviews produced by Underwood and Underwood. This is an area in which new research could lead to a much more satisfactory understanding of how images produced for consumption by outsiders could also be used by those within a society for their own purposes.[31]

The fact that news of the invention of photography reached an Ottoman newspaper within two months of the initial announcement of the invention in Paris indicates the degree to which developments in Europe were followed in the Ottoman capital. While the original impetus for the spread of the technology within the empire may have come from a tourist market, photography continued to grow in popularity long after tourists were able to produce their own photographs. Photographs appear in a similar range of uses in an Ottoman context as we might find in Europe or North America in the same decades. This congruence of use should not be understood as a simple borrowing of a cultural product by one society from another, for photography, as a new art form and new product in Europe and North America, was evolving in those contexts as well. Although aspects of the use of photography, for example, formal portraits, look very much alike from one place to another, in the absence of any proof to the contrary, we should not assume similar, culturally nonspecific meanings for those portraits, or any other images.

Much, if not most of the history of photography in the Ottoman Empire remains to be written. At this point, it is clear that the Ottomans were quick to see the value of a new technology, to learn how to use that new technology, and to develop their own meaning and uses for the objects which could be produced. Portraits, of individuals and groups from a range of social classes and ethnic groups, surveillance photographs, documentary photography, to mention only the most obvious kinds of images, were created and imbued by Ottoman photographers and subjects with specific meanings and understood to have certain uses and values. Perhaps as more photographs and more related documentation comes to light, this picture can be completed.

Notes

1. Most, but not all, of the photographs and photographers discussed in this paper come from Istanbul. There is more information available concerning photography in the Ottoman capital, and thus one can construct a more detailed view of photography in that context. While it is possible or even likely that many aspects of the production and use of photographs were similar throughout the Ottoman Empire, we will not know this for sure without a great deal of additional research.

2. I am particularly indebted to Donald Quataert, who convened the conference from which these papers have resulted, for his comments about

my work, and to Sherry Vatter, whose job it was to serve as discussant for my paper and who made a number of very valuable suggestions for ways of thinking about the photographs. My ideas about the issues which are addressed in my paper and others were shaped, at least in part, by my participation in the conference and ensuing discussion. Of course any shortcomings of my work are my responsibility alone.

3. In the course of doing research for a forthcoming book on photography in the nineteenth-century Middle East, I have looked at hundreds of unpublished photographs in museums and archives. While that experience has certainly had an impact on this paper, most of those collections of photographs were assembled by tourists or other visitors to the Middle East, not the Ottoman residents of the empire, who are my focus here.

4. The Abdul Hamid albums are discussed below in more detail.

5. Despite the obvious significance of photographs as a widely available object of consumption, they have not so far been the focus of a study from the point of view of consumption per se. While there is a very large bibliography in nineteenth-century photo history, primary areas of interest have been the relationship between painting and photography, the careers of individual photographers, the analysis of specific formats (daguerreotypes, calotypes, and so on), and the study of meaning. There are numerous works however which are of use in understanding how photographs functioned from the point of view of the consumer, these focus, for example, on topics such as family photography, amateur photography, the business aspects of commercial photography, and various uses to which photographs were put by political and social institutions in Great Britain and North America.

6. That task, thankfully, falls to Donald Quataert. Please see his introductory essay in this volume.

7. The ideas surrounding emulative consumption are discussed at length in McKendrick, Brewer, and Plumb (1982).

8. Please see the bibliography for complete citations of these two articles.

9. Kopytoff (1986), 68.

10. Underwood and Underwood, a very successful firm based in New York, marketed stereoviews produced by their team of photographers, or purchased them from other photographers. Stereoviews (the image in Figure 1 is half of a stereo view) are discussed in more detail below.

11. See Wigh (1984), 32, for a discussion of the circumstances of the taking of the picture, as recounted by one of the participants.

12. Graham-Brown (1988) has an interesting discussion of the problems of interpretation in her chapter on family portraits, as well as providing some specific information about the subjects pictured in Figure 3.

13. Çizgen (1987) 20.

14. Henisch and Henisch (1990), 23.

15. Roger Fenton is a well-studied figure in the history of British photography. For an account of his Crimean War photography, see Helmut and Alison Gernsheim, *Roger Fenton, Photographer of the Crimean War: His Photographs and Letters from the Crimea.* London, 1954 (reprinted 1973).

16. James Robertson has been the subject of two articles, Henisch and Henisch (1984)(1990), and one book, Öztuncay (1992). His work is also mentioned in numerous other works on photography in the Middle East.

17. Allen (1990).

18. Please see the bibliography for complete information for the books and articles listed here.

19. While there are portraits of many Ottoman court women in various collections, little is known about the circumstances in which they were made. For the most part, these representations should probably not be regarded as portraits in the conventional sense since the artists generally did not have access to their sitters, and thus produced idealized or imaginary depictions. Furthermore, in most cases we do not know how these "portraits" were intended to be used, whether in the Ottoman court or elsewhere.

20. The clearest discussion of the complex transition in painting styles which took place in the Ottoman empire is found in Renda et al. (1988), 15–236. See Boppe (1911) for information on portraits painted in a European style for Ottoman patrons.

21. The advertisement is reproduced, translated, and discussed in Çizgen (1987), 64–66.

22. Çizgen (1987), 65.

23. According to Çağman, who published the photograph (1994), 249.

24. The importance of the Imperial School of Engineers (Mühendishane-i Berri-i Hümâyun) in training Muslim Ottoman photographers is discussed briefly in Çizgen (1987), 43, and in more detail in Çizgen (1989), 33–35.

25. While there has been no explicit discussion of gender in this paper, it is clear that the Ottoman adoption of photography took place in a social context in which women's roles and identities were a subject of endless discussion among many different groups. Photography had a place in that discussion, with the production of images as varied as the stereotypical harem women for the tourist market, the privately commissioned formal portraits, and family photographs. I would argue that photography allowed women to experiment with different roles, trying them on, as it were, if even only for the time needed to produce a photograph.

26. The Research Centre for Islamic History, Art and Culture (IRCICA) has a complete set of copy prints and negatives of the original albums, which are in Istanbul University Library. I would like to thank the director general of IRCICA, Prof. Dr. Ekmeleddin Ihsanoğlu, and department head, Dr. Hidayet Nuhoğlu, for their generosity in allowing me to look through the entire collection.

27. This is a careful estimate of the contents of the Yıldız notebooks which contain copy prints of the original albums, now in the Istanbul University Library. There are many duplicate photographs in the albums, so this number is not a count of the total number of different images. Also, there are many breaks in the numerical sequences of the albums, probably indicating that there were more albums in the collection originally, but that some have been lost over time.

28. The Abdul Hamid albums are the subject of Volume 12 (1988) of the *Journal of Turkish Studies,* which also provides access to other relevant bibliography. John Tagg has written widely on various aspects of photography; for his work on the connections between nineteenth-century photography and surveillance, see especially *The Burden of Representation,* 1988, chapters 2 and 3.

29. The albums which make up the last three notebooks of photographs are mostly labeled only *Karışık Fotografları,* rather than indicating a particular subject for each album. Several of these albums seem to be collections of photographs of criminals, but it is impossible to know for sure without examining the originals.

30. The 1992 volume, *Les Arméniens dans l'empire Ottoman à la veille du génocide,* presents a valuable corpus of material which demonstrates the range of uses to which photographs were put within the Armenian community in the period from about 1880–1920. The authors have done a commendable job of assembling a vast number of different kinds of photographs from a variety of sources; although they state in their introduction that they will privilege the image, and integrate it into the text, in fact the images are presented as a kind of parallel text, with no accompanying information and virtually no connections to the written text. The photographs are of such variety—postcards documenting traditional lifestyles and costume, records of Armenian institutions such as churches, orphanages, and schools, topographic views, street scenes, and group portraits, that some information about the sources of the images and their possible uses at the time they were produced would have added immeasurably to their usefulness. However, even given this lack of detail, it is clear from the photographs themselves that members of this community understood the value of photography for documenting aspects of their public lives. It is ironic (but also an important statement about the shifting meanings which photographs acquire through time) that the photographs which were most likely produced by outsiders

for the consumption of outsiders—that is, the many postcards documenting Armenians involved in traditional modes of production or in traditional dress—are now being used by the descendants of the original subjects, in diaspora, to reconstruct their own history.

31. In the late 1990s, Orientalist paintings and postcards from the nineteenth century are once again being marketed to tourists in Turkey as postcards. No doubt this is partly because these images sell very well, but it also seems to be part of a continuing dialogue that the Turkish people are carrying on with their own past, part of a continuing redefinition of who they were and are, a dialogue in this case informed to some extent by images of their past constructed by foreigners intended for foreigners.

9

Goods in the *Mahalle:* Distributional Encounters in Eighteenth-Century Istanbul

Madeline C. Zilfi

Ottoman Istanbul's incomparable site and diverse population always dazzled visitors. If Istanbul was a "world," as the historian Hâkim called it,[1] it was a world of many cities, perhaps especially in the eighteenth century. The monumental city drew admirers in great numbers and to more lasting effect than ever before. An unprecedented wave of European artists made their way to Istanbul in the seventeen hundreds to produce an indelible record of extended stays.[2] The ruling imperial city, the seat of government, attracted its own set of visitors and petitioners, an assemblage that in the eighteenth century reflected the presence—sustained and more empowered—of ever more Europeans.

The older diplomatic missions—French, English, Austrian, Venetian, and Dutch—added to their staffs to accommodate expanded commercial interests. Relative newcomers like the Prussians and Russians built permanent residences and local networks of their own. The districts of Galata and Pera, home to the capital's Westerners and emerging as a ruling subset in themselves,[3] were an early point of entry for European habits and fashion. Across the Bosphorus in Asia, Üsküdar and Kadıköy gathered in eastern travelers attending to business in and around Istanbul proper. But however distinct the assorted *mahalle*s or neighborhoods may have regarded themselves, their populations held common membership in the capital's "world of goods," buying and selling, trading and withholding, giving and receiving, coveting and disdaining, goods of value.

The population, perhaps 600,000 people in the eighteenth century,[4] was as likely as the landscape to excite curiosity. Rich and poor, male and female, free and slave, and especially the costumed distinctions that marked off each nation or confession—Muslims, Christians, and Jews, and among those, Turks, Persians, Tatars, Greeks, Armenians, Bosnians, Albanians, Circassians, Gypsies, Kurds, Syrians, Arabians, Egyptians, Moroccans, and Yemenis—invariably turned up in sourvenir costume albums. In the eighteenth century, Istanbul society was becoming more expansive as the city and its byways became more accessible to outsiders.

Some of the older considerations of the population were cut through by new categories. With the European powers extending their official favor to preferred Christians—by means of *berat*s or patents of immunity—over the course of the century, their formal protection conferred alternative or hybrid identities upon increasing numbers of individuals within the favored clienteles.[5] At the same time, the growing domestic market for consumer goods, especially new varieties of textiles, was beginning to suggest a reconfiguration of the population according to popular tastes and inclinations rather than according to officially prescribed identities. Merchants and traders, foreign and native, were alert to changes in fashion, favor, and resources in their search for consumerist Istanbulites. For its part, the Ottoman regime sought to manage the marketplace, to reap the benefits of an active commerce without undermining either Ottoman sovereignty or the *Ständestaat* social order on which it relied.

The capitation tax on non-Muslims, sumptuary laws and customs, and the regime's categorial rhetoric—often seconded by the non-Muslim leaderships—reinforced confessional difference and encouraged separation along religious lines. The status of "slave" in Islamic law, and the legal provisions setting off free from unfree, formalized another boundary. The regulation of women's clothing and mobility, along with the law's gendered positions on family and personal status matters, added another. But legal categories do not always produce boundaries even when they are intended, and complete separation is difficult to achieve in any case.

Making a life in a vast, complex city, amid increasingly overlapping neighborhoods and interests, tested the meanings of difference. The marketplace, and the confessionally shared neighborhoods and workshops that were not uncharacteristic of Istanbul and its suburbs in the first half of the eighteenth century,[6] furnished opportunities for cooperation and reciprocity across prescribed identities.[7] They also occasioned conflict. The intensification of dependent arrangements with

European states, an expanding economy,[8] and emerging patterns of consumption strained communal relationships already caught between manifold prescriptive norms and such workaday realities as supply, demand, and deprivation. For individuals, these processes could be apprehended in the daily exchange of goods, and in the concrete and symbolic uses to which goods were applied.

The two incidents discussed below are, in broad outline, crime and punishment stories. But they are also urban stories, with origins rooted firmly in the primary and secondary markets of the imperial capital of the mid-eighteenth century. At the heart of both stories is a multilayered market nexus that confounds the simple polarities prescribed for Ottoman society. The mechanism that set the incidents in motion was the distribution—and redistribution—of valuable goods. As with murder and mayhem elsewhere, the stories cannot be said to represent everyday reality. Their exceptionalism nonetheless reveals much about the ordinary as well as the uncommon in social encounters across normative divides. In that light, the stories are representative of two urban realities—the problematic intersections between prescription and practice, and the role of goods of exchange in exposing them.

Slavery

The first incident concerns Istanbul's large slave population.[9] Early in the *Hicrî* year 1176, around July 1762, a Circassian *cariye* or slave girl was, "in the customary manner," delivered to an Istanbul slave dealer to be sold on the owner's behalf.[10] The girl was lodged in the dealer's house with several other *cariye*s, but soon proved to be ungovernable—an unmarketable trait in any subordinate. When the lady of the house chastised her, presumably with blows as well as words, the girl grabbed a knife and stabbed the woman to death. Once the girl was detained, it was decided that, as a warning to others who might harbor similar ideas, she should be hanged in the slave market *(Esir Pazarı)*. The market in question, in the central commercial district on the city's main thoroughfare,[11] was the principal location for slave sales from the mid-seventeenth century until the abolition of such public sales in the nineteenth century. Under normal circumstances, the display of human beings for sale always drew idle spectators along with buyers and sellers. The public execution of a young woman murderer—perhaps especially a Circassian with ethnic ties to the large Circassian community in Istanbul—added more drama to what was already a tourist destination for natives and foreigners alike.

Under Islamic law, homicide, was a civil injury normally negotiated between the person responsible and the victim's family. In the rare circumstances here, where a slave was the murderer, the victim's relatives could seek compensation, *diya* or "blood money" (from the owner who had consigned the girl to the dealer), or the slave's death.[12] If the survivors agreed to financial compensation, the authorities could invoke the public interest and order the death penalty.[13] Given the inversion of the master-slave relationship and the lurid violence of this case, the family was unlikely to opt for compensation. The government in any case was bound to reckon that public order was at issue. A contemporary account proclaimed that the girl's public execution should be "the essential point" *(maye-i itibar)* of the episode, the message that the other slaves and the city as a whole should carry away with them.[14]

The sketchiness of the story reminds us that we know little about the lives of ordinary domestic slaves. Male or female, domestic slaves and humble servants, remain all but invisible in the narrative histories unless their transgressions, or the transgressions of others toward them, aroused interest—this despite the fact that thousands of slaves were bought, sold, and resold in the capital, the largest of the empire's many markets for unfree labor. The unfree servants of the elites, like their masters, left a more substantial paper trail than did slaves belonging to—and reflecting the status of—the commoner classes. Thus we know something about the lives of special categories of slaves such as slave soldiers and other males handpicked for the imperial palace or notable households. We are especially apt to know more about those slaves—like Melek Ahmed Paşa—who rose to acquire power of their own. To be sure, there is much that we do not know about the elite unfree. The personal histories of the vast majority of slaves of the imperial palace, including many who rose to some fame, are unrecoverable. Nonetheless, the *categories* of elite unfree—janissaries, mameluks, palace pages, and the female slaves *(cariye, odalık)* of the imperial harem—are relatively well marked in the literature in contrast to the nonelite categories submerged in the generic terms of *esir, abd, köle, and rık,* among others. The stories of individual "elite slaves" are less well marked, but are abundant compared to the biographies of the far more numerous ordinary slaves. Among slaves of any sort, as within society as a whole, we know less about women's lives and experience—individually and in terms of socio-economic or status categories—than about comparable men.[15]

Slaves

The slave girl here, like many other young people sold in Istanbul every year, was a Circassian. From the seventeenth century through the nienteenth century, the northern Black Sea and Caucasus regions provided Istanbul's dealers with the bulk of their human merchandise.[16] Prince Selim—the future Selim III and the son of Mustafa III—whose birth had been celebrated a year earlier in 1761/1175, had been born to a Georgian slave. Some of the youths who ended up for sale in the capital were brought to the city by relatives, who trained their charges and guarded their virginity in the hope of securing a good price and, equally important for slave and seller, access to a powerful household. The seventeenth-century author Evliya Çelebi recounts the slave origins of his own mother, an Abkhazian with roots in the great slave reservior of southern Russia. Abkahazian men competed with the Circassians, Tatars, Georgians, and their own, for male and female captives to ship to the Ottoman markets.[17] Evliya's mother and her Istanbul-born male cousin were in fact groomed in Abkhazia for Ottoman service. Back in Istanbul, the two were presented as gifts to Sultan Ahmed I (1603–1617). The offering of slaves to superiors or their bestowal upon inferiors put one of society's most expensive commodities to use in the gift-exchange rites of patrimonialism.[18] The slave-gift's human capacities held the further promise of creating a lasting tie between giver and recipient. In this case, Sultan Ahmed bestowed the girl on a favorite servitor, Evliya's father, the court goldsmith. The girl's cousin remained in the sultan's service, in 1650, rising, as Melek Ahmed Paşa, to become grand vezir. The links among all of them, givers and gifts, lasted until their deaths.[19]

The Circassian slave girl who ends so badly in this story may not have had a hope of reaching the palace. She was probably young and presentable, however, and was thus lodged in the dealer's house in order to ensure her value. Away from the exhibition rooms in the Slave Hall *(Esirhanı),* she and the other girls could be sheltered from vulgar view. The term that is used for the girl, *cariye,* was generic usage for "slave girl," but it could also be applied, in contrast to *molade* or *halayık,* to females at the "high end of the market," those destined for light household duties and personal service or for concubinage.[20] Female slaves of pleasing appearance, especially virgins, could be expected to fetch a good price from male and female buyers alike.[21] Those possessing particular grace or talent also did better on the market. Slave dealers, and the owners who consigned their slaves to them, tried to enhance their charges' appeal—and value—by training them in domestic service and entertainments.[22] Here the story touches on the role of merchants' wives with respect to the dichotomies between slave and free, and between the male workaday world and the private or domestic sphere of their mates.

We do not know the details of the falling-out between the dealer's wife and her murderer—indeed we do not know the extent to which even the outlines of the story are true. Did the confrontation begin not with the girl's contrariness but with the husband's or a son's overtures, or with a wife's jealousy? Did the girl "have a history"? Had she been brought to the dealer by an unhappy owner? Almost anything is possible. The story as written, however, bears on the embeddedness of domestic slavery in Ottoman urban life. The most striking evidences of domestic slavery's importance are well known: that the domestic slave trade weighed heavily in the Black Sea economy as a whole; that slavery was pervasive in Ottoman society, but manumission appears to have been common in all periods; that domestic slaves were sometimes critical to city-centered commerce and skilled production;[23] that domestic slaves, particularly eunuchs, served class and gender interests by supplying the labor necessary for maintaining the gender segregation of the harem system, particularly in wealthy households;[24] and that female slaves played roles that frequently equalled or surpassed those of freeborn women. The possession of slaves to be sure meant access to labor, an additional pair of hands, but it also signified social power. The possession of many slaves satisfied the need for competitive display,[25] the public presentation of valuable countables, in this case in one's human entourage. Even for owners of only one slave—perhaps *mostly* for them—the possession of a slave may have legitimated claims to gentility. But slaveholding was not merely labor-saving, or ornamental, or symbolic of superior wealth or standing. It was also part of the "intelligible universe"[26] of Ottoman elite society, perhaps especially for its women, in the relationship between women of wealth and female domestic slavery. For women, the use of female slaves, although linked to labor and display, also possessed gendered meanings.

The story of the Circassian slave girl bears on how female slaves, as merchandise and as personnel, attached the traffic in women to the household. Even the organized selling of female slaves as here—with guild licensing and prescribed transaction site—nonetheless took place across the supposed divides between workplace and home, and public and private. In effect, slaves—some of the most valuable goods on any market—were warehoused in the dealer's house. The *cariye*s awaiting sale ate, slept, and set about their tasks under instruction, carping or kind, from the women of the household.[27] In preindustrial economies, given the nature of production and the physical convergence between home and workshop, it is hardly surprising that wives of urban producers—shoemakers, clothiers, coppersmiths, and the like—helped in their husband's work. In the case here, however, the slave dealer appears to have possessed some wealth and a formally separate work location. That is, we understand him to have been one of the hundred or so dealers licensed to operate at the central *Esir Pazarı,* where most of Istanbul's slave sales were supposed to take place.[28] He dealt in valuable merchandise in the amount of at least the several slaves of the story. As a licensed trader, he more than likely had working quarters in the market area, a room of some kind, perhaps one of the fifty-four rooms in the *Esirhanı* itself. Notwithstanding the commercial formalities of the slave trade and societal encouragement of separate female and male domains, the wife of this relatively substantial house supported her husband in the family business, readying goods for the market.

In fact, the female slave trade lent itself to women's participation, not only as objects of exchange but as sustaining agents of female slave consumption. The same sociolegal arrangements that pointed women toward home, family, and harem strengthened women's claims to special expertise with regard to members of their own sex. This was true for professions in what we might call the female service sector—midwives, foster mothers *(sütninesi),* bath attendants, matchmakers, and sellers of clothing and novelties come to mind. It was also true of the domestic slave trade, which gave scope to women's expertise even among the upper classes.

In families of middling or modest wealth, women like the slave dealer's wife served as helpmates to their husbands. Other women, from a variety of economic circumstances, operated more or less on their own, as dealers, investors, and entrepreneurs. In terms of the formal marketplace, a small number of women figured among the recognized dealers of the capital.[29] They reportedly specialized in selling women to households and, it was sometimes charged, in procuring slave women for prostitution and other illicit use.[30]

All over the eastern Mediterranean, a substantial informal trade in slaves of both sexes also operated. The trade was carried out privately by occasional dealers, men and women for whom slave trading was a sideline to their principal pastimes.[31] Soldiers, brigands, pilgrims, merchants, tinkers, migrants, and tribespeople were especially well positioned through their journeys in or near the hunting grounds and war zones of the Black Sea, the Caucasus, and Africa. Although women pilgrims and migrants might acquire slaves much as did their male counterparts, it was not proximity to slaving areas but knowledge of demand close to home, and the private, unsupervised nature of the informal market, that lent themselves to women's participation. In their home cities and social circles, women involved themselves in the market in a variety of profitable ways, virtually all of which fostered the continued appropriation of unfree women.

Many of these occasional traders were women of wealth and social standing. Many were former slaves themselves. As wives, sisters, and daughters of notable households, they were—like their menfolk—chiefly consumers of involuntary female labor. But some of the women also invested in young girls, marketed them through relatives and personal contacts in other households, and sold them at a profit.[32] Slave girls, sometimes only seven or eight years old, were commonly given as holiday or wedding gifts, to become personal servants and companions to the wealthy.[33] Many such "gifts" were treated as tenderly as any child of the family. Nonetheless, many slaves, whether obtained by purchase or by gift, were nurtured and polished in the feminine arts of the upper classes until their mistresses could arrange to sell or present them to a comparable household. Although similar to brokering a good marriage for a beloved daughter, the placement of "one like a daughter" in a new, possibly conjugal, home, could bring in a neat cash profit. For the slave who was sold, of course, like the free daughter given in marriage, the best or the worst was possible in a new home and master.

The role of women in molding and managing the domestic slave institution can only be suggested here. The study of inheritance, testaments, and the manumission of slaves, the patterns of Ottoman slavery and the variable of class, and the intermingling of slave and free in the institutions—and psychology—of marriage and gender relations are among the themes that must be set side by side. For the moment, it is clear that the interrupted workday of the murdered wife represents only one mode of women's agency (not very successful in her case) in the redistribution of unfree females. The affluent ladies who bought and sold from their harems represent another. In the nineteenth century, after the slave trade was officially banned, the demand for female slaves persisted, and perhaps even rose with the new middle classes' ability to acquire the symbols of their aspirant social claims.[34] With the disappearance of public auctions, the informal market assumed even greater importance in the distribution of slaves. It is far from clear that women's roles as actors in the trade kept pace in the new configuration, although anecdotal evidence suggests that upper-class harem ladies played an even more central role in securing and training *cariye*s for the upper class.[35]

Clothing Wars

The second urban story comprises scenes from what we might call the "Ottoman clothing wars." In the eighteenth century, sumptuary laws, particularly restrictions on clothing, were issued and reissued, expanded and refined, as Ottoman subjects were recalled to the colors, styles, and fabrics that they were legally suffered to wear. The general lines of complaint had been heard in other centuries. In the eighteenth century, it was their frequency that was the novelty, at least in part a sign of heightened anxiety over state power and communal identities.

As a rule, the various military corps and other categories of Ottoman officials were entitled to special cuts and fabrics whose use was denied the common population.[36] Luxury textiles like brocades, fine velvet, and silver- or gold-threaded silks *(kemha, çatma, seraser)* as well as furs like sable, ermine, fox, and lynx were reserved for the highest officials, "grand vezirs, great mollas, and ranking government officers," as the decrees usually put it.[37] Since the highest officials, not to mention the imperial family itself, were Muslim, the regulation in theory restricted the rarest and costliest merchandise to Muslims, at least insofar as outdoor garb was concerned.

On the whole, commoners, both Muslim and non-Muslim, seem to have honored the status divide by staying clear of the official elites' clothing insignias. They wore instead the styles and colors associated with their particular religious community. Legal stipulations varied over the centuries—sometimes non-Muslims could wear red; at other times certain shades of red were forbidden them. The outdoor uniform for male commoners was an inconspicuous variety or robe (or for the lower orders, workmen's garb) along with the special headgear associated with one's religious community. Among commoners, differences in station and wealth were signaled by the quality or amplitude of fabrics more than by differences in cut or design. Thus rich commoners might simply look like more substantial versions of their humbler co-religionists.

The core of sumptuary regulation was differentiation (Ar., *ghiyar*), a principle that long had served to justify such laws.[38] For much of the Ottoman period, the principle was applied largely along religious lines, and largely with the assent of the various religious communities. That is, regulated subject communities might have wanted complete freedom of choice in the selection of clothing; but with or without state interference, they already were inclined to distinctive communal costumes. These and hairstyles were customary markers of community. The state's interest in regulation lay largely in justifying and expressing power relationships. Subject groups—or at least their religious leaders—had an interest in separate confessional identities as a means to preserving the community and, for its leaders, their own place within it.

As the attention to clothing and female modesty indicates, the body was a contested site,[39] and as the focus on headgear suggests, the Ottoman head was especially so. In theory, turbans were exclusive to Muslim males in the period. Christians wore hats, and Jews bonnets, distinctive to their communities and limited to them.[40] For Muslims, the link between headgear and the presentation of the public self was virtually carved in stone through Ottoman funerary practices. Stone turbans—in shapes from modest wraps to eye-catching towers—top the graves of male Muslim state servants, calling to mind the modest or eye-catching station that the deceased had achieved in life. Not surprisingly, the tombs of well-to-do Muslim women often display headstones wreathed in veils. While there was a good deal of ambiguity about the coats and robes worn by members of the various communities, sartorial laws demanded that headgear, especially male headgear, unequivocally indicate sectarian allegiances. The laws thus affirmed the dominance of Islam and the Muslim community, and the prerogatives of society's ruling members.

Ottoman clothing regulations tended to address women as a class or group unto themselves, "womankind" *(taife-i nisvan),* as the legislation proclaimed them. When in public, all women, regardless of religion, were supposed to dress so as not to offend public (Muslim) standards of modesty. Regulations sometimes also stipulated that women's dress be communally distinctive, that non-Muslim women refrain from wearing a particular shoe or color reserved for Muslims.[41] But above all, the law was concerned with women's bodies, the presentation of women's physical selves, rather than their associational identities.[42] Although the decrees expressed a variety of economic as well as social concerns,[43] the stated intention of most legislation on women was the enforcement of "modesty"—unobtrusiveness, bodily anonymity, an unattracting appearance. Head-to-toe coverage and somber colors were thus the order of the day for all women. The preferred streetwear in the eighteenth century was the *ferace,* a long, plain, dust coat, usually collared, worn with a kerchiefed headpiece and veil *(yaşmak),* which non-Muslims also wore.[44] Since government officials combined imperial authority with Muslim-community responsibility, they were more exacting about the dress of Muslim women than of non-Muslim women; the latter were subject to their own communities' standards. In addition, since non-Muslims were somewhat more relaxed on the subject of female public dress than their Muslim counterparts, non-Muslim women of the affluent classes could be more experimental about their clothing. In the eighteenth century, elaborate headdresses became the vogue. Women perhaps consciously imitated European wear, which was directly observable among the Europeans in Istanbul and was available as well through the descriptions of merchants and clothiers. When Muslim women—it is impossible to know who they were or how many—began to follow the trend, another spate of regulations ordered women to return to more "modest" versions of the veil. Berating Muslim women for imitating Istanbulite and European nonbelievers, the new regulations threatened physical punishment if they did not halt the practice.[45]

In fact over the long term, millinery fashion in Europe and the Islamic east reflected reciprocal borrowings as well as simultaneous invention.[46] In the eighteenth century, Ottoman women's coifs resembled upper-class Ottoman male heads as much as any "Western" coiffure. That is, Ottoman women of wealth, Muslim and non-Muslim, often aimed for bigness, most especially high-ness, a rich look. They did not have to gaze on Europeans to connect highness with social rank. The Ottomans and the Safavis of Iran, as well as the Fatimids and Mameluks before them, were at the cutting edge of big-headedness. For Ottoman women of the eighteenth century, the Ottoman upper-class male head—big, bold, and ubiquitous in ceremony—was a model immediately at hand. One thinks especially of the lofty and widely imitated janissary *kalafat*s and *külah*s, and the beach-ball-sized *örf* turbans of the *ulema* and sultans on parade.[47] Ottoman regulators of the eighteenth century, although sometimes uncertain about the origins of these headdress transgressions, are of one mind in the middle of the century in denouncing female big-headedness, specifically those women who wore "big heads" in public places and thereby presumed on male elite prerogatives.[48]

Sultans Osman II (1754–1757) and Mustafa III (1757–1774) were the driving forces behind the sartorial legislation of the 1750s and 1760s. Determined to rout out disobedience and uphold customary distinctions, the two issued a barrage of clothing decrees and periodically roamed the streets in search of malefactors. For much of the two reigns, the Ottoman Empire was at peace. However, the problem of foreign trade, with increasing dependence on European shipping and goods, made for a sharp peacetime contest that the Ottomans were losing as of mid-century.

Of immediate relevance to Osman and Mustafa's sartorial sensibilities were the everyday effects of the contest. These could be seen—or imagined—under their noses. European goods, notably textiles, were growing in popularity. Sometimes European-made fabrics were cheaper or of higher quality than local products, or they might simply be more available. Thanks to technical innovations based on Indian designs and dyeing processes, European versions of Indian patterned cottons and calicoes made a stunning entry into the markets of Europe and the Ottoman east.[49] Among other things, the new fabrics opened the way for persons of middling wealth to enjoy, sometimes at lower prices, a version of the rare figured weaves worn by the upper classes.

Although the timing and relative weight of the sultans' motivations require more investigation, their policies were a response to the new diplomatic and trading imbalances that gave Europeans unprecedented entry into Ottoman society. The European orbit in Istanbul encompassed a growing body of European personnel and consumer goods. It also increasingly embraced more local clients, particularly Christians. Local employees and liaisons of every variety, from cooks and stableboys to interpreters and merchants, attached themselves to the foreign embassies and trading houses. They acquired legal and economic advantages not available to the bulk of the population.[50]

On the material level, the European presence affected an even larger number of middle-class consumers. Perhaps these were concentrated in the non-Muslim communities, but Muslims were also enthusiastic buyers of new European products, most especially textiles. And, as the legislation of the time charges, many Muslims were using European styles to show off the new fabrics. Muslim imitation of non-Muslims, or of foreigners generally, was only one of the concerns of the period's regulations. Imitation of the perquisites and prerogatives of the official (male) elites was another. Whether through the use of new fabrics or by indulging in forbidden local luxuries, men and women seemed to be testing the right of the monarch to determine status. Like other regimes grounded in social regulation, the Ottomans treated sartorial imitation as a statement of identification. A subject population's seemingly imitative identification with either non-Muslim or privileged Muslim was an act of transgression, morally and politically sinister.

To inspect his capital, Mustafa III took to dressing in the uniform of an imperial guardsman *(bostancı)*. Unlike his subjects, the sultan had perfect freedom in clothing matters. But being wise in the ways of his own capital—where street violence was often traceable to the misbehavior of his own troopers—Mustafa made sure not to "dress down" below the protections offered by imperial livery.[51] If his hope was to unearth wrongdoers, he was seldom disappointed. Derelict guardsmen, dishonest bakers and moneylenders, public smokers, spies, and immodest women were only some of those he condemned to flogging or execution on his rounds.[52]

In late spring of 1758 (Ramadan 1171), soon after his accession, the disguised Mustafa set out in search of lawbreakers in the neighborhoods of Aya Kapısı (originally Aya Kilise Kapısı), located on the Golden Horn between the districts of Un Kapanı and Balat. His victims on this occasion were a Christian and a Jew, not a surprising haul given the preponderance of non-Muslims in those neighborhoods.[53] The two men were caught wearing Muslim garb. One of them was found to have on the yellow leather boots *(sari mest pabuç)* that the law reserved for Muslims alone.[54] The man's crime was compounded by the fact that the soft, shin-high kidskin footwear was not only communally specific but an indicator of wealth and high station. In addition, the sultan had only months before issued decrees spelling out in detail the various restrictions.[55] A story is told about this case, or one much like it around the same time, that the man was a beggar, and that the boots in question, old and all but worn out, had been given to him as an act of charity by a well-to-do Muslim. The beggar told his story hoping for mercy, but he and the other captive were hanged.[56]

The incident points up a few of the strains and ambiguities in the regulation of the capital during the century. In the first place, social regulations almost always were being flouted. Ottomans themselves complained of it, and historians have concluded as much from the constant reissuing of decrees. Sultan Osman's and Mustafa's prowlings could have other causes rather than a rise in sumptuary street crime. In the years when the superbly capable Grand Vezir Mehmed Raghib Paşa (d. 1763) managed foreign affairs, domestic regulation was left to his sovereign. It is also likely that the sultans, however much encouraged by Raghib Paşa or other statesmen to direct their regulatory energies away from their own high officials, were genuinely outraged by evidences of a disorderly realm. Ottoman chronicles record contemporary complaints about the problem of disobedience of the law. The historian, Şem'dâni-zâde (d. 1779/1193), the angry male of the 1700s, complains that defiance of clothing prohibitions was routine. In his view, the government should have demonstrated its commitment by executing lawbreakers at every opportunity. Instead, he says, the authorities exerted themselves for a few days and then looked the other way.[57] Osman and Mustafa were out to put some backbone into enforcement, if only temporarily. Perhaps conservative elements in society demanded at least that much, although it clearly was not enough for Şem'dani-zâde.

The mutability of the law was also evident in the marketplace. The wearing of certain kinds of garments was mandated by law, if not always successfully. The purchase and possession of such garments were another matter entirely. Plenty of supposedly regulated clothing circulated throughout society, in the "wrong" hands. The very nature of clothing as a familiar and manipulable good, plus the simple straight-seam cut of most Ottoman styles, probably meant that stitching up and altering clothing were widespread practices.[58] Items of clothing to be worn in the home or exchanged among relatives, close friends, slaves, and ex-slaves would have moved outside the regulatory gaze. The secondhand market and hand-me-downs would be especially difficult to control, unless the sultans thought their exemplary punishments would curb secondary as well as primary exchanges.

For their part, European visitors bought clothing as souvenirs. Those in residence for longer periods also made sure to keep Ottoman dress on hand in order to travel outside their own compounds without attracting notice. The portfolios of Jean-Baptiste Van Mour and Jean-Étienne Liotard, among other artists, testify to the possession of regulated wear by non-Muslims, local as well as foreign. Van Mour and Liotard earned their bread and butter by painting portraits of prosperous men, and some women. Their biggest commissions came from European ambassadors and merchants as well as native non-Muslims (usually merchants), and the occasional Muslim. If lighting and detail are any measure, clothing and costume are the subject of the paintings as much as the men and women who appear in them. Native non-Muslims made up a large number of the European painters' commissions in Istanbul. The wealthy men and women who look out from the paintings in furred robes and handsome turbans were in many cases tied to the merchantmen who served as local agents for Russian furs, French cottons and tulle, Indian cashmere, British wools, and Persian and domestic silks. They had easy access to the forbidden goods and they possessed the means to buy them for their own use. That they also wished to be memorialized in opulent garb is clear from their portraits. Dressed in the fabrics of privileged Ottoman officialdom, they offer an eastern counterpoint to the familiar north European image of bourgeois well-being.[59]

That non-Muslim visitors from abroad actually owned the garments in which they were painted, as opposed to wearing stock items from the artist's wardrobe, is confirmed in their diaries and correspondence. The letters of Lady Mary Wortley Montagu, wife of the English ambassador earlier in the century, are exceptional for their time in that they detail every item of souvenir finery down to underwear.[60] Travelers were also known to wear turbans, *şalvars*, and robes back home, for masquerades to be sure, but also as exotic loungewear. The artist Liotard, who had grown accustomed to Ottoman caftans and mantles, wore them at home in Vienna following his stay in Istanbul.[61] Footwear was also for sale to those who had the price or the connections. Julia Pardoe informs us that when she visited Istanbul in the early nineteenth century, purple slippers were designated for Jews, red for Armenians, and yellow for Muslims. She was nonetheless able to obtain a pair of the yellow Muslim boots for herself.[62] Clearly the seller's desire to make a sale, or simply to please, could offset the law.

The Ottoman regime sought to regulate the streets and streetwear. In general it did not concern itself with what transpired within the home of Muslim or non-Muslim. Officials were even less inclined to look for trouble among diplomats with immunity from local regulation or among those protected by them. Residents of Istanbul who could afford luxury goods could enjoy them in private. It was only when they took them onto the streets, in public, or otherwise brought attention to themselves, that they ran the risk of detection, either by the authorities or by jealous neighbors. But the eighteenth century was witnessing growing fraternization between local non-Muslims and the Europeans now among them. When wealthy Christians visited ambassadorial residences, or each other's homes, they might do so wearing luxury attire. If they possessed legal immunity, they were free of clothing regulations and could dress as they liked. If not, they could conceal indoor clothing under sanctioned overgarments. Or, in areas where non-Muslims predominated, they might hope to pass unnoticed, particularly if the authorities and their neighbors, Muslim and non-Muslim, were indifferent. The slippery slope to open public display is not far to see in the new mix of social opportunities.

Social relationships between Europeans and non-Muslim natives predated the widespread acquisition of legal immunity by local non-Muslims. The spread of immunity altered social relationships in ways rather different from the less formal processes described here. For our purposes, one can say that the development of fashionable, or at least foreign and hence privileged enclaves, offered native non-Muslims a bit of shelter from Ottoman social regulations and some incentive to depart from them. This was manifestly true of the nineteenth century, of course. But a mixed fashionable society, with Europeans and native

Ottomans, especially non-Muslims, spending time together, not just in the occasional individual friendship or as a function of business, had its beginnings in the mid-eighteenth century. Nonetheless, there were numerous confrontations when a native subject's violation took direct, face-to-face, form. How the letter of the law was implemented depended on circumstances and personalities.

The beggar with the boots had the excruciatingly bad luck to come face to face with the sultan. How he came to be in the sultan's path—or who put him there—or how the sultan came to be in Aya Kapısı at all is difficult to know. Aya Kapısı lies within the city proper, but apart from its shoreside location, it is indistinguishable from dozens of other neighborhoods. According to an eighteenth-century observer, its dock was not a busy one, with just a few skiffs to be seen and only a few shops nearby. Further up the shore, however, between Aya Kapısı and Fener and Balat to the north, were residences of wealthy Greeks, including the Greek Orthodox patriarch and a number of privileged Ottoman Christians who served in the administration of the Moldavian and Wallachian principalities.[63] Ordinary non-Muslims may have felt more secure in these religiously more homogeneous districts, in the shadow of powerful co-religionists. Ottoman suspicions about relationships between European and Russian representatives and native Orthodox grandees, however, put a spotlight on just those districts.

What role these considerations played in the sultan's visit is a mystery. He may have gone because laxity had been reported, or because laxity had *not* been reported. He may have sought to reassure himself of his authority without directly confronting the powerful elements that challenged it. On the other hand, he may have been encouraged to head in the direction of Aya Kapısı because members of one palace faction hoped to embarrass a rival group that was in one way or another linked to the area. Janissaries and bostancıs, for example, the main policing officials for such neighborhoods, were only two of many factional possibilities. Whatever the sultan's particular motives, his movements were political, and in Istanbul as elsewhere, all politics are arguably local politics. European power and minority pretensions were chronic background anxieties; we can only guess at the local politics that helped shape the day. The message to the general population, however, was not unlike that in the slave girl's hanging. The sultan demanded obedience to the law and conformity to its social regulation. And in this case, there was no excuse for defiance—not even poverty nor an accident of charity.

The incognito monarch inspecting his realm is an old story. Energetic autocrats since Nebuchadnezzar had indulged in it. Mustafa had ample precedent among his own ancestors. Like them, Mustafa monitored his city in part because he did not trust his deputies. The beggar lost his life, but the city's officials were put on notice. Aya Kapısı had a small janissary guardhouse *(kulluk)*, as well as shore patrols, religious leaders, and other officials who should have made the sultan's visit unnecessary.

In fact, the sultan was putting all of his subjects on notice, and his legislation said as much. Or at least it said almost as much. His decrees listed all those directly affected. The category of transgressor included servants, tradesmen, boatmen, tailors, and others whose vocation or station excluded them from the entitled ranks and offices of officialdom. Women are named as well—all women, Muslim and non-Muslim, virtuous or not, lest any woman think she was exempt. The decrees also listed the parties responsible for ensuring obedience. These included assorted Ottoman police and watchmen, and European ambassadors, and privileged non-Muslim locals like Greek Orthodox and Armenian clerics, the latter to monitor their co-religionists. The decrees also note the aggrieved: the sultan, and the grandees at the top of the social pyramid whose prerogatives the lawbreakers were seemingly usurping. What the regulations fail to say is that the aggrieved parties were also among the greatest transgressors of the law.

Every rank within the official privileged caste had its own illegal specialty when it came to the unenforceable and unpopular restrictions on clothing. At the lowest levels, police and *mahalle* officials overlooked infractions, sometimes for a fee or favor. Some sold or gave away parts of their own regalia. The wealthier sorts, however, enjoyed a far wider range of opportunities. The "great men of state" *(rical-i devlet)*, especially the military-administrative element, accumulated huge inventories of luxury goods in the course of their service. Rare fabrics and furs were as good as gold and treated as such. Stored in treasuries and vaults, they were handled by special household servants—the keeper of the caftans, the furrier, the turban keeper, and so on. And they circulated among the elite almost as readily as coins in the market. Although the premier fur- and fabric-giver was the sultan,[64] the sultan's subordinates in turn distributed fabric packages *(bohça)* to superiors, inferiors, intimates, and strangers, with and without regard for the law's restrictions. Since their status was enhanced to the degree that they monopolized luxury attire, theoretically they undermined that status whenever they gave regulated furs and cloth to underlings. But the greats of the realm also derived prestige from their roles as patron-commanders of armies of servants, attendants, and soldiers. They projected their political and social weight not only through the numbers of their clients but also through the latters' accoutrements, perhaps especially in these times through the richness of servants' costumes. Among such clients were many non-Muslims—bankers, furriers, physicians, and other favorites. Like their Muslim counterparts, they were awarded cloth and furs for good service; they were thus also protectively clothed in their patron's prestige.

Sultan Mustafa's Grand Vezir, Raghib Paşa, was one of those who showered his attendants with costly favors. Around the time of Mustafa's encounter with the beggar, Raghib apparently decided to rein in his gift-giving by divesting his own aghas and physicians of the notorious ermine, lynx, and sable which he had accustomed them to wearing. A clothing decree of 1174/1760 alludes to how widespread the infractions were by lauding the magnanimity of the Grand Vezir's gesture.[65] It goes unsaid that Raghib was finally acting in conformity with the law, which had for years denounced the befurred servitors of the wealthy. In the 1760 decree, Raghib is seen to be setting an example for others to follow. The fact that it took him some time to reform his own entourage suggests that previously, whether under Osman or earlier in Mustafa's reign, he had not needed to take the matter seriously; he was, after all, the sultan's deputy, thus as the sultan's premier representative, if not on his own account, he was arguably entitled to dress his men accordingly. The contingent political context is not precisely known, but the episode in a larger sense underlines the jagged interface between a consistent imperial legality and the mechanisms of patronage and emanation.

That the great men of state were of two minds in upholding the law is also evidenced by the sultans themselves. Apart from Osman III and Mustafa III, the eighteenth-century sultans were lackadaisical about sumptuary regulation. Other domestic and foreign concerns weighed more heavily with them, and they seemed to recognize that the availability of both consumer wealth and luxury goods made the law all but unenforceable in the city. In any case, the sultans always reserved the right to exempt their own subordinates from sumptuary legislation if they so chose. Given that many of the official upholders of the law also benefited from the bans—by taking payment to overlook infractions or to illegally sell patents of immunity—supporters of the law no doubt included some who were more interested in personal advantage than in public morality.

Elements of a consumer economy had become established in Istanbul by mid-century. The regime exploited that economy to the extent that it was able and, through foreign trade arrangements, even made its expansion possible. At the same time, the state attempted through prescriptive legislation to impede the destabilizing effects of new forms of wealth and social mobility by insisting on palace patrimony, with its nonmonetary status system of mutual obligations and the hierarchical distribution of scarce goods. The regulatory clothing wars tried to deny the combined force of an expanded marketplace, new patterns of consumption, and European diplomatics in the very decades that are commonly regarded as a turning point in the losing battle to stave off European domination. In the nineteenth century such domination led to the abolition of Istanbul's slave markets. The slave trade continued unofficially, to a great extent driven indoors, giving wider scope to households and, perhaps, to women's networks.[66]

The issue of legal prescription brings us back to the venues of conflict in urban society. The examples presented here do not summarize the range of social strains at work in the mid-eighteenth century. They do, however, testify to the elasticity of lawful prescription and to the disturbing circulation of merchandise in a heavily prescribed capital city. They center specifically on the more intimate zones of consumption, in the realm of personal encounters, between slave and mistress, beggar and benefactor, sultan and vezir, and other versions of master and servitor. To some extent the various encounters turned on assertions of self, of personal exceptionalism, whether in habits of dress, acts of charity or largess, murder, or the sovereign's will. There is no direct evidence that the more peaceful sorts of private desires here constructed a notion of public rights at this point. The link between sumptuary legislation and punishments on the one hand and the surge in the demand for foreign-conferred patents of extraterritoriality, especially as these affected Ottoman religious minorities, requires closer study. The patents were an alternative source, under foreign auspices, of the kind of advantage that might be acquired piecemeal, and less securely, through Ottoman patrons or bribery. But the drive to obtain such patents, although fueled by the tax exemptions they conferred, can also be viewed as an implicit will to rights. Until that history can be tested, however, we can only say that the cases here reflect the capacity of individuals to test the limits of authority—even the sultan had obligations to the law—and to remake the rules. This is in any event where the two main cases began.

Mischance and miscalculation brought the two cases to the general public. Their protagonists were delivered up as examples, and their stories transformed into cautionary tales. If we are to believe the texts of the time, the regime acted to reaffirm its unchallenged authority, recouple obedience with authority, and mark off, once again, lines of deference and the boundaries of privilege. Different segments of the population no doubt drew varying conclusions from the two executions with respect to the nature of authority and justice in the Ottoman Empire. Regardless of intent or reception, the two cases define social vulnerability and expose a social system built on relationships of inequality. Although the sultan's role as guarantor and beneficiary is asserted throughout the stories and the legal texts, the cases reveal the fragility of his authority, and the fluid contesting, foundations on which it stood.

Notes

1. Hâkim, 484/2, 227.

2. Boppe (1989), for Jean-Baptiste Van Mour, Jean-Étienne Liotard, Antoine Ignace Melling, and others.

3. Mantran (1962), 74–76; Ortaylı (1989), 131–38; Rosenthal (1980), passim.

4. For Istanbul and its suburbs in the eighteenth century, population figures range from 400,000 to a high of around 800,000; Issawi (1977), 152–53.

5. On commercial privileges, diplomatic immunity, and the *berat* system, see İnalcık (1960); Bağış (1983); and Sonyel (1993).

6. Although some quarters of the city were populated almost exclusively by a single confessional group (İnalcık 1973, 151), the comingling of Istanbul's populations in the later centuries is often contrasted to the situation in the Arab provinces. (Mantran 1962, 24).

7. They also provide evidence from *sicil*s on interconfessional cooperation/interaction.

8. Genç (1995), 177-80.

9. On the Ottoman slave trade generally, see İnalcık (1979) and Fisher (1978a, 1978b, 1980); and for the nineteenth century particularly, Toledano (1982), Erdem (1997), and Baer (1969). Local studies include Sahillioğlu (1985), Jennings (1987), Sak (1989), and Limam (1981).

10. The principal narrative occurs in Hâkim, TKS, B233, fol. 143a; see also Şem'dani-zâde (1976–1981), IIa:41.

11. On Istanbul dealers and their markets, see: Eyice (1965), 209–10; Toledano (1982), 51–52, who also cites numerous firsthand Western accounts; Mantran (1962), 506–7; Kütükoğlu (1983), 257–58; and Pakalın (1946–1954), I:552–55.

12. If the slave dealer owned the girl outright, the question of blood money would presumably not arise. The Maliki school of Islamic law allowed

slaves guilty of murder to be turned over to the victim's family, who could dispose of them as they saw fit. The other schools left final responsibility with the owner, who could surrender the slave or pay the required compensation.

13. Regarding homocide and the doctrine of *siyasa shar'iya,* which upheld the sovereign's intervention, see Coulson (1964), 18, 129–32.

14. Hâkim, TKS, B233, fol. 143a.

15. See, however, Peirce (1993), Reindl-Kiel (1991), and Seng (1996).

16. Sak (1989), 162; Toledano (1982), 17–42 and passim; and Erim (1991), 133.

17. Abdülaziz Bey (1995), 2:314–15; Pakalın (1946–1954), I:554–55.

18. On gift-giving as a binding element of incorporation and identification, see Mauss (1967), 6–16 and passim; cf. Zilfi (1993).

19. Dankoff (1991), especially 8–10, 272–75.

20. On these usages, see Pakalın (1946–1954) and Abdülaziz Bey (1995), II:315. Mernissi (1996) speculates on the *cariye* (Ar., *jariye*) phenomenon and political authoritarianism.

21. The price of comely slaves of either sex sometimes outpaced urban real estate; Sak (1989), 162, 168; Abdülaziz Bey (1995), II:315; Mantran (1962), 508; F. Davis (1986), 104. See also F. Davis (1986), 105–7 for the training of female slaves in the nineteenth century.

22. For taxes and commissions in various periods, see İnalcık (1994), 283–84; Fisher (1978a), 15–16; F. Davis (1986), 105; Pakalın (1946–1954), I:260–61; Toledano (1982), 73; Mantran (1962), 507.

23. İnalcık (1979a), 9–12; Sahillioğlu (1985); Faroqhi (1994), 19–24.

24. Recent studies that have considered the issue include Ahmed (1992), and Marmon (1995).

25. Veblen (1934).

26. Douglas and Isherwood (1996), p. viii.

27. It is uncertain whether or not the lady of the house was his legal wife. The term *hatun,* meaning "woman," sometimes with overtones of "lady," appears in the account, but the usage is ambiguous.

28. Kütükoğlu (1983), 255–58; Kazıcı (1987), 125–26.

29. Kütükoğlu (1983), 256–57, names eight women dealers *(esirci)* among the "more than 100" men and women listed in 1640 as members of Istanbul's slave dealers' guild.

30. Kütükoğlu (1983), 257; Kazıcı (1987), 121–22.

31. Toledano (1982), 39–40, 45.

32. Ahmed (1992), 121–22; F. Davis (1986), 103, 108.

33. Pakalın (1946–1954), I:259–60; Halide Edip Adıvar (1963), 94–96, tells the poignant story of a frightened Ethiopian child transported to Istanbul as a special holiday gift for the young Halide.

34. Pakalın (1946–1954), I:260.

35. See the late nineteenth-century memoirs and accounts discussed in F. Davis (1986), 99–118, passim.

36. Binark (1968).

37. See, for example, Hâkim, TKS B233, fol. 184a, for a decree from 1754/1177.

38. *Encylopaedia of Islam,* 2nd edition, s.v. "Ghiyar," and "Libas."

39. See Şeni (1984) on the semiotics of the female body and urban space.

40. Ercan (1990); Heyberger (1994), 51–53. Clothing practices conformed generally to these broad categories, but there was considerable variation within the confessions because of regional origins or ethnicity (e.g., Greek Orthodox islanders and Muslim Tatars), or religious subsect (Catholic and Gregorian Armenians, or Karaite, Ashkenazi, and Sephardic Jews). On such variations in women's dress, see Scarce (1987), 90–131.

41. For example, red or green *ferace*s for Muslims, but only black for non-Muslims (Hâkim, TKS, B233, fol. 10b).

42. Zilfi (1996); Şeni (1984).

43. Zilfi (1996).

44. For a richly illustrated history of women's dress, see Scarce (1987).

45. Hâkim, TKS, B231, fol. 234b, for 1759/1173; cf. Refik [Altınay] (1988c), 87, regarding 1138/1726. Of course, social legislation reflected economic worries (and often said as much) about frivolous expenditure, excessive imports, guild rivalries, and class jealousies; Zilfi (1993) and (1996).

46. See, for example, the turban styles (usually achieved by cut rather than by wrapping) of fashionable European and American women in seventeenth- and eighteenth-century portraiture (e.g., La Tour, "Le Tricheur," the Louvre).

47. Illustrations in Binark (1968), İnalcık (1973), and Reyhanlı (1989) are particular vivid.

48. Hâkim, TKS, B231, fol. 234b.

49. Owen (1977), 149–50; Raymond (1977), 185–91 and passim; İnalcık (1993b); Braude (1979); Genç (1995); Kütükoğlu (1974), 53. Colored prints,

called *indiennes* in France, had been introduced into England by the late seventeenth century, but commanded attention in a variety of markets only in the eighteenth century. When the cloth entered France, competing guilds reportedly pressured the French government to punish those who manufactured it and the women who wore it; officials were instructed to rip clothes off women's backs if necessary (Challamel 1882, 156).

50. İnalcık (1960).

51. A point made by Şeni (1984), 81.

52. Şem'dani-zade (1976–1981), IIa:37–38; Hâkim, TKS, B231, fols. 270a–b, 290a–291a.

53. İnciciyan (1956), 14, 118–19.

54. Hâkim, TKS, B231, fol. 270a.

55. Hâkim, TKS, B231, fols. 290a–291a.

56. D'Ohsson (1788–1824), IV.

57. Şem'dani-zâde (1976–1981), IIa:36.

58. Mickelwright (1987b), 37; see also Denny (1972), 64 and passim; Scarce (1987), patterns and sketches, passim.

59. Boppe (1989), 12–95, and passim.

60. Montagu (1971), 124–27, 161–62.

61. *Cornucopia* (1992–1993), 10.

62. Pardoe (1839).

63. İnciciyan (1956), 118.

64. For cloth and clothing in imperial gift-giving, see Zilfi (1993), 184–91.

65. Decree of 1174 Safer, quoted in Hâkim, TKS, B233, fol. 48a.

66. I am pursuing this theme in a separate work that hypothesizes a certain "feminization of slavery" in this period.

Bibliography

Abdel Nour, Antoine. 1982. *Introduction de l'histoire urbaine de la Syrie ottomane (XVIe–XVIIIe siècle).* Beirut.

Abdullah Şeref. 1336/1917. "Istanbul'da Mekulat Müzayakası," *Tarih-i Osmani Encümeni Mecmuası.* no. 40.

Abdülaziz Bey. 1995. *Osmanlı Âdet, Merasim ve Tabirleri (Âdât ve Mersim-i Kadime Tabirât ve Muamelât-ı Kavmiye-i Osmaniye).* Transl. and eds. Kâzım Arısan and Duygu Arısan Günay. İstanbul.

Abu-Lughod, Janet L. 1989. *Before European Hegemony: The World System* A.D. *1250–1350.* Oxford.

Achaya, K. T. 1994. *Indian Food. A Historical Companion.* Delhi.

Adamson, Melitta Weiss, ed. 1995. *Food in the Middle Ages: A Book of Essays.* New York.

Adıvar, Halide Edip. 1967. *Mor Salkımlı Ev.* İstanbul.

Ahmed Refik. 1332/1913. "Sultan Süleyman Kanuni'nin Son Senelerinde İstanbul'un Usül-ü İaşesi ve Ahval-i Ticariyesi," *Tarih-i Osmani Encümeni Mecmuası.* no. 37.

———. 1932. *Lâle Devri.* İstanbul.

———. 1988a. *Onaltıncı Asırda İstanbul Hayatı (1553–1591): İstanbul'un fikri, içtimai iktisadî ve ticari ahvalile evkaf, belediye, iaşe ve gümrük işlerine dair Hazine-i Evrak'ın gayri matbu' vesikalarını havidir.* İstanbul. Reprint.

———. 1988b. *Hicri Onbirinci Asırda İstanbul Hayatı (1000–1100): İstanbul'un fikri, içtimaî, iktisadî ve ticari ahvalile evkaf, belediye, iaşe ve gümrük işlerine dair Hazine-i Evrak'in gayri matbu' vesikalarını havidir. İstanbul.* Reprint.

———. 1988c. *Hicri Onikinci Asırda İstanbul Hayatı (1100–1200): İstanbul'un fikri, içtimaî, iktisadî ve ticari ahvalile evkaf, belediye, iaşe ve gümrük işlerine dair Hazine-i Evrak'in gayri matbu' vesikalarını havidir. İstanbul.* Reprint.

———. 1988d. *Hicri Onüçüncü Asırda İstanbul Hayatı (1200–1255): İstanbul'un fikri, içtimaî, iktisadî ve ticari ahvalile evkaf, belediye, iaşe ve gümrük işlerine dair Hazine-i Evrak'in gayri matbu vesikalarını havidir. İstanbul.* Reprint.

See also Altınay, Ahmed Refik.

Ahmed, Leila. 1992. *Women and Gender in Islam: Historical Roots of a Modern Debate.* New Haven.

Akdağ, Mustafa. 1995. *Türkiye'nin İktisadî ve İçtimaî Tarihi.* Cilt 1: 1453–1559. İstanbul.

Akgündüz, Ahmed. 1995. *İslâm Hukukunda Kölelik-Cariyelik Müessesesi ve Osmanlı'da Harem.* İstanbul.

———, et al. 1988–89. *Şeriye Sicilleri.* 2 vols. İstanbul.

———. 1991. *Osmanlı Kanunnâmeleri. Cilt 1: Fatih Devrinde Anadolu Eyâleti ve Sancakları.* İstanbul.

Aktan, Hamza. 1991. *Mukayeseli İslâm Miras Hukuku.* İstanbul.

Aktepe, M. Münir. 1952. "Damad İbrahim Paşa Devrinde Lâle," *İstanbul Üniversitesi Edebiyat Fakültesi Tarih Dergisi* IV, 7: 83–126.

———. 1953. "Damad İbrahim Paşa Devrinde Lâle," *İstanbul Üniversitesi Edebiyat Fakültesi Tarih Dergisi* V, 8.

———. 1954. "Damad İbrahim Paşa Devrinde Lâle," *İstanbul Üniversitesi Edebiyat Fakültesi Tarih Dergisi* VI, 9: 23–38.

———. 1958a. *Patrona İsyanı (1730).* İstanbul.

———. 1958b. "Damad İbrahim Paşa Devrinde Lâle," *Türkiyat Mecmuası* IX, 1954.

———. 1958c. "XVII. Asrın ilk yarısında İstanbul'un Nüfus mes'elesine dair bazı Vesikalar," *İÜEF Tarih Dergisi* Vol. IX: 1–30.

Aktuğ, İlknur. 1993. *Nevşehir Damat İbrahim Paşa Külliyesi.* Ankara.

Akyavaş, Beynun A., ed. 1993. *Yirmisekiz Çelebi Mehmed Efendi'nin Fransa Sefâretnâmesi.* Ankara.

Alexandrescu-Dersca (Bulgaru), Maria Matilda. 1957. "Contribution à l'ètude de l'approvisionnement en blé de Constantinople au XVIIIe siècle," *Studia et Acta Orientalia,* no. I.

———. 1969. "Quelques donnés sur le ravitaillement de Constantinople au XVIe siècle," *Les Actes du Premier Congrès International des Ètudes Balkaniques et Sud-Est Europèennes.*

———. 1983. "Sur la ravitaillement d'Istanbul au XVIème siècle en relation avec les Principautes Roumaines," *Revue d'Histoire Maghrebine,* nos. 31–39.

Allen, William. 1982. "Lekegian in Constantinople," *History of Photography* 6(2).

———. 1990. "Sixty-five Istanbul Photographers, 1887–1914," in ed., Kathleen Collins, *Shadow and Substance: Essays in the History of Photography,* Bloomfield Hill, Mich.

Altınay, Ahmed Refik. 1930. *Onikinci asr-ı hicride İstanbul Hayatı: 1100–1200.* Istanbul.

Altıner, Avni. 1937. "Tarhala Obasını Tanıyalım, 2." *Gediz* 5: 10–11.

———. 1938. "Tarhala Obasını Tanıyalım, 9." *Gediz* 13: 10–11, 15.

Altınöz, İsmail Haşim. 1995. "Osmanlı Toplumunda Çingeneler," *Tarih ve Toplum* Mayıs 137: 22–29.

Anderson, Eugene N. 1988. *The Food of China.* New Haven.

Anderson, Sonia. 1989. *An English Consul in Turkey: Paul Rycaut at Smyrna, 1667–1678.* Oxford.

Andreasyan, Hrand D. 1964. *Polonyalı Simeon'un Seyahatnâmesi, 1608–1619.* İstanbul.

Andrews, Walter, Najaat Black, and Mehmet Kalpaklı. 1997. *Ottoman Lyric Poetry: An Anthology.* Austin, Tex.

Anhegger, Robert, 1991. "Melling et la sultane Hadidgé, Remarques et commentaires à propos de leur correspondance," in Cornelis Boschma, Jacques Perot, eds., *Antoine-Ignace Melling (1763–1831), artiste-voyageur.* Paris: 28–31.

Anıl, Yaşar Şahin. 1993. *Osmanlı'da Kadılık.* İstanbul.

Anna Komnena. 1996. *Alexiad: Malazgirt'in Sonrası.* Çevirmen Bilge Umar. İstanbul.

Appadurai, Arjun. 1981. "Gastro-politics in Hindu South Asia," *American Ethnologist,* no. 8.

———. 1986. "Introduction: Commodities and the Politics of Value," in Arjun Appaduri, ed., *The Social Life of Things: Commodities in Cultural Perspective.* Cambridge.

Arberry, Arthur J. 1939. "A Baghdad Cookery-Book," *Islamic Culture: An English Quarterly,* no. XIII: 1–2.

Arel, Ayda. 1988. "Gothic Towers and Baroque Mihrabs: The Post-Classical Architecture of Aegean Anatolia in the Eighteenth and Nineteenth Centuries," *Muqarnas* 5: 212–218.

Arıkan, Zeki. 1987. "Bir Kanunnâme Sureti," *Tarih İncelemeleri Dergisi* 3: 49–61.

Arnott, Margaret L., ed. 1975. *Gastronomy: The Antropology of Food and Food Habits*. The Hague.

Artan, Tülay (forthcoming a). "A Mirror for Modesty: Lifestyles and Living Standards in the Eighteenth Century Eyüp in the Light of Probate Inventories," paper presented at The Small Regions of the Ottoman Empire Conference of the Orient-Institute der DMG and the Sudosteuropa-Gesellshaft in Munich, 31 October–2 November 1996, İstanbul.

———. (forthcoming b). "Problems Relating to the Social History Context of the Acquisition and Possession of Books as Parts of Collections of Objets d'Arts in the Eighteenth Century," paper presented at the Xth International Congress of Turkish Art, 17–23 September 1995, Geneva.

———. (forthcoming c). "Aspects of Ottoman Intra-Elite Food Redistributionism in the Light of Eighteenth Century Imperial Kitchen Registers: The Estate-Determination of Diet; the Culinary Determination of Rank and Status," paper presented originally as "Ritual Redistributionism in Food and the Consumption Patterns of the Ottoman Elite in the Light of the Eighteenth Century Imperial Kitchen Registers," at the Symposium on Food, Beverages, and Socialibility in the Ottoman Empire, Bosphorus University, 25–26 March 1996, İstanbul.

———. (forthcoming d). "Fatma Sultan and Damad İbrahim Paşa: Kitchen, Cellar and Marriage," in N. Göyünç ed., *H. İnalcık Festschrift*. İstanbul.

———. 1989. "Architecture as a Theatre of Life: Profile of the Eighteenth Century Bosphorus," Ph.D. dissertation, Massachusetts Institute of Technology, Cambridge.

———. 1993. "From Charismatic Leadership to Collective Rule: Introducing Materials on the Wealth and Power of Ottoman Princesses in the Eighteenth Century," *Toplum ve Ekonomi*, IV.

———. 1995a. "Problems Related to Displaying Material Culture and Standards of Living in the Ottoman World," paper presented at the Workshop on City and Social History Museums, 28–30 June 1995, İstanbul.

———. 1995b. "Courtly Standards of Living and Consumption Patterns in the Ottoman Eighteenth Century," paper presented at the VII. Internationaler Kongres Für Osmanische Wirtschafts und Sozialgeschichte (1300–1920), 25–29 July 1995, Heidelberg.

Artan, Tülay and Halil Berktay, (forthcoming). "What lineages for the 'other' absolutism? The scope, messages, and dimensions of post-classical Ottoman court patronage at the juncture of its own traditions with the challenge of early modernity in Europe," paper presented at the "Court as an Economic Institution," Preliminary Workshop for the

1998 World Economic History Congress, 23–24 March 1997, Fiesole/Florence (to be published in the Proceedings of the A-Sessions at Sevilla, 1998).

Ashtor, Eliyahu. 1975. "An Essay on the Diet of Various Classes in the Medieval Levant," in Robert Forster and Orest Ranum, eds., *Biology of Man in History* (selections from the *Annales ESC*). Baltimore.

Atıl, Esin. 1969. "Surname-i Vehbi: An Eighteenth Century Ottoman Book of Festivals," Ph.D. dissertation, University of Michigan, Ann Arbor.

———. 1993. "The Story of an Eighteenth-Century Ottoman Festival," *Muqarnas* Vol. 10, 181–200.

Atsız, Nihal, ed. 1992. *Aşıkpaşaoğlu Tarihi.* İstanbul.

Ayşe, Fahriye. 1882. *Ev Kadını.* İstanbul.

Ayverdi, M. Ekrem Hakkı. 1950. *XVIII Asırda Lâle.* İstanbul.

Baer, Gabriel. 1969. *Studies in the Social History of Modern Egypt.* Chicago.

Bağış, Ali İhsan. 1983. *Osmanlı Ticaretinde Gayri Müslimler (1750–1839).* Ankara.

Baines, Barbara. 1981. *Fashion Revivals from the Elizabethan Age to the Present Day.* London.

Baker, Patricia. 1986. "The Fez in Turkey: A Symbol of Modernization?" *Costume.* XX.

Baldwin, Gordon. 1990. "Correspondence: Sebah and Joaillier," *History of Photography* 14.

Balta, Evangelia. 1994. "The Bread in Greek Lands during the Ottoman Rule," *Ankara Üniversitesi DTCF Tarih Araştırmaları Dergisi 1992–1994,* no. XVI: 27.

Barber, Benjamin. 1995. *Jihad vs. McWorld.* New York.

Barıştа, H. Örcün. 1984. *Türk İşleme Sanatı Tarihi.* Ankara.

———. 1993. *İstanbul Çeşmeleri.* Ankara.

Barkan, Ömer Lütfi. 1962–3a. "Fatih Cami ve İmareti Tesislerinin 1489–1490 Yıllarına Ait Muhasebe Bilançolar," in "Şehirlerin Teşekkül ve İnkişafi Tarihi Bakımından, Osmanlı İmparatorluğunda İmaret Sitelerinin Kuruluş ve İşleyiş Tarzına Ait Araştırmalar," *İstanbul Üniversitesi İktisat Fakültesi Mecmuası,* no. XXIII: 1–2.

———. 1962–3b. "Ayasofya Camii ve Eyüp Türbesinin 1489–1491 Yıllarına Ait Muhasebe Bilançoları," in "Şehirlerin Teşekkül ve İnkişafı Tarihi

Bakımından, Osmanlı İmparatorluğunda İmaret Sitelerinin Kuruluş ve İşleyiş Tarzına Ait Araştırmalar," *İstanbul Üniversitesi İktisat Fakültesi Mecmuası,* no. XXIII: 1–2.

———. 1962–3c. "Saray Mutfağının 894–895 (1489–1490) Yılına Ait Muhasebe Bilançosu" in "Şehirlerin Teşekkül ve İnkişafı Tarihi Bakımından, Osmanlı İmparatorluğunda İmaret Sitelerinin Kuruluş ve İşleyiş Tarzına Ait Araştırmalar," *İstanbul Üniversitesi İktisat Fakültesi Mecmuası,* no. XXIII: 1–2.

———. 1963. "Şehirlerin Teşekkül ve İnkişafı Tarihi Bakımından Osmanlı Imparatorluğunda İmaret Sitelerinin Kuruluş ve İşleyiş Tarzına ait Araştırmalar," *İstanbul Üniversitesi İktisat Fakültesi Mecmuası,* XXIII, 1–2: 239–296.

———. 1966. "Edirne Askeri Kassamına ait Tereke Defterleri (1545–1659)," *Türk Tarih Kurumu, Belgeler,* III, 5–6: 1–479.

———. 1971. "Süleymaniye Cami ve İmareti Tesislerine Ait Yılık Bir Muhasebe Bilançosu," *Vakıflar Dergisi,* vol. IX.

———. 1972, 1979. *Süleymaniye Cami ve İmareti İnşaatı (1550–1557),* 2 vols., Ankara.

———. 1979. "İstanbul Saraylatına Ait Muhasebe Defterleri," *Belgeler,* no. IX: 13.

Barkas, Janet. 1975. *The Vegetable Passion: A History of the Vegetarian State of Mind.* London.

Bastav, Şerif. 1989. *Bizans İmparatorluğu Tarihi: Son Devir, 1261–1461.* Ankara.

Başkan, Seyfi. 1991. *Ondokuzuncu Yüzyıldan Günümüze Türk Ressamları/Contemporary Turkish Painters.* Ankara.

Batterberry, Michael, and Ariane Batterberry. 1977. *Fashion: The Mirror of History.* New York.

Baudier, Michel, 1626. *Histoire générale du Serrail et de la Cour du Grand Seigneur, Empereur des Turcs, ou se voit l'image de la grandeur Othomane, le Tableau des passions Humaines, et les exemples des inconstances prosperitez de la Cour.* Paris.

Baudrillard, Jean. 1996. *The System of Objects.* London.

Baudrillart, Henri. 1878–1880. *Histoire de luxe privé et publique depuis l'antiquité jusqu'ê nos jours.* 4 vols. Paris.

Baxandall, Michael. 1985. *Die Kunst der Bildschnitzer, Tilman Riemenschneider, Veit Stoß und ihre Zeitgenossen,* tr. by Brigitte Sauerländer. Munich.

Bayly, Christopher A. 1983. *Rulers, Townsmen and Bazaars, North Indian Society in the Age of British Expansion, 1770–1870.* Cambridge.

Baysun, M. Cavid. 1988. "Evliya Çelebi," *İslâm Ansiklopedisi*, 4. İstanbul, 400–13.

Baytop, Turhan. 1994. *Türkçe Bitki Adları Sözlügü*. Ankara.

———. 1992. *İstanbul Lâlesi*. Ankara.

Bedevian, Armenag K. 1936. *Illustrated Polyglottic Dictionary of Plant Names: In Latin, Arabic, Armenian, English, French, German, Italian and Turkish Languages, Including Economic, Medicinal, Poisonous or Ornamental Plants and Common Weeds*. Cairo.

Berkes, Niyazi. 1964. *The Development of Secularism in Turkey*. Montreal.

———. 1978. *Türkiye'de Çağdaşlaşma*. İstanbul.

Bermingham, Ann and John Brewer, eds. 1995. *The Consumption of Culture 1600–1800: Image, Object, Text*. London and New York.

Berry, Christopher J. 1994. *The Idea of Luxury: A Conceptual and Historical Investigation*. Cambridge.

Binark, İsmet. 1968. "XVIII. Yüzyıl Sonlarına kadar Osmanlı-Türk Ordusuna ait Askeri Kıyafet ve Ünvanlar," *Türk Kültürü*, VI, 70.

Black, Jeremy. 1991. *A Military Revolution? Military Change and European Society 1550–1800: Studies in European History*. London.

Blount, Henry. 1636. *A Voyage into the Levant*. London. (Reprint: *The English Experience*, no. 850, 1977. Amsterdam.)

Blunt, Wilfrid. 1950. *Tulipomania*. London.

Boppe, Auguste. 1911. *Les Peintures du Bosphore au dix-huitième siècle*. Paris.

Boran, Behice. (1992 {1945]). *Toplumsal Yapı Araştırmaları: İki Köy Çeşidinin Mukayeseli Tetkiki. Bütün Yapıtlar: III*. İstanbul.

Bostan, İdris. 1995. "Kuyûd-i Mühimmat Defterlerinin Osmanlı Devlet Teşkilat Tarihi Bakımından Önemi," *Osmanlı-Türk Diplomatiği Semineri, 30–31 May 1994*. İstanbul.

Botschantzeva, Z. P. 1982. *Tulips: Taxonomy, Morphology, Cytology, Phytogeography and Physiology*, trans. H. Q. Varekamp. Rotterdam.

Boucher, Francois. 1987. *20,000 Years of Fashion*. New York.

Bourdieu, Pierre. 1977. *Outline of a Theory of Practice*. Cambridge, MA.

———. 1979. *La Distinction: Critique Sociale du Judgement*. Paris.

———. 1984. *Distinction: A Social Critique of the Judgement of Taste*. Cambridge, MA.

Boxer, C. R. 1990. *The Dutch Seaborne Empire, 1600–1800*. London.

Braude, Benjamin. 1979. "International Competition and Domestic Cloth in the Ottoman Empire," *Review*, III.

Brewer, John, ed. 1991. *Consumption and Culture in the Seventeenth and Eighteenth Centuries.* Los Angeles.

Brewer, John and Roy Porter, eds. 1993. *Consumption and the World of Goods.* London and New York.

Brewer, John, and Susan Staves, eds. 1996. *Early Modern Conceptions of Property.* London and New York.

Burke, Peter. 1992. *The Fabrication of Louis XIV.* New Haven.

———. 1994. *Venice and Amsterdam: A Study of Seventeenth Century Elites.* Cambridge.

Burnett, John. 1969. *A History of the Cost of Living.* Harmondsworth/Middlesex.

———. 1979. *Plenty and Want: A Social History of Diet in England from 1815 to the Present Day.* London.

Busbecq, Ogier Ghiselin de, trans. Edward Seymour Forster. 1968 [1927]. *The Life and Letters of Ogier Ghiselin de Busbecq.* London. 2 vols.

See also De Busbecq.

Bushman, Richard. 1992. *The Refinement of America: Persons, Houses, Cities.* New York.

Butel, Paul. 1989. *Histoire du thé.* Paris.

Calhoun, Craig. 1983. "The Radicalism of Tradition: Community Strength or Venerable Disguise and Borrowed Language?" *American Journal of Sociology,* 5: 886–914.

Camporesi, Piero. 1989. *Bread of Dreams: Food and Fantasy in Early Modern Europe.* Chicago.

———. *The Magic Harvest: Food, Folklore and Society.* Cambridge.

———. *Exotic Brew: The Art of Living in the Age of Enlightenment.* Cambridge.

Cannadine, David. 1987. "Introduction: Divine Rites of Kings," David Cannadine and Simon Price, eds., *Rituals of Royalty: Power and Ceremonial in Traditional Societies.* Cambridge, 1–19.

Carson, Cary, Ronald Hoffman, and Peter J. Albert, eds. 1992. *Of Consuming Interest: The Style of Life in the Eighteenth Century.* Charlottesville and London.

Carswell, John. 1977. "From the Tulip to the Rose," in Thomas Naff and Roger Owen, *Studies in Eighteenth Century Islamic History.* Carbondale and Edwardsville, IL, 328–55.

Caspard, P. 1979. "L'accumulation du capital dans l'indiennage au XVIIIeme siècle," in *Revue du Nord* 61: 115–24.

Cevdet, Ahmed. 1892. *Cevdet Tarihi.* 12 vols.

Cezar, Yavuz. 1977. "Bir Ayan'ın Muhallefatı," *Belleten,* XLI, 161: 41–78.

———. 1978. "Osmanlı Devletinin Mali Kurumlarından Zahire Hazinesi ve 1795 (1210) Tarihli Nizamnamesi," *Toplum ve Bilim,* nos. 6–7.

———. 1981. "Osmanlı Devri'nde İstanbul'un İaşesinde Et ve Ekmek," *Yurt Ansiklopedisi,* vol. 5.

———. 1986. *Osmanlı Maliyesinde Bunalım ve Değişim Dönemi.* İstanbul.

Challamel, Augustin. 1882. *The History of Fashion in France,* trans. Cashel Hoey and John Lillie. London.

Chang, Kwang-chih, ed. 1977. *Food in Chinese Culture: Anthropological and Historical Perspectives.* New Haven.

Chaudhuri, K. N. 1985. *Trade and Civilization in the Indian Ocean: An Economic History from the Rise of Islam to 1750.* Cambridge.

———. 1990. *Asia before Europe: Economy and Civilization of the Indian Ocean from the Rise of Islam to 1750.* Cambridge.

Cohen, Stanley and Andrew Scull. 1983. *Social Control and the State.* New York.

Corbett, Wilfred. 1930. "The History of Tomato" in *Fifteenth Annual Report of the Experimental and Research Station.* London.

Coulson, Noel J. 1964. *A History of Islamic Law.* Edinburgh.

Crosby, W. J. 1972. *The Columbian Exchange.* Westport, CT.

Cross, Gary. 1993. *Time and Money: The Making of Consumer Culture.* London and New York.

Crumley, Carole. 1993. *Historical Ecology: Cultural Knowledge and Changing Landscape.* Seattle.

Cunbur, Müjgan. 1982. "Mevlana'nın Mesnevi'sinde ve Divan-i Kebir'inde Yemekler," *Türk Mutfağı Sempozyumu Bildirileri 31 Ekim-1 Kasım 1981.* Ankara.

Cunbur, Müjgan. 1990. "Eski Bir Görgü Kitabında Yemek Kuralları" Türk Mutfağı Özel Sayısı, *Türk Halk Kültürü Araştırmaları,* 1990/1. Ankara.

Curtin, Philip. 1984. *Cross-Cultural Trade in World History.* Cambridge.

———. 1990. *The Rise and Fall of the Plantation Complex.* Cambridge.

Cvetkova, Bistra Andreeva. 1976. "Les registres des celepkeşen en tant que sources pour l'histoire de la bulgarie et des pays Balkaniques," *Hungaro-Turcica, Studies in Honour of Julius Németh.* Budapest.

Çağman, Filiz. 1993. "Women's Clothing," in Günsel Renda, ed., *9000 Years of the Antolian Woman.* Istanbul.

Çeçen, Kazım. 1988. *Mimar Sinan ve Kırkçeşme Tesisleri.* İstanbul.

Çelik, Zeynep. 1986. *The Remaking of Istanbul: Portrait of an Ottoman City in the Nineteenth Century.* Seattle.

Çızakça, Murat. 1985. "Incorporation of the Middle East into the European World-Economy," *Review* 8: 3, 353–78.

Çizgen, Engin. 1987. *Photography in the Ottoman Empire, 1839–1919.* Istanbul.

———. 1989. *Photographer Ali Sami, 1866–1936.* Istanbul.

D'Ohsson, Mouradgea. 1788–1824. *Tableau général de l'Empire Othoman.* Paris.

Dallaway, James. 1797. *Constantinople, Ancient and Modern, with Excursions to the Shores and Islands of the Archipelago and to the Troad.* London.

Dankoff, Robert, tr. and ed. 1983. *Wisdom of Royal Glory (Kutadgu Bilig): A Turco-Islamic Mirror for Princes (of Yusuf Khass Hajib, Eleventh Century).* Chicago.

———. 1990. *Evliya Çelebi in Bitlis: The Relevant Section of the Seyahatname,* edited with translation, commentary and introduction. Leiden.

———. 1991. *The Intimate Life of an Ottoman Statesman, Melek Ahmed Pasha (1588–1662).* Albany.

Dankoff, Robert, and James Kelly, tr. and ed. 1982–85. *Divani Lügat-it-Türk (of Mahmud el-Kashgari, Eleventh Century).* Duxbury, MA.

Davenport, Millia. 1965. *The Book of Costume.* New York.

Davidson, Alan. 1981. *Mediterranean Seafood,* 2nd ed. Harmondsworth.

Davis, Fanny. 1986. *The Ottoman Lady: A Social History from 1718 to 1918.* New York.

Davis, Fred. 1992. *Fashion as Cycle, Fashion as Process.* Chicago.

Dayıgıl, Feyzullah. 1938. "İstanbul Çinilerinde Lâle," *Vakıflar Dergisi.*

de Busbecq, Ogier Ghiselin. 1633. *The Turkish Letters of Ogier Ghiselin de Busbecq.* E. S. Forster, translator (1927). Oxford. *See also* Busbecq.

de Grazia, Victoria, ed., with Ellen Furloung. 1996. *The Sex of Things: Gender and Consumption in Historical Perspective.* Berkeley.

de Groot, A. H. 1978. *The Ottoman Empire and the Dutch Republic: A History of the Earliest Diplomatic Relations, 1610–1630.* Leiden/Istanbul.

De Tott, Baron. 1784. *Memoirs of Baron de Tott Containing the State of Turkish Empire and the Crimea during the Late War with Russia.* 2 vols. London.

de Vries, Jan. 1993. "Between Purchasing Power and the World of Goods: Understanding the Household Economy in Early Modern Europe," in John Brewer and Roy Porter, eds., *Consumption and the World of Goods.* London: 85–132.

———. 1994. "The Industrial Revolution and the Industrious Revolution," *The Journal of Economic History,* June, 249–70.

Delibaş, Selma. 1988. "Behice Sultan'ın Ceyizi ve Muhallefatı," *Topkapı Sarayı Müzesi Yıllık,* 3: 63–104.

Demirel, Ömer. 1990. "1700–1730 Tarihlerinde Ankara'da Ailenin Niceliksel Yapısı," *Belleten* 54, 211: 945–61.

Denny, Walter B. 1972. "Ottoman Turkish Textiles," *Textile Museum Journal,* III.

———. 1983. "Dating of Ottoman Turkish Works in the Saz Style," *Muqarnas* 1: 103–21.

Dermigny, Louis. 1964. *La Chine et l'Occident, le commerce à Canton au XVIIIe siècle, 1719–1833,* 3 vols. Paris.

Develi, Hayati. 1997. "İstanbul'a Dair. Risale-i Garibe," in *İstanbul Araştırmaları,* no. 1.

Diouri, Abdelhai. 1994. "Lahlou: Nourriture sacrificielle des Gnaoua du Maroc," in Manuela Marin and David Waines, eds.

Dobrowolski, Pawel T. 1988. "Food Purchases of a Traveling Nobleman: The Accounts of the Earl of Derby, 1390–1393," *Food and Foodways,* vol. 2.

Douglas, Mary. 1975. "Deciphering a Meal," in C. Geertz, ed., *Myth, Symbol and Culture.* London.

Douglas, Mary. 1976–77. "Structures of Gastronomy," in *The Future and the Past, Annual Report 1976–77, Russell Sage Foundation.* New York.

———. 1977. "Beans Means 'Thinks,' " *The Listener,* 8 September.

Douglas, Mary and Michael Nikod. 1974. "Taking the Biscuit: The Structure of British Meals," *New Society,* vol. 30, no. 637.

Douglas, Mary and Baron Isherwood. 1979. *The World of Goods: Toward an Anthropology of Consumption.* New York.

———. 1996. *The World of Goods: Toward an Anthropology of Consumption.* London. Reprint with a new introduction of 1979 edition.

Doumani, Beshara. 1995. *Rediscovering Palestine: Merchants and Peasants in Jabal Nablus, 1700–1900.* Berkeley.

Downing, Brian M. 1992. *The Military Revolution and Political Change: Origins of Democracy and Autocracy in Early Modern Europe.* Princeton.

Drummond, Jack C. and Anne Wilbraham. 1994. *The Englishman's Food: Five Centuries of English Diet.* London.

Duby, Georges. 1974. *The Early Growth of the European Economy: Warriors and Peasants from the Seventh to the Twelfth Century*, tr. Howard B. Clarke. Ithaca.

Duman, Yüksel. 1998. "Notables, Textiles and Copper in Ottoman Tokat, 1750–1840." Ph.D. dissertation, Binghamton University, State University of New York.

Dumas, Alexandre. 1993. *The Black Tulip.* Oxford.

Düzdağ. 1972. *Şeyhülislâm Ebussuûd Efendi Fetvaları Işığında 16. Asır Türk Hayatı.* İstanbul.

———, M. Ertuğrul. 1983. *Şeyhülislâm Ebussuûd Efendi Fetvaları Işığında 16. Asır Türk Hayatı.* İstanbul. Second printing of 1972 edition.

Dyer, Christopher. 1983. "The English Diet in the Later Middle Ages," in T. Aston, P. R. Cross, C. Dyer, and J. Thirsk, eds. *Social Relations and Ideas: Essays in Honouor of R. H. Hilton.* Oxford.

———. 1989. *Standards of Living in the Latter Middle Ages.* Cambridge.

———. 1994. *Everyday Life in Medieval England.* London.

Edwards, Elizabeth, ed. 1992. *Anthropology and Photography, 1860–1920.* New Haven.

Eicher, Joanne B., and T. V. Erekosima. 1980. "Distinguishing Non-Western from Western Dress: The Concept of Cultural Authentication," in *Proceedings. Association of College Professors of Textiles and Clothing National Meeting.*

Eldem, Sedad Hakkı. 1977. *Sa'adabad.* Istanbul.

Elias, Norbert. 1969. *The Court Society.* Oxford.

———. 1978. *The Civilizing Process*, v. 1: *The History of Manners.* Oxford.

———. 1982. *The Civilizing Process*, v. II: *State Formation and Civilization.* Oxford.

———. 1983. *The Court Society.* Oxford.

Emecen, Feridun M. (forthcoming). "Şehzadenin Mutfağı: III. Mehmed'in Şehzadelik Dönemine Ait Bir Mutfak Masraf Defteri," paper delivered at the symposium on Food, Beverages, and Socialability in the Ottoman Empire, Bosphorus University, 25–26 March 1996. İstanbul.

———. 1989. "XVI. Asrın İkinci Yarısında İstanbul ve Sarayın İaşesi İçin Batı Anadolu'dan Yapılan Sevkiyat," *Tarih Boyunca İstanbul Semineri Bildirileri.* İstanbul.

———. 1989a. *XVI. Asırda Manisa Kazâsı,* Türk Tarih Kurumu Yayınları XIV. Dizi Sayı: 6. Ankara.

———. 1989b. "Evliya Çelebi'nın Manisa'ya Dair Verdiği Bilgilerin Değeri." *Türklük Araştırmaları Dergisi,* 4: 215–23.

———. 1979. *Unutulmuş Bir Cemaat: Manisa Yahudileri.* İstanbul.

Ercan, Yavuz. 1990. "Osmanlı İmparatorluğunda Gayrimüslimlerin Giyim, Mesken ve Davranış Hukuku." *OTAM,* I, 1.

Erdem, Hakan. 1997. *Slavery in the Ottoman Empire and its Demise.* New York.

Erdemir, Ayşegül Demirhan. 1991. "Hekim Zeynelabidin b. Halil'in Şifa al-Fuad Adlı Eserinin Türk Tıb Tarihindeki Yeri ve Bazı Orijinal Sonuçları," *Türk Dünyası Araştırmaları,* 71.

Erdoğan, Muzaffer. 1958. "Osmanlı Devrinde İstanbul Bahçeleri," *Vakıflar Dergisi,* 4: 149–82.

Erim, Neşe. 1991. "Trade, Traders and the State in Eighteenth-Century Erzurum," *New Perspectives on Turkey,* 5–6.

Erol, Aydil. 1992. *Şarkılarla Şiirlerle Türkülerle ve Tarihi Örneklerle Adlarımız.* Türk Kültürünü Arştırma Enstitüsü, genişletilmiş geliştirilmiş 2. baskı. Ankara.

Ertaylan, İsmail Hakkı. 1960. *Tabiat-name.* İstanbul.

Establet, Colette and Jean-Paul Pascual. 1994. *Familles et fortunes à Damas, 450 foyers damascains en 1700.* Damascus.

Evans, Guy. 1988. "From East to West," *Hali,* 38, March/April.

Evin, Ahmet Ömür. 1973. "Nedim: Poet of the Tulip Age: The Beginning of Western Influence and Westernization in Turkey: 1718–1730," Ph.D. dissertation, Columbia University.

———. 1983. *Origins and Development of the Turkish Novel.* Minneapolis.

Evliya Çelebi. 1314/1896–97 to 1938. *Seyahatnamesi.* İstanbul.

Eyice, S. 1965. "İstanbul'un Mahalle ve Semt Adları" *Türkiyat Mecmuası,* XIV.

Fairchilds, Cissie. 1993. "Consumption in Early Modern Europe, A Review Article," *Comparative Studies in Society and History,* July, 35, 3: 851–58.

Farb, Peter and Armelagos, George. 1980. *Consuming Passions: The Anthropology of Eating.* Boston.

Faroqhi, Suraiya (forthcoming). "Vom Sklavenmädchen zur Mekkapilgerin: Lebensläufe Bursaer Frauen im späten fünfzehnten Jahrhundert," in Christoph Neumann, ed., *Festschrift Nejat Göyünç.* İstanbul.

———. 1979–80. "Istanbul'un İaşesi ve Tekirdağ Rodoscuk Limanı," *METU Gelişme Dergisi,* no. 2.

———. 1984. *Towns and Townsman in Ottoman Anatolia: Trade, Crafts, and Food Production in an Urban Setting, 1520–1650.* Cambridge.

———. 1987. *Men of Modest Substance, House Owners and House Property in Seventeenth-Century Ankara and Kayseri.* Cambridge.

———. 1991. "Wealth and Power in the Land of Olives: Economic and Political Activities of Müridzade Hacı Mehmed Agha, Notable of Edremit" in Çağlar Keyder and Faruk Tabak, eds., *Landholding and Commercial Agriculture in the Middle East.* Albany.

———. 1994. "Part II Crisis and Change, 1590–1699" in Halil İnalcık with Donald Quataert, eds., *An Economic and Social History of the Ottoman Empire,* Cambridge.

———. 1994a. "Labor Recruitment and Control in the Ottoman Empire (Sixteenth and Seventeenth Centuries)," in Donald Quataert, ed., *Manufacturing in the Ottoman Empire and Turkey, 1500–1950.* Albany.

———. 1994b. *Pilgrims and Sultans: The Hajj under the Ottomans, 1517–1683.* London.

———. 1994c. "Trade: Regional, Inter-regional and International" in "Crisis and Change, 1590–1699" in İnalcık with Quataert, eds.

———. 1995. *Kultur und Alltag im Osmanischen Reich: Vom Mittelalter bis zum Anfang des 20. Jahrhunderts* München.

Feldman, Walter. 1997. "Imitatio in Ottoman Poetry: Three Ghazals of the Mid-Seventeenth Century," 41–58, *Turkish Studies Association Bulletin* 21, 2.

Fellows, Charles. 1975 [1852]. *Travels and Research in Asia Minor.* New York, George Olms Verlag.

Fenton, Alexander, and Eszter Kisbán, eds. 1986. *Food in Change: Eating Habits from the Middle Ages to the Present Day.* Edinburg.

Fenton, Alexander, and Trefor M. Owen, eds. 1981. *Food in Perspective.* Edinburg.

Fisher, Alan. 1978a. "Chattel Slave Procurement in the Ottoman Empire." Paper Presented at the Twelfth Annual Meeting of the Middle East Studies Association, Ann Arbor, Mich.

———. 1978b. "The Sale of Slaves in the Ottoman Empire: Markets and State Taxes on Slave Sales," *Boğaziçi Üniversitesi Hümaniter, Bilimler Dergisi,* VI.

———. 1980. "Studies in Ottoman Slavery and Slave Trade, II: Manumission," *Journal of Turkish Studies,* IV.

Flandrin, Jean-Louis. 1981. "Différences et différenciationi des goûts: Réflexion sur quelques examples européénnes entre le 14e et le 18e siècle," *Oxford Symposium Proceedings.* Oxford.

———. 1983a. "La diversité des goûts et des pratiques alimantaires en europe du 16e ou 18e siècle," *Revue d'histoire moderne et contemporaine,* no. 30.

———. 1983b. "Le goût et la nècessitè: Sur l'usage des graisses dans les cuisines d'Europe occidentale (XIV–XVIIIe)," *Annales ESC,* 2.

———. 1992. *Chronique de platine: pour une gastronomie historique.* Paris.

———. 1996. "Mealtimes in France before the Nineteenth Century," *Food and Foodways,* vol. 6.

Flandrin, Jean-Louis and Philip Hyman. 1986. "Regional Tastes and Cuisines: Problems, Documents, and Discourses on Food in Southern France in the sixteenth and seventeenth Centuries," *Food and Foodways,* vol. 1

Flandrin, Jean-Louis and Massimo Montanari, eds. 1996. *Histoire des Alimentations.* Paris.

Fleet, Kate. 1993. "The Treaty of 1387 between Murad I and the Genoese," *Bulletin of the School of Oriental and African Studies,* 56, 1: 13–33.

Fleischer, Cornell H. 1990. "The Lawgiver as Messiah: The Making of the Imperial Image in the Reign of Suleyman," in Gilles Veinstein, ed., *Soliman le manifique et son Temps Acts du Colloque de Paris, 7–1983.*

Fontenay, Michel (forthcoming). 1994. "Le commerce des Occidentaux dans les échelles du Levant vers la fin du XVIIe siècle," Proceedings of the Symposium in Tours on *Chrétiens et Mussulmans à la Renaissance,* 4–9 July.

Foote, Kenneth E., Peter J. Hugill, Kent Mathewson, and Johnathan M. Smith, eds., 1995, *Rereading Cultural Geography.* Austin.

Forster, Robert and Orest Ranum, eds. 1975. *Biology of Man in History (Selections from the Annales ESC).* Baltimore.

———. 1979. *Food and Drink in History (Selections from the Annales ESC).* Baltimore.

Foust, Clifford M. 1992. *Rhubarb: The Wondorus Drug.* Princeton.

Fragner, Bert. 1994a. "From the Caucasus to the Roof of the World: A Culinary Adventure," in Sami Zubaida and Richard Tapper, eds., *Culinary Cultures.*

———. 1994b. "Social Reality and Culinary Fiction: the Perspective of Cookbooks from Iran and Central Asia," in Sami Zubaida and Richard Tapper, eds., *Culinary Cultures.*

Freeman, Michael. 1977. "Sung," in K. C. Chang, ed., *Food in Chinese Culture.* New Haven and London.

Freeman, Sarah. 1989. *Mutton and Oysters. The Victorians and Their Food.* London.

Frierson, Elizabeth B. 1995a. "Is There any Future for Us in Trying to be Ladylike? The Ethnic Politics of Late-Ottoman Dress and Manufacture," presented to the Davis Center Seminar, Princeton University.

———. 1995b. "Unimagined Communities: Educational Reform and Civic Identity among Late-Ottoman Woman," *Critical Matrix* 9: 2, Fall.

———. 1996. "Unimagined Communities: State, Press and Gender in the Hamidian Era, 1876–1909," Ph.D. dissertation, Princeton University.

Fukusawa, Katsumi. 1987. *Toilerie et commerce du Levant, d'Alep à Marseille.* Paris.

Garcia, Expiración. 1994. "Las conservación de los productos vegetales en las fuentes agronómicas andalusies," in Manuela Marin and David Waines, eds., *La alimentacion.*

Garnett, Lucy M. J. 1891. *The Women of Turkey and Their Folklore: Jewish and Moslem Women,* vol. 2, London.

Gavin, Carney E. S., ed. 1988. "Imperial Self-Portrait: The Ottoman Empire as Revealed in the Sultan Abdul Hamid II's Photographic Albums," *Journal of Turkish Studies,* vol. 12.

Geissler, Catherine, and Derek J. Oddy, eds. 1993. *Food, Diet and Economic Change: Past and Present.* Leicester.

Genç, Mehmet. 1975. "Osmanlı Maliyesinde Malikâne Sistemi" in Osman Okyar and Ünal Nalbantoğlu, eds. *Türkiye İktisat Tarihi Semineri, Metinler-Tartışmalar, 8–10 Haziran 1973.* Ankara.

———. 1987. "Enterprise d'Etat et Attitude Politique da l'industrie Ottomane au XVIIIe siècle," in Jacques Thobie et Jean-Louis Bacqué-Grammont, eds., *L'Accession de la Turquie à la civilisation industrielle: Facteurs Internes et Externes.* Istanbul. 6–23.

———. 1989. "Osmanlı İktisadî Dünya Görüşünün İlkeleri," *Sosyoloji Dergisi İstanbul Üniversitesi Edebiyat Fakültesi,* 3rd Ser., 1: 176–85.

———. 1994. "Ottoman Industry in the Eighteenth Century: General Framework, Characteristics, and Main Trends," in Donald Quataert, ed., *Manufacturing in the Ottoman Empire and Turkey, 1500–1950.* Albany.

———. 1995. "L'Economie ottomane et la guerre au XVIIIe siècle," *Turcica,* XXVII.

Genç, Reşat. 1982a. "XI. Yüzyılda Türk Mutfağı," *Türk Mutfağı Sempozyumu Bildirileri 31 Ekim Kasım 1981.* Ankara.

———. 1982b. "Eski Türk Ziyafetleri," *II. Milletlerarası Türk Folklor Kongresi Bildirileri,* vol. IV. Ankara.

Gerber, Haim. 1988. *Economy and Society in an Ottoman City: Bursa, 1600–1700.* Jerusalem.

Gerelyes, Ipolya. 1995. "Métiers et ateliers artisanaux tures en Hongrie aux XVIe et XVIIe siècles," in Daniel Panzac, ed., *Histoire économique et sociale de l'Empire ottoman et de la Turquie (1326–1960), Actes du sixième congrès international.* Paris and Louvain: 185–94.

Gernsheim, Helmut, and Alison. 1954. *Roger Fenton, Photographer of the Crimean War: His Photographs and Letters from the Crimea.* London.

Gervers, Veronica. 1982. *The Influence of Ottoman Turkish Textiles and Costume in Eastern Europe.* Toronto.

Gibb, E. J. W. 1967. *A History of Ottoman Poetry,* volume IV, ed. by Edward G. Browne. London.

Godechot, Jacques. 1974. "La ville devient une ville rouge (1789–1815)," in Philippe Wolff, ed., *Histoire de Toulouse.* Toulouse: 445–94.

Goffman, Daniel. 1990. *Izmir and the Levantine World, 1550–1650.* Seattle.

Goldthwaite, Richard. 1993. *Wealth and the Demand for Art in Italy, 1300–1600.* Baltimore.

Golombek, Lisa. 1988. "The Gardens of Timur: New Perspectives." *Muqarnas* 5: 137–47.

Golombek, Lisa, and Maria Subtelny, eds. 1985. *Timurid Art and Culture: Iran and Central Asia in the Fifteenth Century.* Leiden.

Goodman, Jordan, Paul E. Lovejoy, and Andrew Sherrat, eds. 1995. *Consuming Habits.* London.

Goody, Jack. 1982. *Cooking, Cuisine and Class.* Cambridge.

———. 1993. *The Culture of Flowers.* Cambridge.

Gopin, Seth A. 1994. "Jean-Baptiste Vanmour, a Painter of 'Turqueries,' " Ph.D. diss. Rutgers, State University of New Jersey.

Göçek, Fatma Müge. 1996. *Rise of the Bourgeoisie, Demise of Empire, Ottoman Westernization and Social Change.* New York and Oxford.

Gökçe, Turan. 1994. "Anadolu Vilâyeti'ne Dâir 919 (1513) Bir Kadı Defteri," *Tarih İncelemeleri Dergisi* 9: 215–59.

Gökçen, İbrahim. 1946. *Manisa Tarihinde Vakıflar ve Hayırlar (Hicrî 954'den 1060'a)*, 1. Cilt. İstanbul.

———. 1947. "Muharrem Resmî Çelebi." *Gediz* 96: 4–5.

———. 1950. *Manisa Tarihinde Vakıflar ve Hayırlar (Milâdî 1650'den sonra)*, II. Cilt. İstanbul.

Göksel, Aslı. 1983. "The 'Surname' of Abdi as a Sample of Old Turkish Prose," MA Thesis, Bosphorus University, İstanbul.

Gökyay, Orhan Şaik, ed. 1978. *Gelibolulu Mustafa Ali: Görgü ve Toplum Kuralları Üzerinde Ziyâfet Sofraları (Mevâidü'n-nefâis fâis fi kavâidi'l mecâlis)*, 2. Cilt. İstanbul.

———. 1985. "Sohbetname," *Tarih ve Toplum*, vol. 2, no. 14.

———. 1987. "Divan-ı Et'ime," *III. Milletlerarası Türk Folklor Kongresi Bildirileri*, vol. V. Ankara.

Göyünç, Nejat. 1994. "Das Mevlevihane in Samsun," *Osmanlı Araştırmaları*, vol. XIV.

Graham-Brown, Sarah. 1988. *Images of Women: The Portrayal of Women in Photography of the Middle East, 1860–1950*. New York.

Greene, Molly. 1993. "Kandiye 1669–1720: The Formation of a Merchant Class," Ph.D. dissertation, Princeton University.

Greenwood, Anthony. 1988. "İstanbul's Meat Provisioning: A Study of the Celepkeşan System," Ph.D. dissertation, University of Chicago.

Grewe, Rudolf. 1987. "The Arrival of Tomato in Spain and Italy: Early Recipes," *The Journal of Gastronomy*, 3.

Grimm, Veronika E. 1996. *From Feasting to Fasting: The Evolution of a Sin: Attitutes to Food in Late Antiquity*. London and New York.

Grosrichard, Alain. 1979. *Structure du sérail: La fiction du despotisme asiatique dans l'Occident classique*. Paris.

Güçer, Lütfi. 1949–50. "XVIII. yüzyıl ortalarında İstanbul'un iaşesi için lüzumlu hububatın temini meselesi," *İstanbul Üniversitesi İktisat Fakültesi Mecmuası*, no. XI.

———. 1954. "XVI. yüzyıl sonlarında Osmanlı İmparatorluğu dahilinde hububat ticaretinin tabi olduğu kayıtlar," *İstanbul Üniversitesi İktisat Fakültesi Mecmuası 1*, no. XIII.

———. 1964. *Osmanlı İmparatorluğunda Hububat Meselesi ve Hububattan Alınan Vergiler*. İstanbul.

Güran, Tevfik. 1984–85. "The State Role in the Grain Supply of İstanbul: The Grain Administration, 1793–1839," *International Journal of Turkish Studies*, no. 3.

Güvemli, Zahir. 1987. *Sabancı Resim Kolleksiyonu.* Istanbul.

Hadiye Fahriye. 1342/1923. *Tatlıcı Başı.* İstanbul.

Hâkim, Mehmed. n.d. a "Hâkim Tarihi." Topkapı Saray Müzesi Arşivi, Bağdat 231, 233. İstanbul.

———. n.d. b "Hâkim Tarihi." Arkeoloji Müzesi, 484. İstanbul.

Halaçoğlu, Yusuf. 1991. *XIV–XVII. Yüzyıllarda Osmanlılarda Devlet Teşkilâtı ve Sosyal Yapı.* Ankara.

Halıcı, Feyzi, ed. 1992. *Ali Eşref Dede'nin Yemek Risalesi.* Ankara.

Hamilton, Earl. 1947. *War and Prices in Spain.* Cambridge, MA.

Hamilton, Jean. 1990. "Silkworms of the East Must Be Pillaged: The Cultural Foundations of Mass Fashion," *Clothing and Textiles Research Journal,* XVIII, 4.

Hançerlioğlu, Orhan. 1984. *İslâm İnançları Sözlüğü.* İstanbul.

Hanioğlu, Şükrü. 1995. *The Young Turks in Opposition.* Oxford.

Hanna, Nelly. 1991. *Habiter au Caire aux XVIIe XVIIIe siècles.* Cairo.

Harvey, J. H. 1976. "Turkey as a Source of Garden Plants," *Garden History* 4: 21–42.

Hattox, Ralph S. 1985. *Coffee and Coffeehouses: Origins of a Social Beverage in the Medieval Near East.* Seattle.

Heath, Deborah. 1992. "Fashion, Anti-Fashion, and Heteroglossia in Urban Senegal," *American Ethnologist,* XIX, 1.

Hengirmen, Mehmet, ed. 1983. *Güvahî: "Pend-Nâme."* Ankara.

Henisch, B. A. and H. K. Henisch. 1984. "James Robertson of Constantinople," *History of Photography* 8.

———. 1990. "James Robertson of Constantinople: A Chronology," *History of Photography* 14.

Henish, Bridget Ann. 1994. *Fast and Feast: Food in Medieval Society.* Philadelphia.

Herzfeld, Michael. 1991. *A Place in History: Social and Monumental Time in a Cretan Town.* Princeton.

Heyberger, Bermard. 1994. *Les Chrétiens du Proche-Orient.* Rome.

Hezarfen, Ahmet. 1995. "18.yy'da Eyüb'te Lâle Yetiştirenler," *Tarih ve Toplum* 137, (Mayıs): 300–302.

Hobsbawm, Eric, and Terence Ranger. 1983. *The Invention of Tradition.* Cambridge.

Hovhannesyan, Sarkis Sarraf. 1996. *Payitaht İstanbul'un Tarihçesi,* trans. Elmon Hançer. İstanbul.

Hughes, Diane Owen. 1983. "Sumptuary Law and Social Relations in Renaissance Italy," in John Bossy, ed., *Disputes and Settlements: Law and Human Relations in the West.* Cambridge.

Hunt, Alan. 1996. *Governance of the Consuming Passions: A History of Sumptuary Law.* New York.

İnan, Abdülkadir. 1948. "Göçebe Türk Boylarında Evlâtlık," *Ankara Üniversitesi Dil Tarih Coğrafya Fakültesi Dergisi* 6:127–37.

İnciciyan, P. G. 1956. *XVIII. Asırda İstanbul.* Istanbul.

İhsanoğlu, Ekmeleddin. 1996. *Büyük Cihad'dan Frenk Fodulluğuna.* İstanbul.

İnalcık, Halil. 1960. "Imtiyazat," in *Encyclopedia of Islam,* new edition.

———. 1970. "The Ottoman Economic Mind and Aspects of the Ottoman Economy" in Michael A. Cook, ed., *Studies in the Economic History of the Middle East.* London.

———. 1973. *The Ottoman Empire: The Classical Age, 1400–1600.* London.

———. 1979a. "The Question of the Closing of the Black Sea under the Ottomans," *Symposium on the Black Sea, March 18–20, 1978, Archeion Pontou,* 35: 74–110.

———. 1979b. "Servile Labor in the Ottoman Empire," in A. Ascher et al., eds., *The Mutual Effects of the Islamic and Judeo-Christian Worlds.* New York.

———. 1979–80. "Osmanlı Pamuklu Pazarı, Hindistan ve İngiltere: Pazar Rekabetinde Emek Maliyetinin Rolü," *ODTÜ Gelişme Dergisi, Türkiye İktisat Tarihi Üzerine Araştırmalar,* special issue, 1–65.

———. 1987. "When and How British Cotton Goods Invaded the Levant Markets," 374–83 in Huri İslamoglu-İnan, ed. *The Ottoman Empire and the World-Economy.* Cambridge. Translation of Inalcık, 1979–80.

———. 1993a. *The Middle East and the Balkans under the Ottoman Empire.* Bloomington, Ind.

———. 1993b. "The Ottoman Cotton Market and India: The Role of Labor Cost in Market Competition," in *The Middle East and the Balkans under the Ottoman Empire.* Bloomington, Ind.

———, with Donald Quataert, eds. 1994. *An Economic and Social History of the Ottoman Empire, 1300–1914.* Cambridge.

Israel, Jonathan, 1989. *Dutch Primacy in World Trade, 1585–1740.* Oxford.

Issawi, Charles. 1977. "Population and Resources in the Ottoman Empire and Iran," T. Naff and R. Owen, eds., *Studies in Eighteenth Century Islamic History.* Carbondale, Ill.

İsvan, Nurhan. 1990–91. "Illegal Local Trade in the Ottoman Empire and the Guilds of Istanbul, 1725–1726: Suggested New Hypotheses," *International Journal of Turkish Studies* 5, 1 and 2: 1–27.

Itzkowitz, Norman, and Max Mote, (tr. and ann.). 1970. *Mübadele: An Ottoman-Russian Exchange of Ambassadors.* Chicago.

İz, Fahir. 1989. "Evliya Çelebi ve Seyahatnâmesi," *Belleten* 53, 207–8: 709–34.

Jardine, Lisa. 1996. *Worldly Goods.* London.

Jellicoe, Susan. 1976. "The Development of the Mughal Garden," in *The Islamic Garden*. Washington, D.C., 107–36.

Jennings, Ronald C. 1976. "Urban Population in Anatolia in the Sixteenth Century: A Study of Kayseri, Karaman, Amasya, Trabzon and Erzurum." *International Journal of Middle East Studies* 7: 21–57.

———. 1987. "Black Slaves and Free Blacks in Ottoman Cyprus, 1590–1640," *Journal of the Economic and Social History of the Orient,* XXX.

Jerome, Norge V., Randy F. Kandel, and Gretel H. Pelto, eds. 1980. *Nutritional Anthropology: Contemporary Approaches to Diet and Culture.* New York.

Jirousek, Charlotte. 1995. "More than Oriental Splendor: European and Ottoman Headgear, 1380–1580." *Dress,* 22.

———. 1997a. "Dress as Social Policy: Change in Women's Dress in a Southwestern Turkish Village," *Dress,* 23.

———. 1997b. "From 'Traditional' to 'Mass Fashion System' Dress among Men in a Turkish Village," *Clothing and Textiles Research Journal,* 15.

Johnson, J. P. 1977. *A Hundred Years of Eating: Food, Drink, and the Daily Diet in Britain Since the Nineteenth Century.* Dublin.

Kafadar, Cemal (forthcoming a). "What Is a Good Curse and Who Deserves It? A Seventeenth-Century Guide to Bad Manners in Ottoman Society."

———. (forthcoming b). "Meşhuratnâme."

———. 1986. "When Coins Turned into Drops of Dew and Bankers Became Robbers of Shadows: The Boundaries of Ottoman Economic Imagination at the End of the Sixteenth Century," Ph.D. dissertation, McGill University, Montreal.

———. 1989. "Self and Others: The Diary of a Dervish in Seventeenth Century Istanbul and Firstperson Narratives in Ottoman Literature," *Studia Islamica,* LXIX.

———. 1991. "On the Purity and the Corruption of the Janissaries," *Turkish Studies Association Bulletin* 15: 273–80.

Kahane R., and Andreas Tietze. 1958. *The Lingua Franca in the Levant: Turkish Nautical Terms of Italian and Greek Origin.* Urbana.

Kaplan, Steven L. 1976. *Bread Politics and Political Economy in the Reign of Louis XV*, 2 vols. The Hague.

———. 1984. *Provisioning Paris. Merchants and Millers in the Grain Trade during the Eighteenth Century.* Ithaca and London.

———. 1996a. *The Bakers of Paris and the Bread Question, 1700–1775.* Durham and London.

———. 1996b. "The Times of Bread in Eighteenth-Century Paris," *Food and Foodways*, vol. 6.

Karal, Enver Ziya. 1950. "Ahmed III (1673–1736)," *İslâm Ansiklopedisi* vol. 1, 165–68. İstanbul.

Karaman, Hayreddin. 1985. *Anahatlarıyla İslâm Hukuku.* Cilt 2: Hususî Hukuk, İstanbul.

Karpat, Kemal. 1977. *An Inquiry into the Social Foundations of Nationalism in the Ottoman State: From Social Estates to Classes, from Millets to Nations.* Princeton Research Monograph no. 9.

Kayra, Cahit, Erol Üyepazarcı, eds. 1992. *İkinci Mahmut'un İstanbulu, Bostancıbaşı Sicilleri.* İstanbul.

Kazıcı, Ziya. 1987. *Osmanlılarda İhtisab Müessesesi.* İstanbul.

Keller, Arthur S., Oliver J. Lissityzn, and Federick J. Mann. 1938. *The Creation of Rights of Sovereignty through Symbolic Acts, 1400–1800.* New York.

Kévorkian, Raymond, and Paul Paboudjian. 1992. *Les Arméniens dans l'empire ottoman à la veille du génocide.* Paris.

Khare, Ravindra S., and Rao M. S. A. 1986. *Aspects in South Asian Food Systems: Food, Society and Culture.* Durham.

Kınalızâde, 'Ali Çelebi. d. 1572. *Ahlâk-ı, 'Alâ'i Bulaq* iii, Book q 1833.

Kızıltan, Mübeccel. 1987. "The 'Surname' of Mehmed Hazin as a Sample of Old Turkish Prose," unpublished MA thesis, Bosphorus University, İstanbul.

Kidwell, Claudia. 1974. *Suiting Everyone: The Democratization of Clothing in America.* Washington, D.C.

King, Donald, and David Sylvester. 1983. *The Eastern Carpet in the Western World*, Exhibition Catalogue. London.

Kinross, John. 1977. *The Ottoman Centuries: The Rise and Fall of the Turkish Empire.* New York.

Kitsikis, Dimitri. 1996 [1985]. *Türk-Yunan İmparatorluğu: Arabölge Gerçeği Işığında Osmanlı Tarihine Bakış.* İstanbul.

Koçu, Reşat Ekrem. 1939. *Seyid Vehbi. Surname (Üçüncü Ahmedin Oğullarının Sünnet Düğünü).* İstanbul.

———. 1969. *Türk Giyim Kuşam ve Süslenme Sözlüğü.* İstanbul.

Kolodzicjezyk, Dariusz (forthcoming). "Food Served to Polish Ambassadors," paper presented at the Symposium on Food, Beverages, and Sociability in the Ottoman Empire, Bosphorus University, 25–26 March 1996. İstanbul.

Koloğlu, Orhan. 1992. *Basınımızda Resim ve Fotoğrafın Başlaması.* İstanbul.

Kopytoff, Igor. 1986. "The Cultural Biography of Things: Commoditization as a Process," in Arjun Appaduri, ed., *The Social Life of Things: Commodities in Cultural Perspective.* Cambridge.

Koşay, Hamit Zübeyr. 1982. "Eski Türklerin Ana Yurdu ve Yemek Adları," *Türk Mutfağı Sempozyumu Bildirileri 31 Ekim-1 Kasım 1981.* Ankara.

Koşay, Hamit Zübeyr, and Akile Ülkücan. 1961. *Anadolu Yemekleri ve Türk Mutfağı.* Ankara.

Kömürciyan, Eremya Çelebi. 1988. *İstanbul Tarihi,* tr. and ed. by H. D. Andreasyan. İstanbul.

Köprülü, M. Fuad. 1979. "Bâc." *İslâm Ansiklopedisi,* Cilt 2, 187–90. İstanbul.

Köymen, Mehmet Altay. 1982. "Alp Arslan Zamanı Türk Beslenme Sistemi," *Türk Mutfağı Sempozyumu Bildirileri 31 Ekim-1 Kasım 1981.* Ankara.

Kum, Naci. 1954. "Ruhî Tedavide: Karaca Ahmedler Hakkında İncelemeler, Düşünceler." *Türk Folklor Araştırmaları* 55, 5, 3: 1500–1502.

Kumbaracılar, I22ET *Serpuşlar.* İstanbul. 1979.

Kunt, Metin. 1975. "Kulların Kulları," *Boğaziçi Üniversitesi Dergisi Hümaniter Bilimler,* vol. III.

———. 1986. "Ottoman Names and Ottoman Ages," *International Journal of Turkish Studies* 10: 227–34.

Kuran, Aptullah. 1990–1991. "The Evolution of the Sultan's Pavilion in Ottoman Imperial Mosques," *Islamic Art: An Annual Dedicated to the Art and Culture of the Muslim World* IV. Genoa and New York, 1992: 281–301.

Kurat, A. N. 1976. "The Retreat of the Turks, 1683–1730" in M. A. Cook, ed. *A History of the Ottoman Empire to 1730.* Cambridge.

Kut, Günay. 1984. "13. Yüzıla Ait Bir Yemek Kitabı," *Kaynaklar,* no. 3.

———. 1985. "Tabiat-name ve Tatlılar Üzerine Bir Yazma Eser: 'Et-Terkibat fi Tabhi'l-Hulviyyyat," *Folklor ve Etnoğrafya Araştırmaları.*

———. 1986. *Et Terkibat fi Tabbi'l-Hulviyyyat (Tatlı Pişirme Tarifleri).* Ankara.

———. 1987a. "Kanuni'nin Oğulları Sultan Bayezit ve Sultan Cihangir'in Sünnet Düğünlerindeki Kına Gecesi Ziyafeti. *Catering Gourmet.*

———. 1987b. "Şehzade Cihangir ve Bayezid'ın Sünnet Düğünlerindeki Yemekler Üzerine," *III. Milletlerarası Türk Folklor Kongresi Bildirileri,* Ankara.

———. 1988. "Şirvani'nin Yemek Kitabı Çevirisine Eklediği Yemekler Üzerine," *I. Milletlerarası Yemek Kongresi Bildirileri.* Ankara.

———. 1996. "Turkish Culinary Culture," in *Timeless Tastes.* İstanbul.

Kut, Turgut. 1985. *Açıklamalı Yemek Kitapları Bibliyografyası (Eski Harfli Yazma ve Basma Eserler).* Ankara.

———. 1990. "A Bibliography of Turkish Cook Books up to 1927," *Petits Propos Culinaires,* no. 17.

Kütükoğlu, Mübahat S. 1974. *Osmanlı-İngiliz İktisâdî Münâsebetleri (1580–1838).* Ankara.

———. 1978. "1009 (1600) Tarihli Narh Defterine Göre Istanbul'da Çeşitli Eşya ve Hizmet Fiyatları," *Tarih Enstitüsü Dergisi:* 59–83.

———. 1983. *Osmanlılarda Narh Müessesesi ve 1640 Tarihli Narh Defteri.* İstanbul.

———. 1995. "Son Devir Osmanlı Resmi Ziyafetleri," *Prof. Dr. Hakkı Dursun Yıldız Armağanı.* Marmara Üniversitesi, İstanbul.

Labarge, Margaret W. 1965. *A Baronnial Household of the Thirteenth Century.* London.

Lambert, Coline, ed. 1992. *Du manuscrit á la Table: Essais sur la cuisine au Moyen Ágee répertoire des manuscrits médiévaux contenant des recettes culinaires.* Montreal.

Lang, K., and G. Lang. 1965. "Fashion: Identification and Differentiation in the Mass Society," in Mary Ellen Roach and Joanne B. Eicher, eds., *Dress, Adornment and the Social Order.* New York.

Laurioux, Bruno. 1985. "Spices in the Medieval Diet: A New Approach," *Food and Foodways,* vol. I.

———. 1989. *Le Moyen Age: A Table.* Paris.

Lawson, Julie. 1988. "Dr. John Kirk and Dr. William Robertson: Photographers in the Crimea," *History of Photography* 12.

Le Roy Ladurie, Emmanuel. 1981. *Carnival in Romans.* Harmondsworth.

Lentz, Thomas, and Glenn D. Lowry, eds. 1989. *Timur and the Princely Vision: Persian Art and Culture in the Eighteenth Century.* Washington.

Lévi-Strauss, Claude. 1966. "The Culinary Triangle," *New Society*, December 22. London.

———. 1969. *The Elementary Structures of Kinship*. Boston.

———. 1970. *The Raw and the Cooked*. London.

———. 1973. *From Honey to Ashes*. London.

———. 1978. *The Origin of Table Manners*. London.

Lewis, Bernard. 1961. *The Emergence of Modern Turkey*. London.

———. 1963. *Istanbul and the Civilization of the Ottoman Empire*. Norman, OK.

Liman, R. 1981. "Some Documents Concerning Slavery in Tunisia at the End of the Eighteenth Century." *Revue Histoire Maghrébine*, 23–24.

Lis, Catharina, and Hugo Soly. 1979. *Poverty and Capitalism in Pre-Industrial Europe*. Brighton/Sussex.

Mann, Michael. 1986. *The Sources of Social Power*, vol. 1, Cambridge.

———. 1993. *The Sources of Social Power*, vol. 2, Cambridge.

Mantran, Robert. 1962. *Istanbul dans la second moitié du XVIIe siècle d'histoire institutionelle, économique et sociale*. Paris.

Marcus, Abraham. 1983. "Men, Women and Property: Dealers in Real Estate in Eighteenth-Century Aleppo," *Journal of the Economic and Social History of the Orient*, 26: 137–63.

Mardin, Şerif. 1973. "Center-Periphery Relations: A Key to Turkish Politics?" *Daedalus* 102:11: 169–90.

———. 1974. "Superwesternization in Urban Life in the Ottoman Empire in the Last Quarter of the Nineteenth Century," in Peter Benedict, Erol Timurtekin, and Fatma Mansur, eds., *Turkey: Geographic and Social Perspectives*. Leiden.

Marin, Manuela, and David Waines, eds. 1994. *La alimentación en las culturas islámicas*. Madrid.

Marmon, Shaun. 1995. *Eunuchs and Sacred Boundaries in Islamic Society*. New York.

Matalas, Antonia-Leda, and Louis E. Grivetti. 1994. "The Diet of Nineteenth Century Greek Sailors: An Analysis of the Log of the Konstantinos," *Food and Foodways*, vol. 5.

Matthee, Rudi. 1995. "Exotic Substances: The Introduction and Global Spread of Tobacco, Coffee, Cocoa, Tea and Distilled Liquor, Sixteenth to Eighteenth Centuries," in *Drugs and Narcotics in History*, Roy Porter and Mikulas Teich, eds. Cambridge, 24–51.

Maury, Bernard, André Raymond, Jacques Revault, and Mona Zakary. 1983. *Palais et maisons du Caire,* vol. II: *Epoque ottomane (XVIe–XVIIIe siècles).* Paris.

Mauss, Marcel. 1967. *The Gift: Forms and Functions of Exchange in Archaic Societies.* Trans. Ian Cunnison. New York.

McChesney, R. D. 1991. *Waqf in Central Asia: Four Hundred Years in the History of a Muslim Shrine.* Princeton.

———. 1996. "Barrier of Heterodoxy? Rethinking the Ties between Iran and Central Asia in the Seventeenth Century," in Charles Melville, ed., *Safavid Persia: The History and Politics of an Islamic Society.* 231–68. London.

McGowan, Bruce. 1994. "The Age of the Ayans," in İnalcık with Quataert, 637–758.

McKendrick, Neil, John Brewer, and John H. Plumb. 1982. *The Birth of Consumer Society: The Commercialization of Eighteenth-Century England.* London.

McNeill, William H. 1982. *The Pursuit of Power.* Chicago.

Mehmed Kamil. 1844. *Melceü't-Tabbahin.* İstanbul.

Mehmed Tevfik (Çaylak Tevfik). 1891. *İstanbul'da Bir Sene. İkinci Ay. Helva Sohbeti.* İstanbul.

Meisami, Julie Scott. 1996. "Nasir-i Khurau and the Homiletic Qasida" in "Poetic Microcosms: The Persian Qasida to the End of the Twelfth Century," pp. 137–83; *Qasida Poetry in Islamic Asia and Africa,* volume one: Classical Traditions and Modern Meanings. Brill.

Melek Hanım. 1996. *Haremden Mahrem Hatıralar,* tr., İsmail Yerguz. İstanbul.

Melikian-Chirvani, Asadullah Souren. 1975. "Recherches sur l'école du bronze ottoman au XVIe siècle," *Turcica,* VI: 146–67.

Melikoff, Irene. 1967. "La Fleur de la Souffrance: Recherche sur le Sens Symbolique de Lale dans la Poésie Mystique Turco-Iranienne," *Journal Asiatique* CCLV.

Melling, Antoine-Ignace. 1819. *Voyage pittoresque de Constantinople et des rives du Bosphore d'après les dessins de M. Melling.* Paris.

Mennell, Stephen. 1984. "Food at the Late Stuart and Hanoverian Courts," *Petits Propos Culinaires,* v. 17.

———. 1996. *All Manners of Food: Eating and Taste in England and France from the Middle Ages to the Present.* London.

Mernissi, Fatima. 1996. *Women's Rebellion and Islamic Memory.* London.

Mertes, Kate. 1988. *The English Noble Household, 1250–1600.* Oxford.

Mickelwright, Nancy. 1987a. "Tracing the Transformation in Women's Dress in Nineteenth-Century Istanbul," *Dress,* XIII.

———. 1987b. "Tracing the Transformation in Women's Dress in Nineteenth-Century Istanbul," *The Annual Journal of the Costume Society of America,* XIII.

———. 1992. "Dervish Images in Photographs and Paintings," in Raymond Lifchez, ed., *The Dervish Lodge: Architecture, Art and Sufism in Ottoman Turkey.* Berkeley.

Milbank, Caroline. 1985. *Couture, the Great Designers.* New York.

Mintz, Sidney W. 1985. *Sweetness and Power.* New York.

———. 1988. *Power of Sweetness and Sweetness of Power.* Deventer.

———. 1993. "The Changing Roles of Food in the Studies of Consumption," in John Brewer and Roy Porter, eds., *Consumption and the World of Goods.* London and New York.

———. 1996. *Tasting Food, Tasting Freedom: Excursions into Eating Culture.* Boston.

Monstereul, Sr. de la Chesneé. 1654. *La Florist François.* Paris.

Montagu, Lady Wortley. 1837, ed. Lord Wharncliffe, *The Letters and Works of Lady Wortley Montagu,* 2 vols. Philadelphia.

———. 1971. *Letters from the Levant during the Embassy to Constantinople, 1716–1718.* New York.

Montanari, Massimo. 1994. *The Culture of Food.* Oxford and Cambridge, MA.

Mroueh, Sahban, and Kaj Öhrnberg. 1987. *Kitab al-tabikh,* Studia Orientalia no. 60. Helsinki.

Mukerji, Chandra. 1983. *From Graven Images: Patterns of Modern Materialism.* New York.

———. 1993. "Reading and Writing with Nature: A Materialist Approach to French Formal Gardens," in ed., John Brewer and Roy Porter, *Consumption and the World of Goods.* London 441–43.

Murcott, Anne, ed. 1983. *The Sociology of Food and Eating.* Hants.

Murphey, Rhoads. 1988. "Provisioning İstanbul: The State and Subsistence in the Early Modern Middle East," *Food and Foodways,* vol. 2.

Musset, Lucien. 1975. *The Germanic Invasions: The Making of Europe,* AD *400–600,* tr. by Edward and Columba James. London.

Naff, Thomas, and Roger Owen, eds. 1977. *Studies in Eighteenth Century Islamic History.* Carbondale and Edwardsville, Ill.

Necipoğlu, Gülru. 1986. "The Süleymaniye in Istanbul: An Interpretation," *Muqarnas,* III: 92–117.

———. 1989. "Süleyman the Magnificent and the Representation of Power in the Context of Ottoman-Hapsburg-Papal Rivalry," *Art Bulletin* 71, 3: 401–27.

———. 1991. *Architecture, Ceremonial, and Power: The Topkapı Palace in the Fifteenth and Sixteenth Centuries.* Cambridge, MA.

———. 1997. "The Suburban Landscape of Sixteenth Century Istanbul as a Mirror of Classical Ottoman Garden Culture," in Attilio Pettruccioli, ed., *Gardens in the Time of the Great Muslim Empires.* Leiden.

Nouveau Traité pour la Culture des 1674 Fleurs qui enseigne la manière de les cultives, multiplier et les conservé selon leurs Espèce, avec leurs Proprietez merveilleuses et les Vertus Medicinales divisée en 3 livres. Paris, chez Charles De Sercy.

Nutku, Özdemir. 1972. *IV. Mehmet'in Edirne Şenliği (1675).* Ankara.

Nystrom, Paul H. 1928. *Economics of Fashion.* New York.

Olson, Robert. 1974. "The Esnaf and the Patrona Halil Rebellion of 1730: A Realignment in Ottoman Politics?" *Journal of the Economic and Social History of the Orient* 17:3: 329–40.

Ongan, Halit. 1974. *Ankara'nın İki Numaralı Şer'iye Sicili.* Ankara.

Onno, Ydema. 1991. *Carpets and their Datings in Netherlandish Paintings, 1540–1700.* Zutphen, The Netherlands and Woodbridge, Suffolk.

Onur, Oral. 1995. "Çingeneler," *Tarih ve Toplum* 137: 16–21.

Oral, Zeki M. 1957. "Selçuk Devri Yemekleri ve Ekmekleri," *Türk Etnoğrafya Dergisi,* nos. I–II.

Ortaylı, İlber. 1980. "Anadolu'da XVI. Yüzyılda Evlilik İlişkileri Üzerine Bazı Gözlemler." *Osmanlı Araştırmaları* I: 33–40.

———. 1989. "Onsekizinci-ondokuzuncu Yüzyıllarda Galata," in *Tarih Boyunca İstanbul Semineri.* Istanbul.

Owen, Roger. 1977. "Introduction to Part II," in Naff and Owen, eds., *Studies in Eighteenth Century Islamic History.* Carbondale, Ill.

Oxford Symposium [on] National and Regional Styles of Cookery. (1981) 1981. *National and Regional Styles of Cookery.* Oxford.

Oxford Symposium on Food and Cookery. (1984–1985) 1986. *Cookery: Science, Lore and Books.* London.

Oxford Symposium on Food and Cookery. (1986) 1989. *The Cooking Pot.* London.

Oxford Symposium on Food and Cookery. (1989) 1990. *Staplefoods.* London.

Oxford Symposium on Food and Cookery. (1990) 1991. *Feasting and Fasting*. London.

Oxford Symposium on Food and Cookery. (1991) 1992. *Public Eating*. London.

Oxford Symposium on Food and Cookery. (1992) 1993. *Spicing up the Palate: Studies of Flavorings, Ancient and Modern*. London.

Oxford Symposium on Food and Cookery. (1993) 1994. *Look and Feel: Studies in Texture, Appearance and Incidental Characteristics of Food*. Harlan Walker, ed., Devon.

Oxford Symposium on Food and Cookery. (1994) 1995. *Disappearing Foods: Studies in Foods and Dishes at Risk*. Harlan Walker, ed., Devon.

Oxford Symposium on Food and Cookery. (1995) 1996. *Cooks and Other People*. Harlan Walker, ed., Devon.

Oxford Symposium on Food and Cookery. (1996) 1997. *Food on the Move*. Harlan Walker, ed., Devon.

Öhrnberg, Kaj. 1994. "Ibn Sattar al Warraq's Kitab al-Wusla ila al-Habib/ Kitab al-Tabbakh, Another Ms of Ibn Sayyar al-Warraq's Kitab al-Tabikh" in *La Alimentación en las culturas islámicas*. Madrid.

Özakbaş, Ayşe. 1996. "17. Yüzyılda Yazılan Bir Tıb Kitabı: 'Şifa'ü'l-Fuad li-Hazreti'is Sultan Murad. Istanbul Kütüphanelerindeki Nüshaları ve Muhtevası," *Türklük Bilgisi Araştırmaları*, 20.

Özdemir, Rıfat. 1990/1991. "Tokat'ta Ailenin Sosyo-Ekonomik Yapısı (1771–1810)," *Belleten* 54, 211: 993–1052.

Özel, Mehmet. 1992. *Folklorik Türk Kıyafetleri*. İstanbul.

Öztuncay, Bahattin. 1992. *James Robertson: Pioneer of Photography in the Ottoman Empire*. İstanbul.

Pakalın, Mehmet Zeki. 1946–54. *Osmanlı Tarih Deyimleri ve Terimleri Sözlüğü*. İstanbul.

———. 1993. *Osmanlı Tarih Deyimleri ve Terimleri Sözlüğü*. Istanbul. 3 vols. (reprint of 1946–54 edition).

Pardailhé-Galabrun, Annik. 1988. *La naissance de l'intime, 3000 foyers parisiens, XVIIe–XVIIIe siècles*. Paris.

Pardoe, Julia. 1839. *The Beauties of the Bosphorus*. London.

Paviot, Jean. 1991. "Cuisine grecque et cuisine turque selon l'expérience des voyageurs (XVe–XVIe siècles)," in A. A. M. Bryer and Michael Ursinus, eds., *Manzikert to Lepanto: The Byzantine World and the Turks, 1071–1571* (Byzantinische Forschungen XVI). Amsterdam.

Payne, Blanche, Geitel Winakor, and Jane Farrell-Beck. 1992. *The History of Costume.* New York.

Peirce, Leslie. 1993. *The Imperial Harem: Women and Sovereignty in the Ottoman Empire.* Oxford.

Pekin, Ersu, and Ayşe Sümer, eds. 1996. *Timeless Tastes.* İstanbul.

Perez, Nissan. 1988. *Focus East: Early Photography in the Near East, 1839–1885.* New York.

Perlin, Frank. 1983. "Proto-Industrialization and Pre-Colonial South Asia," *Past and Present* 98 (Feb.), 30–95.

Petersen, Christian. 1995. *Bread and the British Economy, ca. 1770–1870.* Brookfield, Vermont.

Peterson, T. Sarah. 1994. *Acquired Taste: The French Origins of Modern Cooking.* Ithaca and London.

Petsopoulos, Yanni, ed. 1982. *Tulips, Arabesques, and Turbans: Decorative Arts in the Ottoman Empire.* New York.

Plumb, John H. 1952. "Sir Robert Walpole's Food," *Wine and Food,* no. 74.

Pool, Daniel. 1993. *What Jane Austen Ate and Charles Dickens Knew: From Fox Hunting to Whist: The Facts of Daily Life in Nineteenth Century England.* New York.

Porter, Glenn, and Harold C. Livesay. 1971. *Merchants and Manufacturers: Studies in the Changing Structure of Nineteenth-Century Marketing.* Baltimore.

Poster, Mark. 1997. *Cultural History and Post Modernity: Disciplinary Readings and Challenges.* Columbia.

Posthumus, N. W. 1929. "Notes and Documents: The Tulip Mania in Holland in the Years 1636 and 1637," *Journal of Economic and Business History* I, 3 (May): 433–65.

Pounds, Norman J. G. 1989. *Hearth and Home: A History of Material Culture.* Bloomington and Indianapolis.

Preto, Paolo. 1975. *Venezia ed i Turchi.* Milan.

Prochazka-Eisl, Gisela. 1995. *Das Sûrname-i Hümayun: die Wiener Handschrift in Transkription, mit Kommentar und Indices versehen.* İstanbul.

Pulaha, Selim, and Yaşar Yücel. 1988. "I. Selim Kanunnâmesi (1512–1520) and XVI. Yüzyılın İkinci Yarısının Kimi Kanunları," *Belgeler,* no. XII/16.

Pullar, Phillipa. 1970. *Consuming Passions.* London.

Quataert, Donald. 1993. *Ottoman Manufacturing in the Age of the Industrial Revolution.* Cambridge.

———. 1994. "The Age of Reform," in Halil İnalcık with Donald Quataert, eds., *An Economic and Social History of the Ottoman Empire, 1300–1914*. Cambridge.

———. 1997. "Clothing Laws, State and Society in the Ottoman Empire, 1720–1829," *International Journal of Middle Eastern Studies* 29: 403–25.

Raby, Julian. 1982. *Venice, Durer, and the Oriental Mode*. Totowa, New Jersey.

Rásonyi, Lazlo. 1988. *Tarihte Türklük*, İkinci Baskı. Ankara.

Raşid Mehmed. 1865. *Tarih-i Raşid*, 6 vols. Istanbul.

Raymond, André. 1973–74. *Artisans et commerçants au Cairo au XVIIIe siècle*. 2 vols. Damascus.

———. 1977. "The Sources of Urban Wealth in Eighteenth Century Cairo," in Naff and Owen, eds. *Studies in Eighteenth Century Islamic History*.

Redhouse, James W., Sir. 1890. *A Turkish and English Lexicon, Showing in English the Significance of the Turkish Terms*. Constantinople.

Rehman, Abdul. 1997. "Garden Types in Mughal Lahore According to Early 1997 Seventeenth Century Written and Visual Sources," 164–65 in Attilio Petruccioli, ed. *Gardens in the Time of the Great Muslim Empires: Theory and Design*, Leiden.

Reid, Anthony. 1988. *Southeast Asia in the Age of Commerce, 1450–1680, I*. New Haven.

Reindl-Kiel, Hedda (forthcoming). "Taam-ı Paşayan ve Büyük Ziyafet," paper presented at the Symposium on Food, Beverages, and Sociability in the Ottoman Empire, Bosphorus University, 25–26 March 1996, İstanbul.

———. 1991. "Mord an einer Haremsdame." *Münchner Zeitschrift für Balkankunde*, VII–VIII.

———. 1995. "Wesirfinger und Frauenschenkel. Zur Sozialgeschichte der türkischen Küche," *Archiv für Kulturgeschichte*, 77. Heft 1.

Relation des deux Rebellions arrivées à 1737 Constantinople en MDCCXXX. et XXXI, dan la Depositions d'Achmet III et l' Elevation au Trône de Mahomet I: Composée sur des Mémoires originaux reçus de Constantinople. A la Haye chez Jean Neaulme, M.DCC.XXXVII.

Renda, Günsel. 1977. *Batılaşma Döneminde: Türk Resim Sanatı, 1700–1850*. Ankara.

———. 1987. "Traditional Turkish Painting and the Beginning of Western Trends," in S. Pınar, A. Mill, and I. Altıntaş eds. *A History of Turkish Painting*, Istanbul.

Renda, Günsel. et al. 1988. *A History of Turkish Painting*. Seattle.

Revel, Jean-François. 1982. *Culture and Cuisine.* New York.

Reychman, Jan, and Ananiasz Zajoczkowski. 1968. *Handbook of Ottoman-Turkish Diplomatics.* Revised and expanded translation by Andrew S. Ehrenkreutz. Ed., Tibor Halasi-Kun. The Hague.

Reyhanlı, Tülay. 1989. "Nicolas de Nicolay'ın Türkiye Seyahatnâmesi ve Desenleri." *Erdem,* V.

Richards, Audrey. 1932. *Hunger and Work in a Savage Tribe.* London.

———. 1939. *Land, Labour and Diet in Norther Rhodesia.* London.

Robertson, Una A. 1987. "A Taste of Hopetoun: Food and Drink in a Scottish Household, 1754–55," *Food and Foodways,* vol. 2.

Roche, Daniel. 1989a. *The Culture of Clothing: Dress and Fashion in the Ancien Regime.* New York.

———. 1989b. *La culture des apparences: Une histoire du vêtement XVIIe–XVIIIe siècle.* Paris.

Rodinson, Maxime. 1949. "Recherches sur les document arabes relatifs à la cuisine," *Revue des etudes Islamiques,* no. 17.

———. 1965. "Ghıdha," *Encyclopaedia of Islam.*

Rogers, J. M. 1995. *Empire of the Sultans: Ottoman Art from the Collection of Nasser D. Khalili.* Geneva and London.

Rosenthal, Steven T. 1980. *The Politics of Dependency: Urban Reform in Istanbul.* Westport, Conn.

Rosselló-Bordoy, Guillermo. 1994. "Arqueologia e información textual: El utillaje en la cocina andalus" in Manuela Marin and David Waines, eds., 1994.

Rotenberg, Robert. 1995. *Landscape and Power in Vienna.* Baltimore and London.

Rubiera Mata, Maria Jesús. 1994. "La dieta de Ibn Quzman: Notas sobre la alimentación andalusi a travós su literatura" in Manuela Marin and David Waines, eds.

Russell, Dougals A. 1983. *Costume History and Style.* Englewood Cliffs, N.J.

Rypka, Jan. 1968. *History of Iranian Literature.* Dordrecht, Holland.

Sabban, Françoise. 1986. "Court Cuisine in Fourteenth-Century Imperial China: Some Culinary Aspects of Hu Suhui's Yinshan Zhengyao," *Food and Foodways,* vol. 1.

Sahillioğlu, Halil. 1985. "Slaves in the Social and Economic Life of Bursa in the Late Fifteenth and Early Sixteenth Centuries," *Turcica,* XVII: 43–112.

Said, Edward. 1978. *Orientalism.* New York.

Sak, İzzet. 1989. "Konya'da Köleler (16. Yüzyıl Sonu-17. Yüzyıl)." *Osmanlı Araştırmaları* IX.

Salaman, Radcliffe. 1985. *The History and Social Influence of the Potato.* Cambridge.

Salzmann, Ariel. 1993. "An Ancien Régime Revisited: Privatization and Political Economy in the Eighteenth Century Ottoman Empire," *Politics and Society,* 21: 4:393–423.

———. 1995. "Measure of Empire: Tax Farmers and the Ottoman Ancien Régime, 1695–1807," Ph.D. dissertation, Columbia University.

Sarı, Nil. 1982. "Osmanlı Sarayı'nda Yemeklerin Mevsimlere Göre Düzenlenmesi ve Devrin Tababetiyle İlişkisi," *Türk Mutfağı Sempozyumu Bildirileri 31 Ekim–1 Kasım 1981.* Ankara.

Savaş, Saim. 1992. *Sivas Ali Baba Zaviyesi Tekkesi: Bir Dinî ve Sosyal Tarihi.* İstanbul.

———. 1993. "Fetva ve Şer'iye Şicillerine Göre Ailenin Teşekkülü ve Dağılması," in Hakkı Dursun Yıldız, ed., *Sosyo-Kültürel Değişme Sürecinde Türk Ailesi,* Cilt 2, Ankara.

Sayers, William. 1990. "A Cut Above: Ration and Station in an Irish King's Hall," *Food and Foodways,* vol. 4.

Sayers, William. 1994. "Diet and Fantasy in Eleventh-Century Ireland: The Vision of Mac Con Glinne," *Food and Foodways,* vol. 6.

Scarce, Jennifer. 1980. "Turkish Fashion in Transition," *Costume,* XIV.

———. 1987. *Women's Costume of the Near and Middle East.* London.

———. 1988. "Principles of Ottoman Turkish Costume," *Costume,* XXII.

Schama, Simon. 1987. *The Embarassment of Riches, an Interpretation of Dutch Culture in the Golden Age.* New York.

Schimmel, Annemarie. 1976. "The Celestial Garden in Islam," in Richard Ettinghhausen, ed., *The Islamic Garden,* 11-40. Washington, D.C.

———. 1988. "The Genius of Shiraz: Sa'di and Hafez" in *Persian Literature,* Ehsan Yarshater, ed. Albany, 214–25.

Schoonover, David E. 1992. *The Khwan Niamut, or Nawab's Domestic Cookery.* Iowa City.

Schwartz, Stuart B., ed. 1994. *Implicit Understandings: Observing, Reporting, and Reflecting on the Encounters between Europeans and Other Peoples in the Early Modern Era.* Cambridge.

Scott, James C. 1985. *Weapons of the Weak, Everyday Forms of Peasant Resistance.* New Haven and London.

Scully, Terence (tr. and ed.) 1986. Chiquart's "On Cookery." *A Fifteenth Century Savoyard Culinary Treatise.* Frankfurt am Main.

———. 1987. "Aucune science de l'art de cuysinerie et de cuisine: Chiquart's Du Fait de Cuisine," *Food and Foodways,* vol. 2.

———. 1995. *The Art of Cookery in the Middle Ages.* Suffolk and Rochester.

Sefercioğlu, Nejat. 1985. *Türk Yemekleri. XVIII. Yüzyıla Ait Yazma Bir Yemek Risalesi.* Ankara.

Seng, Yvonne J. 1991. "The Üsküdar Estates *(tereke)* as Records of Daily Life in an Ottoman Town, 1521–1524," Ph.D. dissertation, University of Chicago.

———. 1996. "Fugitives and Factotums: Slaves in Early Sixteenth-Century Istanbul," *Journal of the Economic and Social History of the Orient,* XXXIX.

Shammas, Carole. 1990. *The Pre-Industrial Consumer in England and America.* Oxford.

Shay, Mary Lucille. 1944. *The Ottoman Empire from 1720 to 1734: As Revealed in Despatches of the Venetian Baili.* Urbana, Ill.

Sılay, Kemal. 1994. *Nedim and the Poetics of the Ottoman Court: Medieval Inheritance and the Need for Change.* Bloomington, Ind.

Simoons, Frederick J. 1994. *Eat Not This Flesh: Food Avoidances from Prehistory to Present.* Madison, Wisc.

Singer, Amy. 1994. *Palestinian Peasants and Ottoman Officials: Rural Administration around Sixteenth-Century Jerusalem.* Cambridge.

Sirman, Ayşe Nükhet. 1988. "Peasants and Family Farms: The Position of Households in Cotton Production in a Village of Western Turkey," Ph.D. dissertation, University College, London.

Skilliter, S. A. 1977. *William Harbourne and the Trade with Turkey, 1578–1582.* London.

Smith, Andrew F. 1992. "Authentic Fried Green Tomatoes," *Food History News,* no. 4.

———. 1994. *The Tomato in America.* Columbia, South Carolina.

Smith, Grace Martin, and Nedret İşli. 1984. "Foodcustoms at the Kaadirhane Dergah in İstanbul" in Orhan Şaik Gökyay Armağanı, *Journal of Turkish Studies,* no. VII.

Smith, Robert E. F., and David Christian, and 1984. *Bread and Salt: A Social and Economic History of Food and Drink in Russia.* Cambridge.

Soboul, Albert. 1970. *La civilisation et la Révolution française.* Paris.

Sonyel, Salâhi R. 1993. *Minorities and the Destruction of the Ottoman Empire.* Ankara.

Soucek, Svat. 1996. *Piri Reis and Turkish Mapmaking after Columbus: Studies in the Khalili Collection,* volume II. Oxford.

Soustiel, Jean. 1985. *La Ceramique Islamique.* Freibourg.

Sönmez, Neslihan. 1997. *Osmanlı Dönemi Yapı ve Malzeme Terimleri Sözlüğü.* İstanbul.

Spence, Jonathan D. 1992. "Food," in *Chinese Roundabout.* New York.

Spufford, Margaret. 1984. *The Great Reclothing of Rural England: Petty Chapmen and their Wares in the Seventeenth Century.* London.

Stillman, Yedida, and Nancy Micklewright. 1992. "Costume in the Middle East," *MESA Bulletin,* 26: 13–38.

Stirling, Paul. 1965. *A Turkish Village.* New York.

Stoianovich, Traian. 1970. "Model and Mirror of the Premodern Balkan City," in *Studia Balcanica,* III: *La ville balkanique, XVe–XIXe siècle,* 83–110. Sofia.

Stoianovich, Trajan. 1951. "Le mais," *Annales ESC,* no. 6.

———. 1966. "Le mais dans le Balkans," *Annales ESC,* no. 21.

Subrahmanyam, Sanjay. 1990. *The Political Economy of Commerce: Southern India, 1500–1650.* Cambridge.

———. 1997. "Connected Histories: Notes toward a Reconfiguration of Early Modern Eurasia," *Modern Asian Studies* 31, 3: 735–62, *Studia Iranica:* 167–217.

Sumner-Boyd, Hilary, and John Freely. 1989. *Strolling through Istanbul: A Guide to the City,* fourth edition. İstanbul.

Sunguroğlu, İshak. 1966. "Harput'da Evlenme ve Düğünler, 4: Nişan Bohçası, Gelin Elbisesi, Kına Hamamı, Cehiz Yazma," *Türk Folklor Araştırmaları:* 4137–40.

Sutton, Ann. 1991. "Order and Fashion in Clothes: The King, His Household, and the City of London at the End of the Fifteenth Century," *Costume,* 22, 2.

Sweetman, John. 1988. *The Oriental Obsession: Islamic Inspiration in British and American Art and Architecture, 1500–1920.* Cambridge.

Symposium Review on Cooking, Cuisine and Class. 1989. *Food and Foodways,* vol. 3.

Symposium Review on Sweetness and Power. 1987. *Food and Foodways,* vol. 2.

Şahin, M. Süreyya. 188, *Fener Patrikhanesi ve Türkiye.* İstanbul.

Şem'dânîzâde, Fındıklılı Süleyman. 1976–81. *Şem'dânîzâde Fındıklılı Süleyman Efendi Târihi Mür'i't-Tevârih,* ed., M. Münir Aktepe. İstanbul.

Şemsettin Sami. 1899–1900. *Kamus-i Türki: kaffe-yi lügat-i Türkiye ile lisan-i Türkide müstamil kelimat ve ıstılat-ı Arabiye ve Farisiye ve ecnebiye-yi cami olarak lisanımızın mükemmel lügat kitabıdır.* İstanbul.

Şeni, Nora. 1984. "Ville ottoman et représentation du corps féminin," *Les Temps Moderns,* XLI.

———. 1995. "Fashion and Women's Clothing in the Satirical Press of Istanbul at the End of the Nineteenth Century," in Şirin Tekeli, ed. *Women in Modern Turkish Society: A Reader.* London.

Şirvanlı Ahmed Hamdi Efendi. 1993. *Şirvanlı Mahmud Kemaliyye: Giriş, İnceleme, Cümle Bilgisi, Metin, Sözlük.* Ed., Muhammet Yelten. İstanbul.

Tabak, Faruk. 1996. "Ars Longa, Vita Brevis? A Geohistorical Perspective on *Pax Mongolica,*" *Review,* XIX, 1: 23–48.

Tagg, John. 1988. *The Burden of Representative: Essays on Photographies and Histories.* Amherst, MA.

Tannahill, Reay. 1988. *Food in History.* Harmondsworth.

Tarım, Zeynep. 1987. "Matbah-i Amire Müessesesi ve 1105–1106 Muhasebe Defteri," MA thesis, Marmara Üniversitesi, Istanbul.

Tapper, Richard, and Sami Zubaida. 1994. "Introduction" in Sami Zubaida and Richard Tapper eds. *Culinary Cultures.*

Tavernier, Jean Baptiste. 1678. *The Six Voyages of Jean Baptiste Tavernier.* London.

Taylor, Paul. 1995. *Dutch Flower Painting, 1600–1720.* New Haven.

Terzioğlu, Arslan. 1992. *Helvahane Defteri ve Topkapı Sarayı'nda Eczacılık.* İstanbul.

Teuteberg, Hans J., ed. 1992. *European Food History: A Research Review.* Leicester.

Tezcan, Hülya. 1992. *19 yy sonunda bir terzi defteri/A Late nineteenth-Century Tailor's Order.* İstanbul.

Tezcan, Hülya, and Selma Delibaş. 1986. *The Topkapı Saray Museum: Costumes, Embroideries, and Other Textiles.* London.

Tezcan, Semih. 1997. "Bir Ziyafet Defteri," in Klaus Kreiser and Christoph Neumann, eds., *Das Osmanische Reich in seinen Archivalien und Chroniken. Nejat Göyünç: zu Ehren.* Leipzig.

Theophano, Janet. 1996. *Household Words: Women Write from and for the Kitchen.* Philadelphia.

Thomas, Ritchie. 1990. "Sebah and Joaillier," *History of Photography,* 14.

Thompson, E. P. 1991. "The Moral Economy Reviewed," *Customs in Common.* New York, 259–351.

Todorova, Maria N. (1993). *Balkan Family Structure and the European Pattern: Demographic Developments in Ottoman Bulgaria.* Washington, D.C.

Tournefort, Joseph Pitton de. 1717–1730. *The Compleat Herbal: Or The Botanical Institutions of Mr. Tournefort . . . Carefully Translated from the Original Latin/ with Large Additions from Ray, Gerarde, Parkinson, and Others,* 2 vols. London.

Toussaint-Samat, Maguelonne. 1992. *History of Food.* Oxford and Cambridge, MA.

Toygar, Kamil, ed. 1993. *Türk Mutfak Kültürü Üzerine Araştırmalar.* Ankara.

Turquie. 1993. *Turquie: Au Nom de la Tulipe.* Toulouse.

Türâbi Efendi. 1864. *Mecmua-ı Et'ime-i Osmaniye. [Turkish Cookery Book: A Collection of Receipts Dedicated to Those Royal and Distinguished Personages, the Guests of his Highness, the Late Viceroy of Egypt on the Occasion of the Banquet Given at Woolich on Board his Highness's Yacht, the Faiz-Jehad, 16th July 1862.* Compiled by Turabi Efendi, from the Best Turkish Authorities]. London.

Uluçay, M. Çağatay. 1942. *XVII. Yüzyılda Manisa Ziraat, Ticaret ve Esnaf Teşkilâtı,* I. C. H. P. Manisa Halkevi Yayınlarından No: 9. İstanbul.

Unat, Faik Reşit, ed. 1943. *1730 Patrona İhtilali Hakkında Bir Eser: Abdi Tarihi.* Ankara.

Uzunçarşılı, İsmail Hakkı. 1945. *Osmanlı Devletinin Saray Teşkilatı.* Ankara.

———. 1961. "Bostancı" 736–38 *İslâm Ansiklopedisi,* vol. 2. İstanbul.

Ünver, Süheyl. 1941. *Anadolu ve İstanbulda İmaretlerin Aşhane, Tabhane ve Misafirhanelerine ve Müsseselerin Ruhî Kemâllerine Dair.* İstanbul.

———. 1942. "Bizde Meyve Yetiştirmeğe Meraklı Son Hekimbaşılar ve Yemişleri," V/19–20.

———. 1948. *Tarihte 50 Türk Yemeği.* İstanbul.

———. 1952. *Türkiye Gıda Hijyeni Tarihinde Fatih Devri Yemekleri.* İstanbul.

———. 1953. *Fatih Aşhanesi Tevzî'nâmesi.* İstanbul.

Valensi, Lucette. 1993. *The Birth of the Despot: Venice and the Sublime Port,* trans. Arthur Denner. Ithaca.

Veblen, Thorstein. 1934. *The Theory of the Leisure Class.* New York.

———. 1979. *Theory of the Leisure Class.* New York. (Reprint)

Waines, David. 1987. "Cereals, Bread and Society: An Essay on the Staff of Life in Medieval Iraq," *Journal of the Economic and Social History of the Orient,* vol. XXX/III.

———. 1988. "Review Article: Kitab al-tabikh" in *Journal of Semitic Studies,* vol. XXXIII.

———. 1994. *In Caliph's Kitchen.* London.

Waines, David, Halil İnalcık, and J. Burton-Page. 1991. "Matbakh," *Encyclopaedia of Islam,* 2nd edition, 807–15.

Wallerstein, Immanuel. 1989. *The Modern World-System III: The Second Era of Great Expansion of the Capitalist World Economy, 1730–1840s.* New York.

Walton, Whitney. 1992. *France at the Crystal Palace.* Berkeley.

Watson, Andrew M. 1983. *Agricultural Innovation in the Early Islamic World: The Diffusion of Crops and Farming Techniques.* Cambridge.

Weatherill, Lorna. 1988. *Consumer Behaviour and Material Culture in Britain, 1660–1760.* London and New York.

Weatherill, Lorna, ed. 1990. *The Account Book of Richard Latham,* 1724–1767. Oxford.

Weiner, Annette B., and Jane Schneider. 1989. "Introduction," Weiner, Annette B., and Jane Schneider, eds., in *Cloth and Human Experience,* 1–10. Washington.

Wescoat, James L. Jr. 1990. "Gardens of Invention and Exile: The Precarious Context of Mughal Garden Design during the Reign of Humayun (1530–1556)," *Journal of Garden History* 10, 2 (April–June), 106–17.

Wigh, Leif. 1984. *Photographic Views of the Bosphorus and Constantinople.* Stockholm.

Wills, John E. Jr. 1993. "European Consumption and Asian Production in the Seventeenth and Eighteenth Centuries," in eds. John Brewer and Roy Porter, *Consumption and the World of Goods,* 133–47. London.

Wilson, Anne C., ed. 1991a. *The Banqueting Stuffe: The Fare and Social Background of the Tudor and Stuart Banquet.* Edinburg.

———, ed. 1991b. *The Appetite and the Eye: Visual Aspects of Food and Its Presentation within Their Historic Context.* Edinburg.

———, ed. 1991c. *Traditional Food East and West of the Pennies.* Edinburg.

———, ed. 1994. *Luncheon, Nuncheon and Other Meals: Eating with the Victorians.* Dover.

———. 1976. *Food and Drink in Britain.* Harmondsworth.

Withers, Robert. 1996 [1650]. *Büyük Efendi'nin Sarayı.* Çeviren Cahit Kayra. İstanbul.

Wolf, Eric. 1990. "Facing Power: Old Insights, New Questions," *American Anthropologist,* no. 92.

Yapp, M. E. 1992. "Europe in the Turkish Mirror," *Past and Present* 137: 134–55.

Ydema, Onno. 1991. *Carpets and Their Datings in Netherlandish Paintings, 1540–1700.* Woodbridge/Suffolk.

Yerasimos, Stephane (forthcoming). "Hypothesis on the Use of Rugs and Carpets in Ottoman Society," *Symposium on Turkish Carpets: Fifteenth–Eighteenth Centuries, 27–28 Eylül 1996.* İstanbul.

Yücel, Hasan Ali. 1937. *Bir Türk Hekimi ve Tıbba Dair Manzum Bir Eseri.* İstanbul.

Yücel, Yaşar. 1988. *Osmanlı Devleti Teşkilâtına Dair Kaynaklar.* Ankara.

Yüksel, Hasan. 1993. "Vakfiyelere Göre Osmanlı Toplumunda Aile," in: Hakkı Dursun Yıldız, ed., *Sosyo-Kültürel Değişme Sürecinde Türk Ailesi,* Cilt 2, 468–503. Ankara.

Yüksel, Hasan, and Saim Savaş. 1993. "Osmanlı Aile Hayatına Ilişkin Fetvalar," in Hakkı Dursun Yıldız, ed., *Sosyo-Kültürel Değişme Sürecinde Türk Ailesi,* Cilt 3, 876–97. Ankara.

Zarinebaf-Shahr, Fariba. 1998. "Women and the Public Eye in Eighteenth Century Istanbul," ed. Gavin R. G. Hambly, *Women in the Medieval Islamic World,* 301–24. London.

Zilfi, Madeline C. 1993. "A *Medrese* for the Palace: Ottoman Dynastic Legitimation in the Eighteenth Century," *Journal of the American Oriental Society,* CXIII.

———. 1995. "Ibrahim Paşa and the Women," in Daniel Panzac, ed., *Histoire économique et sociale de l'Empire ottoman et de la Turquie (1326–1960), Actes de sixième congrès international.* Louvain and Paris.

———. 1996. "Women and Society in the Tulip Era, 1718–1730," Amira El Azhary Sonbol, ed., *Women, the Family, and Divorce Laws in Islamic History.* Syracuse.

Zubaida, Sami, and Richard Tapper, eds. 1994. *Culinary Cultures of the Middle East.* London.

Index